FROM
POOR LAW

TO
WELFARE
STATE

A HISTORY OF SOCIAL WELFARE IN AMERICA

Fifth Edition

WALTER I. TRATTNER

THE FREE PRESS

New York   London   Toronto   Sydney   Tokyo   Singapore

The Free Press
A Division of Simon & Schuster Inc.
1230 Avenue of the Americas
New York, N.Y. 10020

Printed in the United States of America

printing number

   6 7 8 9 10

Library of Congress Cataloging-in-Publication Data

Trattner, Walter I.
    From poor law to welfare state: A history of social welfare in America /
Walter I. Trattner. — 5th ed.
      p.   cm.
    Includes index.
    ISBN 0-02-932714-8. — ISBN 0-02-932713-X (pbk.)
    1. Public Welfare — United States — History.   2. Social service — United
States — History.   I. Title.
HV91.T7 1994
361.973 — dc20   93-29347
                                                      CIP

FOR
STEPHEN, ANNE, AND DAVID

What a pity it is to see a proper gentleman to have such a crick in his neck that he cannot look backward! yet no better is he who cannot see behind him the actions which long since were performed. History maketh a young man to be old without either wrinkles or gray hairs; privileging him with the experience of age, without either the infirmities or inconveniences thereof. Yea, it not only maketh things past, present; but enableth one to make a rational conjecture of things to come. For this world affordeth no new accidents, but in the same sense wherein we call it a new moon, which is the old one in another shape, and yet no other than what hath been formerly. Old actions return again, furbished over with some new and different circumstances.

THOMAS FULLER
The Historie of the Holy Warre,
1639

You often say, "I would give, but only to the deserving."
The trees in your orchard say not so, nor the flocks in your pasture.
They give that they may live, for to withhold is to perish.
Surely he who is worthy to receive his days and his nights, is worthy of all else from you.
And he who has deserved to drink from the ocean of life deserves to fill his cup from your little stream.
And what desert greater shall there be, than that which lies in the courage and the confidence, nay the charity, of receiving?
And who are you that men should rend their bosom and unveil their pride, that you may see their worth naked and their pride unabashed?
See first that you yourself deserve to be a giver, and an instrument of giving.
For, in truth, it is life that gives unto life—while you, who deem yourself a giver, are but a witness.

KAHLIL GIBRAN, *The Prophet*

Contents

Preface
to the Fifth Edition

■ Ordinarily, authors are quite pleased to have the opportunity to revise and update books they had written previously. Certainly that was the case with me, as for example my comments in the Preface to the Second Edition indicate. Unfortunately, however, that was not so this time. For the most part, revising and updating this work proved to be a difficult and depressing task.

The last edition of this book, published in 1989, concluded with George Bush's election to the presidency after eight years, under Ronald Reagan, of unremitting horror for the nation's poor. Since that time, however, as I feared, conditions only have gotten worse. Under Bush, the war on the welfare state continued, poverty intensified, and homelessness and a variety of other related social problems reached new heights. All the while, the occupant of the White House and his supporters, who viewed the needy with indifference, if not scorn, did nothing—or worse: they cut even more holes in the social welfare safety net, such as it was. And while the violence that erupted in Los Angeles in the spring of 1992 thrust the state of America's inner cities and urban poverty into the public consciousness once again, and even rekindled some public debate on these matters, certainly it did not propel them onto the public agenda, at least not yet.

If there is any light at the end of the tunnel, it is the fact that the twelve dark and dismal years of the Reagan–Bush era have come to an end, and—as I indicate in the conclusion to this work—there is hope (although not quite as much now as there was immediately after the 1992 presidential election) for the onset of a new domestic order, one that will allow

Americans to regain their "dignity as a just and compassionate people," as the authors of *The Greatest of Evils: Urban Poverty and the
American Underclass* (1993) put it.

There is, then, a good, if not an entirely happy, reason to bring out
a new, revised edition of this book at the present. Although, as in the
past, this edition contains no sweeping interpretive or major structural
changes, it has been altered considerably in a number of important
ways.

The most obvious and significant changes occurred at the end of
the book, in Chapter 16, which had been the concluding one. Quite a
few revisions were made in the coverage of the Reagan years, especially
in my comments on the 1988 Family Support Act—and what has
happened to it since its enactment. More important, however, is the
fact that the chapter now covers the Bush administration as well,
including the advent of the "new paternalism." In addition, a Chapter
17, entitled "Toward a New Domestic Order?," was added to the
manuscript. It includes the 1992 presidential campaign and election,
the early months of the Clinton administration, and a brief conclusion.

At the same time, many other important revisions were made in
the book. In fact, changes have been made in every chapter. The most
noteworthy of these occurred in Chapter 14, where I clarified and
added some material on both the Economic Opportunity Act and the
"culture of poverty" theory, and included for the first time material on
the Kerr–Mills Act (which provided the foundation for the Medicare
and Medicaid Amendments to the Social Security Act); in Chapter
13, where I discussed recent allegations about the racist and sexist
nature of the New Deal, especially the Social Security Act, and where
I added a good deal of information on the most current theories about
why the United States lagged behind the rest of the industrialized
world in creating a welfare state, and in Chapter 10, where I expanded
my comments on the gender-specific nature of widows' pensions and
the alleged intentions behind it.

In addition, in Chapter 8 I incorporated material from the most
recent studies of the settlement house movement, including further
discussion of the issues of social control and racism. In Chapter 7,
which had been revised least since the original edition of the book but
which now was changed considerably, I added a great deal of new

material on the drug problem, on the AIDS epidemic, and on the return of tuberculosis and measles as major public health problems in contemporary America. In Chapter 6 I included additional material on child neglect, abuse, homelessness, and other forms of mistreatment (and their causes), which have grown significantly worse over the past five years. In Chapter 5 I added more material on African-American benevolent societies and other efforts at self-help by the beleaguered race. Here and throughout the work (as this list of changes suggests), I tried not only to update the book but, even more so than in previous editions, to address the issues of racism and sexism and to get away from the older ethnocentric and male-oriented history. In addition, of course, the bibliographies at the end of every chapter were revised and updated.

In light of the above, a few more words are in order. Despite all the changes in this and in the prior three editions, which certainly have been important and, I am certain, have made this a better book, it is essential to remind the reader that this edition remains essentially the same in form, in spirit, and especially in intent as the original one. That is, it still is a general account of social welfare in America, "a brief [although much longer] review of America's main social welfare policies and practices from the colonial period to the present," which seeks to "assemble, assimilate, and synthesize the literature that already exists in the field," to quote from the Preface to the First Edition. To reiterate, this book rests largely on the work of others, both those with whom I agree and those with whom I sometimes do not; to them— many of whom are mentioned in the text, some of whom are not, but all of whom I have tried to treat fairly—I am deeply indebted.

Also, as readers of the book will discover, on occasion I have used the term "underclass" with great care and perhaps even with some misgivings, hence always in quotation marks or preceded by the words "so-called." It is a term, of course, that has been used rather widely during the last two decades or so, especially by a variety of social scientists, policy experts, and journalists, to describe those families and individuals, mainly African-Americans and Hispanics, who exist outside the mainstream of the American social and occupational structure and whose behavior appears to threaten the very fabric of American life. That term, however, and what it implies—more specifically, hordes of uneducated and unemployed ghetto residents who are into drugs, gangs, crime, and a variety of other degrading and menacing activities—has evoked a great deal of debate and confusion among scholars. Some argue that the "underclass" represents a new and especially corrosive development in American history, one that must be understood and treated in an untraditional manner. Others argue that the so-called underclass is not a new or menacing phenomenon, that urban poverty and disorganization existed in the past, that the term is nothing more than a euphemism for last century's "immoral" or "undeserving" poor who, like their current counterparts, largely were victims of appalling social and economic conditions over which they had very little control, and that therefore there is no need to panic about their existence or to treat them significantly otherwise than we have the impoverished in the past.*

In all honesty, I really am not certain where I stand on the matter, hence my decision to use the term sparingly and in a guarded manner. In the end, of course, the reader will have to determine for himself or herself whether the term is appropriate—or whether it is at least defined and used in a correct manner.

Before closing, I would like to express my continuing thanks to the many individuals whose assistance I acknowledged in the previous editions of this book. That is especially true of my wife, Joan, and my three children, Stephen, Anne, and David, to whom, from the start, this book has been dedicated. Without their good cheer, encouragement, and help in ways too numerous to mention (and in ways they might not fully understand), the original edition of this work would not have been written, nor would the four revised editions that have appeared since that time. To all of them, I am deeply grateful.

My sincere thanks also are extended, again, to those readers of this book whose comments, from time to time, have made me aware of certain shortcomings in the work or of ways to improve it. I have always welcomed such suggestions and continue to do so.

I also wish to thank some people who, for some inexplicable reason, I am embarrassed to say, I have not acknowledged in the past: the many wonderful, talented, and exceedingly cooperative people at The

---

*The most recent and best single source on the subject, including the scholarly controversy over its history, is Michael Katz, ed., *The "Underclass" Debate: Views from History* (Princeton, N.J.: Princeton University Press, 1993).

Free Press with whom I have worked over the past twenty years. Too numerous to name, I thank them all for the skillful way in which they have handled the manuscript, for continuing to publish the work, for allowing me to make whatever (and however many) revisions in it I deemed desirable over the years, and no less important, for agreeing to retain the Prefaces to the previous editions with each successive one, a costly—and no doubt some would say unnecessary—inclusion. I, however, think they are exceedingly important. They reveal a great deal about my thinking on a variety of matters that are not always spelled out in the text (or in some editions of the text), including, for example, such things as my definition of social welfare for the purposes of the book, the selective nature of the book's contents, the sparing use of footnotes (mainly to elaborate points made in the text rather than to cite sources), my thoughts on social control and the so-called social control thesis, the absence of a precise theoretical framework with which to interpret changing events in American social welfare history, the inevitability that authors' values will influence their perceptions of the past, and my own values concerning the subject matter of this book.

As for that last point, let me add the following, in no uncertain terms: The social welfare system neither created nor exacerbated the problem of poverty in America, nor can it prevent or eliminate it. Furthermore, it has not been the abysmal failure many of its critics claim. On the contrary, over the years it has provided some badly needed assistance to countless Americans who have been subjected to a variety of injustices, hence who have deserved, and who continue to deserve, such aid. That the number of impoverished Americans now is at an all-time high is not the consequence of misplaced altruism, well-intentioned but misguided benevolence, or excessive social action, as current popular wisdom maintains. Just the opposite, these failures, if you wish to call them that, are the consequences of the hostility and the stinginess of opponents who, through their misguided theories and actions, have made sure that the system cannot perform more adequately. The continuation of poverty in America is a matter of choice. To end it, more, not less, action and resources are needed. We can, and I hope we shall, do better.

Besides spelling out important matters that are not always made explicit in the text, the Prefaces to the previous editions also are important historical, and historiographical, documents in their own right; they tell the reader a good deal about what was occurring in the field at the time they were written, at least as seen through my eyes. For those reasons, I encourage users of the book to read through all of them carefully.

Needless to say, I continue to be pleased by the widespread interest in and use of this book, especially by teachers and students of American social welfare history and policy. I certainly hope that continues. At the same time, while most historians refuse to admit it, their fondest hopes—and those of other scholars as well—are that their works "will make a difference." Certainly I do; nothing, in fact, would make me happier than the knowledge that *From Poor Law to Welfare State* proved helpful, in however small a way, to the lives of those about whom it is written, the nation's destitute and dependent citizens. More than ever before, at least in the modern period, they need such help.

W.I.T.
JULY 1993

Preface
to the Fourth Edition

■ At the conclusion of the Preface to the third edition of this book, written in July, 1983, I stated, "Perhaps . . . a later edition of . . . [this] work, should one appear, will have a happier ending." Unfortunately, that is not so. Despite the efforts of the outgoing administration to deny and conceal the fact, millions of American citizens remain mired in poverty. Indeed, the situation has worsened over the last eight years. In point of fact, there now are more Americans—especially women and children—who are poverty-stricken and in many cases homeless and hungry than there were when Ronald Reagan took office. In addition, in cities all across the nation, there has developed a demoralized "underclass," comprising school dropouts, gang members, hustlers, criminals, drug addicts, drifters, and other marginal and functionless people who often prey upon and terrorize innocent citizens and threaten the very fabric of American life.

This new edition gave me the opportunity to take account of, and analyze, these developments and to put them into historical perspective. In so doing, I came to realize that "Reaganism" was not merely the continuation of policies initiated during the Nixon, Ford, and even Carter administrations, as I had believed (and written) earlier. In retrospect, it became clear that the period from 1969 to 1981 was a transitional era between the Kennedy–Johnson administrations, with their idealistic and grandiose social policies, and the Reagan administration, with its far more punitive and restrictive measures—measures that, for the first time, were designed to undermine and undo the welfare state that had emerged in America dur-

ing the prior half-century. The major changes, then, in this edition are
twofold: the first is a revised chapter on the Nixon–Ford–Carter years
which not only contains a great deal more information than the previous one but which was written from a much more sympathetic perspective; the second is an entirely new chapter on the Reagan years,
entitled "War on the Welfare State," which concludes with a discussion of the recently enacted Family Welfare Reform Act and the 1988
presidential campaign and election.

In addition to these changes—in substance, in interpretation, and
in structure—at the end of the book, there are numerous other differences between this edition and the previous one. In fact, modifications have been made in every chapter (in addition to revising and
updating the bibliography at the end of each). The most significant
of these are in Chapter 6, on child welfare, which deals with children's institutions, with the rising infant mortality rate, and with the
recent upsurge in poverty and homelessness among the young; in
Chapter 9, on mental health, which relates to treatment of the
retarded and to developments since the end of World War II, especially deinstitutionalization and its consequences; in Chapter 10, on
the renaissance of public welfare, which analyzes the demise of the
Sheppard–Towner Act and discusses the role of the private sector in
the emergence of the welfare state; in Chapter 13, on the depression
and a New Deal, which includes new material on self-criticism
among social workers and their attitudes toward rural poverty and
the Lundeen bill; and in Chapter 14, on the years from World War II
to the Great Society, which, among other things, analyzes the "culture of poverty" idea and discusses further the improved treatment of
the elderly.

Apart from these changes, there is good reason to bring out a new
edition of this work: the need to understand the history of social welfare in America is as great, or perhaps even greater, today as it was five
(or more) years ago. In the introduction to the new edition of his
work on the subject, James Patterson pointed out an interesting irony.
The Reagan administration's continued assault on the welfare state
and the appearance in the nation's cities of a menacing group of people who have been cast out of society (in part by the social and economic policies of that administration) have made the poverty and welfare problems sources of greater discussion and controversy than at

any time since the 1960s.[1] On the one hand, that is heartening, for these problems cannot be solved without first acknowledging their existence. On the other hand, it is rather discouraging, for it is evident that the problems remain misunderstood, misrepresented, and mistreated. The United States is the only Western democracy in the world without a system of family (or children's) allowances and without a national system of health insurance. It has the highest infant mortality rate in the Western world. One out of five of its children are living in poverty and in many cases on its city streets. Thirty-eight million of its citizens, or about one-sixth of its population, have no health insurance, and millions of others only have very limited coverage. Close to seven million of its wage earners are unemployed (while several million others who have given up searching for work and thus are left out of the statistics also are jobless) through no fault of their own, and approximately thirty-two million of its citizens are living below the poverty line. It spends less per capita on "welfare" than virtually every other advanced capitalist nation in the world. Yet, the American people continue to deceive themselves into believing that "workfare"—the forcing of welfare recipients, mainly women with young children, into the job market—somehow will right those wrongs. Perhaps more than ever before, then, the public needs to understand what frequently is referred to as "the welfare mess"—why and how welfare programs have developed over time, how they have gone astray, and what really needs to be done to help the destitute and dependent. Only then can this blot on society be eliminated.

Hopefully, this book will continue to be a small and improved contribution to that educational and corrective process. Given the current state of affairs, however, including the recent election—during which the "L word," or liberal(ism), was in disrepute and the President-elect demonstrated no concern for, let alone understanding of, the seriousness of the poverty problem, and which, if anything, seemed only to confirm Christopher Lasch's contention that we now are living in an age of narcissism[2]—I am considerably less optimistic

---

[1]James T. Patterson, *America's Struggle Against Poverty, 1900–1985* (Cambridge, Mass.: Harvard University Press, 1986).

[2]Christopher Lasch, *The Culture of Narcissism: American Life in an Age of Diminishing Expectations* (New York: Norton, 1979).

about the fate of the needy than I was when I concluded the third edition of this book.

Before closing on that rather gloomy note, let me happily inform readers that this edition, like the previous ones, rests largely on the work of other scholars, some of whom have published new studies, others of whom have revised older ones, on the subject during the last five years or so. Most of these people are cited in the text; to them, and to the others who are not mentioned, I am deeply indebted. As always, however, I of course am solely responsible for any errors—in fact or interpretation.

W.I.T.
DECEMBER 1988

Preface
to the Third Edition

■ Less than two decades ago, during the "booming" 1960s, a consensus existed in America regarding the welfare state. Few people on either side of the political aisle opposed strengthening the Social Security system or even declaring "war on poverty." It was widely believed that the federal government was responsible for the well-being of all citizens, including their basic economic security and their physical and mental health.

Now, in the midst of a long period of low productivity, deep recession, near-record levels of unemployment, high inflation, and widespread and growing suffering, the welfare state is under severe attack. In the forefront of that attack is the Reagan administration, with its neo-conservative philosophy. After his landslide victory in the fall of 1980, Ronald Reagan and his business-oriented advisors came into office intent on altering the direction of public affairs, particularly with regard to the scope and costs of federal activities and the relationship between the public and the private sector, especially in the area of social welfare. Since that time, they have consistently sought, with great success, to eliminate some federal and federally subsidized welfare programs and to cut back on others in a concerted attempt to reverse the steady drift toward Washington's greater involvement in the nation's social welfare system.

The assault against the welfare state has come from the left as well as from the right, from radical scholars and activists as well as from conservative politicians, businessmen, and working class Americans. During the past fifteen years or so, the literature on social welfare, in fact, has been dominated by critics from the left, those who advocate the so-called social control thesis—the argument that the middle and upper classes have devised and used the nation's welfare institutions and agencies not to help but to control the needy in order to safeguard the existing class system, perpetuate capitalism, and serve their own interests.[1] In fact, so pervasive had such a view become that David Rothman, one of the authors of a widely cited statement on the "limits of benevolence," rightly indicated that there even existed a widespread and acute suspicion of the very idea of doing good: "Whereas once historians and policy analysts were prone to label some movements reform, thereby assuming their humanitarian aspects," Rothman wrote in 1978, "they are presently far more comfortable with a designation of social control, thereby assuming their coercive quality. . . . "[2]

Activists of all kinds also see the needy less as beneficiaries of a benevolent society and more as victims of an all-controlling state; such activists include radicals who preach "participatory democracy" and "community control," liberals fed up with big government and the federal bureaucracy, and even some social workers and members of the other helping professions who are convinced that the "experts" or "helpers" do not really help, that their professional knowledge, techniques, and institutions have been used to promote a sort of societal imperialism designed to keep the needy in a dependent position in order to perpetuate and enhance the professionals' own role in society.[3]

This, then, is an exciting and challenging (if not very encouraging) time to be thinking and writing about American social welfare history and the social work profession—and one of the justifications for a new edition of this work. This revised text is a product, at least in

---

[1] I do not mean to imply that all those who espouse or tend to support the social control thesis are "leftists" (members of the New Left or otherwise), but many are. For a representative list of such works and their authors, see Walter I. Trattner, ed., *Social Welfare or Social Control?* (Knoxville: University of Tennessee Press, 1983), note 3, pp. 11–12.

[2] Willard Gaylin, Ira Glasser, Steven Marcus, and David Rothman, *Doing Good* (New York: Pantheon Books, 1978), p. 83.

[3] For excellent examples of such criticisms from the right and the left, respectively, see George Gilder, *Wealth and Poverty* (New York: Basic Books, 1981), and Ivan Illich, *Tools for Conviviality* (New York: Harper and Row, 1973), or *Medical Nemesis* (New York: Pantheon Books, 1976).

part, of the many things that have happened in the field, intellectually and practically, since the appearance of the last edition in 1979. While, like its predecessor, it contains no sweeping changes in substance or perspective, the book has been revised in many significant ways; in fact, there are far more revisions in this edition than there were in the previous one.

Perhaps it would be appropriate to begin by saying a few more words about "social control," a matter, for good or for bad, that may be becoming passé. Faced by an administration intent on, and to a degree succeeding in, cutting welfare expenditures and returning care of the needy to the states and localities and to the private sector—dismantling the welfare state, in other words—more people are concerned now with *what* the dependent will receive, if anything, than with the motivation, or aim, of the provider, whoever it happens to be. Even Frances Piven and Richard Cloward, authors of *Regulating the Poor*, clearly the most forcefully presented and influential of the works stressing social welfare as a means of social control, suggested in their most recent work, *The New Class War* (1982), that the issue of social control no longer is as significant as it was previously—that it is more relevant to the past than to either the present or the future.[4]

Let me say something about the relevance of the social control concept to this book, particularly this edition. Reviewers and others rightly have placed this work in the liberal tradition, or school, of history. The book suggests, for the most part, that the development of American social welfare policy has been progressive, both in intentions and in results—a purposeful adaptation of state power to the needs of its citizenry (at least its white citizens). A careful reading of the second edition, however, should reveal at least some ambivalence on the matter; in places, I state that social control, with its evil connotations, was a motivating factor, or may have been, of the "reformers" and others working with persons in need. This edition reflects much

---

[4]See Frances F. Piven and Richard A. Cloward, *The New Class War* (New York: Pantheon Books, 1982), esp. p. xi. I should add, though, that their major point is that the welfare state is so entrenched in America—primarily in the form of various income maintenance entitlements—that the Reagan administration (or anyone else) will not be able to undo it and thereby control the poor. *Regulating the Poor*, then, which (as mentioned in the Preface to the second edition) describes a cyclical pattern of providing aid and then cutting it back, characterizes the past, not the future, according to Piven and Cloward.

more thinking about the matter (in light of critiques of the social control writings, the more recent literature on social welfare, current developments in the field, etc.) and, I hope, less wavering on it.

As I indicate in the text, the term "social control" originally had benign rather than sinister connotations. At the outset, it was used to describe those processes in a society that supported a level of social cohesiveness sufficient for the society's survival, including measures that enabled the needy and the helpless to survive and function within the social order—the very things we now call social work or social welfare. Social controls, then, always are present in society; they enter every aspect of organized human activity. The question is not whether one group will seek to regulate, or control, the behavior of others but how that control is exercised and for what reason. As David Rothman has put it: "To attach a label of social control . . . and let the matter rest there hardly represents an advance." It is, he added, essential to ask, "Social control by whom? For what purposes? And why in this form rather than in another?"[5]

To begin with, then, I believe that social controls operated, perhaps even often, but usually they were the work of well-intentioned people seeking not their own self-interest but the betterment of their charges and of society. We might not like what they did, nor did their efforts always turn out well—indeed, on occasion they even may have done more harm than good—but to impugn their motives as a result does them and the historical process a disservice.

Furthermore, social control advocates or believers in effect operate from the assumption that human affairs always are reasoned responses to specific developments, responses about which the historian or the social scientist can be certain—that history, in other words, is similar to the physical world; it is a determinate order about which statements that are unshakable and testable can be framed. I repudiate this notion, too. Even more so than previously, I am convinced that human affairs are too vagarious, disordered, unstructured, uncertain, and diverse to permit facile generalizations about social control or other matters.

I repeat, therefore, what I stated in the Preface to the previous edi-

---

[5]David Rothman, "Social Control: The Uses and Abuses of the Concept in the History of Incarceration," *Rice University Studies* 67 (Winter 1981): 16.

tion of this work: "no simple 'scientific' formula can be devised to interpret the history of social welfare in America." As I believe this work (and others) demonstrates, American social welfare policy has been the product of a wide variety of factors, including, no doubt, paternalism and self-interest, whether they reflect a desire to maintain capitalism or other motives. But our social welfare policy has been more the product of a wide variety of other factors, including good intentions (which have no place in the social control scheme), economic forces (prosperity as well as recession or depression), religious beliefs, cultural values, demographic changes, and such political and institutional developments as the nationalization of politics, the growing number and influence of pressure groups, and the bureaucratic expansion of established agencies and programs.[6]

As far as other changes in the book are concerned, clearly the most obvious and important occur in the last chapter, previously entitled "Where Do We Go from Here?" and now called "A New Era: Disenchantment and Retreat." Chapter 15 not only has been brought up to date but also has been completely restructured and rewritten in light of developments during the past few years—and the opportunity to put much of the material into historical perspective. As a result, whereas the concluding chapter previously began in the 1970s, it now opens with Richard Nixon's election in 1968, the start of a "new era."

Chapters 14 (formerly "The War and Postwar Years" and now "From World War to Great Society") and 13 ("Depression and a New Deal") also have been extensively revised. The former includes a great deal more material on the 1950s, the Kennedy–Johnson years, and the growing disenchantment with the Great Society; the latter includes discussion of the new assessments of Herbert Hoover, extensive revision of the material on Franklin D. Roosevelt, from a slightly less favorable perspective, new material on rural poverty, a more extensive discussion of the Civil Works Administration ("the best of the New

---

[6]For the best general refutation of the social control thesis (especially Piven and Cloward's *Regulating the Poor*) and discussion of "liberal incrementalism" as an important factor in the making of American social welfare policy, see James T. Patterson, *America's Struggle Against Poverty, 1900–1980* (Cambridge, Mass.: Harvard University Press, 1981). For another good discussion of the problems with the social control thesis (and the progressive outlook as well), see David A. Rochefort, "Progressive and Social Control Perspectives on Social Welfare," *Social Service Review* 55 (December 1981): 568–92.

Deal relief measures"), and, especially, material on opposition to the administration from the left wing within the social work profession.

Rather than recite all the other changes made in this edition, suffice it to state, once again, that there are a great many; in fact, significant revisions were made in virtually every chapter, with the exception of the one on public health. In general, additional material was included, new interpretations were either incorporated into the text or alluded to for the readers' knowledge or consideration (see the discussions of the institution in the early nineteenth century, the settlement house movement in the early twentieth, and the alleged "psychiatric deluge" of the 1920s, for example), and the narrative was brought up to date, or at least closer to the present (see the chapters on child welfare and the mental health movement, for instance). Two specific changes, however, should be mentioned: the material on the early twentieth-century social insurance movement was broadened considerably and moved from Chapter 8 to Chapter 10, for reasons that will be self-evident; moreover, the bibliographies at the end of each chapter were revised and updated.[7]

This new edition, then, is an attempt to bring to the reader the best, the most thoughtful, and the most recent material on the subject of American social welfare history, as defined in the Preface to the original work. I hope I have succeeded in so doing. Of course, there still will be those who differ with what has been said here or lament what has been left unsaid; that is inevitable. I welcome readers' comments on these or other matters relating to American social welfare history and should add that I have profited greatly from such comments in the past. In fact, I wish to thank publicly all those people who took the time to write to me, whether to express satisfaction with the work, to call errors to my attention, or simply to query me about one thing or another.

I also wish to acknowledge, once again, my continuing gratitude to those cited in the first two editions of this work, especially my wife and children, who continue to be sources of inspiration and pride, as well as enormous help in all sorts of ways. In addition, I would like to

---

[7]For a more extensive guide to sources, see the first comprehensive bibliography in the field: Walter I. Trattner and W. Andrew Achenbaum, eds., *Social Welfare in America: An Annotated Bibliography* (Westport, Conn.: Greenwood Press, 1983).

thank the many scholars—some of whom are mentioned in the text, others of whom are not—whose works proved helpful in the revisions found in this edition. And, finally, but by no means least important, I would like to express my continuing debt to someone I am embarrassed to say I somehow failed to pay tribute to, at least publicly, in the past—Professor Emeritus Robert C. L. Scott of the History Department at Williams College. It was Professor Scott, an inspiring teacher, who introduced me to the study of history, especially American social and intellectual history, and who, unbeknownst to either of us at the time, turned me (and quite a few others) into a historian.

Needless to say, I have been pleased by the widespread interest in the earlier editions of this book. Apparently quite a few students and teachers of American social welfare history and policy, and others, found them useful; I hope this edition proves a worthy successor to those works. While I did not write this book with the intention that it be applicable to current developments, but rather that it provide some historical perspective to those interested in such matters, I nevertheless confess to the hope that it might have some constructive impact on the nation's social welfare system, however small, and ultimately on the lives of the nation's needy citizens. Perhaps, then, a later edition of the work, should one appear, will have a happier ending.

W.I.T.
JULY 1983

Preface
to the Second Edition

■ Readers who are acquainted with the first edition of this work will quickly discover that this new, revised version contains no sweeping changes in content or interpretation. The book, however, has been improved in a number of important ways.

The initial version, completed early in 1973, brought the account of social welfare in America up to the start of this decade. To leave it at that critical juncture would be to shirk an obligation to readers who have witnessed the important, often complex occurrences since then and who seek to know how they are related to prior events. One of the most significant elements in the new edition, then, is the addition of a chapter on the 1970s, "Where Do We Go from Here?"

I was especially pleased to have the opportunity to bring the text up to date because, writing some five or six years ago, I ended the manuscript on a rather optimistic note. For reasons discussed in the work, I suggested that "as 1970 approached, all was not bleak"; despite the lack of progress, "there were rays of hope." Events over the past half-decade have proved me unduly sanguine, as the new concluding chapter indicates. Perhaps a future edition of this work will see the restoration of my confidence in the future; I hope so.

The revision also offered me the opportunity to rectify a few errors and obscurities in the original edition and to rewrite my account of "the Postwar Decades," clearly the weakest part of the original study, as some reviewers indicated. Writing about the eventful decade of the 1960s from the vantage point of only two or three years later was a hazard that I was mindful of but chose to confront. The time elapsing since has permitted me to place that period in better perspective. Another significant change, then, involves the inclusion of additional material in, and the rewriting of, Chapter 14, now entitled "The War and Postwar Years."

Two other modifications in the new edition deserve special mention. In the interest of a more balanced treatment of the subject, I have added more material on the nation's minority groups, especially blacks. In addition, when appropriate, I have tried to incorporate, or at least take into account, the new scholarship and fresh points of view that have appeared since publication of the original work. I hasten to add, however, that there have been few scholarly works on the subject in the intervening years, and, for the most part, those that have appeared have lent support to the interpretations already presented. Where they have not—as, for example, in the case of the settlement house movement—I was particularly careful to call this matter to the reader's attention.

With these and a few other exceptions—a slight reorganization of the material in Chapters 4 and 5, the inclusion of a discussion of changing concepts of childhood and human development in Chapter 6, the redrafting of pages or paragraphs here and there, and the updating of the bibliographies—the work remains essentially the same in form and spirit. It is still a general account of social welfare in America, "a brief [although slightly longer] review of America's main social welfare policies and practices from the colonial period to the present," which seeks to "assemble, assimilate, and synthesize the literature that already exists in the field," to quote from the original Preface.

Two other matters warrant comment here, especially since they evoked the concern of some of those who read the original work. The first involves the question of objectivity. As is generally accepted, it is impossible for the historian to be completely objective. His or her background, upbringing, education, and numerous other factors invariably affect the work, if only in deciding what to study or what to include or omit from that study. I am no exception; my experiences and values have affected my judgment and, although I have endeavored to be as fair and as judicious as possible, parts of this work undoubtedly reflect a point of view. The reader should be aware of this problem and approach the book with an appraising and critical attitude as well as an open mind.

Another matter of concern to some reviewers of the original edition, especially to political scientists, was its lack of a clear conceptual framework to explain changing events. As one critic put it, the book failed "to reflect the impact of a scientific approach to the subject matter." To that charge I plead guilty—although without regret.

In my opinion, no simple or "scientific" formula can be devised to interpret the history of social welfare in America. Welfare programs, which to some degree involve the redistribution of resources from the "haves" to the "have-nots," are contingent upon a society's ability to pay for them. They depend in large part on the economic forces or realities that prevail at any given time. However, they are not determined on economic grounds alone. Society's response to its needy citizens is affected by numerous other, sometimes related, factors, including inherited (but changing) customs and traditions, religious attitudes and beliefs, social values, the political climate, the degree of social stability or instability, and the importance attached to the family as a basic social institution. Consequently, broad generalizations about American social welfare history are, to say the least, difficult to come by. To those brave enough to attempt such a venture, I wish good luck. I have chosen to let the "facts" speak for themselves.

Two courageous souls who have pursued the risk-strewn path are Frances F. Piven and Richard A. Cloward, whose important and widely read book *Regulating the Poor* appeared after the completion of my original work. Piven and Cloward argued that, historically, relief systems have served—and continue to serve—two main functions: (1) to maintain social and political tranquility, and (2) to enforce work. Assistance has been given to the poor less out of concern for their plight than out of concern for the stability of the social and political order and out of a desire to maintain the work ethic. Relief, thus, has been an effective way of manipulating the poor—keeping them under control and occupied in low-income, menial labor. To quote Piven and Cloward:

Relief arrangements are initiated or expanded during the occasional outbreaks of civil disorder produced by mass unemployment, and are then abolished or contracted when political stability is restored. Expansive relief policies are designed to mute civil disorder, and restrictive ones to reinforce work
norms. In other words, relief policies are cyclical—liberal or restrictive
depending on the problems of regulation in the larger society with which
government must contend.*

Although I allude to this work and its thesis in discussing the dramatic increase in welfare cases and expenditures in the 1960s, I have
not attempted to substantiate or refute it. A general introductory
work which presupposes that its readers have no wide technical
knowledge of social welfare programs and services is hardly the place
to do so. Still, the reader, with all the evidence before him or her, may
wish to decide whether regulation of the poor was and is the primary
motivating factor behind the development of the nation's social welfare system.

Before closing, I would like to indicate my continuing obligation
to those whom acknowledgment was made in the first edition, including the many scholars on whose work so much of this book rests, and
Freeman Cleaves of Millburn, New Jersey, who was kind enough to
read and correct parts of the revised as well as the entire original manuscript. It is also appropriate to mention again the debt I owe to my
wife, Joan, and to my children, Stephen, Anne, and David. Without
their consistent good cheer and assistance, manifested in ways too
numerous to cite, this work would have been neither written nor
revised. My sincere thanks are also extended to many readers and
reviewers, friends and unknown associates, whose personal comments
or published critiques have made me aware of certain shortcomings in
the original edition. Among these, I would like to express my special
gratitude to Ralph Pumphrey of Washington University in St. Louis;
his helpful comments are appreciated.

I have made every effort to take full advantage of the suggestions
and criticisms voiced in reviews of the first edition. I hope that these
efforts have been successful, and that this revised work will remain

---

*Frances F. Piven and Richard A. Cloward, *Regulating the Poor: The Functions of Social
Welfare* (New York: Pantheon Books, 1971), p. xiii.

useful to those interested in American social history, to social workers and members of the other helping professions, and especially to students and teachers of social welfare history and policy.

W.I.T.
JANUARY 1978

Preface
to the First Edition

■ Despite the great bulk of social welfare literature, the widespread concern about poverty and social justice, the current reassessment of our public assistance programs, and the growing number of historians turning their attention to the field, there is no interpretive history of social welfare in America from the colonial period to the present. There have been state and local studies, there have been accounts of various chronological periods in American history, and there have been histories of specific developments within the field—housing reform, the social settlements, child labor reform, the struggle for social security, and so on—but no attempt has been made to synthesize these into a broad account of American social welfare. This book is intended to fill that gap.

It is important to do so for several reasons. First of all, social welfare is an important aspect of American social history. As Merle Curti, the eminent historian, has suggested, it is a vital part of the American character; thus it should be brought into the mainstream of American history.

Also, while professional social work and our present social welfare institutions are products of the twentieth century, their antecedents go far back into history. From the beginning of recorded time, people have shown a concern for others; individually and collectively, they have tried to deal with insecurity and human need and to help those fellow men found unable to meet the minimum requirements of society. Perspectives on those attempts and the development of a variety of social welfare activities associated with such terms as alms, charity, poor relief, philanthropy, social reform, and the like may help us appreciate how far we have come.

It may also help us realize how far we still have to go. This would be especially helpful for social workers, who, like most people in the helping professions, tend to be absorbed with the burdens of those they are trying to help. Thus, they seldom look back to learn how they arrived where they are, or to obtain perspective on the magnitude and character of the problems they are dealing with. I hope that this book will help them gain that knowledge. An awareness of the rich tradition behind modern social work should also add to their professional security and philosophy and help them, and others, in planning for future social action.*

In addition, a general history of social welfare in America is needed for classroom purposes, especially for students enrolled in social welfare history, social policy, and other similar courses taught at schools of social work and elsewhere. This work was written, in part, to fill that need. I have taught the history of American social welfare for several years and, along with my students, have been frustrated at times by the lack of a text-like book that could be used for the course; this work grew, in part, from that experience.

This, then, is a history of social welfare in America. Since social welfare functions within and is determined by the larger setting of which it is a part, the book is set against the background of certain developments in American history, especially social and intellectual trends. And because so much that has happened in America in this field has been derived from or been influenced by the British experience, some attention has been given to English developments.

This is by no means a definitive or comprehensive account of the entire field; to cover all aspects of the subject would require many volumes. Rather, it is a brief review of America's main social welfare policies and practices from the colonial period to the present—one that

---

*On the role of history in social work see: Clarke A. Chambers, "The Discipline of History in a Social Welfare Curriculum," mimeographed paper prepared for the Minnesota Resource Center for Social Work Education, 1971; Karl de Schweinitz, "Social Values and Social Action—the Intellectual Base as Illustrated in the Study of History," *Social Service Review* 30 (June 1956): 119–31; Philip Seed, "The Place of History in Social Work," *Case Conference* 15 (February 1969): 407–8; and Elizabeth Wisner, "The Uses of Historical Material in the Social Work Curriculum," *Social Service Review* 34 (September 1960): 265–72. See also Merle Curti, "American Philanthropy and the National Character," *American Quarterly* 10 (Winter 1958): 420–37.

attempts to bridge the gap between a topical survey and a mono-graphic study. Naturally, some developments are alluded to only briefly, such as the role of religious and ethnic groups and the whole field of corrections, and others have been omitted, particularly American social service overseas, measures for the physically handi-capped, recent efforts to stimulate self-awareness, and the like. Still, the book embodies what I believe to be the essence of social welfare history and its significance in the American experience. There is little here that is new, for I have tried mainly to assemble, assimilate, and synthesize the literature that already exists in the field; I hope that the work, nevertheless, will have value.

Perhaps a word on the footnotes is in order. As stated, this book grew in part out of my classroom experience. Since it contains infor-mation accumulated from many sources (including my students) over a period of years, it would be impractical and impossible to cite all the material used. Moreover, the source of a quotation here, or a state-ment there, would not do justice to the associated material and the whole process of reflection that has gone into my course and into the manuscript. So I have used notes sparingly, and, for the most part, only to elaborate points made in the text. At the end of each chapter, however, I have included a bibliography in which the reader may locate sources. (Although many of the sources could have been listed in several places, for reasons of space I have listed each only once, in that place where I think it would be most useful.) These include many of the titles that my students have found helpful, as well as those I have relied on in preparing both my classroom lectures and this study.

Finally, the obvious should be mentioned—"social welfare" is a broad term that has no precise definition. Agricultural programs, for example, which were designed to provide financial help and other forms of assistance to poor farm families (but which too often have become methods of subsidizing the rich) may be considered part of our social welfare system. The same may be said of education or, to go a little afield, of political machines which, by distributing food baskets or fuel in winter, often helped the needy. In other words, almost any-thing can fall within its scope, as William Graham Sumner, the pio-neer sociologist, indicated in an essay entitled "Sociology," written in 1881: "In truth," Sumner declared in objecting to treatment of the matter as a novel issue, "the human race has never done anything else

but struggle with the problem of social welfare. That struggle consti-
tutes history, or the life of the human race on earth." Since this book
is not a history of the human race, perhaps I should define "social welfare." As used here, the term embraces those social security, social service, and health programs, activities, and organizations, public and
private, intended primarily to promote the well-being of individuals
who society felt needed and deserved help.

At first, the objective of those efforts was simply to care for those
in need—either as individuals or in groups. Later on, it became a
matter of preventing destitution and other social ills and of restoring
those in need to economic and social self-sufficiency, of bringing them
up to a standard of living consonant with that of others in the community. Still later, social workers fought for the creation of constructive programs aimed at ensuring a more secure and abundant life for
all. Our social welfare system today, then, acts not only to support
and enhance the well-being of needy individuals and groups, but also
to improve community conditions and help prevent and solve social
problems affecting all citizens. To use current terms, it plays an "institutional" as well as a "residual" role in society. To follow the development of these activities is to trace the evolving concept of man's
responsibility to man and of the community's and the government's
responsibility for the well-being of all citizens.

Far too many debts have been incurred in the preparation of this
book for me to attempt to list all of them here. As indicated, much of
this work rests upon the scholarship and ideas of others, including
many students in my social welfare history course at the University of
Wisconsin–Milwaukee. I am certain they will understand that adequate personal acknowledgment is not possible. I have attempted,
however, to indicate in the text those authors and works from which I
have borrowed most.

I do wish to acknowledge the special assistance of a number of
people. Among these, I would like to express my special gratitude to
Freeman Cleaves of Millburn, New Jersey, who read the entire manuscript and improved it in many ways. Another discerning critic who
read the entire manuscript and suggested changes that I was happy to
incorporate in the final revision is Clarke A. Chambers of the
University of Minnesota. I am also heavily indebted to Charles
Harbaugh, my research assistant, who did an excellent job reading and

analyzing articles in various social work journals. For the funds to engage Mr. Harbaugh, and for me to spend the summer of 1971 working on the manuscript rather than in the classroom, thanks is due to the Graduate School of the University of Wisconsin–Milwaukee. My gratitude is also extended to the secretarial staff of the U.W.M. Department of History, and especially to Kathy Poplawski, for typing various drafts of the manuscript with speed, accuracy, and good cheer.

Once again, I owe a special debt to my wife, Joan, who not only provided the atmosphere and the encouragement without which this book would not have been written, but who also took the time to improve its prose. Finally, I would be remiss if I did not mention my children, to whom this book is dedicated—Stephen, Anne, and David; never once did they complain about the long working hours, and irritabilities, of an author. For that I am deeply thankful.

While all of those mentioned helped me, the writer is solely responsible for any errors in fact, interpretation, and style.

W.I.T.
January 1973

CHAPTER 1

The Background

■ The basic tenets and programs of any social welfare system reflect the values of the society in which the system functions. Like all other social institutions, social welfare systems do not arise in a vacuum; they stem from the customs, statutes, and practices of the past. Therefore, one cannot understand current efforts to help the needy without first comprehending the foundations on which they were built. And since the practice of assisting people in need as we know it in America did not originate in this country but was transplanted from the Old World to the New during the colonial period, we must go back in time, perhaps even to antiquity, to begin our study of American social welfare.

Hospitality to strangers, for example, was recognized as a virtue even among primitive peoples. Hammurabi, the famed ruler of Babylonia some two thousand years before Christ, made the protection of widows and orphans, and the weak against the strong, an essential part of his code. Buddhism, founded about 400 B.C., taught that all other forms of righteousness "are not worth the sixteenth part of the emancipation of the heart through love and charity."

The ancient Greeks and Romans frequently discussed the matter. Aristotle (384-322 B.C.) spoke of man as a social animal and, as such, one who had to cooperate with and assist his fellow men. He also said it was more blessed to give than to receive. Then there was Cicero (106-43 B.C.), the famed Roman, who wrote: "Justice commands us to have mercy on all . . . , to consult the interests of the whole human race, to give everyone his due," rich and poor alike. In fact, the words "philanthropy" and "charity," and the concepts for which they stand—love of mankind, love of humanity, brotherhood—are of Greek and Latin origin.[1] It is not surprising, then, that the ancient Greeks, and the Romans after them, had a variety of ways of relieving distress and helping those in need. Some of those we might not recommend today, such as infanticide, slavery, concubinage, and euthanasia. On the other hand, they also had such other practices as daily allowances or pensions for the crippled, public distribution of grain for the needy, and institutions for the custodial care of various unfortunates, especially youngsters orphaned as a result of fathers lost in battle.

Even more important for the history of American philanthropy and social welfare are the ancient Jewish doctrines which teach the *duty* of giving and, equally important, the *right* of those in need to receive. Throughout the Old Testament, the ancient Hebrew collection of historical books, laws, proverbs, psalms, and prophetic writings that go as far back in time as the late eleventh century B.C., one finds commandments to be charitable to the unfortunate—the sick, the old, the handicapped, and the poor.[2] Thus, the Scriptures not only state that "one might break off his iniquities" by showing mercy to the poor, but command that "thou shalt not harden thy heart nor shut thy hand" to the poor, and note that "it is forbidden to turn away a poor man . . . empty-handed." Moreover, such "charity should be given with a friendly countenance, with joy, and with a good heart."

Not only is everyone who can afford to do so obliged to contribute to charity, but according to the Old Testament, all those in need are obliged to take it. Thus, as Maimonides (1135-1204), the Jewish scholar and philosopher, put it: "Whosoever is so much in need of charity that he cannot live unless he receives it—as, for instance, a man who is old or sick or in constant pain—but takes none out of

---

[1]Philanthropy comes from the Greek words *philo*, or love, and *anthropos*, or mankind; charity comes from the Latin word *caritas* (or *carus*), or love (brotherly love), although there is some evidence that it may be derived from the Greek word *haris* (or *harieis*), which technically means grace but may imply brotherly love or its equivalent.

[2]This is especially true of the Pentateuch, the first five books of the Old Testament, sometimes called the Torah. Within the Pentateuch, the book of Deuteronomy, the law book (in which the God of the Israelites is described as one who "loveth the stranger, in giving him food and raiment"), is most important for these purposes.

pride, is guilty of bloodshed and is responsible for his own life; so that he has nothing for his suffering, save punishment and sin."

The Talmud, a collection of Jewish law and tradition (based upon biblical texts and rabbinical commentaries on those texts) codified around A.D. 500 and still considered the source of authority among orthodox Jews today, prescribes exactly how charitable funds are to be collected and distributed, including the appointment of *gabbaim*, or tax collectors, to administer the system.

How much should be given a poor man? The Talmud provides the answer: "Sufficient for his needs in that which he wanteth." Thus, if someone is hungry, "he should be fed; if he needs clothing, he should be clothed; if he lacks household utensils, they should be purchased for him. . . . [E]ach and every one should be supplied with what he needs."

Christianity carried on this tradition. Its emphasis upon good deeds, love of one's enemies, and entry into heaven through mercy and charity stemmed, of course, from Old Testament doctrine and Hebraic law and custom. Since Jesus, Peter, Paul, and the other founding fathers of the Christian church—including the first fifteen bishops in Jerusalem—were Jews, it is not surprising that the New Testament no less than the Old contains many verses that stress charity.[3] The text that perhaps more than any other weaves together the threads of early Christian-New Testament teaching on charity is the description of the Day of Judgment in St. Matthew, especially: "And the King shall answer and say unto them, Verily, I say unto you, Inasmuch as ye have done it unto one of the least of these my brethren, ye have done *it* unto me."

The Decretum, a compilation of papal decrees, canons of church councils, and commentaries of church lawyers codified in the twelfth century which, along with subsequent decrees and writings, is considered the authoritative source of law for Christians, contains an elaborate discussion of the theory and practice of charity. Study of the

---

[3]It should also be mentioned that the seventh-century Koran, the sacred text of Islam, or Mohammedanism, exhorts the believer to show charity to widows, orphans, wayfarers, and the unfortunate, and specifies various "right" ways of giving. Almsgiving is one of the Five Pillars of Islam (along with confession of faith, prayer, pilgrimage, and fasting during the holy month of Ramadan), and those who perform such good deeds are promised paradise.

Decretum reveals that the leading principle underlying early Christian social welfare policy was similar to the Hebrew idea that preceded it—poverty was not considered a crime. And while discretion was to be observed in bestowing assistance, and careful rules were elaborated for discriminating among the various classes of needy people,[4] generally speaking, evidence of need overrode all else. It was assumed that need arose as a result of misfortune for which society, in an act of justice, not charity or mercy, had to assume responsibility. In short, the needy had a right to assistance, and those who were better off had a duty to provide it.

In practice, these ideas operated in a variety of ways. At the outset, when the church was small and its early followers owned no private property, there was little need to establish any formal social services. While there was some poverty, it was not a social problem. Those suffering misfortune were among close friends and associates who came to their assistance as a matter of course; mutual aid, in other words, sufficed to meet the needs of the faithful.

With the passage of time, the end of persecution (as marked by Emperor Constantine's conversion to Christianity in the fourth century), an increase in members and wealth, and greater ease of travel, church fathers found it more and more necessary to establish a formal system of charities. Beginning in the sixth century, the monasteries that emerged served as basic agencies of relief, especially in rural areas. Some monastic orders, in fact, were organized to help the needy. Receiving income from their lands and from donations, legacies, and collections, they not only gave generously to those who came to their doors, but carried food and other provisions to the poor in the community.

By the eleventh century, with the evolution of feudalism, a system of government in which those who possessed landed estates also held political power, there was little uncared-for distress, at least in theory. Most people lived on feudal manors as serfs, protected by their liege lords or masters against such hazards as sickness, unemployment, and old age. In return for imposing a strong measure of constraint on individual freedom, feudalism, in other words, provided a form of social insurance against the exigencies of life.

---

[4] A man's first responsibility was to his family, especially his parents, then to his neighbors, and after that, to strangers. Even among strangers, however, a rather elaborate hierarchy existed.

Those who received no such protection, especially in the rapidly emerging cities, were often helped by social, craft, and merchant guilds. While for the most part the guilds provided benefits for their own members (who, because of their craft or trade, were somewhat removed from the immediate threat of poverty), they also provided assistance to others. Thus, many maintained "works of charity" for the town poor—they distributed corn and barley yearly, fed the needy on feast days, provided free lodgings for destitute travelers, and engaged in other kinds of intermittent and incidental help.

A more important source of aid to the needy during the Middle Ages was the hospital. Medieval hospitals did not merely provide medical assistance to the ill; rather, they housed and cared for weary travelers, for orphans, the aged, and the destitute, and in general provided a variety of services for all those in need. Most early hospitals were attached to monasteries or were found along main routes of travel. Soon they appeared in cities and later were taken over by municipal authorities, thus forming a link between ecclesiastical and secular charity. By the middle of the fourteenth century, there were hundreds of such institutions in England alone. They varied in size from those caring for a dozen or so people, to others accommodating up to several hundred.

Most important in terms of administering medieval poor relief was the aid dispensed by ecclesiastical or church authorities at the diocese or parish level. The bishop of each diocese was charged with the duty of feeding and protecting the poor within his district. He was directed to divide the total revenue of the diocese, which came from the church tithe, and distribute a fixed portion—from a third to a fourth—to those in need. In most cases, though, the diocese was divided into several parishes, and in practice it was the parish priest who became directly responsible for relieving distress.

Most priests were diligent in carrying out their duties, and the money available for care of the poor was sufficient for the need. By the "high" Middle Ages, then, a highly developed and effective system of poor relief had been established. Because the church was a *public* institution and the tithe a *compulsory* tax, it could be argued that the system as regulated by the church was the prototype of the one that arose under the famous English Poor Law of 1601. With the rise of the modern state, which in the middle of the sixteenth century absorbed the church, civil authorities naturally became responsible for administering the system of poor relief conducted earlier by church officials.

In any case, medieval poor relief, it must be remembered, was governed by the time-honored beliefs that poverty was a permanent and inescapable feature of society and that the better off were obliged to share some of their riches with their poorer brethren. Furthermore, it was practiced in an environment of localism and social stability in which strangers and mass destitution were absent; relief, for the most part, had to be provided only for members of the community with unusual cases of poverty occasioned by accident, illness, death, or some other calamity that strained the resources of families, landlords, and voluntary associations.

In the meantime, however, certain social and economic upheavals occurred that altered the situation greatly. The general dissolution of feudalism and the manorial system resulted, on the one hand, in an increase of individual freedom but, on the other hand, in social disorder, uncertainty, and serious hardship for many, especially agricultural laborers forced from the land. The growth of commerce and international trade and the rise of a money economy with its elements of capital investment, credit, interest, rent, and wages also affected the incidence and nature of poverty. So too did the Industrial Revolution and development of the factory system, which led to the decline of rural handicrafts and the rise of urban masses with limited skills who experienced not only seasonal but also cyclical unemployment and other social and economic hazards over which they had no control. Subsistence, in other words, depended much less now than previously on the individual, or on work itself, as on the farm or in the home, than on employment by those who owned the resources, on the factory whistle and the time clock—and on the state of the market.

In England, conditions were made worse by the so-called enclosure movement, which resulted from the growth of the woolens industry. As the demand for wool increased, and with it the price, it became extremely profitable for landowners to turn their fields into pastures and to raise sheep. Since sheep-raising could not be done on small fields, this upset the earlier feudal system of tillage, which rested on landlords dividing their estates into small tracts and parceling them out to tenants (or serfs) in return for certain specified services. Thus, enclosure led to the further destruction of rural homesteads, the scattering of many more cottagers, and a sizable increase in the number of unattached persons without the traditional means of support and therefore forced into wage labor in search of a livelihood.

Then a series of natural calamities—crop failures, famine, pestilence, and especially the dread Black Death (or bubonic plague), which occurred in 1348–49 and killed almost a third of England's population—produced further suffering and hardship for many. Finally, the growth of corruption and the general decay of the church in England and elsewhere ultimately led to the Protestant Reformation and, in 1536, to the dissolution of the monasteries and other church property by Henry VIII; many of those who had lived or had been employed in ecclesiastical institutions were turned out and forced to join the ranks of poor wanderers.

Taken together, these developments—the breakdown of the medieval economy, the social structure with its relatively fixed order of things, and the church with its entire framework of charity—meant for many people the loss of the economic security given to a serf by his master, and the social, economic, and spiritual security given by the church to its members during the Middle Ages. This, in turn, resulted in a tremendous increase in unemployment, poverty, vagabondage, begging, and thievery, especially in the growing commercial centers to which many of the needy gravitated in search of work and higher wages. New social arrangements were required to mitigate these hardships, to reduce uncertainty, and to stabilize community life. It was in this context that the modern institution of social welfare emerged.

As early as the mid-fourteenth century, the state began to intervene where the church had no dominion. Kings, lords, and rising businessmen perceived mendicancy, widespread population movement, and labor shortages as problems. In an effort to do something about these conditions, especially to suppress the restless wandering of the landless and to keep laborers in the state of servitude from which they were just emerging, Edward III, as early as the mid-fourteenth century, initiated a series of restrictive measures. Although sometimes considered the beginning of parliamentary involvement in welfare policy, they were basically repressive statutes aimed more at immobilizing laborers and thereby recreating a subservient work force than at assisting the needy. Among these, the most important was the Statute of Laborers. Proclaimed in 1349 (a year after the Black Death, which killed so many people that it caused severe labor shortages and demands for higher wages among the poorer classes as well as widespread fears of potential carriers of the plague), the measure fixed maximum wages, placed travel restrictions on impotent and unemployed persons, and in effect compelled the jobless to work for any employer willing to hire them. The law also forbade the giving of charity to "sturdy" and "valiant" alms-seekers, a practice which allegedly induced mobility or laziness and unemployment; all able-bodied persons would be forced to work in their place of residence at a rate of wages fixed by law and hence would be unable to exploit the more favorable labor market conditions resulting from the Black Death—and perhaps spread the dread disease.

The social and economic changes that occasioned the statute, however, were far more powerful than the law designed to stop them. The progress from feudalism toward a capitalistic-democratic society—one of the most profound upheavals civilization has known—continued, not always peaceably. As a result, in the sixteenth century other measures were enacted which further attempted to repress vagrancy and mobility. In 1531, Parliament passed a statute that provided severe punishment for able-bodied beggars. They were to be brought to the market place and "there to be tyed to the end of a carte naked and be beten with whyppes throughe out . . . tyll [their bodies] . . . be blody by reason of suche whypping."

The act, however, also contained constructive features concerning relief of the poor; it decreed that mayors, justices of the peace, and other local officials "shall make diligent search and inquiry of all aged poor and impotent persons which [sic] live or of necessity be compelled to live by alms of the charity of the people," and assign such people areas where they may beg. While still primarily a punitive and repressive measure designed to limit begging, by making a distinction between the able-bodied who refused to seek work and the poor who could not work and thus needed relief, and authorizing the latter to beg, and even setting aside areas where they might do so, the state took the first step toward administering an organized network of relief.

In 1536, with the passage of the Act for the Punishment of Sturdy Vagabonds and Beggars—the Henrician Poor Law—the government exercised further responsibility for the relief of persons in economic distress. While the measure made the penalties for begging even more severe (including an elaborate schedule of branding, enslavement, and execution for repeated offenses), it also ordered local public officials to obtain resources, through voluntary contributions collected in churches, to care for the poor, the lame, the sick, and the aged. Instead of merely setting up machinery for legalizing begging and confining it to the impotent poor, as the previous statute had done, this measure attempted to eliminate the need for alms-seeking, making the parish the unit of local government for poor relief.

Furthermore, the act permitted local officials to use the funds they collected to provide work for "such as be lusty or having their limbs strong enough to labor." A perceptive and novel feature of the measure, then, was its recognition of the fact that the able-bodied were not always able to find jobs. In such cases, parish officials could furnish work for those in need. They were also given the authority "to take . . . children under the age of fourteen years and above the age of five years, in begging or in idleness, and to appoint them to masters of husbandry or other crafts or labors to be taught, by which they may get their living when they shall come of age." By the provisions of this act, then, the state, through civil and church authorities, assumed legal responsibility for the relief of *all* its poor, old and young, impotent and able-bodied alike. It was a serious attempt to cope with the economic and social problems of the age.

Although local officials—"mayors, governors and head officers of every city and the church wardens or two others of every parish"— were required to provide assistance to the destitute, funds for the purpose were to be raised through voluntary contributions in churches. The next logical step was introduction of a compulsory assessment when donations proved insufficient. This came in 1572 with the enactment of a measure stating that the justices of the peace and other local officials "shall by their good discretions tax and assess all and every the inhabitants dwelling in all and every city,

borough, town, village, hamlet and place" for the care of those in
economic distress. The statute also created a new public official, the
overseer of the poor, who was charged with the duty of providing
work relief for the able-bodied unemployed, a job more clearly
defined and made mandatory by the provisions of yet another measure, enacted four years later.

By the late sixteenth century, then, the government had perceived
that punitive measures directed at vagrants were insufficient to preserve order, let alone the general good of the realm, or, in the words
of R. H. Tawney, that "the whip had no terror for the man who must
either tramp or starve." Based on the idea that poverty was an economic rather than a personal matter and that the state should help
those people who could not provide for themselves, a series of measures relating to poverty, vagrancy, and relief of the poor had been
enacted that attempted to deal with the problem of economic security in light of the changing religious, social, and economic conditions
of the period. The principle of relief locally financed and administered for local residents had been established. Public officials administered a system of assistance that included both direct grants-in-aid
to the unemployable and a policy of apprenticeship for the young
and work relief for able-bodied adults. Taken together, these measures embodied most of the principles written into the renowned
Poor Law of 1601.

The immediate background of the famous statute was the worsen-
ing times of the 1590s—a decade of food scarcity and widespread
famine, of inflation and high prices, of insecurity and great suffering.
Rioting, thievery, and social disorder again became widespread.
Lawmakers, not only fearful of insurrection (especially since England
had no standing army at the time), but also compelled to recognize
the existence of large-scale involuntary idleness and suffering due to
difficult conditions, felt the need to act.

This, too, was the age of mercantilism, an era of paternalism, and
of faith in the government's capacity (and need) to arrange the
affairs of mankind. The interests of the state—especially the desire
to build up a strong, self-sufficient economy—were dominant. And
since the means of accomplishing this were by "setting the poor to
work" and turning the country into "a hive of industry," direct and

active government intervention was required to overcome the threat of insecurity and the prevailing social disorder; hence, the Poor Law of 1601.[5]

Like its predecessors, the Elizabethan Poor Law, which was to stand with but minor revisions for almost 250 years, embodied the conflicting strain between the desire to reinforce the feudal structure and the increasing assumption by civil government of responsibility for the downtrodden. Thus it had some harsh, repressive features (or at least features that today would be considered harsh). Parents—insofar as they had the means—were legally liable for the support of their children and grandchildren. Likewise, children were responsible for the care of their needy parents and grandparents. More important, vagrants refusing work could be committed to a house of correction; whipped, branded, or put in pillories and stoned; or even put to death. And the measure did not provide for the right of "appeal" by recipients—or potential recipients—of relief if they felt aggrieved.[6] On the other hand, the measure had many constructive features—especially its assumption that the state had a responsibility to supplement ordinary efforts to relieve want and suffering and to insure the maintenance of life. It further conceded that there were helpless or needy people who not only deserved such assistance but who had a legal right to it. In addition, the statute defined three major categories of dependents—children, the able-bodied, and the impotent—and directed the authorities to adapt their activities to the needs of each: for needy children, apprenticeship; for the able-bodied, work; and for the incapacitated, helpless, or "worthy" poor, either home ("outdoor") or institutional ("indoor") relief.

---

[5]Although the 1601 Act is the most famous and is thought of as the most important poor law, it was in fact anticlimactic. In 1597 and 1598, a comprehensive poor law was enacted which brought together all the previous legislation on the matter; about the only thing the latter measure added to its predecessor was the extension of liability for support to grandparents. As Karl de Schweinitz has pointed out, the 1601 statute has been considered a landmark in the relief of economic distress largely because it was the last rewriting of the total law.

[6]The right of appeal against a decision made by the overseers of the poor was granted to the needy in England in 1796.

The law firmly established the principle of local responsibility, at the lowest level, for the care of those in need. In executing the measure, the parish was to act through its church wardens and a small number of "substantial householders" who would be appointed annually by the justices of the peace to serve both as overseers of the poor and as collectors of the revenue—a wholly secular or civil position. Funds necessary for carrying the act into effect were to be raised by taxing every householder in the parish, with the threat of imprisonment for those who failed to pay such taxes.[7]

So while the basic principles of public assistance did not originate in 1601—for poor relief had been a matter of public concern long before that time—the Elizabethan Poor Law brought together, in a single coherent statute, the "inconsistent and erratic relief legislation of the previous" years, firmly placing its operation in the hands of civil authorities and establishing a definite system of obligatory financing outside of the church. According to Karl de Schweinitz, author of *England's Road to Social Security*, it culminated a development that started in 1531, or perhaps as early as 1349.[8]

Written to bring order out of chaos and with an eye toward preserving stability in case of future social and economic crises, the statute recognized the existence of involuntary unemployment and of need, and firmly established the individual's right to public assistance. For the most part it was a broad, permissive act. From what evidence we have, we can say that it was put into effect throughout England with a fair degree of efficiency and success. Although it did not eliminate all human suffering, many of the needy were helped, the able-bodied put to work, children apprenticed—and society remained rela-

---

[7]The justices of the peace, who fixed the rate of assessment, also had the authority to raise revenue from other parishes should local funds prove to be insufficient and to levy fines against overseers of the poor for being negligent in their duties.

[8]Perhaps it should be pointed out that a number of statutes enacted after the Poor Law of 1601 perpetuated some of the repressive features of the Acts of 1349 and 1531, including the Law of Settlement of 1662, which was designed to restrict the movement of the poor from their parishes. Another such measure, passed in 1772, provided for the establishment of workhouses, which were to act as deterrents to home relief for the able-bodied. On the other hand, there were Gilbert's Act of 1782, which mitigated the demoralizing effects of such workhouses, and the Speenhamland system, discussed in Chapter 4.

tively tranquil.[9] The statute also provided the pattern for the poor laws in the American colonies, in the original thirteen states, and in the subsequent ones as they entered the Union.

Bibliography

BEER, MAX. *Social Struggles in Antiquity*. New York: International Publishers, 1925.

———. *Social Struggles in the Middle Ages*. New York: International Publishers, 1929.

BEIER, A. L. "Vagrants and the Social Order in Elizabethan England," *Past and Present* 64 (August 1974): 3–29.

BOSWELL, JOHN E. "*Expositio* and *Oblatio*: The Abandonment of Children and the Ancient Medieval Family," *American Historical Review* 89 (February 1984): 10–33.

BRUNO, FRANK J. "New Light on Oriental and Classical Charity in the Pre-Christian Era," *The Family* 25 (November 1944): 260–65.

CAMPBELL, ANNA M. *The Black Death and Men of Learning*. New York: Columbia University Press, 1931.

COLL, BLANCHE D. "Perspectives in Public Welfare: The English Heritage," *Welfare in Review* 4 (March 1966): 1–12.

COULTON, G. G. *The Medieval Village*. Cambridge, U.K.: Cambridge University Press, 1931.

COURTENAY, WILLIAM J. "Token Coinage and the Administration of Poor Relief During the Late Middle Ages," *Journal of Interdisciplinary History* 3 (Autumn 1972): 275–96.

---

[9]It should be mentioned that while the state gave notice (through passage of this act) that the poor were to be cared for from public funds, the state was quite willing, if not anxious, to allow parishes to look after their poor through voluntary (or private) relief, if they elected to do so. The same Parliament that passed the Poor Law of 1601 encouraged private philanthropy through enactment, the same year, of the Law of Charitable Uses which, in the words of W. K. Jordan (*Philanthropy in England, 1480–1660*), "was far more important to the history of Tudor-Stuart philanthropy than the great Elizabethan Poor Law of the same year." According to Jordan, until 1660, the mainspring of the English charity system remained private, in both organization and in financing. The Trust Law directed the spirit of generosity into the founding of numerous free private schools, hospitals, almshouses, dispensaries, and the like. In short, private philanthropy at least complemented public relief at this time, providing a second cluster of institutions and services for the needy.

DE SCHWEINITZ, KARL. *England's Road to Social Security*. Philadelphia: University of Pennsylvania Press, 1943.

FEINBERG, LOUIS, ed. *Section on Charity from the Shulhan Arukh*. New York: Charity Organization Society, 1915.

FLETCHER, JAMES L. "Enlightenment England: The Background and Development of Its Poor Law System," *Enlightenment Essays* 1–2 (Spring 1970–71): 1–13.

HANDS, A. R. *Charities and Social Aid in Greece and Rome*. Ithaca, N.Y.: Cornell University Press, 1968.

JORDAN, W. K. "The English Background of Modern Philanthropy," *American Historical Review* 66 (January 1961): 401–8.

———. *Philanthropy in England, 1480–1660*. New York: Russell Sage Foundation, 1959.

LEONARD, E. M. *The Early History of English Poor Relief*. Cambridge, U.K.: Cambridge University Press, 1900.

MARSHALL, DOROTHY. *The English Poor Law in the Eighteenth Century*. London: Routledge, 1926.

MARTS, ARNAUD. *The Generosity of Americans*. Englewood Cliffs, N.J.: Prentice-Hall, 1966.

———. *Man's Concern for his Fellow-man*. Geneva, N.Y.: Marts and Lundy, 1961.

MENCHER, SAMUEL. *Poor Law to Poverty Program*. Pittsburgh: University of Pittsburgh Press, 1967.

MOLLAT, MICHAEL. *The Poor in the Middle Ages*. New Haven: Yale University Press, 1986.

NICHOLS, SIR GEORGE. *A History of the English Poor Law*. 3 vols. London: King, 1900.

NIEBUHR, REINHOLD. *The Contribution of Religion to Social Work*. New York: Columbia University Press, 1932.

OWEN, DAVID. *English Philanthropy, 1660–1960*. Cambridge, Mass.: Harvard University Press, 1964.

"POOR LAW," *Encyclopaedia Britannica*, Vol. 18 (Chicago: Benton, 1971): 226–32.

SALTER, FRANK R., ed. *Some Early Tracts on Poor Relief*. London: Methuen, 1926.

STILLMAN, NORMAN A. "Charity and Social Service in Medieval Islam," *Societas* 5 (Spring 1975): 105–16.

TAWNEY, RICHARD HENRY. *Religion and the Rise of Capitalism*. New York: Harcourt, Brace, 1937.

THORNDIKE, LYNN. "The Historical Background," in Ellsworth Faris et al., eds., *Intelligent Philanthropy*. Chicago: University of Chicago Press, 1930.

TIERNEY, BRIAN. *Medieval Poor Law*. Berkeley: University of California Press, 1959.

ULLMAN, WALTER. "Public Welfare and Social Legislation in the Early Medieval Councils," in *Councils and Assemblies*. Cambridge, U.K.: Cambridge University Press, 1971.

WEBB, SIDNEY AND BEATRICE. *English Local Government: English Poor Law History, Part I, The Old Poor Law*. New York: Longmans, Green, 1927.

———. *English Poor Law Policy*. New York: Longmans, Green, 1910.

CHAPTER 2

Colonial America

■ Widespread destitution, which existed in many parts of the Old World, was not present in the New. The combination of abundant resources and a sparse population contrasted sharply with conditions in Europe, especially in England. Labor was at a premium; thus, unemployment was not a major social problem. Moreover, a liberal system of land tenure enabled many of those without property to acquire it, while commonage for grazing or tillage added to the possible sources of a livelihood. All in all, there was real opportunity for success in the New World.

Yet, the picture of America portrayed by early promoters of settlement—a land abounding in wealth and good auspices, indeed a new Paradise, a veritable Garden of Eden—was hardly true. Those who came to the colonies (land proprietors, tax-dodgers, and a handful of others excepted) were of moderate or poor means. The English practice, as authorized by Parliament and the transportation laws, of shipping to America thousands of rogues, convicts, political prisoners, beggars, vagrants, orphans, the unemployed, and other undesirables hardly helped. Then there was the trip across the Atlantic; not only a prolonged but also a debilitating experience for many. Passengers were packed into tiny ships with filthy and foul-smelling quarters, lack of adequate food and drinking water, and exposure to disease. Many did not survive the wretched conditions of the voyage; those who did frequently reached shore ill or infirm.

Once in America, life was so severe, so full of hardship and deprivation, that many were forced to live in poverty or so close to it that any misfortune might reduce them to that state. As a result, despite favorable chances for acquiring land or for earning a living in other ways in the New World, they did not escape poverty and many of the other social ills that plagued them in the Old World. Each colony soon had to deal with the problem of caring for the poor, the aged, the blind, the sick, the lame, the mentally ill, the lazy, the destitute of all kinds.

At the outset, as in all closely knit communities, especially in pioneer settings where there was no recourse to other forms of assistance, neighborly kindness, or mutual aid, sufficed; as Governor William Bradford's account *Of Plimouth Plantation* indicates, sheer survival depended upon it. As the population increased, however, and as the social life of the colonies grew more varied, the problem of dependency became more complex and the need for a permanent, carefully regulated poor relief policy and system became more acute, especially around the middle of the seventeenth century. By that time, so many indigent colonists were about—idlers, misfits, tramps, criminals, widows, the sick, and so on—especially in growing towns such as Boston, Newport, and Philadelphia, that their care had to become a community function and responsibility. As one would expect, the colonists turned to the manners and customs, the social and legal institutions that were part of their cultural baggage, to meet the need—the English Poor Law of 1601.

Conditions in the New World seemed to invite the adoption and nurture of the relief policies of the mother country. There were neither private charitable trusts nor ecclesiastical welfare institutions in the New World. The hardships of frontier life and the isolation and self-containment of the early settlements led to the development of a strong sense of social obligation and community solidarity which, in turn, provided a sufficient rationale for local responsibility, especially in New England where the system of local self-government prevailed.

In addition, as David and Sheila Rothman have pointed out, for seventeenth-century Americans need was in the order of things, a natural and inevitable part of the human condition. The poor, mere pawns in a divinely destined universe and hence not responsible for their condition, were always present—in America as elsewhere. This, however, was not a necessary evil, but rather a blessing, a God-given opportunity for men to do good—to serve society and their Creator.

According to God's scheme, a well-ordered society was hierarchical;

it had a series of ranks ranging from top to bottom. Some people "the great ones, high and eminent in power and dignity," were at the top, others, "the poor and inferior sort," at the bottom. Each had special privileges and obligations; the poor to work hard and to respect and show deference to those above them, the well-to-do to be humble and to aid and care for those below them. Disparities in wealth and condition existed not to separate and alienate people from one another but to make them have more need of each other—to bind them closer together "in the bond of brotherly affection" so that they might "improve [their] . . . lives to do more service to the Lord," as John Winthrop, the noted Puritan leader, put it—or perhaps militate against class antagonism and thus maintain order, as more recent observers have suggested.

In any event, social theory and theology gave meaning to poverty in colonial America. Its presence did not indicate a flaw in society, or in the needy, something to be feared and eliminated. Its victims, permanent and integral parts of the community, were to be pitied and helped. It is not surprising, therefore, that the colonial assemblies quickly acknowledged public responsibility for those unable to care for themselves or those whose families, extending through three generations (as in England), were unable to care for them, making the taxpayers of each locality responsible for their support.

The Plymouth Colony adopted such provisions in 1642, Virginia in 1646, Connecticut in 1673, Massachusetts in 1692, and so on. The colonial poor laws not only were patterned after the Elizabethan legislation, but often retained many of its specific provisions, in some cases *in toto*. Thus, the first session of the Rhode Island colonial legislature announced that the doctrine of local care for the needy was to be implemented and that overseers of the poor were to be appointed to assess a tax and collect the money to care for the poor "according to the provisions of the law of England."

In marked contrast with the practice of applying the Elizabethan Poor Law in a simple matter-of-fact way, was the case of New Amsterdam. Settled in 1609 by the Dutch, the colony set up an ecclesiastical system of poor relief; officers of the Dutch Reformed Church were vested with the authority to raise the necessary money through voluntary collections and then to distribute it to the needy. However, when the colony came under English rule in 1664, its relief policies were transformed to conform to the English pattern—public assistance through compulsory taxation.

Colonial administration of the poor laws was left to the smallest unit of government. In New England, the town was responsible for executing the statute. The Town Meeting made the decisions, which were carried out by the selectmen, tithingmen, or overseers of the poor, civil officials. In the southern colonies where, as in England, the Anglican church was established, the parish was the administrative unit. There, the board of vestry, a group of men, usually twelve in number, chosen by the freeholders to oversee the religious affairs of the parish, was also charged with the responsibility of caring for the poor. Although the entire board assessed and collected the taxes, two vestrymen served as church wardens or the "executive arm" of the body and actually distributed the aid, which was raised through a compulsory tax designed specifically for that purpose.

The simplest method of aiding the poor, especially those unable to care for themselves, was for each family to care for a destitute person during a part of the year. Thus, in Massachusetts, the Hadley Town Meeting voted in 1687 that a certain widow should be sent "round the town" to live two weeks with each family "able to receive her." Others, particularly those who needed only temporary or partial assistance, were provided with outdoor aid. The most common seventeenth-century practice, however, was to place the poor in private homes at public expense.[1] While this usually involved the payment of a fixed sum agreed upon for each person, with the town often supplying clothing and medical care besides, it was not unusual to auction off the needy (usually at the village tavern on the Saturday evening following the Town Meeting), who went to the lowest bidder. In all cases, the family and the private home, considered to be the foundation of the social order, was the setting in which the assistance was provided.

Another form of relief was abatement of taxes or parish dues. For example, on October 29, 1656, the Boston Town Meeting agreed that a "Mr. Wales hath six shillings abated of his [tax] rate for this year in regard to his poverty." Moreover, the poor were usually provided with

---

[1] In some instances, the needy were so maintained for long periods of time—up to thirty years, and more.

free medical attention.[2] Towns and parishes employed doctors to treat those who could not afford to pay medical bills. Hence, in 1664, Boston's selectmen paid Dr. Thomas Oliver five pounds "for seven months attendance upon . . . Thomas Hawkins," a needy person. Other doctors had their taxes remitted or reduced for performing such services.

While townsmen relieved neighbor's needs rather generously, and without suspicion, they showed considerably less compassion for the plight of strangers—people who might be a source of social and political as well as financial difficulty for the community. As the number of people without means of support steadily increased, as did transiency, some communities began to restrict immigration, or the movements of strangers. As early as May 1636, Boston's selectmen prohibited citizens from entertaining strangers for more than two weeks without first securing official permission; if the visitors seemed likely to stay longer and become a public burden, such permission was denied. Those who came anyway, or perhaps were already present, were "warned away," or told to leave by the selectmen or overseers of the poor; those who did not go willingly were forcibly removed by the constable.[3] Three years later, Boston officials required that some townsman provide security for any newcomer in order "to save the town from charge," as the ordinance read, again with the threat of warning away those not so covered.[4] The frequency of these and other regulations indicates that Boston and other communities continually

---

[2]On occasion, towns and parishes even paid for the sick poor to visit health spas. Thus, one Virginia record reads: "Ordered that the Church Wardens Agree with some person on the best terms they can to carry Rich Sentale to the Spring on New River for the Recovery of his health."

[3]In "warning out" those likely to become public dependents, the town was merely exercising a right that existed because of the English theory of inhabitancy, or right to live in a certain settlement. Each town was considered a corporation established by free consent; its residents, therefore (so the reasoning went), had the sovereignty to admit or exclude their own inhabitants. "Warning out," or banishment, was perceived to be especially necessary because towns had no police forces to maintain control over such "dangerous" people.

[4]The practice of requiring strangers to post bond before being allowed to settle in a community continued until the time of the American Revolution and was revived again during the era of restrictive legislation in the late nineteenth century.

faced the problem of caring for unwanted strangers who became public charges.

Establishment of residency requirements to determine eligibility for—or "entitlement" to—public assistance originated in the Plymouth Colony. There, as elsewhere, each town was obliged to support its resident poor, but, by the provisions of its poor relief statute of 1642, the status of an "inhabitant" or "resident" was defined to apply only to those who remained in a community for three months without being asked to leave.[5] Another safeguard against the influx of needy persons was a statute that prohibited the sale of land to strangers without first obtaining official approval. Also, residents who brought servants into a town had to agree to maintain them if the latter became ill, lame, or impotent.

In New York, no stranger could be harbored in a private home or in a tavern for more than one night without first registering with the town recorder. Constables in each ward were instructed to seek out strangers and present a list of their names and addresses to the mayor.

The Rhode Island Assembly empowered town councils to expel all nonresident vagrants and indigents and to accept or reject bonds from strangers. Those who returned after having been expelled were subject to heavy fines and severe whipping. These and similar restrictions

---

[5]Residency as a factor in determining eligibility for public assistance was declared illegal by the U.S. Supreme Court on April 21, 1969, in the case of *Shapiro* v. *Thompson*. Earlier, a number of states had abolished the requirement. The first to do so was Rhode Island, which acted in 1944, during World War II, when manpower shortages meant that laborers had to be more mobile and welfare administrators could not spend as much time verifying settlement and residency requirements—a time-consuming and costly venture. The Rhode Island experience indicated: (1) that people do not move in order to secure public assistance; they move in order to secure a better life for themselves, to be with relatives and friends, etc,; and (2) that the cost of assisting the needy is usually less than the administrative costs of implementing residency requirements.

As mentioned earlier, residency as a requirement for eligibility for public assistance formally began in England in 1662 with enactment of "The Law of Settlement and Removal." Patterned after the fourteenth-century Statute of Laborers, the measure prohibited parish relief to any but official parish residents—those who had obtained a legal "settlement." Such status might be acquired by birth, land ownership, taxpaying, or apprenticeship. In part, at least, this measure was a reflection of the English Revolution of 1660, which weakened the central power of the state and thus brought about less national attention to social problems. It never really was very rigidly enforced, however, because labor immobility was dysfunctional to an economically growing society.

were carried out, especially in the seventeenth and eighteenth century, as the frequency of town disputes concerning the care of dependents and the great deal of time and money spent in litigation over such matters indicate. Later, however, especially after Massachusetts terminated the warning out system in 1767, "settlement" provisions were not as rigidly enforced, for they proved impractical in an economically expanding society.

Meanwhile, seaborne paupers entering large port towns such as Newport, Boston, and New York was a related problem. In Boston, the sea was watched by a special official who warned away poor newcomers. Forty-nine of these newcomers were not permitted to disembark from the ship *Elizabeth*, which arrived in Boston Harbor from Ireland in November 1719.

The Massachusetts General Court and other colonial legislatures even required masters of all vessels to post a bond for each person they brought to the colonies. In 1721, the New York Assembly passed a similar measure requiring ship captains to file passenger lists with the town recorder within twenty-four hours after docking. Then they had to post fifty pounds security for each passenger who might become a public charge or else return that person to his or her port of embarkation. Again, in most places, ship captains were required to post bonds for sick mariners left in port.

Finally, the influx of impoverished refugees from frontier settlements during times of trouble, such as Indian wars (or from small inland towns as a result of being warned away), created a stubborn problem in some areas, especially in wealthy seaport towns. These victims of misfortune (often widows and orphans) posed more of a problem for some coastal communities than did aliens. Early during King Philip's War (1675–77), Boston officials reported that sixty-two people who had come to town were public charges and should be warned away, and no doubt many others escaped detection. Officials asked the legislature for more power to prevent such persons from residing in Boston, for those who came "thither for relief and shelter in time of war . . . had already proved a great expense to the town" and should be removed.

Fugitives from the frontier pouring into Newport at this time exhausted that town's charitable resources. More than 500 such persons arrived there in 1675 alone, and some 800 pounds had to be spent on their care. It was this problem of the "unsettled poor" in times of trouble that led to the first important change in the practice of local responsibility.

Faced with the prospect of having to care for large numbers of those driven from their homes during King Philip's War, Boston authorities appealed urgently to the General Court which provided funds from the colonial treasury to succor the nonresidents. Such was the beginning of "state" aid, in whole or in part, for the needy—veterans excepted, who from the start were wards of the various colonies rather than their localities—a practice that gradually expanded. Thus, beginning in 1701, local communities were reimbursed by the colonial treasury for the relief of "unsettled persons" with contagious diseases—people who, if sent away, would endanger other communities. In the meantime, other colonies began assigning funds to localities for the care of certain nonresidents.

As Englishmen with a poor law heritage, and as religious people for whom the injunctions about the sacredness of human life had sense and meaning, most colonists felt an obligation to help those members of their community who were unable to care for themselves. At the same time, their Calvinistic ideas about the virtue of hard work and the sin of idleness—their concept of the "calling" made work sacred—their desire to avoid an unduly heavy burden of taxes, and, perhaps more important, the existing need for labor in the colonies, convinced many that all able-bodied persons should and could work. Thus, powerful religious and economic forces converged to see to it that there would be little sympathy for "sturdy beggars." As the Puritan divine Cotton Mather put it: "For those who indulge themselves in idleness, the express command of God unto us is, that we should let them starve."

In this spirit, the Virginia Assembly, as early as 1619, ordered the apparent slothful bound over to compulsory labor. A few years later, the Massachusetts Bay settlers told Governor John Endicott that "no idle drone [should] be permitted to live amongst us." The General Court followed that, in 1633, with a decree inflicting harsh punishment on those who spent their time "idly or unprofitably." So, in the American colonies (as in England), voluntary idleness was regarded as a vice, and the able-bodied unemployed were either bound out as indentured servants, whipped and run out of town, or put in jail; in short, they were viewed not only as odious but as criminal, threats to themselves as well as to the entire community. Later, toward the latter seventeenth and early eighteenth century, many were placed in workhouses as they began to appear.[6] The great era of institution building, however, did not come until the following century.

Having red skin was also considered a vice by most of the colonists, who did not really understand the Indians, especially their love of nature, their communal life, and their concept of collective land ownership. Although the Indians had attained a high level of civilization long before the Europeans came to the New World, they were assumed to be savages, especially by the property-conscious and land-hungry English settlers. When efforts to "civilize" the Indians failed, a policy of extermination followed, usually justified on moral and religious grounds. Cotton Mather, in his major work, *Magnalia Christi Americana* (1702), described what happened to one Indian tribe that repudiated Christianity and the white man's ways:

> The Nation of Narragansetts was one of the most populous among the Indians, and once filled this mighty wilderness. Unto that woeful nation the gospel of our Lord Jesus Christ was freely rendered, but they with much affront and contempt, rejected it. . . . The glorious Lord Jesus Christ, whom they had slighted, was with our army. . . . Their city was laid in ashes. Above twenty of their chief captains were killed; a proportionable desolation cut off the inferior savages, mortal sickness and horrid famine pursued the remainders of them, so that we can hardly tell where any of them are left alive on the face of the earth.

Needless to say, there was little social welfare for native Americans during the colonial period—or later on, for that matter; most of those who survived were forced onto the nation's worst lands where, out of

---

[6]As time passed and some people began to prosper, philanthropic citizens began to make bequests to towns for various charitable purposes, including the building of workhouses. In Boston between 1656 and 1662 at least three, and probably more, probated wills included bequests to the town for the relief of the poor; these were combined and a workhouse was built with the funds. Before long, other communities did the same. This trend resulted in part from developments in England, where it was believed that putting the poor to work was both morally therapeutic and beneficial to the economy. Such institutions, however, also were used on occasion to house nonresident poor persons who were too sick or too old to be warned away.

sight, they were either ignored despite their poor plight, or placed on federal reservations administered by corrupt and uncaring officials.

Then there were blacks, who were also viewed by most colonists as uncivilized and permanently inferior—children of Satan not entitled to the same rights as white people and hence excluded from the social welfare system. Black slaves were the responsibility of their masters and were prohibited from receiving aid under most of the poor laws; free blacks, for the most part, were simply denied assistance and forced to develop their own informal self-help mechanisms.

For pauper, illegitimate, and orphaned white children, the colonies enacted typical Elizabethan legislation—apprenticeship. Indeed, the town had the authority to remove children from their parents and apprentice them out if they were not being taught a trade, as this inscription in the Boston records for November 25, 1656, indicates: "It is agreed upon the complaint against the son of Goodwife Samon, living without a calling, that if she dispose not of him in some way of employ before the next [town] meeting, that then the townsmen will dispose of him to some service according to law."

Apprenticeship was widely used for a number of reasons. As mentioned, it was a well established English practice, one that coincided nicely with the common belief that all people should be attached to a family. Also, it was argued that it was a good method of disciplining children. In addition, the practice relieved the town fathers of the burden of caring for needy youngsters, keeping public outlays and the poor rate down. And, finally, the system provided a sound means of social and economic control—it reduced idleness and it trained young workers for the needs of a growing town or colony, including the most menial and least lucrative trades, at a time when the demand for labor often exceeded the available supply of adult workers.

Finally, there were the mentally ill. Although there is no way to know the exact number of such persons during the colonial era, it is evident from scattered references that many were present in the colonies. They did not cause widespread public concern, nor were they accorded much special treatment. With the exception of the separate "mental section" in the newly established Pennsylvania Hospital, opened in 1756, and a state hospital at Williamsburg, Virginia, founded in 1773, no special facilities were provided for the mentally ill prior to the American Revolution.

Because insanity and dependency were intimately related—it often disrupted family relationships and undermined the means of support—and because specific therapies were lacking, mental disease was viewed primarily as an economic and social rather than as a medical problem.[7] Its victims came under the jurisdiction of the local community as a result of the poor laws. And except for those who were especially troublesome and deemed threats to public safety, who were usually confined to quarters, the mentally ill were regarded simply as other needy people unable to care for themselves.[8] Residents were boarded, at public expense, in the homes of relatives or others, or housed in public institutions as they began to appear. Nonresident insane indigents were warned away or, on occasion, returned home, as a note in John Winthrop's *Journal*, dated December 11, 1634, indicates: "One Abigail Gifford, widow, being kept at the charge of the parish Weldsen in Middlesex near London, was sent by Mr. Ball's ship to this country, and being found to be somewhat distracted and a very burdensome woman, the governor and assistants returned her back by warrant . . . to the same parish in the ship *Rebecca*. . . ."

The first statute concerned specifically with providing special care for the insane was enacted in Massachusetts, in 1676, when the General Court noted a rise in the number of "distracted persons" and problems stemming from their behavior. It read:

> Whereas there are distracted persons in some towns that are unruly, whereby not only the families wherein they are, but others suffer much damage by them, it is ordered by this Court that the Selectmen in all towns where such persons are, are hereby empowered and enjoined to take care of all such persons that they do not damnify others.

---

[7] The responsibility for determining insanity was always placed with civil officers—governors, selectmen, church wardens, vestrymen, etc., depending upon the political structure of the colony—never with medical men; so, too, was guardianship of estates.

[8] To quote from the most highly regarded work on the subject: "There is little evidence . . . to substantiate the oft-repeated allegation that the insane were singled out for harsh and inhumane treatment. Given the living standards in the colonial period, the limited resources and the lack of medical knowledge and facilities, there is no reason for believing that the condition of the insane was appreciably worse than that of other dependent groups within colonial society." See Gerald Grob, *Mental Institutions in America: Social Policy to 1875* (New York: Free Press, 1973), p. 12.

The act recognized that the mentally ill, at least those who were seriously disturbed, needed to be treated in a special way—less for their own good than to prevent them from annoying or "damnifying" others. The care provided at least some of the insane poor under the provisions of this statute was revealed in a vote of the residents of Braintree, Massachusetts, who, in 1689, agreed to pay for the construction of a house seven feet long and five feet wide in which one member of the community could "secure his sister and goodwife Wittey, [both] being distracted." However poor the care provided under its provisions, the statute was at least a beginning. Its principle that some kind of special care should be provided for the mentally ill was important; eventually, the care provided under this and similar statutes would improve.

By the end of the seventeenth century, it was quite evident not only that poverty was a natural product of the human situation and an inevitable concomitant of urban growth, but also that it would get worse. Yet, for the most part, the American colonists were attacking the problem seriously. Although the poor increased in number and skilled administration was lacking, most communities expressed genuine sympathy for the needy and tried to improve their methods and facilities for helping them. One should not dwell on the shortcomings or the harsher aspects of their efforts. Most localities had so many of their own poor to maintain and were forced to spend so much money for their aid that it is understandable that they denied assistance to those who clearly were able-bodied but lazy and that they pursued a vigorous policy of attempting to exclude poor strangers. Recent scholarship has suggested that there was a clear connection between the public response to poverty and the factor of age—at least in seventeenth-century Massachusetts. In general, those who received aid tended to be older, and widowed, while those who were not given assistance tended to be younger. This, though, should not be surprising, for older persons, especially women, were more likely to become dependent through no fault of their own than were younger males. The most noteworthy fact is the apparent readiness with which the colonists accepted responsibility for so many of their indigent; they did not allocate blame for poverty nor, for the most part, did they punish or isolate the needy. On the contrary, they usually tailored the means of assistance to fit the needs of the recipient.

Most communities attacked the problem of poverty with a high degree of civic responsibility. The large amount of money spent on public relief (and, as time passed, the philanthropies of private individuals and voluntary associations) is evidence of a consciousness of the problem and a real attempt to meet it. In the American colonies, where natural resources were abundant and labor was scarce, human life was held in esteem; the wisdom of providing for the poor was rarely, if ever, seriously challenged. On the contrary, the colonials were more interested in providing good treatment for the poor than they were in economizing on welfare costs. And what evidence we have indicates that they were fairly successful in doing so; while they did not design programs to eradicate poverty, there was little suffering for lack of support.

By the eighteenth century, then, the problem of poverty had been defined and the lines of attack against it were marked out. In many areas, selectmen, county justices, overseers of the poor, constables, church wardens, or whoever the authority happened to be, made regular surveys of their areas to determine the condition of the population and to call attention to those who needed assistance. (Failure to do so was punishable by a fine, the proceeds of which went to the support of the poor.) The care provided those individuals was beginning to become more sophisticated, in some cases taking on an element of rehabilitation and prevention. By and large, the poor—at least the white poor—were dealt with humanely and often wisely, even when measured by English standards, and especially when compared to later developments. Furthermore, the needy were quite conscious of their rights within the law and were not merely pawns, or powerless victims, of the system and its administrators; they actively used it to meet their needs. Yet the vicissitudes of colonial life, especially in the larger towns, made the problem appear to be permanent, one likely to grow rather than diminish in the years ahead.

Bibliography

BERNHARD, VIRGINIA. "Poverty and the Social Order in Seventeenth-Century Virginia," *Virginia Magazine of History and Biography* 85 (April 1977): 141–55.

BRADFORD, WILLIAM. *Of Plimouth Plantation*. New York: Capricorn Books, 1962.

BROWN, ROY M. *Public Poor Relief in North Carolina*. Chapel Hill: University of North Carolina Press, 1928.

COLDHAM, PETER W. *Emigrants in Chains*. Baltimore: Genealogical Publishing Company, 1992.

CRAY, ROBERT E., JR. *Paupers and Poor Relief in New York City and Its Rural Environs, 1700–1830*. Philadelphia: Temple University Press, 1988.

CREECH, MARGARET. "Some Colonial Case Histories," *Social Service Review* 9 (December 1935): 699–730.

———. *Three Centuries of Poor Law Administration: A Study of Legislation in Rhode Island*. Chicago: University of Chicago Press, 1936.

DAIN, NORMAN. *Disordered Minds: The First Century of Eastern State Hospital in Williamsburg, Virginia, 1766–1866*. Williamsburg, Va.: Colonial Williamsburg Foundation, 1971.

DEUTSCH, ALBERT. "Public Provision for the Mentally Ill in Colonial America," *Social Service Review* 10 (December 1936): 606–22.

GROB, GERALD. *Mental Institutions in America: Social Policy to 1875*. New York: Free Press, 1973.

GUEST, GEOFFREY. "The Boarding of the Dependent Poor in Colonial America," *Social Service Review* 63 (March 1989): 92–112.

HALL, PETER. "A Model of Boston Charitable Benevolence and Class Development," *Science and Society* 38 (Winter 1974–75): 464–77.

HEFFNER, WILLIAM C. *History of Poor Relief Legislation in Pennsylvania, 1682–1913*. Cleona, Pa.: Holzapfel, 1913.

HOSMER, JAMES KENDALL, ed. [Governor John] *Winthrop's Journal "History of New England" 1630–1649*. New York: Scribner's, 1908.

JERNEGAN, MARCUS W. "The Development of Poor Relief in Colonial America," *Social Service Review* 5 (June 1931): 175–98.

———. *Laboring and Dependent Classes in Colonial America, 1607–1783*. Chicago: University of Chicago Press, 1931.

———. "Poor Relief in Colonial Virginia," *Social Service Review* 3 (March 1929): 1–18.

JIMINEZ, MARY ANN. "Madness in Early American History: Insanity in Massachusetts from 1700 to 1830," *Journal of Social History* 20 (Fall 1986): 25–44.

JONES, DOUGLAS. "The Strolling Poor: Transiency in Eighteenth-Century Massachusetts," *Journal of Social History* 8 (Spring 1975): 28–54.

KELSO, ROBERT. *The History of Public Poor Relief in Massachusetts, 1620–1920*. Boston: Houghton Mifflin, 1922.

KLEBANER, BENJAMIN J. "Pauper Auctions: The 'New England Method' of Public Poor Relief," *Essex Institute Historical Collection* 91 (1955): 195–210.

KLEIN, RANDOLPH S. "Medical Expenses and the Poor in Virginia," *Journal of the History of Medicine* 30 (July 1975): 260–66.

LEE, CHARLES R. "The Poor People: Seventeenth-Century Massachusetts and the Poor," *Historical Journal of Massachusetts* 9 (January 1981): 41–50.

———. "Public Poor Relief and the Massachusetts Community, 1620–1715," *New England Quarterly* 55 (December 1982): 564–85.

MCCAMIC, CHARLES. "Administration of Poor Relief in the Virginias," *West Virginia History* 1 (April 1940): 171–91.

MACKEY, HOWARD. "The Operation of the English Old Poor Law in Colonial Virginia," *Virginia Magazine of History and Biography* 73 (January 1965): 29–40.

MORGAN, EDMUND. *The Puritan Dilemma: The Story of John Winthrop*. Boston: Little, Brown, 1958.

MORRIS, RICHARD. *Government and Labor in Early America*. New York: Columbia University Press, 1946.

MURDOCK, KENNETH B., ed. *Selections from Cotton Mather*. New York: Harcourt, Brace, 1926.

PARKHURST, ELEANOR. "Poor Relief in a Massachusetts Village in the Eighteenth Century," *Social Service Review* 11 (September 1937): 446–64.

PUMPHREY, RALPH AND MURIEL, eds. *The Heritage of American Social Work*. New York: Columbia University Press, 1961.

RIESENFELD, STEFAN. "The Formative Era of American Assistance Law," *California Law Review* 43 (May 1955): 175–233.

ROTHMAN, DAVID AND SHEILA, eds. *On Their Own: The Poor in Modern America*. Reading, Mass.: Addison-Wesley, 1972.

SCHNEIDER, DAVID M. *A History of Public Welfare in New York State, 1607–1867*. Chicago: University of Chicago Press, 1938.

———. "The Patchwork of Relief in Provincial New York, 1664–1775," *Social Service Review* 12 (September 1938): 464–94.

SMITH, ABBOTT E. *Colonists in Bondage: White Servitude and Convict Labor in America, 1607–1776*. Chapel Hill: University of North Carolina Press, 1947.

TRACY, PATRICIA. "Reconsidering Migration Within Colonial New England," *Journal of Social History* 23 (Fall 1989): 93–113.

WATSON, ALAN D. "Public Poor Relief in Colonial North Carolina," *North Carolina Historical Review* 54 (October 1977): 347–66.

WINTHROP, JOHN. "A Model of Christian Charity," in Perry Miller, ed., *The American Puritans*. New York: Doubleday, 1956.

WISNER, ELIZABETH. "The Puritan Background of the New England Poor Laws," *Social Service Review* 19 (September 1945): 381–90.

———. *Social Welfare in the South*. Baton Rouge: Louisiana State University Press, 1970.

CHAPTER 3

The Era of the American Revolution

■ It is impossible to determine exactly how many people received public assistance during the late seventeenth and early eighteenth centuries. The number, however, was large. By 1691, the care of the poor consumed so much of the selectmen's time in Boston, for example, that they turned the work over to four full-time officers—the town's first overseers of the poor. The number of sermons delivered on "doing good" rose dramatically during these years. And in 1712, the Reverend Cotton Mather noted in his diary: "The distressed Families of the Poor [in my congregation] are now so many, and of such daily occurrence, that it is needless for me to . . . mention them."

Not only was the number large but each year it increased, as did relief expenditures and taxes. In 1700, the residents of Boston spent about 500 pounds on public relief; by 1715, the annual expenditure was more than 2000 pounds, half of what it would be some twenty years later. By 1753, poor relief expenditures in Boston climbed to 10,000 pounds per year, and the figure continued to increase even more rapidly each year thereafter through the 1770s, even though the population was relatively static by that time.

The same was true for New York. By 1752, the needy so burdened that city's residents that in order to care for them, poor law officials had to borrow 150 pounds against the following year's taxes. So it went elsewhere. Gary Nash, in an article on "Poverty and Poor Relief in Pre-Revolutionary Philadelphia," concluded that on the eve of the war "poverty . . . blighted the lives of a large part of the population." In 1772, for example, one out of every four free men in that city could be "classified as having been poor or near poor by the standards of that time." Nash and others have suggested that widespread poverty in the late colonial period—when most large cities were spending on poor relief about three times per capita (after inflation) the amount they had spent thirty years earlier and when, in the North and the South alike, poor relief consumed on the average anywhere from 10 to 35 percent of all municipal funds, the single largest annual outlay— may have been a major cause of the American Revolution: widespread poverty probably "eroded the allegiance of many urban dwellers to the British mercantilistic system and also to their own internal social systems." Poverty and the charitable impulse it fostered also helped break down localism and proved to be a spur to national unity in that way as well, according to these observers.[1]

In any case, many factors contributed to the rising rate of indigency during these years. A number of needy immigrants continued to come to America each year. Frequent wars or military skirmishes, especially with the French and Indians, added disabled soldiers and refugees from the frontier and from Canada to the multitude of others—the aged, the ill, the improvident, and so on—for whom care had to be provided. For example, about 1000 Acadians, after being expelled from Nova Scotia during the French and Indian Wars (1754–63), settled in Massachusetts, where for a long time they were dependent upon public support.

Another very real problem, particularly in New England, was the large number of widows and orphans bereft by husbands and fathers lost at sea. Then there was the seasonal nature of many jobs. Fisherman, seamen, longshoremen, craftsmen who worked out of doors, and others went without pay several months each year. A steady rise in the number of illegitimate children—who, until the late nineteenth century, were defined as *filius nullius*, or the "child and heir of no one," neither their mother nor their father, and thus were the responsibility of the town or parish in which they were born—

---

[1] See Gary Nash, "Urban Wealth and Poverty in Pre-Revolutionary America," *Journal of Interdisciplinary History* 6 (Spring 1976): 582, and *The Urban Crucible: Social Change, Political Consciousness, and the Origins of the American Revolution* (Cambridge, Mass.: Harvard University Press, 1979); Peter Virgadamo, "Charity for a City in Crisis: Boston, 1740–1775," *Historical Journal of Western Massachusetts* 10 (January 1982): 22–33.

contributed to swollen poor lists. Colonel Lawrence Smith, a Virginian, complained in 1699 of the "excessive charge" that was brought to the parishes "by means of bastards," a problem that obviously did not disappear; fifty years later, half the annual poor relief expenditures in some of that colony's parishes went to families caring for illegitimate children. That, however, was not a local or a regional problem; the North had its share of illegitimacy as well. In fact, it has been estimated that during the Revolutionary era one-third to one-half of *all* recorded first births were the result of premarital sexual intercourse.

Economic depressions disrupted trade and caused financial hardship for many. Destructive fires further increased the ranks of the distressed, as did recurring illnesses, diseases, and epidemics of all kinds—smallpox, dysentery, measles, and the like. Thus, in 1749, the village of Waterbury, Connecticut, lost 130 people in a single dysentery epidemic, while 800 to 900 residents of Charleston, South Carolina, died from measles in 1772. These and other accumulated misfortunes caused poverty to be an ever present and even alarming problem at times in the eighteenth century. So, too, did growing overcrowdedness in the colonies' major cities, which, with the passage of time, became more stratified and contained an increasing proportion of propertyless and impoverished persons.

Although the towns and parishes spent a good deal of money to care for the needy, the problem was so large that it demanded (and received) assistance from private sources as well. Private charity began early in American history, as a notation in John Winthrop's *Journal*, dated August 16, 1635, indicates: "In the tempest a bark was cast away. . . . None were saved but one Mr. Thatcher and his wife. . . . The General Court gave Mr. Thatcher £26.13.4 towards his losses and divers good people gave him besides." In the seventeenth century, though, private charity was rather limited in scope; donors with great resources to distribute in philanthropic ventures were few and far between. By the eighteenth century, however, as wealth increased in general and a growing number of people began to accumulate sizable fortunes, individuals and private groups proved of enormous service. Sometimes they supplemented public relief activities, at other times assisted individuals or families whose need had not yet been recognized as a public responsibility, and on occasion even attacked some of the causes of poverty.

In the North, the names of Benjamin Franklin,[2] Thomas Bond, founder of the Pennsylvania Hospital, Benjamin Rush, physician and reformer, Stephen Girard, merchant, banker, and philanthropist, and others became synonymous with "doing good." In the Anglican South, private efforts, especially large-scale giving, were even more sustained. There, Calvinist principles of hard work were less pressing than in the North and many large landholders, imbued with a spirit of noblesse oblige and trying to maintain a social system not unlike that of feudalism, felt that aiding the needy was more a personal than a civic responsibility.

Typical in this respect was George Washington, who, even while leading the military struggle against Great Britain, could not neglect that obligation. In November 1775, he wrote a letter to the agent of his estate at Mt. Vernon that stressed, in effect, open house:

> Let the hospitality of the house, with respect to the poor, be kept up. Let no one go away hungry. If any of this kind of people shall be in want . . . supply their necessities . . . ; and I have no objection to your giving my money in charity to the amount of forty or fifty pounds a year. . . . What I mean by having no objection is that it is my desire that it should be done.[3]

Not only individuals but private groups of all kinds aided the needy. Churches frequently took up collections for their own needy members, and others. Thus Boston's South Church raised some 260 pounds for the relief of sufferers from a great fire of 1711, and an

---

[2]Perhaps a few words about Franklin are in order. Certainly, he did not like public assistance or the poor laws. He believed that economic want was necessary to prevent sloth, wastefulness, and dissipation, and that industry and thrift were sufficient to meet the economic needs of life. Rather than aiding the needy financially or materially, then, he helped them in other ways—by working for social betterment in order "to establish conditions in which all people would be able to care for themselves," as he put it. In his preventive approach and in other ways—he was an astute student of community organization, for example—he was quite farsighted and even modern in his approach to matters of social welfare

[3]Letter from George Washington to Lund Washington, November 26, 1775, in Worthington Chauncey Ford, ed., *The Writings of George Washington*, Vol.3 (New York: Putnam's, 1889), pp. 236–37.

equally large amount for those afflicted during a smallpox epidemic of 1752. Other churches did likewise.

Then there were the Quakers, who spent an enormous amount of time, effort, and money aiding the needy. Looking upon themselves as bound together through love and fellowship, and believing that whatever the differences among people all were children of God, carriers of his seed and spiritually equal in his sight, Quakers were concerned about the problem of need the world over, extending help first to their own, but then to others as well. Thus, each Quaker meetinghouse or congregation had a permanent poor fund for the use of its members, but in time of general calamity or widespread suffering of any kind, they were among the first to raise additional funds for the unfortunate, whoever or wherever they happened to be.

It may well be, as Sydney James has suggested, that the Quakers were motivated less by humanitarianism than by other goals—self-interest, a desire to avoid giving up their place in society. As a result of various eighteenth-century developments—social, political, and religious—the sect was thrown on the defensive; it was vulnerable to a "challenge by power, votes, and competitive religiosity," to use James's words. Humanitarianism was the Quaker response to this attack by colonial society. Benevolence helped solidify the church and give it a place in American society:

> By benevolent activities . . . [Quakers] found a way to win a place for themselves in American society without either sacrificing their strict fidelity to their distinctive code of behavior or compromising with worldliness. . . . They purified their own conduct, maintained the solidarity of their church, and by offering examples of philanthropic action for the national welfare in ways which they believed it their special duty to do, showed the way in virtue and public policy to fellow Americans.

Be that as it may, the Quakers (and many other "private" groups), whatever their motives, proved enormously helpful in times of stress. Of all their relief work, perhaps the most notable Quaker effort came during the British siege of Boston in 1775. Their belief in the divinity or sacredness of each individual led them to insist that no people could remain Friends if they participated "in the spirit of war." Most members of the group, therefore, refused to bear arms in the struggle, a practice that did not endear them to many of their fellow countrymen. Persecuted as a result, they nevertheless contributed to the cause—in peaceful ways. Even before the war broke out, New England Friends had organized "The Meeting of Sufferings," composed of Quaker delegates from all the colonies and designed to deal with the hardships likely to arise from the impending struggle. The group raised several thousand pounds, which, when the fighting began, its members distributed to those in need, in and out of Boston, without respect to religious or political belief.

In addition to religious bodies, numerous other private organizations—nationality groups, fraternal societies, social organizations, and the like—aided the unfortunate. Appealing to common sense and self-interest as well as compassion, these bodies gave their members a sense of economic security through mutual aid while performing charitable services for others as well.

The first, and in some ways the most important, of these "friendly societies" was the Scots Charitable Society, organized in 1657 by twenty-seven Scotsmen living in Boston. The group was founded, according to its charter, for the "relief of ourselves and any other for which [sic] we may see cause." By 1690, it had 180 members, including several wealthy merchants in Boston and elsewhere. Largely based on ties of common nationality in a strange land, the society aided its poor, provided for its sick, and buried its dead, reducing the number of public dependents at a time when official agencies were heavily burdened.

More important, the society, still functioning today, became the model for countless similar bodies that sprang up throughout America in the eighteenth and succeeding centuries. In 1754, fifty-four Boston Anglicans founded the Episcopal Charitable Society of Boston, distributing private charity to needy members of the Church of England in that city. Thirteen years later, the Charitable Irish Society of Boston was born. Soon the German Society of New York came into existence, as did the French Benevolent Society, and so on.

Clearly then, at this time, social welfare was a partnership. Private philanthropy complemented public aid; both were part of the American response to poverty. While, from the outset, the public was responsible for providing aid to the needy who, in turn, had a right to such assistance, as soon as they could afford to do so, private citizens and a host of voluntary associations also gave generously to those in distress—orphans, widows, debtors, needy mariners, the religiously oppressed, new residents of communities who were not covered by the poor laws, and others who could not care for themselves. In view of the antagonism later thought to exist between public assistance and private charity, this cooperative approach to the problem is one of the more noteworthy aspects of American colonial history.

The men and women who took part in these philanthropic activities were moved, no doubt, by a variety of impulses—to prove to themselves and to others that they were worthy of respect and admiration, to rub shoulders with distinguished citizens, or to control the poor. Clearly, however, many possessed a genuine concern for others, for this was an age of humanitarianism, not only in America but in much of the western world. In America, the urge to help the distressed was particularly strong because of certain social phenomena, such as the Great Awakening, the Enlightenment, and the American Revolution.

Briefly, the Great Awakening was a series of emotional religious revivals which began in the late 1720s and reached a climax about fifteen years later. Put in its simplest terms, it rested on the doctrines of faith, repentance, and above all, regeneration, or being born again—a concrete, ascertainable conversion experience, one however, which laid increasing emphasis on *human* responsibility rather than the work of God alone. The movement thus not only strengthened individual piety but also encouraged a spirit of religious independence to such an extent that it weakened the authority of the established churches; thousands upon thousands of adherents flocked to great outdoor meetings to hear itinerant preachers.

At the same time, by stressing the potential salvation of all human beings—Christ died not for the elect alone, but for all people, its adherents claimed—the Great Awakening, a mass movement, fostered humane attitudes and popularized philanthropy at all levels of society, especially among the poorer classes. In the words of the social welfare historian Robert Bremner, it transformed "do-goodism from a predominantly upper- and middle-class activity—half responsibility, half recreation—into a broadly shared, genuinely popular avocation." As another student of the period, Raymond Mohl, put it, "Pious men everywhere seemed to transcend interest in their own souls in an aggressive concern for the salvation of others"—or perhaps to exhibit their own Christian spirit. Whatever, the result was the same—benevolent efforts to improve and purify the human condition.

The humanitarian impulse found in the Great Awakening was personified by its leading figure, George Whitefield, who constantly spoke about the misery of the poor as well as the suffering of the damned and made the collection plate as important as the mourner's bench. Wherever he preached, Whitefield, who had a tremendous ability to move the purses as well as the hearts of his listeners, took up collections for poor debtors, for victims of disaster, for hard-pressed colonial colleges, and for a variety of other good causes, including his pet project, an orphanage in Georgia.[4] Even Benjamin Franklin, the author of *Poor Richard's Almanac* and other writings on economic individualism, who was never noted for being careless with his money, fell before Whitefield's spell as he heard the revivalist speak, and he emptied his pockets, "gold and all" for the cause.[5]

Whitefield also provided assistance, of other sorts, to many blacks. including slaves. Although he was interested in the souls rather than in the bodies of those in bondage and he never attacked the institution of slavery, many slaves were, in Gary Nash's words, "deeply moved" by George Whitefield's message, which "minimized the importance of rank, emphasized the special virtue of 'Christ's poor,' and called for the participation of the individual in his [or her] own salvation." So, too, were others, including some slaveholders, who heeded the itinerant preacher's pleas to educate blacks—essential for Protestant indoctrination—and to expose them to Christian doctrine and rituals, including church marriages and baptisms. Whatever the

---

[4]Georgia, the last of the American colonies to be settled (in the 1730s), was itself a unique experiment in philanthropy. Besides serving as a buffer to the other colonies against Spanish, French, and Indian attacks, it was created to serve as a haven for English debtors and ex-prisoners.

[5]In his autobiography, Franklin wrote:

> I happened . . . to attend one of [Whitefield's] . . . sermons, in the course of which I perceived he intended to finish with a collection, and I silently resolved he should get nothing from me. I had in my pocket a handful of copper money, three or four silver dollars, and five pistoles in gold. As he proceeded I began to soften, and concluded to give the coppers. Another stroke of his oratory made me ashamed of that, and determined to give the silver; and he finished so admirably, that I emptied my pockets wholly in the collector's dish, gold and all.

motivation, the result was that many blacks, free and enslaved alike, not only found new meaning in life thanks to Whitefield and the Great Awakening, but learned to read and write as well.

The so-called Enlightenment, which resulted mainly from the growth of science, especially Sir Isaac Newton's studies of the planets (which established the notion of a mechanical, harmonious, law-governed universe that could be understood by human beings through the use of their reason), and John Locke's treatises on psychology (which held that people are born without any innate ideas, original sin, or anything else—they are blank, plastic beings who will be molded by their environment), also challenged the public to alleviate the lot of the poor; its belief in boundless progress wore away the rather grim determinism of Calvinism and the notion that misery and want were inevitable.

Advocates of the Enlightenment argued that all people possess reason and therefore are, or can be, equal; that there is no need for supernatural revelation, for men and women, through the use of their reason, can comprehend the universe; and that since they were not evil but good (or had the capacity for being good) and could test social institutions by virtue of their reason and reform them according to its light, they can attain salvation here on earth. Poverty was not natural and incapable of being eradicated, something to be tolerated with stoicism and resignation. On the contrary, its elimination, along with that of other injustices and inequities, was both right and just, for the poor had human qualities comparable to those of the more privileged, and had the right to share more adequately in the resources of the nation.

Social reform and humanitarianism followed naturally from these ideas. To quote Mohl again, groups "were formed for every imaginable . . . purpose: to assist widows and orphans, immigrants and Negroes, debtors and prisoners, aged females and young prostitutes; to supply the poor with food, fuel, medicine, [and] employment . . . ; to promote morality, temperance, thrift, and industrious habits; to educate poor children in free schools, Sunday schools, and charity schools; to reform gamblers," drunkards, and juvenile delinquents.

In Boston, the Society for Encouraging Industry and Employing the Poor was created. A society to relieve "every poor person without distinction" was founded in South Carolina in 1764. The Society for Inoculating [and providing medical care for] the Poor Gratis was organized in 1774 by Philadelphia doctors. Marine societies to aid disabled seamen and their families were created throughout the land.

Finally, the American Revolution intensified the sense of humanitarianism and reform that had already gripped many Americans. The Declaration of Independence, with its emphasis upon reason and human equality, naturally tended to call attention to the need to improve the common person's lot. Independence in the New World, where resources were abundant, offered Americans the opportunity, if not the obligation, to root out old errors and vices and erect a society which would be a beacon to the world. At the very least, if the independent republic and democratic rule were to endure, American citizens had to be exempt from such impediments as illiteracy, poverty, and distress to cast their ballots freely and rationally.

And so, even the state became an instrument for advancing the welfare of the entire population, resulting in many reforms, including the separation of church and state. There were widespread attacks on slavery, which came to be banned in the northern states. Imprisonment for debt was attacked and the criminal codes revised. Public and private groups associated with these and countless other reforms multiplied.[6]

At the same time, the social and economic dislocations caused by the Revolution created special problems, including an increase in need and the breakdown of poor law measures in many communities. The relief of refugees from the invaded and wasted areas of some of the colonies proved difficult to handle on a local basis. It became neces-

---

[6]Two quite interesting bodies were the humane societies of Boston and Philadelphia. Their main concern was the rescuing and reviving of those suffering from "suspended animation;" i.e., people who appeared to be dead but were not. While there were various causes of the condition, the primary cause was drowning. The societies provided special life-saving equipment and stored it at wharves and taverns near the waterfront. Such equipment included bellows for inflating and deflating the lungs, drag hooks, and medicines. Long a favorite with these humane societies was the fumigator, an instrument for pumping tobacco smoke into the rectum of someone supposedly drowned but who, it was believed, was really in a state of suspended animation. Regardless of the results, the intention was good and it was typical of the age.

sary for the state to take the reins as a financial, and in some cases
even as an administrative, agency.

In New York, for example, a state body—the Committee on
Superintendence of the Poor—was appointed to administer emergency relief to persons removed from their places of settlement
because of the war. The principle of settlement was thereby relaxed as
a prerequisite for public aid. There arose then, in New York and elsewhere, what had occurred earlier in Massachusetts when Boston was
flooded with victims of Indian skirmishes on the frontier—the category of dependents known as the "state poor," who were not chargeable
to any local unit; while individual towns did "subsist them," they were
reimbursed by the colonial treasury.

To be sure, such special state provision was not a reaction against
or a repudiation of the concept of local responsibility. Rather, it was a
recognition of the inadequacy of the care, if any, given by local
authorities in certain difficult times. So it was that the state began to
assume added responsibility for public relief; in 1796, it allocated
funds to New York City (and then other municipalities) "for the
maintenance and support of such persons as shall not have gained settlement in the state." Before long, it provided special facilities and services for the blind, the deaf, the mentally ill, and other needy groups
with special problems.

National independence brought few immediate changes in the
public welfare system. The poor laws had not been an issue in the
Revolution, so they were not only retained by the original states but
passed on to the western territories and to the new states that were
carved from them. In the North, then, as people migrated from the
eastern seaboard to the areas west of the Appalachian Mountains, they
reenacted amidst the difficulties of frontier life the poor laws they had
brought with them, just as their forefathers had enacted similar
statutes carried from England to the New World. Thus, in 1790, only
three years after its establishment, a poor law based on those of the
northeastern states was enacted in the Northwest Territory; the township was made the administrative unit and overseers of the poor were
appointed to implement the statute. Ohio, the first of the northwestern territories to enter the Union (in 1803), duplicated those provisions. Ohio's poor law served as a model for the new states of Indiana

and Illinois, which in turn influenced the statutes in Michigan and Wisconsin, and so on.[7]

In the South, however, a significant change occurred—a switch from parish and quasi-ecclesiastical to county and completely civil jurisdiction. The southern system of parish administration of poor relief had become unsatisfactory even before the Revolution. The addition of new parishes had not kept pace with the westward migration of population, causing some distress and discontent. Then came the Revolution and the separation of church and state and, with it, the dissolution of the parishes and their vestries.

As the southern states drew up new constitutions, between 1780 and 1785, they created the position of county overseer of the poor, elected by the freeholders within the county to collect and administer relief funds raised through a compulsory tax. Thereafter, in the South as in the North, public poor relief was entirely a secular matter, but on a county rather than a township basis. And beginning with Kentucky in 1793, as new states came into the Union from the Southwest, they followed this pattern.

While the Revolution and its aftermath brought few immediate changes in the social welfare system, many important long-range effects may be traced. Although the "general welfare" clause (Article 1, Section 8) of the U.S. Constitution "has come to mean virtually any purpose for which Congress chooses to exercise its taxing and spending powers," to quote Hugh Heclo, the establishment of a federal political system and the failure to delegate specific responsibility for needy citizens to Washington, tended to give American social welfare some of its most distinctive hallmarks, for good or for bad. Unlike Great Britain, Germany, and other European countries, the United States has had no single legal code affecting social welfare matters throughout the nation. Instead, it has had various state laws and court decisions which, on the one hand, have made for confusion, uncertainty, inefficiency, and tardiness in matters of social welfare, but, on the other, have permitted flexibility.

More important, by stressing states' rights and limited central gov-

---

[7]Likewise, the settlement laws of these new states were influenced by the northern colonies.

ernment, the federal system, until recently, tended to minimize the role of the national government in assuming responsibility for aiding the needy. This is not to say that it assumed no responsibility, but that less was assumed in America than elsewhere.[8] And since the states themselves also supported relatively few measures designed to aid the unfortunate, at least well into the nineteenth century, each town or county (with its relatively limited resources) and private citizens continued to take on most of the welfare burden, in marked contrast to the Old World practice.

The separation of church and state also had a significant effect. The absence of a state church meant that in America many sects would flourish. And since most churches and religious groups have been interested in maintaining their own orphanages, hospitals, aid societies, and other welfare institutions, these have abounded in America. Furthermore, the long experience of promoting social welfare through these and other voluntary associations may have led Americans to feel that there was unique value in such private operations.

The tendency to assume that voluntary associations and institutions were superior in a sense to public ones was furthered by the process of relatively free and unlimited immigration after the Revolution. Just as in prior years, during the nineteenth and early twentieth century numerous ethnic and nationality groups, no less than religious organizations, aided their compatriots in need, and thus served to strengthen the concepts of self-help, mutual aid, and private philanthropy. Perhaps it was this that prompted Lord Bryce, the noted student of Americans affairs, to write in 1888:

> In the works of active benevolence no country has surpassed, perhaps none has equalled, the United States. Not only are the sums collected for all sorts of philanthropic purposes larger relatively to the wealth of Americans than in any European country, but the amount of personal effort devoted to them seem to a European visitor to exceed what he knows at home.

---

[8] The major exception to this was treatment of veterans, who continued to receive special consideration as a result of their service in the armed forces; by the early nineteenth century Congress had taken over (from the former colonies and states) financial support for disabled, needy veterans, veterans' widows, and orphans of veterans. Eventually, the federal government granted such aid, in the form of pensions, to able-bodied, nonneedy veterans (and their dependents) as well.

The opening of the West for settlement after the Revolution also had an effect on American social welfare. To begin with, the frontier, with its creed of individual responsibility and personal achievement, further emphasized the idea of self-help. The frontier also fostered personal mobility, making it difficult for anyone on the rise to be certain of social success. In addition, an abundance of free land and a liberal land policy meant that America could not have a landed aristocracy. Taken together, these conditions encouraged many people to engage in charitable or philanthropic activities (and other voluntary programs of civic concern) in order to win social recognition—or to exhibit the fact that they had the wherewithal to deserve such recognition. Charity work became an index of social status, especially in the late nineteenth century, when metropolitan newspapers, entering their great age, celebrated the activities of "Society."[9]

The frontier stimulated private charity in another way: many of our early philanthropic efforts were motivated by fears of irreligion or loose morality in the West.

And finally, the frontier, with its abundant resources, meant that the nation would become a land of plenty. Many Americans, therefore, rejected the Old World's belief in the inevitability of poverty which, in turn, had a variety of results. At times, it led Americans to act as though distress would cure itself and, when it did not, as though it could, and should, be treated by spiritual rather than by economic means, for in America, with its emerging capitalist economy, everyone could fashion his or her own destiny through moral behavior and hard work. At other times, however, it was a dynamic force for reform. Americans never lacked critics who took them to task for their shortcomings; each generation had its fair share of people who reminded them that in a land of affluence poverty is shameful, not only to those who suffer from it, but also to the society that allows it to exist.

This is not to say that Americans have always agreed on the best way to eliminate poverty, or even to help the poor. Indeed, immigra-

---

[9]Observing America in the 1830s, Alexis de Tocqueville, the noted Frenchman, made much of the "principal of association," as he called it, which drove Americans to establish voluntary organizations of all kinds. Such organizations, he stated, were America's substitutes for the more stable institutions and status relationships of Europe.

tion and rapid urbanization along with higher taxes and changing economic conditions and attitudes generated new ideas concerning poverty and dependency during the early nineteenth century.

Bibliography

ABBOTT, EDITH. *Some American Pioneers in Social Welfare.* Chicago: University of Chicago Press, 1937.

ALEXANDER, JOHN K. *Render Them Submissive: Responses to Poverty in Philadelphia, 1760–1800.* Amherst: University of Massachusetts Press, 1980.

BERNHARD, VIRGINIA. "Cotton Mather and the Doing of Good: A Puritan Gospel of Wealth," *New England Quarterly* 49 (June 1976): 225–41.

BREMNER. ROBERT H. *American Philanthropy.* Chicago: University of Chicago Press, 1960.

BRIDENBAUGH, CARL. *Cities in Revolt: Urban Life in America, 1743–1746.* New York: Knopf, 1955.

———. *Cities in the Wilderness: The First Century of Urban Life in America.* New York: Knopf, 1955.

———. *Rebels and Gentlemen: Philadelphia in the Age of Franklin.* New York: Oxford University Press, 1962.

BRYCE, JAMES. *The American Commonwealth,* 2 Vols. New York: Macmillan, 1889.

COLL, BLANCHE D. "Perspectives in Public Welfare: Colonial Times to 1860, Part I," *Welfare in Review* 5 (November-December 1967): 1–9.

CORNER, GEORGE W., ed. *The Autobiography of Benjamin Rush.* Princeton, N.J: Princeton University Press, 1948.

COWING, CEDRIC B. *The Great Awakening and the American Revolution.* Chicago: Rand McNally, 1971.

CRAY, ROBERT E. *Paupers and Poor Relief in New York City and Its Environs, 1700–1830.* Philadelphia: Temple University Press, 1989.

CURTI, MERLE. *The Growth of American Thought.* New York: Harper, 1964.

DE TOCQUEVILLE, ALEXIS. *Democracy in America,* 2 Vols. New York: Vintage Books, 1957.

HECLO, HUGH. "General Welfare and Two American Political Traditions," *Political Science Quarterly* 101 (Summer 1986): 179–98.

JAMES, SYDNEY V. *A People Among Peoples: Quaker Benevolence in Eighteenth Century America.* Cambridge, Mass.: Harvard University Press, 1963.

JAMESON, J. FRANKLIN. *The American Revolution Considered as a Social Movement*. Boston: Beacon Press, 1956.

JANSSON, BRUCE S. *The Reluctant Welfare State*. Belmont, Cal.: Wadsworth, 1988.

JORNS, AUGUSTE. *The Quakers as Pioneers in Social Work*. New York: Macmillan, 1931.

LEMISCH, JESSE, ed. *Benjamin Franklin: The Autobiography and Other Writings*. New York: New American Library, 1961.

McMASTER, JOHN B. *The Life and Times of Stephen Girard*. Philadelphia: Lippincott, 1918.

MAIN, JACKSON TURNER. *The Social Structure of Revolutionary America*. Princeton, N.J.: Princeton University Press, 1965.

MOHL, RAYMOND A. "Poverty in Early America, A Reappraisal: The Case of Eighteenth-Century New York City," *New York History* 50 (January 1969): 5–27.

NASH, GARY. *Forging Freedom: The Formation of Philadelphia's Black Community, 1720–1840*. Cambridge, Mass.: Harvard University Press, 1988.

———. "Poverty and Poor Relief in Pre-Revolutionary Philadelphia," *William and Mary Quarterly* 33 (January 1976): 3–30.

———. *The Urban Crucible: Social Change, Political Consciousness, and the Origins of the American Revolution*. Cambridge, Mass.: Harvard University Press, 1979.

———. "Urban Wealth and Poverty in Pre-Revolutionary America," *Journal of Interdisciplinary History* 6 (Spring 1976): 545–84.

O'CONNELL, NEIL J. "George Whitefield and Bethesda Orphan House," *Georgia Historical Quarterly* 54 (Spring 1970): 41–62.

RESCH, JOHN P. "Federal Welfare for Revolutionary War Veterans," *Social Service Review* 56 (June 1982): 171–95.

SEAMAN, JOHN W. "Thomas Paine; Ransom, Civil Peace, and the Natural Right to Welfare," *Political Theory* 16 (February 1988): 120–42.

SIMLER, LUCY, AND PAUL CLEMENS. "The 'Best Poor Man's Country' in 1783: The Population Structure of Rural Society in Late-Eighteenth-Century Southeastern Pennsylvania," *Proceedings of the American Philosophical Society* 33 (June 1989): 234–61.

SMITH, BILLY G. "Poverty and Economic Marginality in Eighteenth-Century America," *Proceedings of the American Philosophical Society* 132 (March 1988): 107–25.

SMITH, DANIEL S., AND MICHAEL S. HINDUS. "Premarital Pregnancy in

America, 1640–1971: An Overview and Interpretation," *Journal of Interdisciplinary History* 5 (Spring 1975): 537–71.

SMYTH, ALBERT H., ed. *The Writings of Benjamin Franklin*. New York: American, 1907.

SWEET, WILLIAM WARREN. *Religion in Colonial America*. New York: Harper, 1942.

VIRGADAMO, PETER R. "Charity for a City in Crisis: Boston, 1740–1775," *Historical Journal of Western Massachusetts* 10 (January 1982): 22–33.

VOGT, DANIEL C. "Poor Relief in Frontier Mississippi, 1798–1832," *Mississippi History* 51 (August 1989): 181–99.

WALCH, TIMOTHY. "Catholic Social Institutions and Urban Development," *Catholic Historical Review* 64 (January 1978): 16–32.

WILLIAMS, HOWELL V. "Benjamin Franklin and the Poor Laws," *Social Service Review* 18 (March 1944): 77–91.

WILLIAMS, WILLIAM H. " The 'Industrious Poor' and the Founding of the Pennsylvania Hospital," *Pennsylvania Magazine of History and Biography* 97 (October 1973): 431–43.

CHAPTER 4

∎The Trend Toward Indoor Relief∎

∎ While, as a matter of course, the poor laws spread westward as new lands were opened up after the American Revolution, in the coastal cities they were being questioned for the first time. There, the forces of change—especially large-scale immigration, rapid industrialization, the advent of capitalism and the spread of wage labor, and widespread urbanization—tended to alter the relatively stable and well-ordered society of the colonial years and to bring with them a rising incidence of poverty that caused public relief spending to rise to ever higher levels; year after year, outlays for poor relief continued to top all other items in town and city budgets. This, along with heightened social tensions and general disarray,[1] aroused not only a great deal of concern about poverty but attempts to ferret out its causes and efforts to eliminate it—a clear departure from colonial practice.

The same was true in England, which was also undergoing pronounced and disturbing changes. There, as in America, concern over the poor laws was widespread. First of all, the system's effectiveness and equity were questioned. Local responsibility often led to inadequate and unequal standards, on the one hand, and inefficient and sometimes corrupt administration, on the other. Thousands of unpaid, untrained, and often incompetent overseers of the poor, many of whom gave little time or energy to what they viewed as a

---

[1]Religious denominations and congregations were separating. Deism and secularism appeared to be spreading. The French Revolution threatened to undermine the established classes. The West attracted restless families, stirring mobility and further upsetting settled communities, etc.

49

temporary, burdensome task, did not make for effective administration. More important, because many of the poorer districts had a higher proportion of needy residents and less money to spend on relief than the more prosperous ones, not only was treatment of the poor unequal, but the communities that could least afford it usually had the highest poor rates. Everywhere, however, taxes went up. Between 1760 and 1818, poor relief expenditures throughout England increased sixfold while the population about doubled.

One of the reasons, it was thought, for the higher tax rates was what amounted to an assured annual income, popularly known as the Speenhamland system, or rate-in-aid of wages. Low wages and high prices had caused much distress in late eighteenth-century England, especially in the southern agricultural regions of the country. As a result, in 1795, after several unsuccessful attempts at regulating wages, the district of Speenhamland (and others later) adopted a system by which all laborers paid less than a certain amount, which varied according to the price of wheat, were granted relief allowances. "Every poor and industrious man and his family," the legislation read, "was to have a certain weekly income produced by his own or his family's labor," the cost of which was "to be borne from the poor rates."

As the system spread, it seemed to bring with it higher prices, higher taxes, and the belief that, since the poor were guaranteed a minimum income, they not only were becoming lazy but were encouraged to multiply. Furthermore, it was alleged that since employers, who never paid higher salaries than they were forced to, knew that their workers would not starve, the system invited low wages and perpetuated poverty.

A general subsidy of wages, in which employers paid low salaries and the public footed the bill and which encouraged early marriages and large families certainly would have left a great deal to be desired. But, in reality, the system did not operate that way. Wages were below standard before the program was implemented. To attribute substandard wages to Speenhamland, therefore, was not accurate. Furthermore, those who bore the burden of the system—that is, those who paid the taxes to finance it—were, for the most part, employers of agricultural and industrial labor who therefore had little to gain by cutting wages. Nor, in practice, was it true that the system promoted population growth; at best, it led to a reduction in infant mortality although, as one historian has recently concluded, "not substantially enough to affect the general death-rate or . . . the rate of population growth." Furthermore, population growth in Scotland and Ireland was the same as in England, despite the fact that Speenhamland was not put into operation in those places.

In short, Speenhamland was not responsible for the evils attributed to it. If anything, it was a forward-looking measure that provided financial aid to the destitute according to need as determined by the cost of living. Increased relief expenditures and higher taxes resulted not from Speenhamland but from other factors, especially chronic technological unemployment. Abolition of the system in itself had no salutary effect on the national economy or the condition of the poor. (The drop in relief expenditures after its termination was largely due to good harvests, a boom in railroad building, and a substantial increase in private charity.) Nevertheless, it was widely believed that the poor laws were responsible for these and other evils.

In the meantime, the poor laws had come under attack from another source—the so-called classical economists, who believed that poverty was the natural state of the wage-earning classes. The possession and accumulation of property and wealth, they argued, was a "natural right" with which the state must not interfere; the poor law, an artificial creation of the state which taxed the well-to-do for the maintenance and care of the needy, violated that right and was morally wrong.

Dissatisfaction with the poor law on these grounds and evolution of the laissez-faire philosophy resulted from major social and economic changes that occurred between the seventeenth and nineteenth centuries, changes which had profound consequences for social welfare policy. The dominance of the old landed aristocracy, with its sense of social responsibility and its assumption that the stability of the state required public action to regulate the affairs of mankind, including the discouragement of labor mobility, was waning rapidly under the competitive pressure of the rising business classes, the emergence of a capitalist economy that substituted the price mechanism for the state in determining the status of labor, and the disintegrating relationship between employer and employee caused by industrialization and urbanization. It was held that interference with normal market operations—a fluid national labor force controlled by supply and demand—would threaten, if not overturn, the economic order. In short, the mercantilist philosophy underlying the Elizabethan Poor Law was being replaced by the idea of free and unlimited exchange—a self-regulating market economy, or laissez-faire. All of the restrictions on trade and industry had to be removed. The poor laws and other anachronistic measures would have to undergo major change.[2]

Thus, the system was not only morally wrong, according to economists Adam Smith, David Ricardo, and others, but it was also economically unsound. Residency rules, an inevitable concomitant of the poor law, interfered with the labor mobility required in a free market. In addition, the poor law was socially bad. According to Thomas Malthus (whose famous *Essay on the Principle of Population* was first published in 1798), one of the severest opponents of the poor law and a firm advocate of its abolition, it caused overpopulation, already a serious problem, lowering wages and living standards, causing more misery than it alleviated. Adhering to the "wage-fund" theory—the idea that there existed at any one time a certain fixed sum of money to be used for the wages of *all* workers—the classical economists argued that the money spent to support paupers comprised wages withheld (in the form of taxes) from industrious workers. Public assistance, then, lowered the standard of living; rugged individualism was not only natural, but ideal.

As a result, immediately after the manufacturing interests (who wanted to slash, if not terminate, public assistance in order to force poor, displaced agricultural workers into the newly forming industrial wage earning class) gained power from the landed mercantile classes through the electoral reforms of 1832, Parliament created a Royal

---

[2]Denying the organic concept of society in favor of "natural law" and a belief in the harmony of the universe, the dominant philosophy of the nineteenth century was individualism and laissez-faire. Human happiness, or rather the greatest happiness for the greatest number, was the purpose of life and the goal of society. Society, it was believed, was composed of isolated individuals, each of whom was the best judge of his or her own interest. The sum of each individual's good led to the good of the whole. As a result, any interference with the individual was a blow or an impediment to the social good or welfare. Since wealth was a primary source of happiness, unfettered self-interest and the accumulation of wealth (and property) was the ideal; the economic welfare of the nation was not a matter of predetermined policy, but one of free and natural growth.

Poor Law Commission for Inquiring into the Administration and Practical Operation of the Poor Laws. The commission, dominated by the laissez-faire philosophy and intent upon altering the welfare system to meet the requirements of industrial capitalism—that is, the existence of a national pool of laborers who would work in factories for long hours and low wages—approached its investigation with an a priori attitude, or with its heart rather than its mind, and thus found exactly what it was looking for—that the prevailing poor law system (especially wage supplementation), and the way in which it was being administered, was responsible for debasing the character and energy of the English laboring classes.

Based, then, upon faulty history, gross exaggeration, contemporary social philosophy, and the fears of the day, the commission's report, written by its secretary, Sir Edwin Chadwick, together with some classical economists, and published in 1834, contained two recommendations which were immediately enacted into law.

Recognizing that the problem of relief was larger than that of any single unit, the first called for a national supervisory body with the authority to combine parishes in order to coordinate and thus improve poor law services throughout the land. Within three years, 90 percent of Great Britain's parishes (some 13,264 of them) were combined into 568 units, poor law districts, or unions, as they were called, presided over by boards of guardians, which effected some improvement in the public welfare system.

The second recommendation was for an end to public assistance for able-bodied persons, except in public institutions. While the framers of the report thus did not intend for the principle to be applied to the helpless poor, by implying, among other things, that the reduction of public relief and the cutting of taxes were the ideal, it was carried out indiscriminately. Most of those on public relief—the young and the old, the sick and the disabled, the unemployed and the underpaid, as well as the lazy—would be deprived of outdoor assistance.

Curtailment of home relief also resulted from what was perhaps the most important aspect of the report—its general tone, which implied that poverty was an individual moral matter. An essential corollary to this, written into the report and its subsequent legislation, was the doctrine of "less eligibility"—the notion that the status of those dependent on public assistance "shall not be made really or apparently so eligible [satisfactory] as the situation of the independent laborer of the lowest class." In other words, the condition of all welfare recipients, regardless of need or cause, should be worse than that of the lowest paid self-supporting laborer. While relief should not be denied the poor, life should be made so miserable for them that they would rather work than accept public aid.

Passage of the Poor Law Reform Bill of 1834, which implemented these recommendations, epitomized the punitive attitude toward the poor. Thenceforth, it was publicly known, to use the words of Prime Minister Benjamin Disraeli, that it was "a crime to be poor" in England. Poor relief was redesigned to increase fear of insecurity, rather than to check its causes or even to alleviate its problems. At best, it would prevent starvation or death from exposure, but it would do so as economically and unpleasantly as possible. The measure of the system's soundness would be its deterrent effect—or, to quote Karl Polanyi, a more recent critic, its ability to oil "the wheels of the labor mill."

The trip, then, from the Middle Ages to 1834 brought with it a vast change in the public attitude toward the poor and the way in which they should be cared for. During the Middle Ages, evidence of need overrode all else. It was generally assumed that need arose from misfortune for which society, in all justice, should assume responsibility. The individual's right to public assistance was firmly established. The Elizabethan Poor Law of 1601 endorsed that right, placing the ultimate charge for implementing it upon secular authorities. It also distinguished between the impotent and the able-bodied poor and acknowledged the existence of involuntary unemployment.

By the early nineteenth century, conditions had changed. Industrial capitalism, urbanization, greater poverty, higher taxes, and the laissez-faire philosophy had made the pursuit and accumulation of wealth a moral virtue and dependency a vice. It was assumed that destitution was the individual's fault, and since most of the needy were recipients of help from the public treasury, it followed that public aid was a cause of pauperism and thus inherently bad. If bestowed at all, it should be done so as carefully and as stringently as possible, hence in public institutions where, it was felt, the costs would be lower, the opportunity for control better, the chances for propagation fewer, and the deterrent power greater.[3]

In America, where land was abundant and labor scarce, the Malthusian population theory, one of the most telling arguments used against the British poor laws, had little relevance. Nevertheless, the influence of the classical economists and the laissez-faire philosophy in general, and the idea that public relief tended to pauperize and demoralize recipients and depress the standard of living in particular, had even more rigid acceptance in the United States than in England. There were many reasons for this.

First of all, some of the very influences that led to reform and efforts to help those in need, especially the Enlightenment and the American Revolution, also stimulated distrust of the poor. The Enlightenment, by helping to wear away the notion that misery and want were endemic to society, made it appear as though the poor were personally responsible for their condition. The same was true for the American Revolution; by fostering the belief that poverty need not exist, it encouraged a harsh and suspicious view of the poor. God's will was no longer a satisfactory explanation for defective social conditions, especially in America, a land of abundance and virtually unlimited resources where work was more plentiful than elsewhere, especially crowded England. Observers concluded that no one ought to be poor, and there was little tolerance for the able-bodied pauper. The only cause of such poverty, it was assumed, was individual weakness. As Nathanial Ware, a social philosopher of the early nineteenth century, saw it, the able-bodied man who begged or received public assistance was beyond redemption, having sunk to the level of a mere eating brute. "Humanity aside," reported Ware, "it would be to the best interest of society to kill all such drones." Thus, whereas colonials had

---

[3]Actually, more than 100 years earlier, in 1722, Parliament had enacted a law (Knatchbull's Act) that *permitted* local parishes to build, and use, poorhouses/workhouses rather than outdoor relief as the major means of assisting their needy residents. There was a great deal of opposition to the measure, however, especially among the poor, and very few parishes constructed such institutions; those that did found them very expensive to operate. Sixty years later, passage of Gilbert's Act of 1782 betrayed the prevailing feeling that such methods were inhumane and/or inefficient and that the needy must be helped outside institutions, either through home relief for the disabled or work relief for the able-bodied. A few years later, Speenhamland was developed.

accepted the notion that the poor must always be present and citizens are obliged to do whatever is necessary to help them, by the late eighteenth and the early nineteenth century, Americans began to believe that poverty could, and should, be obliterated—in part, by allowing the poor to perish.

Unconcerned about the inadequacy or uncertainty of wages, such detractors accepted uncritically the prevailing economic doctrines of Adam Smith and his followers. It was assumed that anyone who wanted to could work, and that all those working received or invariably would receive enough wages to support themselves and their families. They failed to recognize that even in America some people could not find jobs, that even in the best of times some branches of industry were depressed and opportunities were limited or below-standard wages prevailed, that seasonal and technological unemployment was inevitable, and that nothing could be done about these ills. Thus, the New York Society for the Prevention of Pauperism, in the midst of the nation's worst depression to date (1821), contended: "No man who is temperate, frugal, and willing to work need suffer or become a pauper for want of employment." Or, in the words of one reformer, the "sober and able-bodied, if industriously disposed, cannot long want employment. They cannot, but in their own folly and vices, long remain indigent."

Stereotypes rather than individuals in need dominated the public mind. Although, on occasion, a verbal distinction was made between the "worthy" and the "unworthy" poor, between those willing to work but who, for one reason or another, were unable to and those who simply chose not to work, most people tended to regard all the needy with contempt. The "worthy" poor soon discovered that no matter how hard they struggled they still were condemned as moral failures. Thus, a New York Humane Society report on the "sources of vice and misery" nowhere mentioned economic causes. "By a just and inflexible law of Providence," the report stated, "misery is ordained to be the companion and the punishment of vice." Pauperism obviously resulted from laziness, extravagance, immorality, or some other moral defect. So, whereas earlier dependency was viewed largely as a social and economic matter, it was now largely viewed as an individual, or personal, matter.

The Protestant ethic, which, as Raymond Mohl has observed,

demanded benevolence of the rich as well as hard work and morality of the poor, complemented the belief that the individual had the power to achieve economic success through his or her own efforts. So, too, did the Second Great Awakening and the growth, once more, of revivalism, which again preached that salvation depended largely on personal factors—diligence, frugality, virtue, and conversion. If a person failed, then, in the religious or the secular realm, it was his or her own fault; idleness, bad habits, and other human frailties were responsible. Poverty and damnation were personal matters; only the individual could overcome them.

This outlook appeared to be borne out by the large number of immigrants entering the country at the time, another reason for the change in attitude toward the poor in America. Some six million foreigners came to the United States between 1800 and 1860, mainly impoverished German and Irish Catholics who landed at entry points between Baltimore and Boston. For the most part, they remained in the North, where they congregated in cities. From the outset, these newcomers, alien to the dominant Protestant middle-class culture, aroused concern. In fact, as early as 1796, the commissioners of New York City's poorhouse complained of the "enormous and growing expense . . . not so much from the increase of our own poor, as from the prodigious influx of indigent foreigners in this city." With time, the situation grew even worse. In 1820, the annual report of New York's Society for the Prevention of Pauperism listed "emigrants to this city from foreign countries" as the largest source of pauperism.

Making matters worse, the Irish and German immigrants, who could hardly enjoy life in their cramped and stuffy tenements, often congregated in neighborhood bars, even on holidays and Sundays. Their drinking habits, observance of the Sabbath, and other customs differed from those of the dominant and alarmed Protestant majority intent upon maintaining order in an increasingly chaotic society. That many of the immigrants were victims of malnutrition, exploitation, the Irish potato famine, the cruel voyage across the sea, thieves and swindlers waiting to fleece them as soon as they stepped off the boat, vile slums and substandard wages, and other wretched living and working conditions, was ignored by the dominant majority who "found it difficult to apply Christian benevolence to [these] ragged, uncouth, 'different,' [un-Christian,] and seemingly immoral newcomers."

Outdoor aid, especially public relief, only aggravated the problem. "The more paupers you support, the more you will have to support," claimed one citizen. To another, public aid was like a drug and was as dangerous: "Very often it creates an appetite which is more harmful than the pain it is intended to relieve," he asserted. "Of all the modes of providing for the poor," declared Boston's Mayor Josiah Quincy, who in 1821 chaired a state commission that investigated public out-door relief, "the most wasteful, the most expensive, and the most inju-rious to their morals and destructive to their industrious habits is that of supply in their own families." By encouraging the poor to rely upon the public dole rather than upon their own energies, and by removing the dread of want, considered by many to be the prime mover of the needy, the poor laws destroyed the incentive to work, causing the poor to become even more idle and improvident.

Equally galling was the attitude it fostered among the needy, the idea that relief was a right; thus, there was no gratitude for those who provided it. Public assistance, then, deprived the giver of the pleasure of observing the supplicant's joy when his plea was granted. Moreover, by compelling people to pay taxes for relief, public assistance dried up (or would inevitably dry up) private charity. Hence, it was unChristian, for charity was a Christian virtue.

So, for these reasons, the abolition of public assistance had many proponents. Its elimination, they contended, would end pauperism. Those who could not contribute labor to the marketplace and thus remained in need would be helped by private charity, which would not lead to the willful lack of productivity; the poor could not inter-pret such assistance as a right for they had no statutory claim to it. Similarly, the private sector would prove less susceptible to political pressures for liberalization of benefits. Too, agents of voluntary agen-cies were better equipped to exert those moral and religious influences that would prevent relief from degenerating into a mechanical pauper-izing dole. And finally, private giving also bound the poor to the well-to-do and had such other desirable characteristics as precariousness and uncertainty.

The system of public aid, however, was too deeply ingrained in the culture to be abolished. As J. V. N. Yates, New York's Secretary of State, who would have liked to abolish it, remarked: "The total want of a pauper system would be inconsistent with a humane, liberal, and enlightened policy," and perhaps domestic peace and tranquility as well. It was up to the private citizen to exercise vigilance to see to it that it was administered as economically and, therefore, as efficiently as possible. To this end, emphasis was placed on the widespread use of institutions—almshouses and workhouses. A sort of division of labor arose. Public assistance would be confined to institutional care, mainly for the "worthy" or hard-core poor, the permanently disabled, and others who clearly could not care for themselves. Also, the able-bodied or "unworthy" poor who sought public aid would be institutionalized in workhouses where their behavior not only could be controlled but where, removed from society and its tempting vices, they presumably would acquire habits of industry and labor and thus prepare themselves for better (i.e., self-sufficient) lives. The institution, in other words, would have a therapeutic as well as a wholesome economic effect. Whether it was possible to serve both of these ends simultaneously remained to be seen. In any event, for the remainder, home relief of a new kind—mainly moral relief administered by private benevolent agencies—would be available.

The greater emphasis on the use of almshouses resulted, in part, from the English experience. More important, however, was a similar, and even earlier, development in America—the Yates Report, the first comprehensive survey of poor relief in the United States and one of the most influential documents in American social welfare history. New York's Secretary of State, J. V. N. Yates, was commissioned by the legislature to conduct a survey of public poor relief throughout the state. His report, based mainly upon the replies to questionnaires sent to poor law officials throughout the state, was presented to the lawmakers in February 1824.

Widely received and considered to be a progressive document during its time, the Yates Report offered an excellent account of prevailing poor relief practices. Yates cited four main methods of public assistance that were used throughout the state—institutional relief, home relief, the contract system, and the auction system—and outlined what he felt to be the cruelty, waste, and inefficiency arising from this chaotic situation. Where the poor were "farmed out," through either the contract or the auction system, they were often treated cruelly, even inhumanely. Moreover, the "education and the morals of children were almost wholly neglected" and, according to Yates, "they grow up in filth, idleness, and disease, becoming early candidates for the prison or the grave." The able-bodied poor were rarely employed; home relief encouraged idleness, and "vice, dissipation, disease and crime" resulted.

For Yates (and others who conducted similar studies in Boston, Baltimore, Philadelphia, Providence, and elsewhere), the ending of home relief and the building of institutions was the solution, especially for dependent youngsters. In public institutions, he argued, children's "health and morals" would be improved and "they would receive an education to fit them for future usefulness." Not content with merely evaluating the system, he made three recommendations for its improvement: that no able-bodied person between the ages of eighteen and fifty be given public assistance; that for the old, the young, and the disabled, institutional relief be supplied; and that the *county*, rather than the town, become the administrative unit.

So it was that in 1824, that same year, the New York State legislature enacted the County Poorhouse Act, a measure that called for one or more poorhouses to be erected in each county of the state. Thenceforth, all recipients of public assistance were to be sent to that institution (unless sickness or infirmity rendered their removal from home dangerous). All expenses for building and maintaining the institution and supporting its inmates were to be defrayed by the county out of tax funds. The act also created a new body of relief officials—County Superintendents of the Poor—whose principal function was to manage the almshouse. The measure, then, marked two significant nineteenth-century trends in American social welfare: the transfer of responsibility for public assistance from towns to counties (in the North, as had occurred earlier in the South) and the general trend toward indoor relief.

While it may be true, as Blanche Coll and others have suggested, that, contrary to popular belief, institutional relief did not monopolize public assistance—it did not become the sole method of providing for the poor—it did increase significantly during this period. In fact, it became fundamental. To use David Rothman's words, "to an extraordinary degree [indoor relief] dominate[d] the public response to poverty."[4] For example, in 1824 Massachusetts had 83 almshouses;

---

[4]David Rothman, *The Discovery of the Asylum* (Boston: Little, Brown, 1971), p. 185, but see pp. 180–205. Interestingly, among those who opposed institutionalizing the needy were some local merchants who lamented a loss in "business" from the practice and some members of the propertied classes who were eager to maintain a reserve of cheap labor in the community.

fifteen years later the number had increased to 180, and by 1860 the total had risen to 219. Although public officials continued to dispense some outdoor assistance to meet emergencies, by the end of the Civil War "four out of every five persons in Massachusetts who received extended relief remained within an institution," and the situation was similar elsewhere; hostility to public outdoor relief was pervasive. Whereas the family and the private home were the settings in which assistance was provided to the needy in the preindustrial era, during the early nineteenth century—as the incidence of poverty increased and the poor population changed largely from older, widowed residents to many younger, foreign-born male transients—social welfare functions were transferred, for the most part, to institutions in the larger community (where, by the way, families often were not kept intact).

Not only was there a greater use of county institutions, but the state began to build its own institutions at this time as well. The growth of state participation resulted from a greater nonresident population, as well as from the evils of county almshouse care.

With regard to the first, the changes in the nation's socioeconomic life—the influx of immigrants, the expansion of an industrial-capitalist economy, the growth of cities and a vast network of canals, railroads, and highways, the increase in travel and mobility, the westward movement, and so on, all of which helped to change the poor from "neighbors" to members of the "lower classes"—made it impossible to maintain a completely local and insular poor relief system. Local officials, continually occupied with nonresident indigents, from home as well as from abroad, naturally demanded state aid to relieve their communities of that burden; as you recall, there was a precedent for such action.

Equally important were the faulty results of the county institution system. While for the most part the public accepted its responsibility for erecting such institutions, oftentimes little or no regard was paid to the type of care provided within their walls. Into many were herded the old and the young, the sick and the well, the sane and the insane, the epileptic and the feebleminded, the blind and the alcoholic, the juvenile delinquent and the hardened criminal, male and female, all thrown together in haphazard fashion. Nakedness and filth, hunger and vice, and other abuses such as beatings by cruel keepers were not uncommon in many of these wretched places, vile catchalls for everyone in need, defined by one contemporary as "living tombs" and by another as "social cemeteries."

Blaming an indifferent public for the foul conditions, a New York State legislative committee in the 1850s said the following about many of New York's rural almshouses:

> It is much to be regretted that our citizens manifest so little interest in the condition even of those in their immediate neighborhood. Individuals who take great interest in human suffering whenever it is brought to their notice, never visit them, and are entirely uninformed, that in a county house almost at their own doors, may be found the lunatic suffering for years in a dark and suffocating cell, in summer, and almost freezing the winter—where a score of children are poorly fed, poorly clothed, and quite untaught—where the poor idiot is half starved and beaten with rods because he is too dull to do his master's bidding—where the aged mother is lying in perhaps her last sickness, unattended by a physician, and with no one to minister to her wants—where the lunatic, and that lunatic, too, a *woman*, is made to feel the lash in the hands of a brutal underkeeper—yet these are all to be found—*they all exist in our State.*

"Common domestic animals are usually more humanely provided for than the paupers in some of these institutions," the committee concluded.

It must be pointed out, however, that conditions varied among county poorhouses. Although many were like those described above— houses of degradation, disease, near-starvation, and the like—others were not. Some, in fact, provided reasonably good care for their inmates, including adequate medical services, administered in a fairly personal and caring way.

Furthermore, recent demographic studies of county poorhouses in New York State and elsewhere have shown that for *most* people such institutions were not places of permanent, or even long-term, residence; rather, they were temporary refuges during times of personal crisis and widespread social and economic distress. They were places in which the poor stayed for a while during the cold winter months; temporary shelters for the jobless during times of depression and widespread unemployment; maternity homes for young, unmarried pregnant women; and places of last resort for orphans and sick, helpless, and childless elderly persons. In other words, whatever the official purposes of such institutions—and the popular image of them—the poor sometimes put them to their own uses; although they generally were dreaded, poorhouses often served as key life supports amidst the harshness and uncertainty of existence in early industrial America. Later on, however, more and more of them became long-term custodial institutions, mainly for the immigrant aged.

There is an ongoing intellectual debate about the effectiveness or the possible effectiveness of such institutions—of all residential institutions, in fact. Scholars like David Rothman and Gerald Grob assert that county poorhouses, mental institutions, and other "asylums" that were created at the time failed—that is, they did not reform or cure their inmates or patients, they were very expensive to maintain, and they quickly degenerated from therapeutic to custodial establishments—because of external factors, including lack of adequate funds, improper training of staff, and poor management. Other commentators, however, such as Erving Goffman, Christopher Lasch, and Michael Katz, have argued that such institutions were and are flawed from the start and hence doomed to failure. The institution itself, rather than inmates' or patients' needs, is the crucial determinant of life within its walls: the administrators' desire to maintain order and insure a smooth daily routine, and to economize on costs, is at odds with the therapeutic goals that supposedly justify operation of the facility, yet the former always takes precedence.

Whether successful or not, and in most cases they were not, whether useful way stations for temporarily distressed citizens or wretched places of long-term confinement for the older poor, and they soon became the latter, these institutions persisted. Before long, humanitarians, journalists, and others (in England as well as in the United States, as some of Charles Dickens's works indicate) began writing shocking accounts of life within those institutions, especially the worst ones. Under such circumstances, it was inevitable that reformers would turn to the state to step in and improve the situation, especially by establishing, and then running, its own institutions for people in need of specialized care or treatment—the young, the delinquent, the defective, the mentally ill, and so on. Thus, the period also witnessed the beginning of the classification and segregation of different types of dependents in state institutions. The institutional ideal, then, was not confined to county poorhouses; the founding of houses of refuge, or orphanages, penitentiaries, and mental hospitals during this period was part of the same movement.

One of the earliest developments along these lines was in the area of child welfare. In 1824, the House of Refuge for Juvenile Delinquents, the first juvenile reformatory in America, supported by state funds, was established in New York City. In 1847, the Massachusetts legislature enacted a law for the founding of a state reformatory, and two years later another was opened in New York. Five years later Ohio followed suit, and so on. In the meantime, many state orphanages were founded, especially after the 1860s when laws were enacted in many states calling for the mandatory removal of all children from county almshouses. Meanwhile, state institutions for the mentally ill and the physically handicapped, as well as for the feebleminded and the deaf and dumb, had come into existence.

Not only did social reformers seek and obtain state aid at this time, but many also turned to Washington for help. That they did so should not be surprising. Population expansion coast to coast and improvements in transportation and communication highlighted the obvious—that the grave problems and malfunctions of sorts that overwhelm people are not matters merely of local or even state concern but are national in scope and, therefore, within the province of the federal government.

Moreover, many social projects were already receiving federal aid of one kind or another. Such aid could be traced back to the eighteenth century. Upon passage of the Northwest Ordinance in 1787, Congress, under the Articles of Confederation, decreed that a portion of the public domain in the Northwest Territory be set aside for the financial support of public education, the first of a long history of federal grants-in-aid. In 1803, when Ohio entered the Union, it received such aid, as did most of the other states that later came into the Union. Proceeds from the sale of public lands given the states by the federal government were used not only for public education, but also for land reclamation, railroad building, and other internal improvements, such as canals and roads.

Then, too, in 1818 Congress had enacted the Revolutionary War Pension Act—the nation's first military pension program, one that

combined features of a pension plan with poor law principles to provide assistance to impoverished Revolutionary War veterans—and
then the veterans of subsequent wars as well. In addition, the federal
government on occasion had made funds and other forms of direct
aid available to civilian victims of fires, floods, and cyclones. Finally,
and perhaps most important, some public and private welfare institutions had appealed for and received federal aid, chiefly on the grounds
that they provided educational as well as custodial services, and that
they cared for out-of-state as well as in-state residents. Thus, in the
spring of 1819, the Connecticut Asylum for the Deaf and Dumb (a
private institution) was granted 23,000 acres of public land which,
when sold, brought the institution some $300,000. And, in 1826,
Congress granted a township of public land to the Kentucky Deaf and
Dumb Asylum (a state institution).[5] So it was that social reformers
began to look for more help from the U.S. government.

The high-water mark in the early-nineteenth-century drive to get
the national government to assume added responsibility in the area of
social welfare centered around the attempt to get federal aid for the
care and treatment of the mentally ill, a movement synonymous with
the name of Dorothea Dix. A great figure in the field of social welfare,
Dix's career offers an excellent example of sustained constructive
action for the downtrodden. Her method of fact-gathering, preparing
memorials and bills, and then rallying public opinion behind them, is
still of value today.

Dorothea Lynde Dix was born in Hampden, Maine, in April
1802. At age twelve, she moved to Boston where, living with her
grandparents, she received a good education and then turned to teaching. First, she opened a fashionable private school for girls, and then a
free school for paupers. She also found time to write several children's
books. But her heavy schedule proved too great a strain, and in 1836
she collapsed. She remained in retirement until 1841, when she heeded a call for a Sunday school teacher for women inmates of the East
Cambridge jail. There she witnessed the crude and barbaric treatment

---

[5]See Walter I. Trattner, "The Federal Government and Social Welfare in Early Nineteenth-
Century America," *Social Service Review* 50 (June 1976): 243–55, and "The Federal
Government and Needy Citizens in Nineteenth-Century America," *Political Science Quarterly*,
103 (Summer 1988): 347–56.

of prisoners and the degradation to which they were subjected, especially those mentally disturbed. Horrified by what she saw, she apparently experienced a tremendous emotional reaction which led her to embark upon one of the most remarkable crusades of the century—an effort to obtain better care and treatment of the mentally ill.

Dorothea Dix was not among the first to work for better treatment of the insane who, like the poor, had fallen victim to the institutionalization movement of the early nineteenth century; they, too, had become odd and even menacing figures no longer accepted in society merely as one group among others whose incapacitating ailment made them dependent upon relatives or the community. Ironically, this opened the door to constructive change. Just as reformers had come to perceive poverty as abnormal and had moved to end it by eliminating home relief and confining the needy to almshouses, so physicians now insisted that insanity was not the inevitable result of God's will but rather was a medical problem and that it could be cured— through kind and gentle treatment in an institution. Much had been accomplished along these lines when Dorothea Dix began her work. Several good private hospitals for the mentally ill had been founded by incorporated bodies, and a number of states and municipalities had opened public institutions as well. Private hospitals, however, were small in size, extremely expensive, and selective in their admissions policies; hence they catered to a small and affluent clientele. Public institutions were few in number and, like almshouses, tended to deteriorate quickly into wretched places. As a result, the overwhelming majority of mentally ill persons, especially the indigent insane (particularly members of ethnic minorities), were either placed in inadequate public mental institutions or, more likely, confined to jails, almshouses, or other institutions where their care and treatment were faulty, to say the least.

Such was the case when Dorothea Dix began her fight for the insane in Massachusetts, where the number of dependent insane was more than twice as large as the total capacity of the three mental institutions—one state, one municipal, one private—in the state. Visiting numerous jails, houses of correction, dreary almshouses, and other places where the bulk of the mentally ill were housed, she set down in detail all she had seen. She described vividly how many of the unfortunate crazed were impounded in cabins, cages, closets, stalls, and other pens of one kind or another, often chained and then abandoned to filth and neglect, or else brutally beaten—a horrifying picture. Having decided that neither private philanthropy nor local responsibility could effectively remedy the situation, she embarked upon a crusade for more and better state care. Possessing a keen sense of political strategy, she embodied her findings in a memorial to the state legislature, which in part read:

> I come to present the strong claim of suffering humanity. . . . I come as the advocate of the helpless, forgotten, insane and idiotic men and women, beings sunk to a condition from which the most unconcerned should stare with real horror. If my pictures are displeasing, coarse, and severe [she continued], it must be remembered [that] . . . the conditions of beings reduced to the extremest states of degradation and misery cannot be exhibited in softened language and adorn a polished page.

After pleading passionately for its adoption, she eventually won her point—that the state should enlarge its facilities for poor mental patients.

Dorothea Dix did not stop there. Convinced that the issue transcended geographical boundaries, that mental illness was no respecter of persons or places, and that the public had a responsibility to provide adequate care for the sick and suffering, she carried her crusade into a dozen other states, including six in the South—Kentucky, Mississippi, Louisiana, South Carolina, Georgia, and Virginia—where tensions over the slavery issue were high and where it was extremely dangerous for a Yankee (especially a woman) to be traveling about. Still, she went on. Journeying by train, stagecoach, lumber wagon, and foot over muddy roads and across swollen rivers to visit places far removed and difficult to get to, she operated throughout on the assumption that proved successful in her home state—that reform comes from patient, factual research. Before starting out, she read widely on the subject and then, wherever she went, studied antiquated and impractical commitment laws, inspected buildings, talked with and observed the patients and their overseers, and so on, confining her thoughts and the harsh facts to writing. Thus armed with numerous case studies and statistics depicting the extent and nature of the problem, she made her appeal. And between 1843 and 1853, the "decade of victory," as her biographer has called it, she became personally responsible for the founding of state hospitals for mental patients in nine states, North and South alike (and quite a few others around the world, it might be added).

Still, the naturally timid and diffident crusader was not satisfied, for she had failed in some instances. She was convinced that her defeats resulted less from an unwillingness of legislators to help the mentally ill than from their inability to do so because of the high costs involved. So, at a time when the government had already allocated some 135 million acres of land for the purposes mentioned (and when not more than one-twelfth of the insane population in America could be accommodated in existing hospitals and asylums), she appealed to Congress to appropriate ten million more acres to the states to help pay for the construction and maintenance of mental hospitals.

A bill based upon research that had taken her some 60,000 miles to visit jails, poorhouses, and mental institutions throughout the country, was introduced in Congress in 1848. After the lawmakers adjourned without acting on the measure, Miss Dix had it reintroduced at the next session. Numerous clergymen, prominent citizens, newspapers, public and private organizations, including the Association of Medical Superintendents for the Insane, and some government officials wrote or acted in support of the measure. Still the bill was not acted upon, for most congressmen were more interested in using the remaining public domain for their own and for land speculators' purposes than for the mentally ill. Undaunted, she kept up the fight, spending the next five years in and out of congressional corridors promoting the measure. Finally, in 1854, it was passed by both houses of Congress.

The promise of a continued, and perhaps expanded, social welfare program stimulated by federal funds was shattered by a veto from the pen of President Franklin Pierce. While expressing "the deep sympathies in [his] . . . heart" for "the humane purpose sought to be accomplished by the bill," Pierce felt compelled to veto it because, in his opinion, it was illegal: "If Congress has the power to make provision for the indigent insane . . . it has the same power for the indigent who are not insane," and thus all the nation's needy. He continued: "I cannot find any authority in the Constitution for making the Federal Government the great almoner of public charity throughout the United States." To do so "would be contrary to the letter and spirit of the Constitution, and subversive of the whole theory upon which the union of these states is founded." As for previous acts of Congress which furnished precedents for the bill, particularly the land grants to the Connecticut and Kentucky institutions, Congress, in his opinion, simply had erred—it had transcended its power. Those examples, declared the President, generally conceded to be a "strict construction-ist" and a wily northern politician courting southern favor in the midst of the states' rights controversy, should "serve . . . as a warning [rather] than as an inducement to tread in the same path." For the most part, Pierce's reasoning was followed; the veto was upheld and federal involvement in social welfare, while not eliminated, was retarded for years to come and confined largely to certain "wards" of the nation—native Americans, former slaves, indigent merchant sea-men, and the like.

Meanwhile, private benevolent societies—which aimed not at pro-viding material aid to the needy but at uplifting them through improving their character—grew in number.[6] Most Americans contin-ued to believe that, since the nation offered unlimited natural resources and opportunities for success, poverty resulted from individ-ual moral failure—idleness, intemperance, immorality, and irreligion. Such shortcomings could be countered only by bringing contrary forces to bear, "by inculcating religion, morality, sobriety, and indus-try" into the poor. If malign influences could be eliminated and beneficent ones substituted, the better nature of the needy would assert itself and the problem would be solved. As a result, many mid-dle-class Americans engaged in a crusade for moral enlightenment. In urban areas throughout the country, agencies sprang up that empha-sized godliness and the salvation of character as a prerequisite to improvement in the condition of the poor—and as a means to mini-mize discontent and social instability among a highly mobile and dis-cordant population.[7]

---

[6]With public assistance frowned upon, private aid necessarily increased. In part, however, pri-vate charity also was an obvious consequence of heavy immigration and a mixed population; each ethnic and sectarian group established its own charitable agencies.

[7]As Clifford Griffin has suggested in his work on religious benevolence and social control in early-nineteenth-century America, in a sense, leaders of these benevolent societies were trans-mitting and enlarging the heritage from their forebears—the idea, first from the colonial theocrats and then from the Federalists, that the upper classes, a small number of people of particular attainments, should shape, govern, and lead society, which included not only caring for the unfortunate but also dictating their conduct and behavior.

Probably the most important of these was the New York Association for Improving the Condition of the Poor; to describe it is to describe all the others. Ironically, the immediate background of this and similar groups was the financial panic of 1837 and the depression that followed, which caused great hardship among the working classes of New York City and elsewhere. Existing relief agencies, both public and private, proved inadequate to the task of relieving the thousands of needy families. Destitution was widespread; beggars and vagrants stalked the streets.

In an attempt to improve the situation, in the winter of 1842-43, some New Yorkers came together to examine the city's charities. Their report portrayed a situation that undoubtedly existed in other cities and which, it was felt, constituted a serious menace. Public institutions were badly overcrowded and their resources seriously strained. More important, a lack of discrimination in the giving of private aid was seen; voluntary agencies, acting independently of each other, not only gave too much to insistent beggars, but at times duplicated their efforts. And, finally, there was inadequate contact between the donors and the recipients of welfare. The New York Association for Improving the Condition of the Poor, a citywide organization, was created in 1843 to remedy the situation; it would repress pauperism and aid the poor through the influence of male volunteers, "paternal guardians"—for the most part, the woman's place, it was still widely believed, was in the home—who would lead the dependent to self-support through instruction in the basic virtues of religious observance, thrift, hard work, and temperance. Through skillful leadership, it evolved into a leading spokesman for an urban middle class bewildered by the rapid spread of poverty and anxious over its possible effects.

Like most people working to ameliorate poverty, members of the A.I.C.P. were mainly white middle-class Protestants—merchants, professional people, real estate developers, shopkeepers, artisans, and so on, the very people responsible for the conditions whose consequences they so emphatically deplored. They were concerned with the problem because, as Christians, they could not ignore the distress suffered by the needy, because the financial drain for supporting the poor fell largely on their shoulders, and because the growing number of dependents (mainly Catholic immigrants) seemed to menace the virtues

they so dearly cherished. Motivated then by a number of impulses—
sometimes contradictory—they approached the poor in a spirit of
Christian benevolence tempered by fear and perhaps a pang of guilt.
On the one hand, they felt a moral obligation to help the needy, while
on the other they feared, and perhaps even despised, them for the
moral faults and imperfections which were supposedly responsible for
their pauperism. How it was possible to love those who were, by all
standards of wealth, education, and virtue, so obviously inferior, they
did not say.

In the final analysis, members of the A.I.C.P. probably loved the
poor less than they feared or perhaps even hated them. Their object
was not so much to help the poor as to remold them into good middle-class citizens, to make them "respectable." Unless steps were taken
to do this, the A.I.C.P. warned, the poor would "over-run the city as
thieves and beggars and endanger the security of property and life—
tax the community for their support and entail upon it an inheritance
of vice and pauperism." Self-interest and social justice, in other words,
went hand in hand.

In effect, then, the A.I.C.P. was no more a charitable agency than
an instrument for reducing relief costs and keeping society orderly,
stable, and quiet. Indeed, according to its constitution, the organization looked to "the *elevation* of the moral and physical condition of
the indigent; and so far as compatible with these objects, the relief of
their necessities" (italics added). Its goal—self-support and the permanent improvement of the condition of the poor—could best be
achieved not through "indiscriminate charity," but through the uplifting of character. "The most effectual encouragement of [paupers] . . .
is not alms . . . or any other form of charity as a substitute for alms,
but that *sympathy* and *counsel* which re-kindles hope and that expres-
sion of respect for character which such individuals never fail to
appreciate," stated an early A.I.C.P. manual.

Charity, it was maintained, only softened the moral fiber of the
poor and intensified the problem. Reeducation, moral suasion, and
individual counseling, not relief-giving, were the objectives. As a
result, the poor were constantly told by their "protectors" that if they
but worked hard, that if they were economical and good Christians,
that if they gave up that glass of beer on the way home from the factory, everything would be all right.

The most important, or leading, causes of poverty in the A.I.C.P.'s view were extravagance, improvidence, indolence, and, above all, intemperance—all noneconomic factors. Drink was clearly the leading cause of want and woe: "We may consider intemperance as the most prolific source of degradation," declared one member. Or, in the words of Robert Hartley, the agency's long-time chief executive, who never tired of denouncing the pernicious evil, "intemperance is the master vice, exerting above all other evil influences a steady and determined opposition to every good word and work."

The A.I.C.P.'s concern with character building led inevitably to what it termed "incidental labors"—activities that later came to be regarded by many as the most important element in social work—an examination of environmental causes of poverty. Entering the homes of the poor, association members quickly discovered that in the slums, where most of the needy were forced to live, all those features of poverty that middle-class citizens found most reprehensible were concentrated and intensified—filth, crime, sexual promiscuity, drunkenness, disease, improvidence, and indolence—serious obstacles to morality. It was difficult to inculcate the virtues of thrift, temperance, diligence, and cleanliness into the unfortunate victims of such wretched living conditions. It was also found that despite all their hints on household management or admonitions on waste, intemperance, idleness, and the virtues of self-help, many persons could not maintain themselves for a lack of jobs or a living wage. Recognizing that the material welfare of the poor was, under such circumstances, of primary concern, the A.I.C.P. began to seek jobs for the unemployed. Before long, its "unflagging commitment to moral uplift [became] a thing of the past," to use Hartley's words, and it even distributed financial aid to the needy. It also engaged in surveys to ascertain mortality rates in slum areas. It built "model tenements" and sought municipal legislation to clean up the slums and to improve the construction of new housing. It strove to prevent adulteration of milk, to establish free medical dispensaries, public baths and washhouses, and, in general, it became a leading advocate of social reform.

The early history of the A.I.C.P. is important, then, less for the problems it solved than for at least defining those problems and, in the process, laying the path for others to follow. Insisting at the outset that if the poor led moral lives their economic problems would disappear, A.I.C.P. members came to argue that the moral improvement of the poor *depended upon the amelioration of their economic condition*. Hence the group became concerned with the relationship between dependency and the environment, turning eventually to the state for the regulation of behavior. It also insisted that assistance must be well planned, that relief methods can be defined and transmitted, and that personal service has value. In so doing, it set important precedents for later generations to follow; it had great impact on the later charity organization movement and, indeed, on the eventual emergence of a social work profession.

In the meantime, most people continued to accept the belief that poverty was an individual moral matter—the result of willful indolence and vice rather than the natural result of misfortune, as had been assumed earlier. To be sure, there were some in Great Britain, as well as in the United States, who, preaching the virtues of an altogether new society, dissented from that view. Robert Owen and other believers in socialist utopias did not subscribe to that idea. Nor, of course, did Karl Marx, who, living then in London, was close to issuing his manifesto for economic and political revolution. Then there were others such as Mathew Carey, a young Philadelphia bookseller, pamphleteer, and economist, and Sarah Josepha Hale, well known editor of *Godey's Lady's Book*, who also founded and headed the Boston Seamen's Aid Society; both Carey and Hale saw the intimate relationship between poverty and low wages and hence the need for public assistance.

The Reverend Joseph Tuckerman, a Unitarian "minister to the poor" in Boston who believed that society had as much to fear from the "licentiousness of wealth" as from the growth of poverty, preferred preventive measures to both public relief and private charity. Recognizing the economic causes of poverty and alcoholism, especially unemployment, he always treated the poor with respect and became a leading champion of social reform. Dr. John H. Griscom, a New York City health officer, also shifted the concept of fault away from the unfortunate sufferer and attached it instead to other things, not only to "physical disability and premature mortality among the lower classes," which were "in a great degree the results of causes which are removable," but also to greedy landlords and to the system under which they operated. Both the landlord and the system, he believed, should be subject to regulation.

Very little was accomplished along these lines. Rather, in an attempt to cope with the disturbing social and economic conditions and to restore a sense of community to urban America, moralism superseded humanism; public aid and private charity were transformed from acts of justice and benevolence into mechanisms for bringing order and stability to a new and unsettling social environment.

This, of course, raises the question of social control, at least the way in which it has come to be used during the past twenty years or so. Whereas originally the term "social control" had benign connotations—it was used approvingly by progressives to describe those processes in a society that supported a level of social cohesiveness sufficient for its survival, including measures that enabled the needy and helpless to function within the social order—more recently it has come to symbolize sinister activities—efforts by the middle and upper classes to manipulate and regulate the behavior of the lower classes in order to promote the former groups' own interests, often through enhancing the capitalist system.

Were these antebellum "reformers," philanthropists, and charity workers so motivated? Were they, in other words, evil people deliberately seeking to promote or protect their own and their class's interests at the expense of others? That, of course, is a difficult question to answer. Human motives, with regard to social welfare or any other matter, usually are complex and difficult to discern; in fact, they may not always be discernible to the individuals involved, let alone to historians many years later. No doubt, however, as some critics now charge, some middle- and upper-class Americans "gave" to the poor or supported efforts at that time and later to uplift them, for reasons of social control; they feared that allowing pauperism to grow or continuing to treat it through the older, more generous welfare system would not only destroy character and erode the will to work but would endanger society and their place (and property) within it. In addition, as Paul Boyer has argued in *Urban Masses and Moral Order in America, 1820–1920*, others participated in philanthropic activities not to safeguard their position in the community but to alter it—to advance by demonstrating to themselves and to others that they had "made it" and thus were worthy of increased admiration and respect.

On the other hand, the evidence also suggests that many people helped the poor because of evangelical piety. They viewed such activity as the handmaiden of religion; they "gave," in other words, to please God. Clearly, for some a sense of civic duty, not self-interest or religion, was the motivating factor. Others possessed a real humanitarian concern for the needy. Some simply enjoyed giving or got involved because a particular appeal touched their hearts. Yet others were moved by cultural nationalism: they wished to fulfill their dream of an enlightened republic free from the evils and inequities that contaminated European society. No doubt other factors operated as well; motives were mixed and many. And whereas today many of these may seem suspect, or even insidious, most early nineteenth-century citizens no doubt believed that the measures they took to promote self-help and social stability would benefit the individuals involved as well as society as a whole. Whatever the motive or motives, the Civil War brought changes in the nation's social welfare needs and practices.

Bibliography

ALTSCHULER, GLENN C. "Clearinghouse for Paupers: The Poor Farm of Seneca County, New York, 1830–1860," *Journal of Social History* 17 (Summer 1984): 573–600.

BECKER, DOROTHY G. "The Visitor to the New York City Poor, 1843–1920," *Social Service Review* 35 (December 1961): 382–96.

BLAUG, MARK. "The Myth of the Old Poor Law and the Making of the New," *Journal of Economic History* 23 (June 1963): 151–84.

———. "The Poor Law Report Reexamined," *Journal of Economic History* 24 (June 1964): 229–45.

BOYER, PAUL. *Urban Masses and Moral Order in America, 1820–1920.* Cambridge, Mass.: Harvard University Press, 1978.

BROWN, ELIZABETH G. "Poor Relief in a Wisconsin County, 1846–1866: Administration and Recipients," *American Journal of Legal History* 20 (April 1976): 79–117.

CARROLL, DOUGLAS G., AND BLANCHE D. COLL. "The Baltimore Almshouse: An Early History," *Maryland Historical Magazine* 66 (Summer 1971): 135–52.

CHADWICK, EDWIN. *Report for Inquiring into the Administration and Practical Operation of the Poor Laws*, reprinted in Roy Lubove, ed., *Social Welfare in Transition*. Pittsburgh: University of Pittsburgh Press, 1966.

CLEMENT, PRISCILLA F. "The Philadelphia Welfare Crisis of the 1820s," *Pennsylvania Magazine of History and Biography* 55 (April 1981): 150–65.

———. *Welfare and the Poor in the Nineteenth-Century City: Philadelphia, 1800–1854*. Rutherford, N.J.: Fairleigh Dickinson University Press, 1985.

COLL, BLANCHE D. "The Baltimore Society for the Prevention of Pauperism, 1820–1860," *American Historical Review* 61 (October 1955): 77–87.

———. *Perspectives in Public Welfare*. Washington, D.C.: Government Printing Office, 1969.

COTTRELL, DEBBIE M. "The County Poor Farm System in Texas," *Southwestern Historical Quarterly* 93 (October 1989): 169–90.

DOYLE, DON H. "The Social Functions of Voluntary Associations in a Nineteenth-Century American Town," *Social Science History* 1 (Spring 1977): 333–35.

ELDER, WALTER. "Speenhamland Revisited," *Social Service Review* 38 (September 1964): 294–302.

FOX, RICHARD. "Beyond 'Social Control': Institutions and Disorder in Bourgeois Society," *History of Education Quarterly* 16 (Summer 1976): 203–207.

GALPER, JEFFREY. "The Speenhamland Scales: Political, Social or Economic Disaster?" *Social Service Review* 44 (March 1970): 54–62.

GOFFMAN, ERVING. *Asylums: Essays on the Social Situation of Mental Patients and Other Inmates*. Garden City, N.Y.: Doubleday, 1961.

GRIFFIN, CLIFFORD S. "Religious Benevolence and Social Control, 1815–1860," *Mississippi Valley Historical Review* 44 (December 1957): 423–44.

———. *Their Brothers' Keepers: Moral Stewardship in the United States, 1800–1865*. New Brunswick, N.J.: Rutgers University Press, 1965.

HANNON, JOAN U. "The Generosity of Antebellum Poor Relief," *Journal of Economic History* 44 (September 1984): 810–21.

———. "Poverty in the Antebellum Northeast: The View from New York State's Poor Relief Rolls," *Journal of Economic History* 44 (December 1984): 1007–32.

HEALE, M.J. "Humanitarianism in the Early Republic: The Moral Reformers of New York, 1776–1825," *Journal of American Studies* 2 (October 1968): 161–75.

———. "The New York Society for the Prevention of Pauperism, 1817–1823," *New-York Historical Society Quarterly* 55 (April 1917): 153–72.

————. "Patterns of Benevolence: Associated Philanthropy in the Cities of New York, 1830–1860," *New York History* 57 (January 1976): 53–80.

HIMMELFARB, GERTRUDE. *The Idea of Poverty*. New York: Knopf, 1984.

HUZEL, JAMES P. "Malthus, the Poor Law, and Population in Early Nineteenth-Century England," *Economic History Review* 22 (December 1969): 430–51.

JIMENEZ, MARY ANN. *Changing Faces of Madness: Early American Attitudes and Treatment of the Insane*. Hanover, N.H.: University Press of New England, 1987.

KATZ, MICHAEL. "Origins of the Institutional State," *Marxist Perspectives* 1 (Winter 1978): 6–23.

KLEBANER, BENJAMIN J. "Poverty and Its Relief in American Thought, 1815–61," *Social Service Review* 38 (December 1964): 382–99.

————. "Public Poor Relief in America, 1790–1860," Ph.D. dissertation, Columbia University, 1952.

LASCH, CHRISTOPHER. "Origins of the Asylum," in *The World of Nations: Reflections on American History, Politics, and Culture*. New York: Knopf, 1974.

LOWENBERG, FRANK M. "Federal Relief Programs in the 19th Century: A Reassessment," *Journal of Sociology and Social Welfare* 19 (September 1992): 121–36.

LUBOVE, ROY. "The New York Association for Improving the Condition of the Poor," *New-York Historical Society Quarterly* 43 (July 1959): 307–28.

McCLOSKEY, DONALD N. "New Perspectives on the Old Poor Law," *Explorations in Economic History* 10 (Summer 1973): 419–36.

MALTHUS, THOMAS. *An Essay on the Principle of Population*. London: Dent, 1914.

MARSHALL, HELEN. *Dorothea Dix: Forgotten Samaritan*. Chapel Hill: University of North Carolina Press, 1937.

MARSHALL, J. D. *The Old Poor Law, 1795–1834*. London: Macmillan, 1985.

MOHL, RAYMOND A. *Poverty in New York, 1783–1825*. New York: Oxford University Press, 1971.

PICCARELLO, LOUIS J. "Social Structure and Public Welfare Policy in Danvers, Mass.: 1750–1850," *Essex Institute Historical Collections* 118 (October 1982): 248–63.

POLANYI, KARL. *The Great Transformation*. Boston: Beacon Press, 1957.

POYNTER, J. R. *Society and Pauperism: English Ideas on Poor Relief, 1795–1834*. Toronto: University of Toronto Press, 1969.

ROSE, MICHAEL E. "The Allowance System Under the New Poor Law," *Economic History Review* 19 (December 1966): 607–20.

————, ed. *The English Poor Law, 1780–1930.* New York: Barnes and Noble, 1971.

ROSENKRANTZ, BARBARA, AND MARIS A. VINOVSKIS. "Caring for the Insane in Ante-Bellum Massachusetts," in Allan Lichtman and Joan Challinor, eds., *Kin and Communities: Families in America.* Washington, D.C.: Smithsonian Institution, 1979.

ROTHMAN, DAVID J. *The Discovery of the Asylum: Social Order and Disorder in the New Republic.* Boston: Little, Brown, 1971.

SCHWARTZ, HAROLD. *Samuel Gridley Howe: Social Reformer, 1801–1876.* Cambridge, Mass.: Harvard University Press, 1956.

SMITH, BRUCE. "Poor Relief at the St. Joseph County Poor Asylum, 1877–1891," *Indiana Magazine of History* 86 (June 1990): 211–18.

SPEIZMAN, MILTON. "Speenhamland: An Experiment in Guaranteed Income," *Social Service Review* 11 (March 1966): 44–55.

TRATTNER, WALTER I. "The Federal Government and Needy Citizens in Nineteenth-Century America," *Political Science Quarterly* 103 (Summer 1988): 347–56.

————. "The Federal Government and Social Welfare in Early Nineteenth-Century America," *Social Service Review* 50 (June 1976): 243–55.

YATES, J. V. N. *Report of the Secretary of State in 1824 on the Relief and Settlement of the Poor, in Assembly Journal,* Appendix B (January 1824): 386–99.

ZAINALDEN, JAMIL S., AND PETER TYOR. "Asylum and Society: An Approach to Institutional Change," *Journal of Social History* 13 (Fall 1979): 23–48.

CHAPTER 5

The Civil War and After—
Scientific Charity

■ Like all wars, the War between the States created enormous relief problems—problems which could not be blamed on the individuals or families involved.[1] As a result, public officials and private citizens responded accordingly; in fact, the war aroused the charitable energies of the American people as never before. Warnings of unwise giving were forgotten as public and private agencies showered assistance on the needy throughout the conflict.

Methods of distributing such assistance varied. Laws were enacted enabling localities to raise funds for the relief of sick, destitute, and wounded soldiers and their families and, in some instances, for the founding of homes for disabled veterans. Beginning in 1862, state legislatures, North and South alike, appropriated large sums of money for the same purposes. Thus, the war brought a temporary reversal of charitable practices; direct public aid, on a grand scale, became available once again.

The war had other effects on social welfare. To begin with, when the fighting broke out, the first contingents of northern troops had to be hurried into battle so quickly that little provision was made for their sanitary or medical care. Consequently, at the outset, the mortality rate from disease alone was so great that it appeared as though the horrors of

---

[1]The Confederacy may have suffered even more than the Union in this regard. One scholar has gone so far as to suggest that the welfare problem was so great in the region that it contributed to desertion in the army and disaffection with the war. See Paul D. Escott, "The Cry of the Sufferers: The Problem of Welfare in the Confederacy," *Civil War History* 23 (September 1977): 228–40.

the Crimean War (1853–56), in which thousands of men died unnecessarily simply for lack of medical supplies and attention, would be reenacted in America; some observers predicted the loss of 50 percent of the fighting force by the end of the first summer. As a result, a group of people—the most important of whom were Dr. Henry W. Bellows, a New York Unitarian minister, Louisa Lee Schuyler, a scion of a wealthy and distinguished New York family and a member of Bellows' congregation, and Dr. Elisha Harris, a well-known sanitary reformer—saw the need to do something about it.

Appalled by the stories of filth and disease in army camps and hospitals and the lack of trained nurses and adequate transportation facilities for the wounded, they sought to establish some sort of voluntary citizen effort to remedy the situation. They organized the U.S. Sanitary Commission, the nation's first important national public health group.

Organized in 1861 and composed chiefly of women, the commission was solely financed and directed by private means.[2] Its chief aim, which was largely realized, was to unite numerous local voluntary relief societies into a national organization that would supplement the work of governmental agencies in meeting the physical and spiritual needs of the men in uniform. At the outset, its work was mainly preventive—to educate inexperienced troops in proper personal hygiene and to inspect and supervise living arrangements in army camps and field hospitals. By so doing, it prevented much needless suffering and death through disease and illness; thousands of lives were saved each year.

Soon it expanded its work in a variety of ways. It distributed bandages, food, and clothing to the army. It recruited and supplied a corps of nurses, maintained special relief lodges and houses for soldiers in transit, and set up channels of communication between the

---

[2]Dr. Bellows drafted the constitution and served as president of the commission. Other prominent members who took part were George Templeton Strong, its treasurer, and Frederick Law Olmsted, its executive secretary. Bellows and others wanted the government to empower the commission with official authority to carry on its work. The army medical department would not hear of this, however, so the U.S. Sanitary Commission was organized without any power to enforce its recommendations. Later, after it had proved its worth, the commission was able to influence the selection of a new surgeon general more in sympathy with its aims and purposes, and thenceforth it enjoyed the respect and close cooperation of the medical corps and other federal officials.

men on the battlefield and the people at home. In short, it undertook most of the wartime duties later assumed by the Red Cross, winning universal acclaim. John Stuart Mill said of it: "History afforded no other example of so great a work of usefulness extemporized by the spontaneous self-devotion and organizing genius of a people altogether independent of the government."

Aside from its material contributions to welfare, the Sanitary Commission (which ultimately had about 500 people working for it and performed approximately $25 million "worth" of services) helped lay the groundwork for progress in public health that followed the war. Among other things, the training in sanitary science and surgical procedures provided young army physicians tended to further medical progress later on. Also, by awakening public opinion to preventive sanitary practices that could save thousands of lives each year, and the ease with which they could be implemented, the work of the commission stimulated public health reform in later periods. Thus, four years after the war ended, the first state board of health came into existence, followed by similar boards in most populous states. Ten years later, in 1879, the federal government recognized the importance of public health activities by creating a National Board of Health which, while short lived, was nevertheless instrumental in setting precedents for future federal activities in the areas of health and welfare.[3]

Moreover, the Sanitary Commission demonstrated that a well organized and coordinated effort by small voluntary groups or committees supported by a central association can educate masses of people, influence public opinion, and effect important reforms; its success confirmed in many persons' minds the value and power of voluntary organizations in promoting the public welfare, and many such organizations were created in the postwar years. To cite just one example, in 1872, Louisa Lee Schuyler organized the New York State Charities Aid Association, a voluntary organization patterned after the U.S. Sanitary Commission, which to this day works for improved public health and social welfare legislation throughout New York State—and the nation.

---

[3]While the founding of the U.S. Public Health Service (the federal agency traditionally responsible for promoting good health) dates back to 1798, the U.S. government assumed almost no interest in public health matters until the 1870s and the creation of the National Board of Health.

The wartime demonstration of private philanthropy's usefulness, especially the part played by civilians in financing and staffing the U.S. Sanitary Commission and similar organizations, also aided the cause of social welfare. Never before had the nation seen such whole-hearted, generous, and sustained sacrifices from the people, and the lesson would be remembered.

So, too, were the efforts of women, who during the war worked valiantly side by side with men in hospitals and even on the battle-field. President Abraham Lincoln, who, along with Secretary of War Edwin Stanton, early in the conflict was not particularly happy over the prospect of having members of the Sanitary Commission, especially women, in the vicinity of the war zone, later remarked:

> I am not accustomed to the language of eulogy and have never studied the art of paying compliments to women, but I must say that if all that has been said by the orators and poets since the creation of the world in praise of women were applied to the women of America, it would not do them justice for their conduct during the war. . . . God bless the women of America.

Their participation in wartime activities and the recognition they won for it, in turn, gave women not only a new self-image but also rising expectations, what William O'Neill, an historian of feminism, has referred to as a "heroic myth"—a claim on the nation, one that, unfortunately, was not fulfilled. Some women, though, did make progress, winning for themselves a stronger voice in public affairs. Finding themselves in service to others, they could not relapse into total domesticity; thus, they got involved in a variety of postwar reform movements. The war, in other words, launched some women on lifelong careers of service.[4]

The political decision settled by the war—that the national government was supreme and the state governments subordinate to it—also had an important effect upon sanitary and social reform. Social welfare,

---

[4]In an 1888 Memorial Day address, a quarter-century after Gettysburg, Clara Barton, head of the American Red Cross, an organization she had created seven years earlier, recalled women's work in the Civil War and declared that because of it the American woman "was at least fifty years in advance of the normal position which continued peace . . . would have assigned." Clara Barton herself, who began her career nursing sick and wounded soldiers during the Civil War, was an excellent example of what she was talking about. So, too, was Louisa Lee Schuyler.

especially public health, is a matter that transcends village, city, and even state boundaries. It flourishes best under strong central authority. So, by establishing, once and for all, the supremacy of the federal government, the Civil War ultimately drew the states together and introduced a greater amount of coordination among them. A health program in one state, as a consequence, was less likely to be jettisoned by the unrestrained acts or negligence of another, and vice versa—a reform in one state usually resulted in many others following suit.

In these and other ways, the Civil War had a constructive impact upon social welfare in America. The same could not be said for the immediate postwar years.

Between the years 1865 and 1900, America underwent a spectacular expansion of productive facilities and output that was without parallel in the history of the world. Statistics tell part of the story. In 1860, approximately $1 billion was invested in manufacturing plants; the annual value of manufactured products was $1,885,000,000; and 1,300,000 workers were employed in American factories. By the turn of the century, the amount of capital invested had risen to more than $12 billion, the yearly value of products to over $11 billion, and the number of workers to 5,500,000. But as Charles and Mary Beard, historians of American civilization, have indicated, statistics barely reflect the developments of the era:

> With a stride that astonished statisticians, the conquering hosts of business enterprise swept over the continent; twenty-five years after the death of Lincoln, America had become in the quantity and value of her products, the first manufacturing nation in the world. What England had once accomplished in a hundred years, the United States had achieved in half the time.

The consequences of this experience, so pervasive as to be referred to as an "economic revolution," were enormous. On the one hand, it enhanced the national wealth, raised the general standard of living, encouraged immigration, speeded up urbanization, and had many other constructive effects. On the other hand, it produced, among other things, periodic cycles of depression and unemployment, a small group of men who controlled the nation's resources and modes of production, wretched living and working conditions, a high incidence of industrial accidents and fatalities, and numerous other unfortunate results that affected every segment of American society.

It was primarily in industry that the effects of this revolution were most apparent. The swift and enormous growth of the factory system, with its simple, repetitive processes, not only eroded the instinct of craftsmanship and a sense of pride in one's work, but also swept more and more people—men, women, and children—into industrial occupations where they were reduced to a mere part in a mechanical process, automata performing the same monotonous operation hundreds of times a day, usually under noisy and exceedingly unhealthy conditions, with long hours and low pay, over which they and the other "hired hands" in the factory had little or no control. Upton Sinclair described the situation this way in *The Jungle*, published in 1905:

> Each one of the hundreds of parts of a mowing machine was made separately, and sometimes handled by hundreds of men. Where [one man] . . . worked there was a machine which cut and stamped a certain piece of steel about two square inches in size; the pieces came tumbling out upon a tray and all that human hands had to do was to pile them in regular rows and change the trays at intervals. This was done by a single [person]. . . . Thirty thousand of these pieces he handled every day, nine or ten millions every year. Nearby him sat men bending over whirling grind-stones, putting the finishing touches to the steel knives of the reaper; picking them out of a basket with the right hand, pressing first one side and then the other against the stone, and finally dropping them with the left hand into another basket. One of these men . . . sharpened three thousand pieces of steel a day for thirteen years.

Many of the unfortunate victims of these cruel, and in some cases even inhumane, conditions would need help. First, however, as the Civil War was coming to an end, an acute but different problem of relief faced the nation—that of aiding the freed men and women, several million of whom, largely uneducated, unskilled, and unprepared for their abrupt change in status, would shortly be roaming the South in search of employment and assistance.[5] To meet the problem—clearly a national problem since it was one that, for the most part, the southern communities and states had neither the resources nor the desire to deal with—in March 1865, two months before the conflict

---

[5]Ironically, the first real casualties of emancipation and the new labor system were those former slaves who could not work for one reason or another—old age, illness, infirmity, etc. Since slaveowners were responsible for their property, they had been "cared for" earlier by their masters and by other slaves on the plantation. The question was, who would assume responsibility for their welfare now, and on what basis?

ended, Congress established in the U.S. War Department the Bureau of Refugees, Freedmen, and Abandoned Lands, the nation's first federal welfare agency. Usually referred to as the Freedmen's Bureau, it was authorized to administer a program of temporary relief for the duration of the war and one year thereafter, a time of unusual stress. However, after a bitter struggle between President Andrew Johnson, who hoped to terminate the bureau and hence vetoed a measure to prolong its life, and Congress, which sought to continue its existence and thus overrode the President's veto, the life of the Freedmen's Bureau was extended for six years.[6]

Under the able direction of General Oliver O. Howard, a West Point graduate who was extremely sensitive to the feelings and needs of the freedmen, the bureau undertook a wide variety of tasks in its effort to aid blacks in the transition from slavery to freedom. It served as a relief agency on an unprecedented scale, distributing twenty-two million rations to needy persons in the devastated South. It served as an employment agency, helping many blacks to obtain jobs and supervising the writing of contracts between them and their employers.

In addition, it served as a settlement agency, leasing certain abandoned properties to black cultivators. In the field of health, it employed doctors and maintained hospitals, reducing the mortality rate among the freed men and women. As an educational agency, it encouraged the founding of black schools and then provided them with financial aid. And finally, it served as a legal agency, maintaining courts in which both civil and criminal cases involving ex-slaves were dealt with in an informal and just manner. While far from perfect and plagued by many problems—financial, bureaucratic, and political— all in all the bureau provided a variety of welfare services that were unavailable from any other source and saved untold numbers of needy blacks (and some poor whites) from additional pain and hardship.

---

[6]Just as Pierce had done earlier with the Dix bill, President Johnson, a southerner who had no love for blacks, vetoed the measure on constitutional grounds: "A system for the support of indigent persons in the United States," he wrote, "was never contemplated by the authors of the Constitution. . . . " Recovery from slavery was, in his opinion, the freedmen's own responsibility. It should be pointed out, however, the fact that the bureau was placed in the War Department (rather than in the Treasury Department, for example, where some wished to house it) indicates that, from the outset, it was viewed as a wartime, or temporary, rather than a permanent agency.

Finally liquidated in 1872, the Freedmen's Bureau had shown that the federal government could provide for the welfare of people on a broad scale when poverty and hardship could (or would) not be treated locally. The bureau, however, was ahead of its time; its impact on the social welfare policies of the era—public and private—was nil. Not until the twentieth century did the federal government again become involved in social welfare in any sustained way. And as Victoria Olds, a historian of the agency, has pointed out, the bureau had little impact on private charity as well. As an emergency relief program concerned primarily with ex-slaves, it seemed to have little relevance or importance for private philanthropy. Since most of the important private charitable agencies were located in the Northeast or Midwest, where they had a predominantly white clientele, most northerners failed to recognize the importance of the bureau, which, centered in the South, had served mostly blacks.[7]

While the Freedmen's Bureau was the major source of public welfare for blacks in the South after the Civil War, the counties and states did make some strides, at least during the period of so-called Radical, or Congressional, Reconstruction (1867–76). For the most part, though, blacks were treated separately from the white poor and in an inferior manner. Thus, while the new state constitutions generally included sections that required the provision of aid to all the needy on an equal basis, usually in state or county institutions, integration rarely occurred in the provision of such assistance.

In 1867, for example, the state of Tennessee made special provision for the black mentally ill when the legislature authorized the Tennessee Hospital for the Insane to construct quarters for Negroes "so as to keep them secure and safe and yet separate from the white patients." More often than not, however, completely separate facilities were provided, usually fewer in number and poorer in quality. In Richmond, Virginia, for example, where the situation was typical, the

---

[7]The oversight persisted well into the twentieth century. Despite the similarities between the Freedmen's Bureau and the Federal Emergency Relief Administration, which was created during the early years of the Great Depression when it was generally recognized that the resources of voluntary agencies and local government were inadequate to meet mass needs, few references to the Bureau were found in the literature of social welfare until recently.

white almshouse was a three-story brick building while the black institution, which normally contained far more residents, was a much
smaller, rickety wooden structure. Nevertheless, opening the doors of
public institutions to blacks in the South, whether in segregated facilities or in inferior separate ones, was a significant break with the past,
one, however, that proved to be rather temporary.

With the termination of Reconstruction, southerners continued to
give verbal support to a segregated (and allegedly equal) welfare program, but in practice they generally reverted to the policy of complete
exclusion. As a result, by the late nineteenth century deprived blacks
were once again left to fend for themselves. Consequently, they were
forced to turn to self-help, or mutual aid.

While, at times, the extended family proved helpful, at the core of
these efforts were Negro benevolent societies of one kind or another—
fraternal orders, women's clubs, mutual benefit societies, and other
organizations, which often were connected to, or were the offspring
of, local churches. In return for small monthly dues, members of these
voluntary associations, which provided outlets for social interaction as
well as much-needed charitable work, were often entitled to some
assistance, including sick benefits and, when necessary, burial fees,
assuring some African-Americans the kind of respect in death that
white society denied so many of them in life.[8] Still, the number of
these societies was not large and, of course, their resources were limited. As a result, while they helped to temper the impact of the exclu-
sionary practices of white-controlled public agencies and institutions,
on the whole black Americans continued to suffer throughout the
period, just as they had done earlier.

So, too, perhaps it should be added, did many whites who resided
in the region, which by far had the highest incidence of poverty in
America. Hard times after 1865 perpetuated a deeply depressed lower
class of white farmers and farm laborers, who, like their black counterparts in the South, suffered greatly from hookworm, pellagra, malnutrition, and a variety of other ailments and problems. As the textile
industry moved south in the late nineteenth century, they straggled

---

[8]One of the first such organizations was the Nashville (Tennessee) Colored Benevolent Society.
Another, located in Atlanta, had as its motto: "We assist the needy: we relieve our sick; we
bury our dead."

into mill villages, where working and living conditions were only slightly better.

In the meantime, especially with the liquidation of the Freedmen's Bureau, the federal government removed itself from the social welfare scene as a provider of services. For the time being, at least, the state would be responsible for public dependents removed from the jurisdiction of local supervisors of the poor and from county almshouses. As a result, state-supported institutions continued to multiply. For the most part, such institutions were administered by separate, independent, unsalaried boards, composed chiefly of prominent citizens and state officeholders appointed by the governors. In theory, the governors and the state legislatures were supposed to supervise and coordinate their efforts. In practice, it did not work that way. The various public officials usually had so many other duties that they had little time, let alone knowledge, to supervise these institutions. Policies were not uniform; extravagance and waste prevailed. Abuses often went unattended.

The situation in Massachusetts was typical. In 1859, the commonwealth had three state mental institutions, a reform school for boys, an industrial school for girls, a hospital, and three almshouses for the state or nonresident poor. In addition, four private charitable institutions— schools for the blind, the deaf and dumb, the feeble-minded, and an eye and ear infirmary—received state aid. Each of these was managed by its own board of trustees. So uncoordinated a system not only increased the cost of operation, but did not provide for a channel of communication between institutions; a reform in one, then, might not be implemented in the others. The situation obviously called for some method of state supervision, as a report of the state legislature's Joint Standing Committee on Public Charitable Institutions indicated:

> If ever there was a system at loose ends [the report stated] it is the present pauper system. . . . There is a fatal want of harmony between the administrative elements. . . . In truth, there is an evident feeling of jealousy prevalent, and a want of centralized authority injurious to the interests of the state. Unison, cooperation, oneness, is eminently desirable.

The legislature responded by creating, in 1863, a Board of State Charities (later called the State Board of Charities), which was charged with the responsibility of investigation and supervising all of the state's charitable and correctional institutions and recommending changes that would bring about their more efficient and economical operation. Thus, Massachusetts was the first state to coordinate and centralize its state welfare activities. Its example was followed by Ohio, New York, Illinois, Wisconsin, Michigan, Kansas, and Connecticut. By 1886 twelve states had such bodies, and four more added them within another decade.

Despite differences in name—State Board of Charities, Board of Public Charities, Board of Charities and Correction, Board of Charitable and Reformatory Institutions, and the like—the various boards were similar in purpose in that they all sought to bring the supervised institutions directly under the aegis of the state—to see to it that they were operated as economically and as humanely as was possible. Although most had some executive power (especially the authority to transfer inmates from one institution to another), their duties were largely supervisory in nature. Nevertheless, they had a profound effect upon social welfare at the state level. And because many of the boards had the authority to recommend whether or not their legislatures should provide aid to county and municipal institutions and, in some cases, even to private agencies, they affected local social welfare as well. Of particular significance were their studies and written documents, such as annual reports to their legislatures. These studies, which dealt with almost every aspect of public relief and institutional treatment, served to educate not only officeholders but also the general public to conditions that required remedial action in the form of corrective legislation and improved standards of care.[9] As Robert Bremner has pointed out, in an age not noted for the excellence of its public servants, the members and secretaries of these boards—Samuel Gridley Howe, Franklin B. Sanborn, Frederick H. Wines, to cite only a few—set high standards of integrity and competence.

---

[9]This was especially true with regard to the mentally ill. The boards not only resumed the struggle to obtain state care for the indigent insane but were largely responsible for getting Congress, in 1882, to make it unlawful for the mentally ill to enter the country. Perhaps it should be mentioned here that between the Civil War and the end of the nineteenth century the states also created boards of health, bureaus of labor statistics, railroad commissions, and other agencies designed to deal with problems of the social and economic order, thereby laying the basis for the later welfare state, at least according to William Brock. See his *Investigation and Responsibility* (New York: Cambridge University Press, 1984).

Public welfare, however, again played second fiddle, so to speak, to private charity where, as we shall shortly see, there was also a trend toward coordinating administration and supervision in a single agency. The idea that distress was an individual moral matter was not only revived but strengthened as the wounds of the Civil War were healed and the nation grew and prospered. The poor were held in contempt in an acquisitive society in which wealth became almost an end in itself. It was not difficult to believe that indigence was simply punishment of the improvident for their lack of industry and morality—the direct consequence of sloth and sinfulness.

This interpretation, which confined the poor to a purgatory of personal failure and made them mere outcasts of society, was strengthened by the pseudoscientific teaching of Herbert Spencer, the English civil engineer turned philosopher, who coined the phrase "survival of the fittest," and others who applied the Darwinian theory of evolution to social conditions and thought. Social Darwinism, as it was called, a happy union of laissez-faire economics and the doctrine of the struggle for existence and survival of the fittest, became the prevailing philosophy of the era.

It was argued that government should confine itself to insuring liberty for individual citizens by protecting them from assault upon their persons and property. Orthodox social Darwinists found no place in their general scheme of things for public support of education, or for sanitary regulation, a public mail system, regulation of business or trade, or, least of all, for public assistance to the needy.

If, as the Spencerians claimed, competition was the law of life, there was no remedy for poverty other than self-help. Those who remained poor were the unfit, who had to pay the price exacted by "the decrees of a large far-seeing benevolence." Any interference in their behalf, whether undertaken by the state or by unwise philanthropists, was not only pointless but hazardous. Protecting the ill-favored in the struggle for existence would only permit them to multiply and could lead to no other result than a disastrous weakening of the species; it would thwart nature's plan of evolutionary progress toward higher forms of social life. "If we do not like the survival of the fittest," declared Spencer, "we have only one possible alternative, and that is the survival of the unfittest. The former is the law of civilization, the latter is the law of anticivilization." "The unfit must be eliminated as nature intended," he opined on another occasion, "for the principle of natural selection must not be violated by the artificial preservation of those least able to take care of themselves." Or as another social Darwinist maintained, "society is constantly excreting its unhealthy, imbecile, slow, vacillating, faithless members to leave room for the deserving. A maudlin impulse to prolong the lives of the unfit stands in the way of this beneficent purging of the social organism." Thus, as one writer in the *Nation* put it in 1894, the only solution to poverty is "nature's remedy—work or starve."

Although these arguments—advanced to justify inequality and, in effect, to condone misery—never went completely unchallenged, the theory that poverty was caused by personal frailty was not easily supplanted; endowed with this new aura of authority, it retained a loyal following for a long time. Nevertheless, most Americans did not carry the idea to its logical extreme. Only a few read Spencer and/or understood the full implications of social Darwinism. More important, America was a Christian nation with a charitable impulse and tradition that was too strong to be eliminated. Even Herbert Spencer, when accused of hardness of heart because of his attitude toward the poor or ill privileged, retreated to the position that voluntary charity could be tolerated in that it encouraged the development of altruism, a Christian virtue. What resulted therefore was further denigration of public assistance.

Those who opposed public relief had another new and potent weapon in political graft and corruption. This was the so-called Gilded Age, when political scandals and raids on the public treasury were common. Legislators and other public officials expected, as a matter of course, to be paid for the "favors" they performed and, unfortunately, departments of public charities were not exempt from the venality. Chicanery linked with public aid came to light in several cities in the 1870s and 1880s. Was it possible for public relief, especially home relief, to be handled honestly, efficiently, and economically?

For most, the answer was no. A system of well-coordinated voluntary organizations staffed by people who would keep accurate records of applicants, distribute aid honestly and carefully, and at the same time help uplift the needy appeared to be the better way to meet the problem. It would insure that welfare remained a charity rather than an entitlement, a political plum, or a source of demoralization. It also would bind the lower to the upper classes and thus avoid potential conflict. As Robert W. deForest, an influential lawyer-philanthropist, contended: "Public outdoor relief makes for class separation and the enmity of classes. Private charity makes for the brotherhood of man."

So, the informal division of labor that arose earlier in the century but was set aside temporarily during the Civil War was put back into effect. Indeed, it was strengthened considerably. Beginning in the 1870s, cities all across America abolished municipal home relief. By 1900, public outdoor assistance had been abandoned in New York, Baltimore, St. Louis, Washington, D.C., San Francisco, Kansas City, New Orleans, Louisville, Denver, Atlanta, Memphis, Charleston, S.C., Cincinnati, Indianapolis, Pittsburgh, and elsewhere. A year later, *Cooperation*, the official organ of the Chicago Bureau of Charities, a private agency, reported with great satisfaction that virtually all of the nation's large cities had taken such steps and lamented that Chicago was the exception to the rule.

The forces that drove people to dependence, however, did not disappear with the abolition of public home relief. Indeed, the evidence suggests just the opposite: the elimination of such assistance led to a significant increase in the breaking up of families, in the placing of children in institutions or foster homes, in "tramping," and in the formation of private charitable agencies.

Public authorities cared only for dependents and defectives who required (or consented to) confinement in asylums, almshouses, and other such institutions. Those in need who remained outside public institutions—the vast majority, for whom "the county" was the last resort—looked first to family, kin, and neighbors for aid, including the landlord, who sometimes deferred the rent; the local butcher or grocer, who frequently carried them for a while by allowing bills to go unpaid; and the local saloonkeeper, who often came to their aid by providing loans and outright gifts, including free meals and, on occasion, temporary jobs. Next, the needy sought assistance from various agencies in the community—those of their own devising, such as churches and religious groups, social and fraternal associations, mutual aid societies, local ethnic groups, and trade unions. Only when these resources were either exhausted or unavailable, as was the case for marginal inhabitants of the neighborhood, including homeless unemployed wanderers (who, by the way, now were subject to imprisonment as state after state began enacting statutes making "tramping" illegal), or immigrants without friends or relatives in the area, did the needy turn to the "official" private charitable agencies in the community—and then with reluctance and anxiety. Nevertheless, such agencies continued to proliferate as public home relief was abolished and the nation's economy witnessed a number of severe dips. In fact, so rapidly did private agencies multiply that before long America's larger cities had what to many people was an embarrassing number of them. Charity directories took as many as 100 pages to list and describe the numerous voluntary agencies that sought to alleviate misery, and combat every imaginable emergency. In Philadelphia alone, in 1878, there were some 800 such groups of one kind or another in existence.

It was inevitable that charity workers and others should become concerned over the magnitude of benevolent work. William Graham Sumner, the Yale professor and social Darwinist, was appalled by the "unlimited supply of reformers and would-be managers of society" he saw all around him. Such conditions, he and others were certain, only led to waste, inefficiency, and, above all, demoralization of the needy.

The hardship and destitution created by the severe depression of the 1870s seemed to confirm these feelings. With some three million laborers thrown out of work, apprehension gripped industrial and commercial centers throughout the country, especially in 1877, when in state after state the militia and even federal troops were mobilized to put down rioting resulting, in part, from unsuccessful efforts by the unemployed in many large cities to get public works programs and other forms of assistance from local and state authorities. The threat of revolution seemed imminent. Private citizens, charitable bodies, and public authorities responded to the crisis by setting up soup kitchens, breadlines, and free lodging houses, and by distributing coal, food, clothing, and even cash to the poor. Little attention was paid to investigation of need, to tests of destitution, to safeguards against duplicity, or to provision of counsel. In time of such social and economic distress, separation of material relief from spiritual relief was inevitable; naturally, the former took precedence over the latter.

Many charity workers, however, were horrified by this "excess" of relief and the chaotic way in which it was distributed. As one put it, "Next to alcohol, and perhaps alongside it, the most pernicious fluid is indiscriminate soup." Or, in the words of another, "It is not bread the poor need, it is soul; it is not soup, it is spirit." They argued not only for the cessation of all public outdoor aid but also for the improvement of all relief operations, especially by paying more attention to the individual needs of those helped. Charity work, they argued, needed to be organized along scientific lines—made more rational and efficient—giving rise to the so-called charity organization movement, or "scientific charity."

The new era in philanthropy dawned in Buffalo, New York, in December 1877, when the Reverend Stephen Humphreys Gurteen, an Englishman by birth, proposed the creation of an agency patterned after the London Charity Organization Society, which he had studied while on a visit to his native land during the previous summer. He assured the residents of Buffalo that such an agency would bring order to their charitable work by combating the indiscriminate relief policies of overlapping private agencies and a municipal relief system which presumably encouraged indolence, pauperism, and fraud.

The promotion of cooperation and higher standards of efficiency among the older relief-dispensing societies was one of the basic aims of the movement, which spread so rapidly that within six years twenty-five cities had such organizations and by the turn of the century there were some 138 of them in existence.[10] The new charity organization societies did not themselves grant relief; there were already too many relief-granting agencies to suit them. Instead they served as clearing houses for all of the operating charitable bodies in the community. They maintained registries of relief applicants, kept detailed records of the aid given to them, and referred to the proper relief-dispensing agency the "helpable" or "worthy" poor.

The organized charity movement aimed not only at eliminating fraud, inefficiency, and duplicity in the field but also at devising a constructive method of dealing with or treating poverty. "We sought to organize the charitable impulses and resources of the community" in order to "develop the special capacities of each [needy] individual,"

---

[10]The organizations went under a number of different names. In some instances they were called Societies for Organizing Charity (Philadelphia); in others they were referred to as Bureaus of Charities (Chicago, Brooklyn) or Associated Charities (Boston). Regardless of title, their function was the same—namely, to organize the sources of private relief in the community and provide moral relief to their clients.

a worker related. In part, the movement hoped to treat poverty by guarding against overlapping, but more important, by having "friendly visitors" look into each case so as to diagnose the cause of destitution. Investigation was the keystone of treatment; granting relief without investigation was analogous to prescribing medicine without diagnosis. Friendly visiting, then, or personal contact between the rich and the poor as a substitute for alms, was the second basic aim of the movement. Along with registration, cooperation, and coordination, it formed the basis of this "science" of social therapeutics that was supposed to relieve philanthropy of sentimentality and indiscriminate almsgiving—to make it a matter of the head as well as the heart—and thereby to eradicate pauperism and, in the words of the Reverend D. O. Kellogg, a tireless C.O.S. propagandist, make "the socialistic and communistic theories now being energetically taught to the people" specters of the past. Or, as the movement's founder put it, if friendly visitors did their job well, "all avoidable pauperism would soon be a thing of the past, and an age of good will would be ushered in, when the poor would regard the rich as their natural friends and not, as now, fair object of their deceit and imposition."

For all their self-proclamation as new or scientific, the charity organization societies were patterned after such earlier bodies as the New York Association for Improving the Condition of the Poor, which were created to coordinate private charitable agencies, to investigate relief applicants, and, if possible, to make the needy self-sufficient. The newer bodies did, however, spend more time organizing and coordinating the charitable resources of a given community and engaging in consultation with the needy. And, in contrast to their predecessors, most agents of the organized charities were women, thanks in large part to their "emancipation" during and after the Civil War.[11] And finally, the older organizations had succumbed to the great evil of

---

[11]These women were less authoritarian than their male counterparts and perhaps a bit more disposed toward humanistic concerns, at least according to John Cumbler. In an interesting article, he suggested that as women moved into positions of control in private charitable agencies, they altered the policies and orientation of those agencies; they paid less attention, for example, to welfare cheaters and more to reforms affecting women and children. More work, however, needs to be done on this subject before one can affirm or deny the proposition. Meanwhile, see Cumbler's "The Politics of Charity: Gender and Class in Late Nineteenth Century Charity Policy," *Journal of Social History* 14 (Fall 1980): 99–111.

becoming relief-giving agencies, something, of course, the organized charities were intent upon avoiding.

In addition, charity organization societies reflected the spirit of their times, the broad developments affecting all aspects of American life during the late nineteenth century.[12] Rationality, efficiency, foresight, and planning were middle-class virtues applied not only to charity but to business enterprise as well. Scientific charity, in its attempt to organize the philanthropic resources of the community and to relieve suffering in as efficient and economic a manner as possible, was similar to the monopolization and trustification of big business. In fact, as one leader of the movement stated, the "same wisdom which has given this generation its wonderful industrial capacity will preside over the administration of charity." (The state boards, of course, also reflected an attempt to apply business methods to charities—in the public realm—and some people, including Josephine Shaw Lowell, served on both.) No wonder scientific charity found its main support in the business and professional classes—and the New York C.O.S., for example, listed among its patrons such names as William Waldorf Astor, August Belmont, Andrew Carnegie, J. Pierpont Morgan, and Mrs. Cornelius Vanderbilt.[13] It also had a good deal of support, at least initially, in the academic community; its emphasis on the need for hard data for the resolution of social problems was related to the emergence of the social sciences in American higher education at this time.

---

[12]The charity organization movement also had deep roots overseas. Early in the nineteenth century, the influential Scotsman Thomas Chalmers had made a plea for the individual and organized approach in his famous work entitled "The Parochial System Without a Poor Rate, the Christian and Economic Policy of a Nation." Chalmers believed that almost every kind of help was deleterious because it interfered with the "natural operation" of the incentive to work, thus making the poor less industrious and resourceful. He was adamantly against public assistance. Like Spencer, he consented grudgingly to private charity because it stimulated altruism on the part of the giver. Another early exponent of this view was Octavia Hill, who thought that the best way to treat the needy was to encourage them, to provide "help without alms," as she stated it, a motto borrowed by the advocates of scientific charity. Then, as mentioned, there was the London Charity Organization Society, under the leadership of Charles Loch, the prototype on which Gurteen based his agency in Buffalo, New York.

[13]Too, as big businessmen increasingly came under attack from "reform Darwinists" and others in the late nineteenth century, they attempted to refurbish their image by demonstrating that their wealth was an inextricable part of the economic system—that it had social as well as per-

Furthermore, the charity organization philosophy rested upon a series of preconceived moral judgments and presuppositions about the poor which were embodied in the "self-help" cult of the Gilded Age. Leaders of the movement believed in the individual-moral concept of poverty; they accepted the prevailing economic and sociological philosophy that attributed poverty and distress to personal defects and evil acts—sinfulness, failure in the struggle for survival, excessive relief-giving, and so on. After all, the road from rags to riches was open to all, wasn't it?

And, finally, scientific charity was based upon a rather pessimistic view of human nature, at least the poor's—the notion that no members of the lower class would exert themselves if they felt secure. Josephine Shaw Lowell, founder of the New York Charity Organization Society and a leader of the movement, spoke for many when she declared:

> Human nature is so constituted that no [working] man can receive as a gift what he should earn by his own labor without a moral deterioration. No human being . . . will work to provide the means of living for himself if he can get a living in any other manner agreeable to himself.

For the stern Mrs. Lowell and her colleagues, the poor had to be forced to endure deprivation in order to be kept at work; deprivation was the essential incentive. When a contributor to the New York C.O.S. asked Mrs. Lowell how much of her money would go to the poor, she replied proudly, "Not one cent!" "NO RELIEF GIVEN HERE," announced signs posted on both sides of the entrance to the Buffalo C.O.S.

The fallacy of relief-giving, for Josephine Shaw Lowell and her colleagues, was "that it is material, that it seeks material ends by material means and therefore must fail. . . . For man is a spiritual being, and if

---

sonal value. They not only sat on boards of trustees of charity organization societies but also organized their own private philanthropies, usually large foundations that bore their names, and staffed them with "experts" who helped them decide how best to grant their funds— another effort by private charity to be "scientific" and businesslike in a corporate-technological age. By the way, in his *In the Shadow of the Poorhouse*, Michael Katz argues that the organized charity movement also was "a bureaucratic resolution of tension over sex roles among the well-to-do in the Gilded Age"; by getting, and keeping, women in charity work, especially as friendly visitors, men could sharply delimit their spheres of action.

he is to be helped, it must be by spiritual means." Rather than alms, therefore, the poor needed supervision to help them combat or overcome intemperance, indolence, and improvidence. The C.O.S. provided, ideally at least, as its motto indicated, "not alms but a friend" (although critics of the movement charged that its motto should be, "neither alms nor a friend").[14]

In carrying out their work, the charity organization societies relied on their corps of friendly visitors. These agents were to investigate appeals for assistance, distinguish between the worthy and unworthy poor, and above all provide the needy with the proper amount of moral exhortation. In the words of the Reverend Mr. Gurteen:

> The basic axiom, the cardinal principle of the charity organization society is diametrically opposed to all systems, all institutions, all charities, all forms of relief whatsoever. . . . The fundamental law of its operation is expressed in one word. "INVESTIGATE." Its motto is "No relief (except in extreme cases of despair or imminent death) without previous and searching examination."

The Reverend R.E. Thompson, in his *Manual for Visitors Among the Poor*, employed similar terms: "The best means of doing the poor good is found in friendly intercourse and personal influence." Gifts or alms, he maintained, are not needed but rather "sympathy, encouragement, and hopefulness." In fact, he added, "Nothing will so much interfere with . . . proper work as to be recognized as an . . . almoner." Mary Richmond agreed: "If you are going to be a *friend*, fertile in helpful suggestions, sympathetic and kind, you cannot be an almoner too," she contended.

Some people, especially more reform-minded or radical individuals, were severely critical of the charity organization societies, composed, as they were, of the "better classes," emphasizing painstaking investigation and individual treatment. Jane Addams, the founder of Hull-House in Chicago, felt that C.O.S. agents were cold and unemotional, too impersonal and stingy, that they were pervaded by a negative pseudoscientific spirit. Their vocabulary, she argued, was

---

[14]At best, relief was a necessary evil, the "final resort" for those who could not compete in the ceaseless struggle for survival—the aged, the infirm, the sick, the orphaned, perhaps the widowed with dependent children. Under any circumstances, it had to be given discriminately and sparingly, in public institutions, for it "should be surrounded by circumstances that shall repel everyone from accepting it," said Mrs. Lowell.

one of "don't give," "don't act," "don't do this or that"; all they gave the poor was advice—and for that they probably sent the Almighty a bill.

Boston's famed Irish-American poet-reformer, John Boyle O'Reilley, noted scathingly: "The organized charity scrimped and iced, In the name of a cautious, statistical Christ." The Reverend James O. S. Huntington of New York condemned the movement for its predilection to judge individual worthiness by business standards, and for establishing standards of truthfulness and labor for the poor which were not applied to the well-to-do. Another clergyman remind-ed the Cleveland Charity Organization Society:

> Your society, with its Board of Trustees made up of steel magnates, coal operators, and employers, is not really interested in charity. If it were, it would stop the twelve hour day; it would increase wages and put an end to the cruel killing and maiming of man. I doubt as I read the New Testament whether the twelve disciples would have been able to qualify as worthy according to your system. And Christ himself might have been turned over by you to the police department as a vagrant without visible means of support.

Echoing these same themes, John Reed, the radical, referred to the charity organization societies as "deadening and life-sapping" agencies that were "unnecessarily cruel . . . [and] uncomprehending:" "There is nothing of Christ the compassionate in the immense business of the organized charity," he declared; "its object is to get efficient results—and that means, in practice, to just keep alive vast numbers of servile, broken-spirited people."

Even political bosses, who often provided the needy with aid with-out the paternalism—or maternalism—and humiliation that often accompanied the charity organization societies' efforts, scorned the efforts of the societies. As George Washington Plunkitt, the "Sage" of Tammany Hall, put it:

> What tells in holdin your grip on your district is to go right down among the poor families and help them in different ways they need help. I've got a regu-lar system for this. . . . If a family is burned out I don't ask whether they are Republicans or Democrats, and I don't refer them to the charity organization society, which would investigate their case in a month or two and decide that they were worthy of help about the same time they are dead from starvation. I just get quarters for them, buy clothes for them if their clothes are burned up, and fix them up till they get things runnin again. Its philanthropy, but its

politics too—mighty good politics. . . . The poor are the most grateful people
in the world.

The charity organization societies remained undaunted by these
attacks. They saw no incompatibility between their profession of being
scientific and their reliance upon voluntary service. On the contrary,
the ultimate goal—self-sufficiency or the cure and prevention of poverty—depended wholly upon the enlistment and use of the volunteer. It
was the volunteer's personal service that not only differentiated scientific benevolence from mere almsgiving or public relief, but made it superior; it was the "heart and soul" of the movement, for charity, like love,
could not be purchased. To work, it had to regenerate character, which
involved the direct influence of kind and concerned, successful and
cultured, middle- and upper-class people upon the dependent.

Friendly visiting, then, assumed the right and the duty of intervention in the lives of the poor by their social and economic betters.
Sensitive to charges of meddling, Mary Richmond wrote: "Some
question our right to go among the poor with the object of doing
good, regarding it as an impertinent interference with the rights of the
individual. But . . . [we] *must* interfere when confronted by human
suffering and need. Why not interfere effectively?" However much
they distrusted the poor and believed that poverty was mainly a consequence of moral failing, many charity organizers felt a sincere responsibility to serve the needy. To them, the question was not whether to
provide aid but how to do so and by whom—or how to get "the right
help to the right people in the right way," to use James Leiby's words.

The poor were not inherently vicious or mean. Rather, they were
wayward children who drifted astray or who were incapable of discerning their own self-interest. They required no resource so desperately, therefore, as the advice of an intelligent friend who would offer
sympathy, tact, patience, cheer, and wise counsel. The visitor's job was
to discern the moral lapse responsible for the problem and then supply the appropriate guidance—something, of course, they were certain
they could do.

There was, however, a great deal of ambiguity in this approach,
and, in the long run, the work of the friendly visitors undermined
their own deeply cherished beliefs. To begin with, it was assumed that
the poor wanted the moral guidance, which was seldom the case

(although, as Jane Addams observed, despite feelings to the contrary, desperate clients would "laud temperance, . . . thrift and religious observance" when the friendly visitor would appear, in order to receive aid). Too, friendly visitors intervened in the lives of the poor by virtue of a presumed wisdom and superiority while, at the same time, professing to conceive of their charges as personal friends—an impossibility, for moral uplift is far from friendship. Friendly visitors did not really consider their clients as equals, or even potential equals, but as objects of character reformation whose lowly condition resulted from ignorance or other deviations from middle-class norms—intemperance, indolence, improvidence, or whatnot. And while it was possible to create a satisfactory *professional* relationship between nonequals (doctor-patient, lawyer-client), it was impossible to establish satisfactory *personal* relationships between "superior" volunteers and "inferior" dependents.

In addition, the charity organization societies and their agents hoped to discourage pauperism and vagrancy by stringent relief policies—another impossibility. Poverty and dependence were not largely expressions of individual moral perversity. Rather, they were manifestations of other things, especially accidents, ill health, premature loss of the family breadwinner, low wages, and technological, cyclical, and other forms of involuntary unemployment. Poverty rooted in ill health, premature death, substandard wages, involuntary unemployment, and other structural forces in the economy was too deep-rooted and complex to be affected very much by *any* relief policy, let alone one of benevolent stinginess.[15]

Friendly visitors (like paternal guardians before them) began to see this, not because they wanted to, but because it was inevitable. They began to see the difficulty, for example, in trying to distinguish between the worthy and the unworthy poor when no amount of verbal effort could raise the income of a family to a subsistence level, or when a depression, which occurred like clockwork in nineteenth- and early twentieth-century America, threw several million people out of work.

---

[15]For a brilliant discussion of the emergence of involuntary unemployment as a fact of life in nineteenth-century America, especially during and after the 1870s, see Alexander Keyssar, *Out of Work* (New York: Cambridge University Press, 1986).

More important, since the organized charities had insisted upon gathering the facts, records were kept and preserved in order to evaluate progress and insure continuity. As a result, the friendly visitors compiled comprehensive data on the social and economic problems of the poor, the real poverty-producing factors that had little to do with the sufferers' character. Their investigations uncovered information on involuntary unemployment, industrial accidents, and low wages, not on intemperance, improvidence, and the like. It became quite clear, then, that preconceived notions about the poor had to be discarded, or at least seriously reconsidered; the needy were not all alike, members of the "dangerous" or "depraved" classes.

George Buzelle, general secretary of the Brooklyn Bureau of Charities, was one of the first to see and publicly admit this. At the 1886 National Conference, he offered friendly criticism of his colleagues in the organized charity movement, especially their proneness to categorize: "Once, some of us would have undertaken to arrange all the human family according to intellect, development, merit, and demerit, in accurate divisions and subdivisions, each with a label, ready for indexing and filing away," he told his audience. But he and others were learning that "the poor . . . have not in common any type of physical, intellectual, or moral development which would warrant an attempt to group them as a class."

Three years later and then again in 1894, with the appearance of his influential *American Charities*, Amos G. Warner, Stanford University professor and former general agent of the Baltimore C.O.S., published studies of the causes of poverty that became landmarks both because of their content and their attempt to be systematic and empirical in reaching conclusions about the needy, conclusions which indicated that in most cases misfortune was more important than misconduct in causing dependency. Other studies did the same—with interesting results. One was conducted by the New York C.O.S. in cooperation with a number of Columbia University professors and students. Based upon the agency's records for the years 1890–97, a period of sharp depression and hard times, it indicated that lack of employment was the most frequent cause of poverty, sickness and accident second, while shiftlessness and intemperance were causes in only about 10 percent of the cases. Even Josephine Shaw Lowell, that remarkable bellwether of C.O.S. opinion, could conclude from the report only that, for most, the causes of distress are "as much beyond their power to avert as if they . . . [are] natural calamities of fire, flood, or storm." Such studies also indicated that the C.O.S. approach did not work; it neither prevented nor relieved mass poverty. According to Robert Hunter, whose classic work *Poverty* was the most careful and objective study to date when it was published in 1904, at least ten million Americans, or one out of every eight, were poor. They lived below a standard of normal existence that was necessary for industrial efficiency, according to Hunter, through no fault of their own: "Poverty was bred of miserable and unjust social conditions," he wrote. The environment had to be reformed!

Beginning, then, with a narrow, moralistic, and individualistic attitude toward poverty and its causes, the charity organization movement ultimately fostered the development of a broader point of view. The knowledge of misfortune experienced by hundreds of different families and thousands of individuals eventually induced many representatives of these private agencies to regard the social and economic causes of poverty as more pressing than personal inadequacy—and to realize that only the public could cope with the widespread dependence endemic to modern industrial society. Thus, in 1895, Robert Treat Paine, president of the Boston Associated Charities, asked whether the charity organization movement had not for too long been content to relieve single cases of distress without asking whether there were "prolific causes permanently at work" to create want, vice, crime, disease, and death which could be eradicated. "If such causes of pauperism exist," he declared, "how vain to waste our energies on single cases of relief when *society* should aim at removing the prolific sources of all the woe" (italics added).[16] And a year later, Josephine Shaw Lowell wrote, in words remarkably similar to many of the movement's longtime critics: "It seems often as if [the] charities are the insults which the rich add to the injuries . . . they heap upon the poor."

Even notions about home relief underwent scrutiny and change,

---

[16]Although many people associated with private charitable organizations remained suspicious of public assistance, not all did, and by the late nineteenth and early twentieth century a growing number of Americans were concluding that only the government had the resources to cope adequately with the misery associated with a modern urban-industrial capitalistic society. See Chapter 10, "Renaissance of Public Welfare."

for they rested upon a conception of pauperism that was no longer credible. Brooklyn Bureau of Charities secretary Samuel Bishop pointed out that, while the slogan of the movement was "not alms but a friend," there was no reason "why a friend may got give alms." Indeed, by 1907, the Buffalo C.O.S., America's first, had become a relief-giving agency. By that time, Edward T. Devine, general secretary of the New York C.O.S. and editor of its publication, *Charities*, had pretty well summed up the distance the movement had traveled when he declared: "We may quite safely throw overboard, once and for all, the idea that the dependent poor are our moral inferiors, that there is any necessary connection between wealth and virtue, or between poverty and guilt."

Finally, in addition to gathering specific information on the real causes of poverty and dependency and fostering new concepts of treating them, organized charity agents contributed to the development of a technique of social service and research—casework—and with it, the growth of a profession. The inevitable tendency of scientific charity, with its individualistic orientation, the very thing so many critics deplored, was to emphasize the objective and factual rather than the deductive and discretionary approach to social questions. This, in turn, made the use of volunteer visitors, however "friendly," harder and harder, for it was increasingly difficult to reconcile untrained, part-time service with sustained individual treatment based on scientific knowledge. It became increasingly clear that the gathering and interpreting of factual material, the technical character of many of the services that had to be performed, and the consistency of effort required in case treatment—really putting the "scientific" into scientific philanthropy, in other words—could be achieved only by fulltime workers with education, experience, and professional discipline. This led to the creation of training schools for charity workers, the demise of volunteer service, and the rise of a social work profession.[17]

The devaluation of volunteers did not take the form of outright rejection, largely because of the long tradition of voluntarism in social

---

[17]Along with their insistence that charity work had or should have a scientific base and thus required intellectual discipline and professional training, the organized charities' demands that social services be efficiently administered and that inter-agency cooperation take place also were significant influences on modern social work practice.

welfare and because professional social workers needed the power, influence, and financial help of volunteers. What occurred, then, was a reversal of roles. Whereas earlier what was considered the real work of the agency, friendly visiting, was conducted by volunteers and the menial labor by paid staff members, by the turn of the century, the opposite was beginning to occur; volunteers did the office work or, by serving as trustees helped shape policy and raise funds, while the work in the field, casework, was in the hands of paid professional agents. Viewed earlier as a civic duty, voluntarism became, instead, a privilege granted by agencies to those who accepted their authority and discipline.

By the turn of the century, the organized charities were establishing training schools for charity workers. In addition, they were taking part in other activities which, if not aimed at altering the social order, at least sought to mitigate some of its worst effects—housing reform, antituberculosis work, publication of reform-oriented journals, and the like, including juvenile court, probation work, and other measures for child welfare. Most Americans realized that the nation's future depended upon the health and welfare of its young people. Interest in child welfare, therefore, was strong.

Bibliography

ADAMS, GEORGE W. *Doctors in Blue: The Medical History of the Union Army in the Civil War.* New York: Schuman, 1952.

AUSTIN, ANNE L. *The Woolsey Sisters of New York, 1860–1900: A Family's Involvement in the Civil War and a New Profession.* Philadelphia: American Philosophical Society, 1971.

BECKER, DOROTHY G. "Exit Lady Bountiful: The Volunteer and the Professional Social Worker," *Social Service Review* 38 (March 1964): 57–72.

———. "Social Welfare Leaders as Spokesmen for the Poor," *Social Casework* 49 (February 1968): 82–89.

BLASSINGAME, JOHN W. *The Slave Community: Plantation Life in the Antebellum South.* New York: Oxford University Press, 1972.

BOSANQUET, HELEN. *Social Work in London, 1869–1912: A History of the Charity Organization Society.* London: Murray, 1914.

BRANDT, LILLIAN. *Growth and Development of the AICP and COS.* New York: Community Service Society of New York, 1942.

BREMNER, ROBERT. *From the Depths: The Discovery of Poverty in the United States.* New York: New York University Press, 1956.

———. "The Impact of the Civil War on Philanthropy and Social Welfare," *Civil War History* 12 (December 1966): 293–303.

———. "The Prelude: Philanthropic Rivalries in the Civil War," *Social Casework* 49 (February 1968): 77–81.

———. *The Public Good: Philanthropy and Welfare in the Civil War Era.* New York: Knopf, 1980.

———. "Scientific Philanthropy," *Social Service Review* 30 (June 1956): 168–73.

BROCK, WILLIAM R. *Investigation and Responsibility: Public Responsibility in the United States, 1865–1900.* New York: Cambridge University Press, 1984.

CHAMBERS, CLARKE A. "Toward a Redefinition of Welfare History," *Journal of American History* 73 (September 1986): 407–33.

CLARK, CLIFFORD. "Religious Beliefs and Social Reforms in the Gilded Age: The Case of Henry Whitney Bellows," *New England Quarterly* 43 (March 1970): 59–78.

COLBY, IRA C. "The Freedman's Bureau: From Social Welfare to Segregation," *Phylon* 46 (September 1985): 219–30.

CROSS, ROBERT D. "The Philanthropic Contributions of Louisa Lee Schuyler," *Social Service Review* 35 (September 1961): 290–301.

CUMBLER, JOHN T. "The Politics of Charity: Gender and Class in Late Nineteenth Century Charity Policy," *Journal of Social History* 14 (Fall 1980): 99–111.

DEVINE, EDWARD T. *The Principles of Relief.* New York: Macmillan, 1904.

ESCOTT, PAUL D. "The Cry of the Sufferers: The Problem of Welfare in the Confederacy," *Civil War History* 23 (September 1977): 228–40.

FINE, SIDNEY. *Laissez-Faire and the General Welfare State.* Ann Arbor: University of Michigan Press, 1964.

FLEMING, DONALD H. "Social Darwinism," in Arthur M. Schlesinger, Jr., and Morton White, eds., *Paths of American Thought.* Boston: Houghton Mifflin, 1963.

FRANKLIN, JOHN HOPE. "Public Welfare in the South During the Reconstruction Era, 1865–1880," *Social Service Review* 44 (December 1970): 379–92.

GETTLEMAN, MARVIN E. "Charity and Social Classes in the United States, 1874–1900," *American Journal of Economics and Sociology* 22 (April 1963): 313–30; 22 (July 1963): 417–26.

————. "Philanthropy as Social Control in Late Nineteenth Century America," *Societas* 5 (Winter 1975): 49–59.

GILMAN, DANIEL C., ed. *The Organization of Charities*. Chicago: International Congress of Charities and Correction, 1893.

GREENBIE, MARJORIE B. *Lincoln's Daughters of Mercy*. New York: Putnam, 1944.

GURTEEN, S. HUMPHREYS. *A Handbook of Charity Organization*. Buffalo: Charity Organization Society, 1879.

GUTMAN, HERBERT C. "The Failure of the Movement by the Unemployed for Public Works in 1873," *Political Science Quarterly* 80 (June 1965): 254–77.

Hand-Book for Friendly Visitors Among the Poor. New York: Charity Organization Society, 1883.

HASSON, GAIL S. "Health and Welfare of Freedmen in Reconstruction Alabama," *Alabama Review* 35 (April 1982): 94–111.

HOFSTADTER, RICHARD. *Social Darwinism in American Thought, 1860–1915*. Boston: Beacon Press, 1959.

HUGGINS, NATHAN. *Protestants Against Poverty*. Westport, Conn.: Greenwood, 1971.

HUNTER, ROBERT. *Poverty*. New York: Macmillan, 1904.

JACKSON, PHILIP. "Black Charity in Progressive Era Chicago," *Social Service Review* 52 (September 1978): 400–417.

KAPLAN, BARRY J. "Reformers and Charity: The Abolition of Public Outdoor Relief in New York City, 1870–1898," *Social Service Review* 52 (June 1978): 202–14.

KARL, BARRY D. "Lo, the Poor Volunteer: An Essay on the Relation Between History and Myth," *Social Service Review* 58 (December 1984): 493–522.

KATZ, MICHAEL. *In the Shadow of the Poorhouse*. New York: Basic Books, 1986.

KEYSSAR, ALEXANDER. *Out of Work: The First Century of Unemployment in Massachusetts*. New York: Cambridge University Press, 1986.

KOGUT, ALVIN B. "The Negro and the Charity Organization Society in the Progressive Era," *Social Service Review* 44 (March 1970): 11–21.

KRAMER, HOWARD D. "Effect of the Civil War on the Public Health Movement," *Mississippi Valley Historical Review* 35 (December 1948): 449–62.

KUSMER, KENNETH L. "The Functions of Organized Charity in the Progressive Era: Chicago as a Case Study," *Journal of American History* 60 (December 1973): 657–78.

LANE, JAMES B. "Jacob A. Riis and Scientific Philanthropy During the Progressive Era," *Social Service Review* 47 (March 1973): 32–48.

LEIBY, JAMES. "Amos Warner's *American Charities*, 1894–1930," *Social Service Review* 37 (December 1963): 441–55.

———. "State Welfare Institutions and the Poor," *Social Casework* 49 (February 1968): 90–95.

———. "Charity Organization Reconsidered," *Social Service Review* 58 (December 1984): 523–38.

LEWIS, VERL S. "The Development of the Charity Organization Movement in the United States, 1875–1900," Ph.D. dissertation, Western Reserve University, 1954.

———. "Stephen Humphreys Gurteen and the American Origins of Charity Organization," *Social Service Review* 40 (June 1966): 190–201.

LLOYD, GARY A. *Charities, Settlements, and Social Work: An Inquiry into Philosophy and Method, 1890–1915.* New Orleans: Tulane University School of Social Welfare, 1971.

LOWELL, JOSEPHINE SHAW. *Public Relief and Private Charity.* New York: Putnam, 1884.

MAXWELL, WILLIAM Q. *Lincoln's Fifth Wheel: The Political History of the United States Sanitary Commission.* New York: Longmans, Green, 1956.

MAY, J. THOMAS. "A Nineteenth Century Medical Care Program for Blacks: The Case of the Freedmen's Bureau," *Anthropological Quarterly* 46 (July 1973): 160–71.

MOWAT, C. L. "Charity and Casework in Late Victorian London: The Work of the Charity Organization Society," *Social Service Review* 31 (September 1957): 258–70.

———. *The Charity Organization Society, 1869–1913.* London: Methuen, 1961.

OLDS, VICTORIA. "The Freedmen's Bureau: A Nineteenth Century Federal Welfare Agency," *Social Casework* 44 (May 1963): 247–54.

PEEBLES-WILKINS, WILMA. "Black Women and American Social Welfare," *Affilia* 4 (Spring 1989): 33–44.

PLECK, ELIZABETH H. *Black Migration and Poverty in Boston, 1865–1900.* New York: Academic Press, 1979.

RABINOWITZ, HOWARD. "From Exclusion to Segregation: Health and Welfare Services for Southern Blacks, 1865–1890," *Social Service Review* 48 (September 1974): 327–54.

RAUCH, JULIA. "The Charity Organization Movement in Philadelphia," *Social Work* 21 (January 1976): 55–62.

———. "Women in Social Work: Friendly Visitors in Philadelphia, 1880," *Social Service Review* 49 (June 1975): 241–59.

RICH, MARGARET. *Josephine Shaw Lowell*. New York: Family Service Association of America, 1954.

RICHMOND, MARY E. *Friendly Visiting Among the Poor*. New York: Macmillan, 1899.

SANBORN, FRANKLIN B. *Recollections of Seventy Years*. Boston: Badger, 1909.

Sanitary Commission of the United States Army, The. New York: n.p., 1864.

SAVETH, EDWARD N. "Patrician Philanthropy in America: The Late Nineteenth and Early Twentieth Centuries," *Social Service Review* 54 (March 1980): 76–91.

SAVITT, TODD L. "Politics and Medicine: The Georgia Freedmen's Bureau and the Organization of Health Care, 1865–1866," *Civil War History* 28 (March 1982): 45–64.

SCHNEIDER, DAVID M., AND ALBERT DEUTSCH. "The Public Charities of New York: The Rise of State Supervision After the Civil War," *Social Service Review* 15 (March 1941): 1–23.

SCOTT, ANNE F. "Most Invisible of All: Black Women's Voluntary Associations," *Journal of Southern History* 56 (February 1990): 3–22.

SHRYOCK, RICHARD H. "A Medical Perspective of the Civil War," *American Quarterly* 14 (Summer 1962): 161–73.

SPEIZMAN, MILTON. "Poverty, Pauperism and Their Causes: Some Charity Organization Views," *Social Casework* 46 (March 1965): 142–49.

STEWART, WILLIAM R. *The Philanthropic Work of Josephine Shaw Lowell*. New York: Macmillan, 1911.

SUMNER, WILLIAM GRAHAM. *What the Social Classes Owe Each Other*. Caldwell, Idaho: Caxton, 1963.

TAYLOR, LLOYD C. "Josephine Shaw Lowell and American Philanthropy," *New York History* 44 (October 1963): 336–64.

TRATTNER, WALTER I. "Louisa Lee Schuyler and the Founding of the State Charities Aid Association," *New-York Historical Society Quarterly* 51 (July 1967): 233–48.

WARNER, AMOS G. *American Charities*. New York: Crowell, 1894.

WATSON, FRANK D. *The Charity Organization Movement in the United States*. New York: Macmillan, 1922.

Child Welfare

■ Of all social welfare activities, none was deemed more important than those dealing with children. Early-nineteenth-century reformers, A.I.C.P. agents, charity organization society friendly visitors, settlement house residents, and almost every other agency or individual working for social betterment saw in children the possibility for constructive altruism. As a result, a broad child welfare movement swept through America from the mid-nineteenth century through the early twentieth, one unlike anything before it or after it.[1]

The movement took many forms, including the removal of dependent, neglected, and delinquent children from almshouses and other institutions and their placement in private homes. It also included the creation of juvenile courts and probation systems, the provision of mothers' or widows' pensions, the passage of compulsory school attendance laws, crusades against child labor, and a host of other activities.

This great interest in child welfare is easy to understand. Aside from the fact that a child in trouble generally makes a strong appeal, a real need for social work on behalf of the nation's young citizens existed. Being more numerous than adults in an age when large families were the rule, children formed one of the largest groups among the ranks of the neglected and needy, especially after tens of thousands of youngsters were orphaned or half-orphaned as a result of the Civil War. In many ways their sufferings were the most griev-

---

[1]Child welfare includes all those activities and services by individuals and public and private agencies for the benefit of dependent, neglected, or delinquent children.

ous, and it was difficult to argue that they were responsible for their condition. Of all those who required help, then, children seemed the most deserving.

Moreover, the social upheaval and family disruption resulting from large-scale immigration and rapid industrial and urban growth were especially hard on children. Casualties in industry, as in war, frequently deprived them, often early in life, of a parent—or sometimes two. And the mobility and anonymity of a swiftly changing urban-industrial society meant that many of these deprived youngsters were left in a strange and sometimes hostile environment.

Low wages, especially those paid to immigrants, and simplified industrial processes resulting from technology and mass production, also drew large numbers of children as well as their mothers into factories, where the accident rates for both were shockingly high and where they worked long hours for a pittance to help supplement the family's meager earnings. Children lucky enough to stay out of industry but whose mothers went to work were deprived of parental supervision and a normal home life, and this resulted in an alarming increase in juvenile delinquency.

A growing concern with child welfare, however, was not merely a matter of pity or compassion. Indeed, it resulted above all from the fact that most citizens viewed the child as the key to social control. If future generations were to possess the strength of mind, body, and character to become good, self-supporting citizens, able to assume the responsibilities and burdens of democratic rule, they had to be protected as children. Youngsters, in other words, were the hope—or the threat—of the future. Safeguarding them was essential to society. As one reformer argued:

> The fate of the world is determined by the influences which prevail with the child from birth to seven years of age. . . . All our problems go back to the child—corrupt politics, dishonesty and greed in commerce, war, anarchism, drunkenness, incompetence, and criminality. We know that much of our labor for the radical betterment of society is costly and fruitless. It is because we are working against nature. We take the twig after it is bent and has stiffened into a tree. We take the brook after it has become a torrent.

Or, as Robert Hunter put it in his classic *Poverty*, published in 1904: "Poverty degrades all men who struggle under its yoke, but the poverty which oppresses childhood is a monstrous and unnatural thing, for it denies the child growth, development, strength; it robs the child of the present and curses the man of the future." Some thirty years later, President Franklin D. Roosevelt expressed the same idea when he remarked: "The destiny of American youth is the destiny of America."

For a long time—from the colonial period until well into the nineteenth century—childhood was not considered a special phase of human development. For the most part, children were considered to be more or less alike, essentially miniature adults who were inherently aggressive and sinful, and hence prone to all sorts of vices, including idleness.[2] Therefore, they required close supervision and stern treatment so that they would grow up to lead industrious, upright, godly lives. As the Pilgrim minister John Robinson put it, "There is in all children . . . a stubbornness and stoutness of mind arising from natural pride" which "must be broken and beaten down. . . ." Or, in the words of Cotton Mather, "Better whipt than Damn'd." That "whipping" and "breaking and beating down," or oversight and restraint essential for proper development, could best be provided, it was believed, by the family, the basic economic as well as social institution in preindustrial America.

By the mid-eighteenth century, this concept of childhood and child-rearing was undergoing significant change. By that time, Enlightenment notions of free will and human progress had begun to challenge the harsh earlier doctrines. Americans had come to accept the theories of John Locke, who, as we have seen, speculated that children were not depraved but that the "souls of the newly born are just empty tablets afterwards to be filled in by observation and reasoning." By the middle of the next century, some Americans—Ralph Waldo Emerson, Henry David Thoreau, and other Transcendentalists, for example—had gone beyond Locke's *tabula rasa* theory to proclaim that children were innately pure and good, perhaps even morally superior to adults, corrupted only by an overbearing society. At the same time, thanks in part to the wave of evangelical religious revivals

[2]Although some historians are now beginning to challenge the notion that colonial Americans treated their children as "miniature adults," I adhere to the older and still prevalent view. For the revisionist interpretation, see the Ross Beales article cited in the bibliography.

and humanitarian sentiment that swept across America in the decades prior to the Civil War—and the replacement of the stern, vindictive Calvinist God by the Unitarian God of love—the idea of "Christian Nurture" emerged, a concept popularized by Horace Bushnell, the liberal minister whose book entitled *Christian Nurture* first appeared in 1846. According to Bushnell, children were plastic creatures who could attain salvation through a healthful (or nurturing) environment, especially one presided over by a loving, watchful mother who provided affection, good example, and gentle guidance as opposed to strict discipline and hard work. So, by the middle of the nineteenth century, emphasis had shifted from the certainty of children's sinfulness to the probability of their goodness—and even to the possibility of their perfection.

In addition, the need of children to exercise their minds and bodies was recognized, thanks largely to Friedrich Froebel, whose ideas began filtering through to the United States by mid-century. The German educator and founder of the kindergarten movement argued that children were not little grownups but special beings who needed careful preparation for adulthood, especially opportunities for recreation and play.

Scientific developments in the second half of the nineteenth century, including the theory of evolution, strengthened these ideas, especially the conviction that children were basically innocent and malleable creatures who needed special treatment, particularly a relaxed and healthy home life. While Darwinism bolstered the idea of inherited traits and capacities, it also presented a developmental view of human growth and behavior, stressing the power of the environment to modify both. Thus it lent support to those who claimed that children's flexible characters, if carefully and gently nurtured, would develop in accordance with proper Christian and American ideals. Then, too, there was Sigmund Freud, the famed Austrian neurologist and founder of psychoanalysis, who stressed the vital importance of sound nurturance in infancy and childhood for the formation of a good character and a healthy personality. And, finally, there was the work of the psychologist G. Stanley Hall, the "father of the child study movement" in America, who began to look closely at what follows the onset of puberty and whose important book *Adolescence*, published in 1904, not only contained a vast amount of information on human development but was a milestone in child study, contributing greatly to the growing tendency to raise the status of children in society. All of these developments had an impact on the field of child welfare.

In the earlier period in American history, however, destitute and neglected children, as we have seen, were placed in private families and put to work or bound out as apprentices (under court supervision, until age eighteen or twenty-one for boys and age eighteen, or marriage, for girls). As in England, the practice was designed to teach them occupations and trades and to inculcate in them the habits of industry and thrift so that they would become self-supporting citizens. The system also helped to relieve the community of their support and, at the same time, to provide the handicrafts with a badly needed and cheap source of labor—a neat admixture of private and public economics, one that coincided perfectly with the prevailing concept of childhood as a brief, unimportant prelude to adulthood and the real business of living. For the children, however (since there were few if any provisions for inspection and supervision), the system was full of abuses. The master's obligation to his young charge—to provide sustenance and an education, religious and secular, as well as vocational training—was rarely carried out. All too often, the children received little or no training in the trades and their education was ignored; poorly fed and clothed, they performed menial tasks and grew up in ignorance.

A reaction set in, first during the antislavery period, when the similarities between apprenticeship and forced bondage were great in the minds of many, and later when the need for skilled labor disappeared with the coming of industrialization and mass production. As a result, while apprenticeship was still used on occasion in the nineteenth century (especially in the South after the Civil War, when whites sought to use it as a means of virtually reenslaving black youngsters and thus securing a cheap supply of labor), most needy children were cared for in the same way as other dependents—in institutions. In the county almshouse, it was widely believed, their "health and morals would be improved," and they "would receive an education to fit them for future usefulness," as New York's Secretary of State Yates put it in his influential report, written at a time when there were still few public schools in America.

Before long, it became evident that these hopes would not be realized. Many almshouses, as we have seen, were vile catchalls for victims of every sort of misery, misfortune, and misconduct who were herded together and badly mistreated. The tales of uneducated, half-starved, tear-stained young outcasts in these wretched institutions—where, due to inadequate diet and lack of proper sanitary facilities, the mortality rates were extremely high—were sorrowful ones.

As a result, again, as we have seen, concerned citizens began to demand reform of these places, especially through the segregation or removal of certain types of inmates. Children were the first beneficiaries of these successful pleas: various groups of disadvantaged children were removed from county almshouses and placed, instead, in separate children's institutions; the institutional ideal, in other words, still dominated the thinking of reformers. Founders of child care institutions shared fully with the proponents of other caretaker institutions—almshouses and mental hospitals, for example—the notion that only careful and diligent training within an institution to cope with the open, freewheeling, and often disordered life of the community would prevent their charges from falling victim to ignorance, vice, and crime.[3]

Actually, the first separate children's institution predated the American Revolution. As early as 1727, a unit was set up at the Ursuline Convent in New Orleans for children whose parents had been slain in an Indian raid. The first permanent orphanage created for the purpose was Bethesda, the noteworthy institution founded in Savannah, Georgia, in 1740 by the Reverend George Whitefield of Great Awakening fame (and still in operation today—as a modern child care center for emotionally disturbed children). To Charleston,

<hr>

[3]At the same time, however (thanks to the changing concept of childhood), they felt themselves to be singularly fortunate, for their clientele was young, impressionable, and not fixed in deviant or dependent behavior. If the young were vulnerable to corruption, they were also eminently teachable. "Youth," said one reformer, "is particularly susceptible to reform. . . . It has not yet felt the long continued pressure which distorts its natural growth. . . . No habit can be rooted so firmly as to refuse a cure," especially under the tutelage of a kind caretaker. It is appropriate to mention here that Michael Katz interprets the removal of children from county poorhouses quite differently. In his opinion, it was designed to break up poor families, to separate lower-class youngsters from their parents. See *In the Shadow of the Poorhouse* (New York: Basic Books, 1986), 104–5.

South Carolina, goes credit for the first public institution solely for children, established in 1790. It was only after the 1830s, however, when people began to demand the removal of children from almshouses, that the number of such places multiplied. By 1861, when Ohio passed the first statute calling for the mandatory removal of all children from county almshouses, there were some seventy-five separate children's institutions in existence. By 1890, however—by which time apprenticeship and indenture had disappeared, child labor was falling into disrepute, and transiency had increased significant- ly—their number had grown to 600, the overwhelming majority of which were privately owned and operated, especially by various reli- gious and ethnic groups.

Although these separate institutions were on the whole superior to the almshouses as places for child care and conditions among them varied, they too had many defects. Most were large, congregate insti- tutions which brought together under a single roof anywhere from fifty to as many as 2000 children. Managers of such institutions put a premium on order, obedience, and precision. The poor wards com- monly slept and ate together in large dormitories or barracks. Their lives were governed by extremely rigid schedules; individuality was suppressed, and the atmosphere was one of monotonous routine. Practice had not yet caught up with changing theory. The institutions were properly named orphan "asylums."

Making matters worse was the so-called subsidy system—the prac- tice of the states providing funds for private institutions, either in a lump sum on an annual basis, or periodically on a per capita basis. While it was cheaper for the states to do this than to build and main- tain their own institutions, they seldom had the power of supervision or control over the appropriations or the agencies to which they were granted. The result was that the private institutions operated indepen- dently on public funds and, as in the county almshouses, abuses abounded.

They often provided poor and protracted care. The retention of children in these overcrowded institutions was in the hands of their managers who ran them as business or profit-making ventures. As many youngsters as possible were brought in, fed and cared for as inexpensively as possible, and retained for as long as possible. The story was often told of the manager of one such place who, each night before going to bed, would pray for more orphans so that he could build a new wing to his institution.

The growth of these child care institutions therefore turned out to be a doubtful blessing. Again, concerned citizens and reformers moved in, this time to displace the asylum or children's institution. A system of placing needy children in private homes gradually developed. Family care, in other words, began to replace institutional treatment. By this time, many of the states were beginning to establish public school systems and even to enact compulsory school attendance laws; the chances of children receiving an education outside an institution, therefore, were far greater than they had been earlier.

The first children's organization in America to adopt family care, or placing-out, as its policy was the New York Children's Aid Society, founded in 1853 by the Reverend Charles Loring Brace, a twenty-seven-year-old missionary in New York's notorious Five Points District. For the next third of a century, he and the N.Y.C.A.S. were synonymous.

While not insensitive to the plight of needy children, Charles Loring Brace was as impelled by other motives as by the suffering of the youngsters with whom he concerned himself. To begin with, he was not very fond of the city. He was particularly alarmed, however, over increasing juvenile delinquency and crime among the young poor of New York and was fearful of what might happen to the property, morality, and political life of the city if nothing was done to relieve the area of its homeless, vagrant, and delinquent children, menaces to society, or the "dangerous classes," as he referred to them in his auto-biography, *The Dangerous Classes of New York and Twenty Years Work Among Them*, published in 1872. Indeed, his appeals for funds for the C.A.S., which he described as a "moral and physical disinfectant," aroused more popular anxiety over the situation than they did sympathy for the unfortunate youngsters. The founding of the agency, he thus wrote in the opening sentence of his first annual report, reflected "the increasing sense among our citizens of the evils of the city," especially the "outcast, vicious, reckless, multitude of . . . boys swarming now in every foul alley and low street" who might "come to know their power and *use* it."

A pragmatist who worked through trial and error, Brace made use of several approaches in his efforts to help needy children, combat delinquency, and safeguard the property of the well-to-do. The program included evening schools, sheltered workshops, industrial education classes (for boys), training schools for sewing machine operators and household servants (for girls), lodging houses for newsboys and bootblacks, penny savings banks, and outings and vacations. But, above, all, he pinned his hopes on foster home placement.[4]

More and more, Brace became convinced of the futility of helping dependent and delinquent children save by transplanting them (while still saplings) to new environments; removal from society became the only answer. Unlike many of his contemporaries, however, who advocated locking up the needy behind the walls of an institution, Brace contrived a way of both securing their removal and capitalizing on the beneficial influences of home life. While this was not entirely new— for it bore resemblances to the apprenticeship system—Brace injected a novel element: the promise of the expanding West. For a long time in American history, "the West" was the medicine prescribed for all those who wished to better their lot. Like many nineteenth-century Americans, Brace took comfort in the belief that the rich and relatively unpeopled area would provide a new opportunity for the disadvantaged and needy, especially young children.

Brace subscribed to two other related ideas widely held at the time, the so-called agrarian myth and the individualistic social philosophy—the notions that the farmer was the ideal individual and citizen; that agriculture, as a calling, was uniquely productive and important to society; that rural life was inherently more moral and virtuous than urban living; that the fewer restraining forces on the individual the better. (He would read Charles Darwin's *Origin of Species* thirteen times and praise the theory of natural selection as "one of the great intellectual" achievements of the age, one that would prove profoundly relevant to the moral and physical history of mankind.) For Brace, the best of all asylums was the home of the farmer, "our most solid and intelligent citizen." He was convinced that the availability of such homes, especially in the West, where

---

[4]Brace disliked institutional care because, as he put it, "asylum life is not the best training for outcast children in preparing them for practical life. In large buildings, where a multitude of children are gathered together, the bad corrupt the good, and the good are not educated in the virtues of real life."

youngsters could nurture their freedom, their creativity, and their "go-gettedness," was almost unlimited.

The language of the Children's Aid Society's first circular detailed, and again betrayed, the purpose of its work:

> The Society has taken its origin in the deeply settled feeling of our citizens that something must be done to meet the increasing crime and poverty among the destitute children of New York. Its objects are to help this class. . . . We hope . . . especially to be the means of *draining the city* of these children by communicating with farmers, manufacturers, or families in the country who may need such employment. When homeless boys are found by our agents, we mean to get them homes in the families of respectable persons, and to put them in the way of an honest living (italics added).

The success of the plan to "drain the city" of destitute children depended, of course, upon the demand for unpaid farm labor. To Brace, that did not lessen the charity of those who gave the children homes. The best charity, he felt, was the opportunity to work, especially in good Christian farm homes. Boys and girls were better off there than in any institution or on the streets of New York City.

The C.A.S. began its "emigrant parties" in 1854 when forty-six boys and girls were taken by train from New York City to a small town in Michigan, where they were disposed of by methods suggested in the following excerpt from an early C.A.S. journal:

> At the close of the sermon the people were informed of the object of the Children's Aid Society. It met with cordial approval of all present and several promised to take children. . . . Monday morning the boys held themselves in readiness to receive application from the farmers . . . and before Saturday they were all gone.

The process was always the same. Despite his conviction that family life was best for the needy child, Brace bypassed the natural family, the child's own parents. Instead, he flooded the western countryside with wayward youths. Operating in a rather casual way, he rarely took the time to investigate the quality of the substitute family and the way in which it cared for the foster child. More often than not, he never heard from the youngsters again; most of them were under fourteen years of age, but some were beyond their teens. After twenty-five years of such practice, Charles Loring Brace and the Children's Aid Society removed more than 50,000 children from New York City. It is not surprising, therefore, that the city—and the state—subsidized their operation.

Nor is it surprising that such a system, or lack of one should have met firm opposition. Although his detractors may have exaggerated their claims, clearly, with the absence of any care and supervision in placement and the lack of any followup, many of the abuses of the apprenticeship system reappeared. Families commonly overworked the children, failed to educate them, fed and clothed them poorly and in general mistreated them. As a result, despite the possible advantages of family care (and the recognized faults of children's institutions, especially their blighting effects), charity workers, who sometimes referred to the program as "the wolf of indentured labor in the sheep's clothing of Christian charity," took up arms against home placement.

Opposition came also from the poor themselves, many of whom did not want their children sent so far from home. In addition, many of the western states became quite unhappy with what they considered to be the dumping of thousands of needy and delinquent children each year within their borders, where many of them—close to 60 percent, according to a study conducted by the secretary of Minnesota's State Board of Charities, Hastings H. Hart—became sources of trouble and public expenditures. Mistreated and overworked in their new homes, many of the youngsters ran away and became public charges. Soon, many of the western states began passing legislation either prohibiting the practice, especially for delinquent, ill, or incorrigible children, or requiring that the C.A.S. post bond for each child in the event he or she became a public burden.

And finally, Brace's practices set off a heated controversy with the Catholic Church. Right or wrong, the Church charged that the C.A.S. was a Protestant device to proselytize the Catholic children of the city. Throughout the period, the Church sought to keep its dependent children within the shelter of its own institutions rather than distribute them in faraway homes, especially in Protestant rural areas where they were likely to lose their faith.

Still, whatever his shortcomings, Brace, who in theory at least believed in the potential redemption of all children, was an important figure in the history of child welfare, having done much to popularize foster home care. And, as Robert Bremner has pointed out, his "preventive 'child-saving' approach, adopted at a time when so much emphasis was placed on correctional or reformatory methods, exercised a wholesome influence on later developments" in the field.

Indeed it did. Toward the end of the nineteenth century, when several child welfare workers—John Finley of the New York State Charities Aid Association, Charles Birtwell of the Boston Children's Aid Society, and Homer Folks of the Children's Aid Society of Pennsylvania—began to develop sound administrative procedures, the placing-out of children spread rapidly. By the turn of the century, it had replaced institutional treatment in a number of cities.

By that time, however, the practice was far different from the "emigrant parties" of the 1850s. Since the family was considered a unit and its importance in molding the life of the child was once again recognized, whenever possible home ties were preserved. When this was not possible, children were placed in private homes, but by licensed authorities and only after being studied by a social worker and a physician, and later by a psychologist and, on occasion, even by a psychiatrist as well. Prospective homes were studied carefully by paid full-time agents in order to guide the agency in making a proper placement; that is, to see to it that the child was placed in a home that was both emotionally and financially able to meet his or her needs. Even then, the placement was probationary until it could be determined whether or not the child and the foster home were suited to each other. Because of the supervision involved, placements were made within the immediate community whenever feasible. In short, the emphasis was on individual treatment, on understanding each child's needs so that the child would be placed in a home where he or she would be happy and would develop soundly.

While legal adoption was the ultimate ideal, this occurred rarely and only after a long waiting period.[5] Furthermore, it was recognized

---

[5]Adoption was unknown to the Common Law of England; as a result, such measures developed in America largely by means of state statutes, beginning in Massachusetts in 1851. Primarily, they were intended to provide a procedure whereby the custody of a child could be legally transferred from the natural parent to the adopting parent. However, as was characteristic of the methods used throughout most of the nineteenth century, little attempt was made to understand the child's needs or the character of the adoptive parents until Michigan, in 1891 (and then virtually every other state in the nation by the turn of the century), recognized the need for a preadoptive investigation. This marked the beginning of child legislation that emphasized the human elements in adoption.

that in some cases adoption was undesirable or unfeasible, giving rise to the "boarding-out" system—which involved the payment of a fee (weekly, monthly, or yearly) for the rearing of a child—a plan justified on economic as well as on altruistic grounds. Welfare workers found, for example, that as children grew in years, the likelihood of their being adopted decreased. Many were unsuitable for adoption because of a physical or mental handicap; few families would adopt such children. And finally, whenever a living parent might want to reclaim the child, it was impractical or impossible for the youngster to be adopted by others. Boarding-out secured for the child the benefits of home life without depriving surviving (although perhaps destitute) parents of the opportunity to visit their children and even to reclaim them if and when circumstances permitted.

In addition, it was argued that a family reluctant to open its home to a needy child free of charge might do so when paid for it, and then grow to love the youngster and eventually to adopt him or her. Moreover, it was less costly to care for dependent children by boarding them out than it was to house and maintain them in institutions. The practice therefore grew in popularity—and was used even with delinquent children.

Through study and investigation, especially at Dr. William Healy's Juvenile Psychopathic Institute, created in 1909, child welfare workers and others found that delinquents were not necessarily from the pauper classes, as was widely assumed, but from a cross-section of the population. The causes of delinquency, which could be determined only through careful, individual study, were many, including physical defects. The most prevalent cause was lack of parental discipline, usually due to the loss of one or both parents.[6] Home care, therefore, rather than confinement in a penal or correctional institution, was the best hope of preventing repetition of the delinquent act—as well as the best way of helping the dependent child.

---

[6]Many studies of the problem came out of the careful research conducted at the Juvenile Psychopathic Institute, which was located at Hull-House in Chicago. Among the most important of these was Dr. Healy's *The Individual Delinquent* (1915), which rejected the theory that delinquency and crime were caused primarily by heredity and instead emphasized environmental or social factors in a multicausal approach. Thus, the eminent University of Michigan sociologist Charles H. Cooley could say with confidence, "The criminal [or delinquent] class is largely the result of society's bad workmanship upon fairly good material."

That the long controversy over the best method of caring for children in need was being resolved by the turn of the century was epitomized by a statement of approved methods and principles issued by the National Conference of Charities and Correction's Committee on Children. Read before the 1899 National Conference by Chairman Thomas M. Mulry, head of the Society of St. Vincent de Paul, the major Catholic relief organization in America and long the leading advocate of institutional care for dependent children, the report urged the preservation of the home wherever and whenever possible. Where that was impossible, the committee recommended placing- or boarding-out of children—after careful investigation and with constant supervision. The nineteenth century, which began with attempts to get needy children into institutions, ended with attempts to get them out of those institutions.

Efforts to remove or keep children from entering almshouses and then other institutions aided the development, late in the nineteenth and early in the twentieth century, of houses of correction, juvenile courts, and probation systems. Earlier, there were few institutions in the United States for the reformation of juvenile delinquents. Children convicted of crimes were either sent to almshouses or, more often, committed along with adult offenders to prisons, most of which were in wretched condition—antiquated, unsanitary, and regulated by brutal officials who cared little and knew less about penal matters. Alexis de Tocqueville, the French prison reformer who visited the United States in the 1830s, was aghast at the "vile nature of American jails"—"schools of crime," as he called them.

Juvenile reformation in America during the nineteenth century can be summarized in a single sentence: Youthful offenders were removed from harsh surroundings and from association with adult criminals and placed in special institutions or private homes where they were treated from an educational and constructive rather than a punitive point of view—as changing concepts of childhood and childrearing dictated.

This did not happen overnight. Early special institutions for juvenile delinquents, usually state reform schools, were, like jails, pretty gruesome. According to Dr. Hastings Hart, an authority on the subject, most "of the juvenile reformatories were, at first, in reality juvenile prisons, with prison bars, prison cells, prison garb, prison labor, prison punishment, and prison discipline." Based on the prevailing nineteenth-century belief that the roots of delinquency were in the individual, who freely chose to act in a deviant manner and thus needed to be "reformed," severe punishment was considered not only a legitimate part of such institutions but also their very function. Even when managers of such institutions came to believe that love and good training were the necessary ingredients for child-saving, such care proved to be difficult, if not impossible, to provide in these over-crowded and underfinanced institutions.

Still, as recent studies of the early years of some of these places indicate—the State Industrial School for Girls at Lancaster, Mass., the Girls Reform School of Iowa, and others—many of the founders and operators of these reform schools were kind, caring people who really believed that their charges would be made into virtuous citizens under their tutelage—and a large number of the children in such institutions were placed there by their parents in an effort to secure food, shelter, training, and, hopefully, future employment for their offspring or, particularly in the case of girls, sanctuary from physically and sexually abusive fathers. In other words, just as poorhouses were used as tem-porary places of refuge for many needy adults during periods of crisis, so, too, juvenile reformatories, which had not yet acquired their later stigma, were used by many poor parents as a means of removing their children from faulty home situations and avoiding the squalid, trou-bled lives to which they seemingly were headed. Indeed, as Eric Schneider has demonstrated in his recent work on the subject, *In the Web of Class* (1992), such institutions sometimes were forced to rethink and reshape their programs to meet the needs, and desires, of such children and their parents.

As time passed, however, a growing number of citizens realized that these institutions were not "way stations" to success. Furthermore, it was realized that punishment did not act as a deter-rent to crime. Nor did it return the offender to society in any way improved as a result of his or her sentence. On the contrary, he or she usually returned to the community bitter and vengeful. Moreover, because a large proportion of those who left such institutions usually wound up back inside them within a rather short period of time, such treatment was not only unwise but uneconomic. An awareness of these factors eventually led to a number of changes, including the development of real houses of correction (which truly emphasized education and training), the use of indeterminate sentences, the introduction of parole and probation, the creation of detention homes and diagnostic centers; and, in more recent years, such methods of treatment as group therapy, counseling, and the like. In short, correctional institutions began to make serious efforts to rehabilitate rather than to punish offenders.

Some of these new ideas were first put into effect with the opening of the New York State Reformatory at Elmira, in 1876. Under the dynamic leadership of Zebulon R. Brockway, a noted corrections reformer and founder of the newly created National Prison Association, Elmira was the first correctional home for young men to adopt the indeterminate sentence. There, free from association with hardened criminals, the inmates helped to determine the length of stay (up to an imposed maximum) through their performance and progress as determined by a professional authority.[7]

When released, they were usually sent to places of employment which had been arranged for them, and for which they had been trained. Also, they remained on parole until their discharge became final; thus, their reentrance into community life was supervised and controlled. After ten years of trial, it was found that four of every five Elmira "graduates" showed complete reformation—or at least did not return to a penal institution. The merits of the system were so obvious that by 1898 eight other states—Massachusetts, Pennsylvania, Ohio, Michigan, Illinois, Minnesota, South Dakota, and Indiana—had established similar juvenile homes.

With the growth of special institutions for youthful offenders, the breaking down of the prison atmosphere, and the growing emphasis on the environmental causes of crime, juvenile delinquency came to be recognized as a social problem that required improved legal as well as correctional machinery. There arose then, especially among enlightened judges, lawyers, public-spirited citizens, and child welfare work-

---

[7]Similar institutions for girls developed less rapidly. Here again, New York led the way when it opened the Western House of Refuge at Albion, in 1893. There were, of course, earlier female reformatories, such as the State Industrial School for Girls at Lancaster, Mass., established in 1856, and the Detroit House of Correction, which opened a separate women's wing when it was created in 1861.

ers, a demand that children no longer be subjected to the Common Law definition of criminal behavior and the harsh procedure of the criminal court—that they be tried differently and apart from adult offenders.

Massachusetts had pioneered in special court procedures for juveniles charged with crimes; in the 1870s it enacted legislation requiring separate hearings for children's cases—although the same judges and courtrooms were used. The world's first fullfledged juvenile court, however, was created in Cook County (Chicago) in July 1899, after an eight-year battle led by the Illinois State Conference of Charities, the Chicago Bar Association, and the city's settlement house residents.[8] Located across the street from Hull-House, the court was presided over superbly during its early, precarious years by Judge Merritt Pinckney. The famous children's court in Denver, Colorado, that Judge Ben B. Lindsey served so well for so long was created a year later.

The object of the juvenile court was to avoid the stigma of crime by creating a new mechanism for dealing with child offenders. Criminal procedure was abolished and replaced by nonadversary or chancery court proceedings, a legal device that went back to medieval England and that was based on the theory that a youngster who commits an illegal act should be considered someone whose social development has been so faulty that the state is warranted in intervening as an authority in order to bring to bear such corrective influences as will compensate for his or her previous upbringing. Instead of a courtroom trial, hearings were held in an informal atmosphere in the judge's private chamber; no lawyers, oaths, or robes were used.

The role of the judge was supposed to be that of a parental guide. As the statute creating the first such court worded it:

> The care, custody, and discipline of the children brought before the court shall approximate as nearly as possible that which they should receive from their parents, and . . . as far as practicable they shall be treated not as criminals but as children in need of aid, encouragement, and guidance.

---

[8]According to one student of the subject, Joseph Hawes, the measure that created that court— An Act to Regulate the Treatment and Control of Dependent, Neglected, and Delinquent Children—was "the single most influential law concerning juvenile delinquents in the United States," one that "marked the end of the essentially penal official approach to juvenile delinquency and the beginning of the flexible 'scientific' and preventive approach."

Reeducation rather than retribution was the aim of the court; it was not to punish offenders but to enlighten and save them. "The State," the long-remembered Judge Ben Lindsey declared, "has come to help and not to hurt, to uplift and not to downgrade, to love and not to hate." In effect, the court was the child's defender, and its petition was changed from "The People Against . . . " to "The People in the Interest of. . . . "[9]

Despite the emphasis on individual treatment and reformation (or perhaps because of it), considerable concern arose over the years regarding the legal limitations on the powers of such courts, especially the question of due process. All too often, children—especially if members of a minority group—were apprehended by police, detained, questioned, given a closed hearing by a juvenile court judge, and then either placed on probation or committed to an institution without regard for their rights or those of their parents.[10] The pretext of reformation, or "the good of the child," sometimes, perhaps even often, proved to be a source of arbitrary authority and a substitute for justice. In fact, there was some question as to whether or not the legal safeguards embodied in the U.S. Constitution were as applicable to the child as to the adult offender.

---

[9]Just as the stern parent of the Victorian era was being superseded by the more lenient parent of the so-called Progressive era, the harsh court of the nineteenth century was being replaced by the more humane court of the twentieth. Moreover, the absolute authority of the father, which came from the Common Law, was being restricted at this time by legislation and judicial action as the state, charged with the obligation of protecting its future citizens, assumed a degree of parental authority—*parens patriae*. Actually, as Joseph Hawes has pointed out in *The Children's Rights Movement* (1991), *parens patriae* was not new. During the colonial period, the state was permitted to remove children from unsuitable parents, i.e., those who were not educating and training their offspring. In practice, however, that rarely was done. colonial poor law officials mainly dealt with abandoned, orphaned, or illegitimate children, not those in intact families. In any event, during the so-called progressive era reformers also worked for, and generally secured at this time, contributory negligence laws giving the court jurisdiction over parents who did not provide proper guidance for their children.

[10]The fact that black youngsters and members of other minority groups as well received harsher treatment than white children in such courts has been well documented. See, for example, T. N. Ferdinand and E. G. Luchterhand, "Inner-City Youth, the Police, the Juvenile Court, and Justice," *Social Problems* 17 (Spring 1970): 510–27, and Sidney Axelrod, "Negro and White Institutionalized Delinquents," *American Journal of Sociology* 57 (May 1952): 569–74. Perhaps it should be added that along with the attack on the children's court came an attack on the indeterminate sentence, for the same reason—it allowed for too much administrative discretion.

In May 1967, the U.S. Supreme Court settled the question, at least with regard to procedural safeguards in cases that might result in commitment to an institution. In the momentous *Gault* decision, it asserted that "neither the Fourteenth Amendment nor the Bill of Rights is for adults alone" and then ruled that timely notice of all charges against a juvenile must be given; that the child has the right to be represented by legal counsel (which must be appointed by the court if the family cannot afford one); that the child has the right to confront and cross-examine complainants; and that the child has protection against self-incrimination.[11]

Pointing to these and other developments at the time, some scholars, most notably Anthony Platt, have argued that the "child savers" of the late nineteenth and early twentieth centuries, especially those middle-class women who worked to create the juvenile court, were influenced less by a concern with child welfare than by other motives, principally a desire to control the children of the "dangerous classes" and to carve out more meaningful lives (including perhaps professional careers) for themselves.

Two useful correctives, or at least counterpoints, to the Platt view and to the entire "social control" thesis in this regard are Ellen Ryerson's *The Best-Laid Plans: America's Juvenile Court Experiment*, published in 1978, and David Rothman's *Conscience and Convenience: The Asylum and Its Alternatives in Progressive America*, published two years later. Ryerson argues, and I think demonstrates, that the children's court (and the entire child welfare movement) represented a sincere, humane effort by dedicated, well-meaning reformers to establish an agency that would make the law and the judicial system constructive influences in the lives of young offenders. Somewhat similarly, Rothman asserts that the neglect of children's rights in juvenile

---

[11]See *In re Gault*, 387 U.S. 1 (1967). Two years later, in *Tinker* v. *Des Moines Independent Community School District*, 393 U.S. 503 (1969), the Court opened the door to even wider rights for children by declaring them "persons" under the Constitution. In the 1970s, there were three other major Supreme Court cases concerning the constitutional rights of children in juvenile courts. In two of those cases—*In re Winship*, 397 U.S. 358 (1970) and *Breed* v. *Jones*, 421 U.S. 519 (1975)—the Court further expanded the application of due process concepts to the children's court, but in the third—*McKeiver* v. *Pennsylvania*, 403 U.S. 528 (1971)—the Court ruled that the right to trial by jury was not an essential ingredient in due process and fundamental fairness which must be included in such a tribunal.

courts was not a callous, self-interested disregard for constitutional principles by the reformers; rather, it was the product of their deep, if naive, faith in the decency of judges and the disinterested benevolence of the state. In other words, the children's court was a product of the progressive era, an institution that its proponents really believed would benefit both the individuals involved and all of society. Although they may have been wrong and in the long run their efforts failed, these reformers were altruists attempting to do good; the origin of the court and the motivations of its originators should not be judged by those later failures.

In any event, if in the past the court sometimes ignored the rights of children (and their families), it no longer could do so after the *Gault* decision, at least in theory. As it stood, the juvenile court was a forum for children in difficulty and a service different in character from other courts (i.e., more flexible and service oriented), but still one in which due process of law provided fully as much protection to the parties involved as was provided to litigants in other courts.

Along with the aim of treatment and education rather than punishment and retribution, the principle of prevention was implicit in the juvenile court movement. One of it major objectives was to check adult crimes by giving a constructive direction to the life of the potential criminal while he or she was still in the formative stage of life. In other words, proponents of the court realized that measures for the protection of individual children were measures for the protection of society. It was no accident, therefore, that the movement occurred during the time of the settlement house movement and the period of preventive social work, when the work of G. Stanley Hall and other child study experts was becoming increasingly popular.

Since at the base of the juvenile court was the theory that the individual child and his or her needs should be considered rather than the offense and its legal penalty, the resort to such legal procedure was naturally part of, and gave added impetus to, the child home care movement. In theory at least, whenever possible children's court judges would hand down suspended sentences and permit offenders to remain in their own homes, where they would receive treatment. Therefore, a necessary adjunct of the court—in fact, its single most important component—was an effective system of probation, the instrument through which the court would apply that treatment.

Probation represented, in the words of one children's court judge, "the keystone which supports the arch" of the system and, according to another, "the cord upon which all the pearls are strung. . . . Without it," he added, "the court could not exist."

Probation was not considered by its advocates to be an act of clemency by the judge. Rather, it was a positive measure for individual and community welfare. It was argued that since individuals were largely products of their environment—for the most part, in other words, they were not free moral agents who willingly chose to break the law, as had been believed previously—when someone was charged with committing an illegal act it was not merely a personal, but also a community, matter. The misdeed was probably brought on by many influences and factors, both personal and social, that had exercised an unfavorable influence upon the offender. The juvenile delinquent (or, for that matter, the adult criminal as well) was someone who needed help in adjusting to community life.

To provide this help, it was deemed best not to remove the child from his or her home and place him (or her) in the artificial environment of an institution. On the contrary, inquiring into the home conditions and helping the offender adapt to them, or changing those conditions to meet his or her needs, was essential. Unfortunately, the more traditional method of dealing with erring children—locking them up—failed to do this; it took into consideration only the individual element in wrongdoing. Probation took into account both the individual and the surroundings, regarded the offense as the product of both, and sought to influence both so that in the future they would work for the good rather than the harm of the child.[12]

This assumed that probation would not be haphazardly administered. Unfortunately, for a long time it was. The Chicago situation was typical. There the court was authorized to appoint "one or more

---

[12]In most cases, however, the emphasis was on the individual, not on his or her surroundings, according to Eric Schneider, a more recent, and slightly different, critic of the juvenile court. Thus, it was "the perfect structural," as opposed to substantive, reform, one that from the outset was outmoded and doomed to failure, for by treating youngsters individually it dealt with them as though they were deviants—pathological cases—who had to be "cured," *even if their illness was the product of faulty environmental conditions.* In many ways, then, it was more a reflection of the nineteenth- than the early-twentieth-century approach to problem solving, according to Schneider.

discreet persons of good character" to serve as probation officers. No money, however, was authorized for the position. Early proponents of the court feared that the cost involved in paying probation officers might defeat the legislation and thus prevent the courts themselves from coming into existence. Too, it was feared that well-paying probation posts might become political plums for those responsible for the appointments—usually the justices.

As a result, at the outset probation was administered on a volunteer basis or paid for, sparingly, by private sources such as the Woman's Club in Chicago. Most officers were untrained citizens, court clerks, or, paradoxically, policemen, who, in many ways, acted like earlier charity organization society friendly visitors. However, the precedent at least had been set, and over the years probation made headway. Eventually, especially after the creation of state probation commissions in most places, beginning in New York in 1907, probation was placed under civil service, so that appointments were made on the basis of personality, training, and experience. As pay levels increased and professional standards gained ground, more competent people were attracted to the field. For the most part, however, "treatment," which seemingly was enhanced by the emergence of child psychiatry and the proliferation of child guidance clinics in the 1920s, did not work; therapy proved no more successful than moralism in solving juvenile delinquency.

Meanwhile, the promise of the *Gault* decision regarding the rights of children in difficulty with the law (and the rights of their parents as well) also was not fulfilled. Priority remained with "rehabilitation" rather than with justice, despite the paucity of resources, which undermined the quality of the facilities and the services that were supposed to rehabilitate the troubled children—and the fact that, in most cases, they were not deviants in need of psychotherapy but rather victims in need of more favorable surroundings.

As a result, juvenile delinquency increased significantly, especially in the years following World War II. Whereas earlier child welfare enthusiasts and psychiatric social workers had dominated the field, more and more sociologists turned their attention to it. Beginning with Robert Park and Clifford Shaw at the University of Chicago in the 1930s, who were particularly interested in neighborhood disorganization and street gangs, a succession of scholars—Sheldon and

Eleanor Glueck, William F. Whyte, Albert Cohen, Lloyd Ohlin, and
Richard Cloward—researched and wrote about juvenile delinquency
and its apparent causes. By the 1960s, prevailing opinion among those
studying the subject was that young people turned to crime largely
out of frustration, which in turn was caused by lack of opportunity.[13]
Delinquency, then, constituted a critique of society; the means of prevention lay in opening up legitimate avenues of success for deprived
youngsters. Thus was born Mobilization for Youth, a pioneer delinquency control project on New York City's Lower East Side.

Funded initially in 1958 by the National Institute of Mental
Health, Mobilization for Youth consisted of employment bureaus,
manpower training programs, remedial educational work, anti-dis-
crimination activities, and neighborhood service centers, designed to
provide greater opportunities for young people in slum neighborhoods. The program's results were mixed, at best.

At the same time, however, benevolent action was becoming
increasingly suspect: a growing number of people were beginning to
question the consequences of social welfare policy, whatever the motivations of the reformers, vis-à-vis children and others. They even went
so far as to suggest that the juvenile justice system might be more
harmful than helpful both to the offender and to society, even under
the best of circumstances, something Sheldon and Eleanor Glueck
had hinted at back in the 1930s, when they published *One Thousand
Delinquents: Their Treatment by Court and Clinic.* Summarizing the
available research for a presidential commission in 1967, sociologist
Edwin Lemert pointed out that youth who come under court jurisdiction commit more, rather than fewer, crimes later in life: "The conclusion that the court processing rather than the [youth's] behavior in
some way helps to fix and perpetuate delinquency in many cases is
hard to escape," Lemert testified. No wonder, then, that some lawyers,
civil libertarians, scholars, and even a handful of social workers placed
"children's rights" as the next item on the social policy agenda.
Children, they argued, need fewer benefactors, not more; they need
fewer child welfare services and facilities, not more; they need, above
all, the chance to make decisions about their lives free from parental

---

[13]See Richard Cloward and Lloyd Ohlin, *Delinquency and Opportunity: A Theory of Delinquent
Gangs* (Gencoe, Ill.: Free Press, 1960).

and state interference.[14] Whether or not they were correct, and whether society would move in that direction, remained to be seen.

In the meantime, however, what was seen, all too clearly, was that the condition of the nation's sixty-four million children was steadily growing worse. Newspaper headlines blared tale after shocking tale of child neglect, abandonment, and other forms of mistreatment, including a tremendous rise in the "battered child syndrome," a term used to characterize a clinical condition in young children who received serious physical abuses, usually from a parent or a foster parent. In addition, there were significant increases in the infant mortality rate, in child poverty, and in homelessness among the young, all, of course, related matters.[15] In the early 1980s, when defense spending skyrocketed and federal spending on virtually all programs affecting poor children was cut significantly, including Aid to Families with Dependent Children, food stamps, Medicaid, and other health and nutrition programs, there was a shocking increase in deaths among infants—a 3 percent rise in 1983, for example, and the number was growing—primarily a reflection of such preventable social and economic conditions as poor nutrition, inadequate housing, faulty sanitary facilities, lack of basic health care (for pregnant women as well as newborn children), and the like. With a 9.8 infant death rate for every one thousand live births (in 1989, the most recent year for which final figures were available), America was one of the worst places in the industrialized world for a child to be born. For African-American and Hispanic children, among whom the death rate was nearly twice as high as among Anglo infants, the chances of surviving the first year of life were less than for babies in many Third World countries.

At the same time, thanks to a dramatic increase in teenage pregnancy and single-parent families, declining wages, growing unemployment, and lower welfare payments, approximately twenty-six million American children—about two out of five of those who survived the

---

[14]Ironically, at the same time the rising crime rate, the urban disorders of 1964–67, and the various disruptive demonstrations made "law and order" a popular slogan—and a new emphasis on punishment and imprisonment followed, at least among many working-class Americans.

[15]In addition, an alarming number of children were contracting such deadly, or potentially deadly, diseases as Acquired Immune Deficiency Syndrome, or AIDS, tuberculosis, and measles, as will be discussed in the next chapter.

first year of life—were living in poverty, an increase of well over 50 percent from the previous decade and the single largest group of destitute citizens in the entire nation. Furthermore, according to a study conducted by the National Academy of Sciences during the late 1980s, the fastest growing group in America with no place to live were those under eighteen years of age, at least 100,000 of whom were homeless on any given night, and their number, too, was growing.

While some Americans tended to attribute these developments—the increased incidence of child abuse, the high infant mortality rate, and the growth in child poverty and homelessness—to the behavior, or misbehavior, of the poor—they are too violent, they have too many babies out of wedlock, they are too lazy to get jobs, the sayings went—others argued that they were the products of a faltering economy and a lack of decent jobs, changing social attitudes toward out-of-wedlock births and single-parenting, a severe shortage of day care and other badly needed facilities, cutbacks in social programs, and, above all, a sense of hopelessness among poor Americans, especially black and Hispanic teenagers. Whatever the cause, or causes, America's children clearly were "at risk," as Marian Wright Edelman of the Children's Defense Fund put it. For all of their rhetoric about child welfare, many questioned their fellow citizens' commitment to the nation's young people; certainly they were investing little in their future. And if in fact the destiny of American children is the destiny of America, they feared that a national catastrophe was in the making.

To go back to an earlier period, however, when most Americans did accord a high priority to the nation's youngsters and campaigned wholeheartedly for their interests, the placing- and boarding-out of dependent, neglected, and delinquent children and the establishment of true houses of correction, juvenile courts, and probation systems were only part of the concern for the problems of childhood. The growing emphasis on the prevention of need and the desire to conserve human as well as physical resources made it increasingly apparent that every effort to achieve what was termed social and industrial justice (indeed, all movements for social betterment) was directly related to child welfare. What was for the welfare of the community was for the welfare of the family and for the welfare of its children—and vice versa.

Thus, the fight for the regulation of child labor was part of the child welfare movement. At one reformer put it: "Effective and adequate child-caring work must include the enforcement of proper child labor laws; they are an essential part of the child caring system." So, too, were the movements for widows' pensions and numerous other reforms, including enactment of the Social Security Act. Clearly, by the early twentieth century there was increasing awareness of the needs of all children and of the necessity to provide a range of services that would afford them the opportunity for full development. Among the most urgent of those services was the need to curtail illness and death—not only of children, but of their parents as well—resulting from preventable disease.

Bibliography

ABBOTT, GRACE, ed. *The Child and the State*, 2 Vols. Chicago: University of Chicago Press, 1938.

ANDERSON, PAUL G. "The Origin, Emergence, and Professional Recognition of Child Protection," *Social Service Review* 63 (June 1989): 222–44.

ASHBY, LEROY. *Saving the Waifs: Reformers and Dependent Children, 1890–1917.* Philadelphia: Temple University Press, 1984.

BEALES, ROSS W. "In Search of the Historical Child: Miniature Adulthood and Youth in Colonial New England," *American Quarterly* 27 (October 1975): 379–98.

BEARD, BELLE B. *Juvenile Probation*. New York: American, 1934.

BLOCK, HERBERT A., AND FRANK T. FLYNN. *Delinquency: The Juvenile Offender in America Today*. New York: Random House, 1956.

BLOCK, MARY R. "Child-Saving Laws of Louisville and Jefferson County, 1854–1894: A Socio-Legal History," *Filson Club History Quarterly* 66 (April 1992): 232–51.

BRACE, CHARLES LORING. *The Dangerous Classes of New York and Twenty Years Work Among Them.* New York: Wynkoop and Hallenbeck, 1872.

BRECKINRIDGE, SOPHONISBA, AND EDITH ABBOTT. *The Delinquent Child and the Home.* New York: Survey Associates, 1912.

BREMNER, ROBERT H., ed. *Children and Youth in America*, 3 Vols. Cambridge, Mass.: Harvard University Press, 1970–74.

BRENZEL, BARBARA M. *Daughters of the State: A Social Portrait of the First Reform School for Girls in North America, 1856–1905.* Cambridge, Mass.: MIT Press, 1983.

BROWN, JAMES. "Child Welfare Classics," *Social Service Review* 34 (June 1960): 195–202.

BRYANT, KEITH. "The Juvenile Court Movement," *Social Science Quarterly* 49 (September 1968): 368–76.

BUCKINGHAM, CLYDE. "Early American Orphanages: Ebenezar and Bethesda," *Social Forces* 26 (March 1948): 311–22.

CABLE, MARY. *The Little Darlings: A History of Child Rearing in America.* New York: Scribner's, 1975.

CAMPBELL, D. ANN. "Judge Ben Lindsey and the Juvenile Court Movement, 1901–04," *Arizona and the West* 18 (Spring 1976): 5–20.

CAVALLO, DOMINICK. *Muscles and Morals: Organized Playgrounds and Urban Reform, 1880–1920.* Philadelphia: University of Pennsylvania Press, 1981.

CLEMENT, PRISCILLA F. "Families and Foster Care: Philadelphia in the Late Nineteenth Century," *Social Service Review* 53 (September 1979): 406–20.

CLOWARD, RICHARD, AND LLOYD OHLIN. *Delinquency and Opportunity: A Theory of Delinquent Gangs.* Glencoe, Ill.: Free Press, 1960.

COHEN, RONALD D. "Child-Saving and Progressivism, 1885–1915," in N. Ray Hiner and Joseph Hawes, eds., *American Childhood.* Westport, Conn.: Greenwood, 1986.

CORDSACO, FRANCESCO. "Charles Loring Brace and the Dangerous Classes: Historical Analogues of the Urban Black Poor," *Journal of Human Relations* 20 (Third Quarter 1972): 379–86.

Crusade for Children, The. New York: Children's Aid Society, 1928.

DEUTSCH, ALBERT. *Our Rejected Children.* Boston: Little, Brown, 1950.

DOWNS, SUSAN WHITELAW, AND MICHAEL W. SHERRADEN. "The Orphan Asylum in the Nineteenth Century," *Social Service Review* 57 (June 1983): 272–90.

DYE, NANCY SCHROM, AND DANIEL BLAKE SMITH. "Mother Love and Infant Death, 1750–1920," *Journal of American History* 73 (September 1986): 329–53.

EARLE, ALICE M. *Child Life in Colonial Days.* New York: Macmillan, 1927.

FLEXNER, BERNARD, AND ROGER BALDWIN. *Juvenile Courts and Probation.* New York: Century, 1941.

FLYNN, FRANK T. "Judge Merritt W. Pinckney and the Early Days of the Juvenile Court in Chicago," *Social Service Review* 28 (March 1954): 20–30.

FOLKS, HOMER. *The Care of Destitute, Neglected and Delinquent Children.* New York: Macmillan, 1902.

FOX, SANFORD J. "Juvenile Justice Reform: An Historical Perspective," *Stanford Law Review* 22 (1970): 1187–1239.

FREY, CECILE P. "The House of Refuge for Colored Children," *Journal of Negro History* 66 (Spring 1981): 10–25.

GLUECK, SHELDON AND ELEANOR. *One Thousand Delinquents: Their Treatment by Court and Clinic*. Cambridge, Mass.: Harvard University Press, 1934.

HALL, G. STANLEY. *Adolescence: Its Psychology and its Relation to Physiology, Anthropology, Sociology, Sex, Crime, Religion, and Education*. New York: Appleton, 1904.

HART, HASTINGS. *Cottage and Congregate Institutions for Children*. New York: Charities Publication Committee, 1910.

———. *Juvenile Court Laws in the United States*. New York: Charities Publication Committee, 1910.

———. *Preventive Treatment for Neglected Children*. New York: Charities Publication Committee, 1910.

HAWES, JOSEPH. *Children in Urban Society: Juvenile Delinquency in Nineteenth Century America*. New York: Oxford University Press, 1971.

———. *The Children's Rights Movement: A History of Advocacy and Protection*. Boston: Twayne Publishers, 1991.

HEALY, WILLIAM. *The Individual Delinquent*. Boston: Little, Brown, 1915.

HELFMAN, HAROLD M. "The Detroit House of Correction, 1861–74," *Michigan History* 34 (December 1950): 299–308.

JACOBY, GEORGE P. *Catholic Child Care in Nineteenth Century New York*. Washington, D.C.: Catholic University, 1941.

JAMES, ARTHUR W. "Foster Care in Virginia, 1676–1796," *Public Welfare* 8 (March 1950): 60–64.

JONES, MARSHALL. "Foster-Home Care of Delinquent Children," *Social Service Review* 10 (September 1936): 450–63.

KAHN, ALFRED. *A Court for Children*. New York: Columbia University Press, 1953.

KATZ, MICHAEL B. "Child-Saving," *History of Education Quarterly* 26 (Fall 1986): 413–24.

LANGSAM, MIRIAM. *Children West: A History of the Placing-Out of the New York Children's Aid Society*. Madison, Wis.: State Historical Society, 1964.

LARSEN, CHARLES. *The Good Fight: The Life and Times of Ben B. Lindsey*. Chicago: Quadrangle Books. 1972.

LINDSEY, BENJAMIN B. *The Dangerous Life*. New York: Liveright, 1931.

———. *Twenty-Five Years of the Juvenile and Family Court of Denver*. Denver: Ben B. Lindsey, 1925.

LOU, H. H. *Juvenile Courts in the United States*. Chapel Hill: University of North Carolina Press, 1927.

LUNDBERG, EMMA. *Unto the Least of These: Social Services for Children*. New York: Appleton-Century, 1947.

MERGEN, BERNARD. "The Discovery of Children's Play," *American Quarterly* 27 (October 1975): 399–420.

MORTON, MARIAN J. "Homes for Poverty's Children: Cleveland's Orphanages, 1851–1933," *Ohio History* 98 (Winter–Spring 1989): 5–22.

NEIGHER, ALAN. "The Gault Decision: Due Process and the Juvenile Court," *Federal Probation* 31 (December 1967): 8–18.

NELSON, KRISTINE E. "Child Placing in the Nineteenth Century: New York and Iowa," *Social Service Review* 59 (March 1985): 107–20.

ODEM, MARY. "Single Mothers, Delinquent Daughters, and the Juvenile Court in Early 20th Century Los Angeles," *Journal of Social History* 25 (Fall 1991): 27–43.

PICKETT, ROBERT S. *House of Refuge: Origins of Juvenile Reform in New York State, 1815–1857*. Syracuse, N. Y.: Syracuse University Press, 1969.

PLATT, ANTHONY M. *The Child Savers: The Invention of Delinquency*. Chicago: University of Chicago Press, 1969.

———. "The Rise of the Child-Saving Movement," *Annals of the American Academy of Political and Social Science* 381 (January 1969): 21–38.

ROMANOFSKY, PETER. "'To Save . . . Their Souls': The Care of Dependent Children in New York City, 1900–1905," *Jewish Social Studies* 36 (July–October 1974): 253–61.

ROSENHEIM, MARGARET K., ed. *Justice for the Child*. New York: Free Press, 1962.

———, ed. *Pursuing Justice for the Child*. Chicago: University of Chicago Press, 1976.

ROSS, DOROTHY. *G. Stanley Hall: The Psychologist as Prophet*. Chicago: University of Chicago Press, 1972.

ROTHMAN, DAVID. *Conscience and Convenience: The Asylum and Its Alternatives in Progressive America*. Boston: Little, Brown, 1980.

RUBIN, SOL. "Trends in Juvenile Court Philosophy," *Social Service Review* 7 (April 1962): 53–57.

RUBIN, TED, AND JACK SMITH. *The Future of the Juvenile Court*. Washington, D.C.: Government Printing Office, 1968.

RYERSON, ELLEN. *The Best-Laid Plans: America's Juvenile Court Experiment*. New York: Hill and Wang, 1978.

SCHLOSSMAN, STEVEN L. *Love and the American Delinquent: The Theory and*

Practice of "Progressive" Juvenile Justice, 1825–1920. Chicago: University of Chicago Press, 1977.

SCHNEIDER, ERIC C. *In the Web of Class: Delinquents and Reformers in Boston, 1810s–1930s*. New York: New York University Press, 1992.

SCOTT, REBECCA. "The Battle Over the Child: Child Apprenticeship and the Freedmen's Bureau in North Carolina," *Prologue* 10 (Summer 1978): 101–13.

SILVERMAN, MARVIN. "Children's Rights and Social Work," *Social Service Review* 51 (March 1957): 171–78.

SLATER, PETER G. "Ben Lindsey and the Denver Juvenile Court," *American Quarterly* 20 (Summer 1968): 211–23.

SPARGO, JOHN. *The Bitter Cry of the Children*. New York: Macmillan, 1906.

SPEIZMAN, MILTON D. "Child Care: A Mirror of Human History," *Children and Youth Services Review* 3 (1981): 213–32.

TEETERS, NEGLEY K. "The Early Days of the Philadelphia House of Refuge," *Pennsylvania History* 27 (April 1960): 165–87.

THURSTON, HENRY W. *The Dependent Child*. New York: Columbia University Press, 1930.

TIFFIN, SUSAN. *In Whose Best Interest? Child Welfare Reform in the Progressive Era*. Westport, Conn.: Greenwood Press, 1982.

TRATTNER, WALTER I. *Homer Folks: Pioneer in Social Welfare*. New York: Columbia University Press, 1968.

———. *Crusade for the Children: A History of the National Child Labor Committee and Child Labor Reform in America*. Chicago: Quadrangle Books, 1970.

VAN WATERS, MIRIAM. *Parents on Probation*. New York: New Republic, 1927.

WERTSCH, DOUGLAS. "Iowa's Daughters: The First Thirty Years of the Girls Reform School of Iowa, 1869–1899," *Annals of Iowa* 49 (Summer–Fall 1987): 77–100.

WHITTAKER, JAMES K. "Colonial Child Care Institutions: Our Heritage of Care," *Child Welfare* 50 (July 1971): 396–400.

———. "Nineteenth Century Innovations in Delinquency Institutions," *Child Care Quarterly* 2 (Spring 1973): 14–24.

WINSTON, ELLEN. "The Shape of Things to Come in Child Welfare—The Broad Outline," *Child Welfare* 45 (January 1966): 5–11.

ZAINALDEN, JAMAIL S. "The Emergence of a Modern American Family Law: Child Custody, Adoption, and the Courts, 1796–1851," *Northwestern University Law Review* 73 (February 1979): 1038–89.

ZELIZER, VIVIANA A. *Pricing the Priceless Child: The Changing Social Value of Children*. New York: Basic Books, 1985.

CHAPTER 7

The Public Health Movement

■ By the middle of the nineteenth century, American cities were disorderly, filthy, foul-smelling, disease-ridden places. Narrow, unpaved streets became transformed into quagmires when it rained. Rickety tenements, swarming with unwashed humanity, leaned upon one another for support. Inadequate drainage systems failed to carry away sewage. Pigs roamed streets that were cluttered with manure, years of accumulated garbage, and other litter. Outside privies bordered almost every thoroughfare. Slaughterhouses and fertilizing plants contaminated the air with an indescribable stench. Ancient plagues like smallpox, cholera, and typhus threw the population into a state of terror from time to time while less sensational but equally deadly killers like tuberculosis, diphtheria, and scarlet fever were ceaselessly at work. Thus, at a time when the general death rate for the nation was around twenty per thousand inhabitants, that of New York and other large cities averaged over twenty-five. In the poorer quarters of most large cities, however, the rate often ranged between thirty and forty per thousand, and was as high as 135 per thousand for children under five years of age. A horrified humanity was forced by such conditions to recognize not only that a sanitary problem existed, but also that the very life of the city was at stake, for if it was to survive the city had to be made a safe and healthy place in which to live. Beginning around the middle of the nineteenth century, then, the nation's first major sanitation program began.

Public health activities were not new.[1] Laws and regula-

---

[1]According to a widely used definition, public health is "the science and art of preventing disease, prolonging life, and promoting physical health and efficiency

tions to prevent the spread of disease go far back in history. Whenever and wherever people gathered together in communities, they felt a need for some kind of regulation to protect the public health; thus, the Massachusetts Poor Law of 1692 gave local authorities the power to remove and isolate infected members of the community. The organized public health movement, however, which included both the improved treatment and the prevention of disease, did not begin in the United States until around the middle of the nineteenth century, nor did it amount to much until after the 1870s, when Drs. Louis Pasteur and Robert Koch discovered the true etiology of disease—germs.

Earlier in the nineteenth century there were two widely held views of disease. The first, held by most people, including many physicians and public health enthusiasts, was that disease, like poverty and disaster (earthquakes, floods, and so on), was a providential matter, usually the visitation of a just God upon a frail and erring person (or people), a direct consequence of undesirable personal or social behavior. The second, held by many others, was that disease resulted from environmental factors, namely dirt and filth—or, in some cases, the odors given off by Irish ditch diggers. If disease was the result of God's wrath, the inescapable consequence of sin, the answer was improved or better behavior. If it resulted chiefly from dirt, filth, and foul air, then by changing the environment through amending or eliminating those factors, one could improve the public health. By engaging in a vast moral crusade and by improving the water supply, building sewers, initiating better street cleaning and garbage removal, draining bogs and swamps, and planting trees (which served as "ventilators" that absorbed pernicious odors in the air and gave off oxygen instead), most problems of public health would be solved. It was on the basis of these beliefs—especially the latter—that Americans began their first crusade for good health.

As in so many other areas, the influence of England was important. As a consequence of its advanced industrialization, which produced sooty cities in the 1830s and 1840s that were even more squalid than

---

through organized community efforts for the sanitation of the environment, the control of community infections, the education of individual principles of personal hygiene, the organization of medical and nursing services for the early diagnosis and treatment of diseases. . . ."

America's, and a series of influenza and typhoid epidemics that ravaged London's population, England gave rise to a number of busy
social reformers who began to wage war against disease. The most
important among them was Edwin Chadwick, author of the Royal
Poor Law Commission *Report of 1834*, who, shortly thereafter, began
to conclude that ill health—the result of deplorable environmental
conditions, not moral ones—was the major cause of poverty and
dependency.

Chadwick spent several years studying urban conditions and gathering material from all over Britain. It all led to the same conclusion:
Surrounded by foul miasmas, deprived of fresh air and water, living in
the midst of overflowing cesspools and privies, even those people who
tried could scarcely abide by the rules of cleanliness and health. The
more Chadwick studied the situation, the more he became convinced
of the need for far-reaching sanitary reform.

In 1842, he published his famous report on *The Sanitary Condition
of the Labouring Population of Great Britain.* Probably no single document so profoundly affected the development of public health as did
this grim, detailed account of the squalid filth and its consequences in
England's slums. This remarkable study not only awakened the public
conscience to the sanitation needs of a growing urban population but
also led to enactment of the Public Health Act of 1848, which marked
the legal birth of modern sanitation reform and set the pattern, both
in Europe and in America, for the war against disease.

Passage of the English Public Health Act of 1848, which created
the world's first modern board of health, encouraged concerned
American sanitarians to press for similar reforms on this side of the
Atlantic. By that time, the unsanitary and wretched living conditions
prevalent in America's older communities not only duplicated, but in
some cases surpassed, those in England; indeed, the mortality rate in
most Atlantic seaboard cities exceeded that of London.

First to be encouraged by the English example was a small group of
public-spirited citizens in Massachusetts who, alarmed by the distressing
state of the nation's health, persuaded the state legislature to finance a
sanitary survey of the Bay State. The resulting report and its recommendations for change (written by Lemuel Shattuck, a Boston city council-
man and public health enthusiast, and published in 1850) was the first
plan for an integrated health program in the United States.

The Shattuck proposals were short-lived, however, in part because of medical indifference, but more important, because the slavery issue preoccupied the public mind. Then, of course, came the Civil War and its important influence on public health reform. Not only did the health problems created by large armies give supporters of sanitation reform a chance to substantiate their claims,[2] but a growing number of laymen gained some appreciation of the purposes of sanitation and the benefits to be derived from the practice of public hygiene.

When the war came to an end, concerned citizens sought to take advantage of the situation. Thus, when sanitarians, public-spirited persons, magazine writers, and some physicians voiced alarm over the distressing state of America's health and urged hygienic measures for its improvement, some notable advances were achieved. In 1866, the New York Metropolitan Health Law was enacted, creating the nation's first real municipal board of health; other major cities soon followed suit. In 1869, Massachusetts created the first state board of health; again, the example was widely followed. In 1872, the American Public Health Association was founded. The federal government passed the National Quarantine Act of 1878, and a year later created the National Board of Health.

Yet these developments did not produce the results that the public had been led to expect. First, most of the new municipal boards of health were not much better than their predecessors—poor, makeshift, ineffective bodies that either took a do-nothing attitude or else did as much harm as good. (New York's new board, it should be said, was better than its predecessor, a body that prompted Mayor C. Godfrey Gunther in the fall of 1865 to reply to a delegation of medical men who pleaded with him to summon it into session in view of an approaching cholera epidemic: "I will not call the Board, for I consider it more dangerous to the city than cholera.")

For the most part, the boards were composed of the mayor and a

---

[2]Here was another example of where the British experience affected American developments, in this case the Crimean War, which had been waged several years earlier. Many sanitarians, doctors, and concerned citizens had studied the reports of the British Sanitary Commission, or excerpts from that report which were printed in American journals, which related the medical history of the campaign, and they were determined to make good use of the sanitary knowledge purchased at such sad cost in the Crimea.

group of political hacks, sometimes the most crooked and least knowledgeable members of the municipal legislature. Of the seven men on Cincinnati's board, for example, six were saloon-keepers. They convened only when compelled to do so, usually during an emergency; seldom, if ever, did they pay due attention to the conditions responsible for endemic disease.

Another reason for the lack of success in improving the public health at this time was that reform met a great deal of opposition, both from the public in general and from certain interested groups in particular. Such improvements as the construction of municipal drains and sewers, for example, cost a good deal of money, which meant higher taxes. And many people, still not yet aware that public health saves money in the long run, objected. (Indeed, there is evidence to suggest that the attack against public relief later in the century was, in part, an effort to keep taxes down, which were being driven up by the cost of these and other municipal improvements and services.)

Moreover, public health reform often meant the destruction of slum dwellings and other profitable private property, so that tenement owners and others objected. And in an age of individualism, of laissez-faire and social Darwinism, these objections carried weight. Then, too, the medical profession often stood in the way of meaningful reforms.

The most important reason for the failure of the early public health program however, was lack of medical knowledge concerning the true cause of disease. As Pasteur, Koch, and others demonstrated, it was germs, not the wrath of God or dirt and filth, that caused disease; bacteria were not the end product of disease, as was widely believed, but rather its causative agent. Specific microorganisms which could be discovered, tracked down, avoided, and destroyed, were responsible for specific diseases. Neither corruption of morals nor putrification and filth (in themselves) could cause epidemics. However clean a city was, it could still be subject to widespread illness. Taste and smell could not be relied upon as judges of purity. Laboratories and microscopes, scientific specialists and their instruments were more important than cleaning the street. When this was understood, discovery of the origin of most of man's most ancient scourges followed rapidly: typhoid, leprosy, and malaria in 1880;

tuberculosis in 1882; cholera in 1883; diphtheria, tetanus, and bubonic plague in 1884; dysentery in 1898; and so on.

Although the knowledge that specific illnesses were caused by specific germs allowed health officers quickly to identify disorders, the "germ theory" of disease and preventive medicine remained in a relatively primitive stage until the importance of the personal factor in contagion was discovered; only after the role of the infected individual in spreading disease was understood did sanitation control operate effectively. This came near the close of the nineteenth century with elaboration of the concept of the "human carrier." Disease germs, it was discovered, are parasites that reside in the human body. The major mode of transmission, then, is contact with an infected person. As a result, personal cleanliness, inoculation, serums, antitoxins, antidotes, the segregation of "carriers" of disease, and the enactment of effective hygienic laws replaced environmental sanitation (and exhortations to conscience) as the basis for reform, resulting in what has been described as the "golden age of public health."

During this period (approximately 1890–1910), municipal and state boards of health began to attract better personnel and to set up diagnostic laboratories to apply the new medical discoveries to the prevention and cure of disease. Medical education was improved and research work was better organized. And, equally important, campaigns were initiated to educate the public in the ways of modern hygiene and persuade it to support change.

In other words, preventive medicine was not merely a matter of pathological research and laboratory diagnosis conducted by medical experts. It also contained social instruments, the most important of which was a well organized program of public health education, essential for success, for despite the great medical and scientific advances, the movement needed popular support to succeed. The public had to be made aware of the new discoveries and the advantages of their application, however costly and inconvenient. Here, charity workers (or social workers, as they were beginning to be called) and others made an enormous contribution to the movement for improved health, for prior to 1900 the war against disease was mainly the business of professional sanitarians, health officials, and medical men. Early in the twentieth century, when social workers and others began to understand the relationship between dependence and ill health, they opened a new line of attack on disease—the mobilization of the lay forces of the community for its control.[3]

Although perhaps not immediately realized, social workers especially had a large stake in medical progress; social work and public health had much in common. They were concerned with essentially the same problem—relieving the home of distress that often resulted from death or illness caused by some preventable disease. As one reformer pointed out, "Social workers and health officers met because their work brought them to the same place, namely, the home in which there was both communicable disease and poverty." Or, in Robert Hunter's words, "Poverty and sickness form a vicious partnership." Broadly speaking, then, social work embraced health work; the interests of social workers overlapped those of physicians. It was no accident that medical social work officially began at this time when, in 1905, Dr. Richard C. Cabot placed a social worker, Miss Garnet Pelton, on the staff of the Massachusetts General Hospital in order "to study the conditions under which patients lived and to assist those patients in carrying out the treatment recommended by the medical staff."[4]

In any event, by the turn of the century, convinced that the conditions making for charity work must themselves be eradicated, reformers studied the sources of dependency. They discovered that, in most cases, acute need resulted from the breakdown of family life, which in

---

[3]One of the first physicians to advocate "social medicine" was the great German pathologist Rudolph Virchon, who as early as 1848 argued that "medicine is a social science." He developed the basic principles that health is a matter of direct social concern, that social and economic conditions have an important effect on health and disease, and that therefore social as well as medical steps must be taken to promote health and combat disease.

[4]Medical social work is a form of casework, the study and treatment of a sick person in light of the social factors that influence recovery. The function of the medical social worker is to aid the physician in the treatment of the ill. He or she does not treat the disease but the person, trying to discover and interpret the social and economic factors involved in the illness and then to regulate them so that they will favorably influence the outcome of the illness. Since a good deal of medical research depends on surveys involving interviewing techniques, an area in which social workers have considerable expertise, the medical social worker also serves as a member of the doctor's research team. Along with Dr. Cabot, the person most responsible for the early growth and development of medical social work was Miss Ida Cannon, who for many years served as chief of the Social Service Department of Massachusetts General Hospital.

turn was caused by poverty—poverty rooted not in immortality and personal failure but in social and economic conditions, especially illness, invalidity, and the premature death of the family breadwinner. "Even the most cursory examination of the causes of destitution," wrote Homer Folks, the noted child welfare worker turned public health crusader, "shows that sickness is always one of the leading causes, and is usually the leading cause of dependency." Or, as another reformer put it: "The relationship between health and dependency is well known. Illness causes poverty by creating economic burdens, and social and economic insecurity in turn increase ill health—a vicious circle which brings self-supporting families to the dependency level and keeps them there." Focusing upon the medical rather than the moral roots of poverty and dependency, social workers began to wage war on injustice through promoting good health. Sanitation science and social reform went together; despite becoming a science with professional methods and objectives, public health work remained, in part at least, reformist in nature.

Tuberculosis was the first disease attacked. The chief cause of death throughout the world, tuberculosis took its greatest toll on persons between the ages of fifteen and forty-four. In that age span, about one-third of all deaths were caused by this one disease, creating havoc among those in their most productive years; it had the highest "social mortality" rate of all the contagious diseases. Since its victims either died or needed medical care precisely at the time their illness deprived them and their dependents of an income, it caused more suffering and greater economic loss than any other affliction. It was, according to Samuel Hopkins Adams, the noted journalist, "The Real Race Suicide."[5]

Earlier, because members of the same families tended to become infected, it was assumed that tuberculosis was hereditary and that therefore not a great deal could be done about it. When it was proven to be a communicable disease, the attitude of medical and lay leaders changed. As the members of one early antituberculosis society put it, "To know that it is *not* an inherited disease should bring hope and

---

[5]The situation was far worse for the nation's black than for its white citizens; in 1900, the annual mortality rate from tuberculosis was three times higher for African-Americans than for whites.

gladness to thousands of tuberculous parents, and to the children of such parents"—and it did.

Still, controlling the disease was no simple matter, for despite the fact that doctors knew the pathology and etiology of tuberculosis, they could not induce any active or passive immunization to it, nor was there any specific therapy other than a healthy diet, fresh air, and rest, and these were helpful only in incipient cases. These limitations, as well as the high costs of medical treatment and the lack of financial support for patients' dependents, highlighted the need for avoiding exposure to the infection—or acting immediately after contracting it.

The general public was more concerned with therapy than with prevention. Treatment appealed to those most immediately concerned, while preventive measures seemed vague, impractical, or of uncertain value. In any event, since there were only a few hospitals available to care for the tubercular, the prospects for controlling the disease appeared dim.

The first comprehensive analysis of tuberculosis in the United States was made by social workers. Undertaken in 1903, it was carried out by the Committee on the Prevention of Tuberculosis of the Charity Organization Society of New York—an agency that had come a long way since the days of "scientific charity." Under the leadership of secretary Edward T. Devine, the committee investigated the social and other nontechnical aspects of the disease. It set out to broadcast the seriousness, incidence, and symptoms of tuberculosis, and to explain how it could be arrested or prevented. In short, the committee sought to arouse the public; its aim was not the enactment of any legislation.

Similarly, in 1904, the National Association for the Study and Prevention of Tuberculosis was organized by a number of socially minded physicians and laymen in order to intensify and coordinate popular knowledge of the disease in the hope that education would lead to its ultimate control. The National Association's functions were chiefly promotional and advisory; it did not locate cases, provide relief, or found hospitals. Instead, it aided in the formation of other volunteer bodies which it hoped would perform those functions. As a result of these activities, the antituberculosis movement began to expand, affiliated bodies were formed, state and local societies and sanitarium facilities multiplied, and, in state after state, organized campaigns against the dread disease were initiated.

The fight against tuberculosis in New York State provides a case study of similar work elsewhere. Beginning in 1907, the New York State Charities Aid Association (the voluntary organization patterned after the U.S. Sanitary Commission that was founded in the 1870s by Louisa Lee Schuyler) led the movement to curtail the disease.

As a start, the group hired John A. Kingsbury, a young Columbia University graduate student of sociology, as a full-time field agent in charge of antituberculosis work. When he hired several assistants, New York became the first state in America which, in effect, had a field staff engaged in antituberculosis work. Next, the S.C.A.A created a Committee on the Prevention of Tuberculosis, composed of laymen and physicians noted for their public health work. The S.C.A.A. then began its work—a statewide educational campaign emphasizing the prevention of tuberculosis.

To be sure, a program of public enlightenment had to rest upon complete and accurate information. Accordingly, Kingsbury and his assistants went from city to city probing the prevalence of the disease and the measures, if any, in operation for the relief of the ill and the protection of those not yet infected. These facts served as the basis of the committee's educational efforts, which were aimed at securing in each locality of the state the most effective means of prevention, including, among other things, free bacteriological examination of sputum, free dispensaries and visiting nurse services, and early regis-tration of cases.

The campaign began in Utica, New York, and from there it was car-ried to most other large cities throughout the state. An exhibit com-prising photographs, statistical tables, charts, and slides showing com-parative death rates, symptoms of the disease, unsanitary dwellings, and preventive measures was carried about. The committee also dis-tributed thousands of leaflets and pamphlets, sponsored lectures, and held meetings for doctors, nurses, teachers, and concerned citizens. Also in attendance were such dignitaries as Governor Charles E. Hughes; Joseph H. Choate, S.C.A.A. board member and Ambassador to Great Britain; Dr. William H. Welch, "dean" of the nation's medical profession; state legislators; and mayors of surrounding communities.

The campaign was also endorsed by President Theodore Roosevelt, whose supporting message was read at each of the gatherings, giving a tremendous impetus to the antituberculosis work.

The reformers were committed to the proposition that saving and prolonging lives was socially desirable—the antithesis of the view held by social Darwinists. They did not repudiate the evolutionary theory, they merely reinterpreted it in a way that made it useful to them. They argued that they were not simply allowing the unfit to exist, but were reviving them and restoring their fitness to serve. They were substituting "rational selection" for natural selection.

They also believed that good health was attainable and that a healthy populace would lead to a sounder society, a more just and humane social order. They sought to utilize the new scientific knowledge and the increasing store of defensive and preventive medicine to battle disease, especially tuberculosis, by making the public aware of its dangers in the hope that people would begin to take the necessary steps to avoid the infection. In a sense, they were propagandists, or medical muckrakers, in their efforts to overcome public ignorance or apathy, an obvious barrier in the way of improved public health.

Thanks to this educational campaign, within a year six tuberculosis dispensaries were opened in New York State, visiting nurse services for consumptives were provided in six cities, and two large hospitals were being built.

Despite this progress, public health reformers knew that statistics and information alone would not solve the problem. It became increasingly evident that however widely disseminated, knowledge alone would not prevent the spread of tuberculosis; contacts within the family were so intimate and prolonged that, even with an awareness of communicability, infection spread to an alarming degree.

Another factor that greatly retarded control of tuberculosis was an unwillingness by the public and the medical profession to report cases. In many communities, tuberculosis was regarded as a disgrace and a public menace; to avoid the stigma attached to it, victims frequently went unattended. To protect the sensibilities of those patients who did seek medical help, physicians often reported cases of tuberculosis as bronchitis or pneumonia. In fact, so untrustworthy were physicians' death reports for tuberculosis (and other communicable diseases), that Chicago's Board of Health began to look to the city's undertakers for information on the causes of death; and it was on the morticians' rather than the physicians' reports that the health authorities relied.

Many doctors also believed that because the disease was so contagious many of its victims might commit suicide if they knew they had it in order to prevent other members of their family from becoming infected. Thus, they had another reason for refusing to report cases. Some physicians justified their reticence on other grounds: "We aren't paid for reporting cases," one doctor admitted bluntly, "why should we be required to work for nothing?"

Yet efficient public health work depended above all upon prompt discovery and registration, and then segregation, of all carriers of the disease—a measure of control, in other words, not simply scientific knowledge and public education. So the next battle in the campaign was to obtain legislation that would bring this about. In 1908, the New York State reformers succeeded in getting a statute through the legislature providing for the mandatory reporting of tuberculosis by physicians, with prosecution for willful violation. It also made local health boards responsible for home supervision of reported cases, free sputum analysis, and the disinfection and renovation of apartments occupied or vacated by consumptives.

About a year later, an equally important measure was enacted—the County Tuberculosis Hospital Law. This statute resulted from an International Congress on Tuberculosis which met in Washington, D.C., in 1908. Attended by leading figures in this country as well as by notable foreign delegates, the congress produced several significant papers which emphasized the futility of home treatment. Most important was a paper read by Dr. Arthur Newsholme, Chief Medical Officer of England's Local Government Board and an authority on vital statistics.

Newsholme demonstrated that the tuberculosis death rate declined directly in proportion to the adequacy of hospital or institutional care. Since the carrier was necessarily a radiating center of infection, treatment of the infected and protection for the uninfected were related; proper hospital care of the sick was the best protection from contagion for those who were well. Many reformers left the congress convinced that, both on humanitarian grounds and in the interest of public safety, no substitute could be found for institutional care.

Like all other states, New York had an appalling lack of proper accommodations for its victims of the "white plague." Most of the afflicted were either in general wards of hospitals (where they spread the disease to other patients), in almshouses, or in their miserable slum flats. In the words of A.S. Knopf, a renowned authority on the subject, "the majority of America's tubercular are going to die, not because they are incurable, but because there is no place to cure them." One investigator estimated that "no city in the whole country has public institutions available for consumptives which would accommodate one in twenty of its citizens actually perishing for the lack of the simplest treatment," and "no state has institutions which could house one in fifty of its tuberculosis victims."

Public health workers realized that it was too costly for private sources to build and maintain the broad network of badly needed hospitals. In any event, it was a public matter; for an individual or a needy family to bear the financial burden of the treatment for tuberculosis or any other deadly disease was, in their minds, the height of social injustice. Moreover, such hospitals would be preventive as well as curative forces in the community; clearly, they were a public responsibility. Thus, in New York, and later in other states, public health crusaders met with legislators to discuss the need for such hospitals.

While humanitarian interests were uppermost in their minds, they also appealed to self-interest, always making the lawmakers aware of the economic and social implications of the situation. It was argued that, in view of the loss of a patient's earning power and the enormous cost of relief to the dependent, it was economical to eliminate tuberculosis. Furthermore, the disease was not class-specific; while the incidence of tuberculosis certainly was greater among the poor, the upper classes were not immune to it. The building of public tuberculosis hospitals, then, was neither extravagant nor paternalistic. Rather, it was a prudent and wise course, a matter of self-interest.

While at first the lawmakers did not see it that way, they eventually passed a statute permitting the counties to tax their citizens for the erection and maintenance of public tuberculosis hospitals. Seven years later, another law made such hospitals (open to all on a first-come, first-served basis) mandatory for all counties within the state that had a population of more than 35,000. And finally, a few years after that, the state erected three tuberculosis hospitals to provide for the needs of those counties too small to build and operate their own institutions. Thus, every resident of New York State had easy access to a public tuberculosis hospital.

But conditions were not quite the same for black and white residents of the Empire State, or elsewhere. At first, most antituberculosis societies, North and South alike, simply ignored blacks. Eventually, however, it became obvious that self-interest—or the public health—demanded an effort to cure blacks, especially in those areas where members of the two races came into frequent contact with one another. Yet, on the whole, blacks were encouraged to take care of themselves. Their efforts proved ineffective. The lack of black physicians and adequately trained nurses, as well as the fact that the black community was too poor to support enough institutions to meet the problem, proved to be a major stumbling block. When public facilities were provided, they tended to be inferior and segregated. Thus the disparity in the tuberculosis mortality rate of the two races remained great throughout the period—about three to one.

Nevertheless, the general effectiveness of the antituberculosis campaign in New York may be readily summed up by a quick glance at some statistics. In 1907, there was no tuberculosis legislation in the state outside New York City; ten years later, it had the most advanced tuberculosis laws in the nation. In 1907, the disease was the greatest single cause of death in the state; the mortality rate per 100,000 population was 152.18. Twenty-five years later, it ranked as far down as seventh in causes of death; the mortality rate per 100,000 people was 59.2, a decline of 61 percent—and falling. Thus, the antituberculosis campaign in New York State alone saved thousands of lives each year. It also prevented thousands of people from becoming severely ill, it saved many wives from becoming widowed, and many children from becoming orphaned; and through lower relief costs and higher tax revenues, it made a substantial contribution to the economic life of the state—and the nation. The movement, in New York and elsewhere, provided vivid testimony to the contention of Dr. C. E. A. Winslow, a public health authority and leader in the effort, that

> the discovery of the possibilities of widespread social organization as a means of controlling disease was one which may almost be placed alongside the discovery of the germ theory of disease itself as a factor in the evolution of the modern public health campaign.

Next, public health crusaders and social workers attacked diphtheria and the venereal diseases, both of which also had relatively high "social mortality" rates and, in view of the knowledge of how to control them, presented good prospects of achieving success, another important factor in the minds of those engaged in the work.

In the 1920s, physicians had a better knowledge of and power over diphtheria than over any other communicable disease; through the use of antitoxin and toxin-antitoxin they had the weapons needed to prevent and treat it, yet diphtheria still occupied third place among the dread communicable diseases, killing thousands of people each year. Syphilis, like tuberculosis and diphtheria, was another communicable disease that could be both prevented and cured. Similar to the "white plague" in certain respects, its early recognition and adequate treatment were major factors in its prevention as well as in its cure; cure was slow and costly while prevention was easy and inexpensive. Yet it, too, continued to victimize many citizens every year.

The story of the battle against diphtheria and syphilis need not be told here. Suffice it to say that the organized attacks upon these diseases were also successful, again demonstrating the effectiveness of modern administrative and educational methods in combating disease.

In the long run, however, the success or failure of the public health movement depended upon the work of public health officials. All the reforms and legislation in the world would be useless if they were not administered properly, as too often was the case—at least at the start.

In general, at the turn of the century, public health officers were incompetent; most were political appointees with little knowledge of the fields. Also, most states had an uncoordinated array of health districts and authorities. In New York alone, for example, health legislation was implemented by some 1400 health officers attached to 500 or 600 separate boards in various towns, villages, and cities throughout the state. Something had to be done to improve and bring order to so faulty and inefficient a system.

Once again, as in so many other health and welfare matters, New York State led the way when in 1913, by means of a Public Health Law, it revamped its entire Health Department and all of its services. Other than certain minor changes, the statute was responsible for some major revisions in the state's health program. First, and most important, was the creation of a Public Health Council, composed of the State Commissioner of Health and six other members appointed by the Governor. The council had two unique powers—to enact and amend a sanitation code for the entire state, and to fix eligibility rules for all public health positions.

Since the subjects of sanitation laws were so complex and technical that they could not be handled properly by politicians in a legislative session, the delegation of ordinance-making power to a small expert administrative body was an enormous advance in public health work.[6] And when the council provided for the appointment and tenure of all public health personnel to be determined solely on the basis of merit (proven experience as well as education and a high mark on an examination), public health work in New York was removed from politics.

The Public Health Council also ordered a satisfactory minimum wage for the State Commissioner of Health and other health officers so that people of merit would be attracted to and remain in the service. Finally, the new body gave direct control over most aspects of local health work, including the power to enforce both the public health law and the state sanitary code, to the State Department of Health and its commissioner, bringing health work throughout the state under the control of a centralized authority.

Speaking of the statute responsible for these changes, Dr. C. E. A. Winslow said that it "unquestionably marked the most important landmark in the history of state health administration in the United States since the creation of the first health department by Massachusetts in 1869." Although amended in its details several times, the 1913 Public Health Law remains the basis of public health work not only in New York but in most other states, all of which reorganized their own procedures according to its provisions.

The remarkable reduction in the morbidity and mortality rates of tuberculosis, diphtheria, syphilis, and other communicable diseases cannot be attributed solely to improved and better administered sani-

---

[6]The council had only quasi-legislative power. Its decrees and resolutions were not necessarily or immediately acts of law. To achieve legal status they had to be promulgated by the State Commissioner of Health and filed by the Secretary of State, neither of whom was obligated to do so. Furthermore, the statutory acts of the council were subject to review by the courts. Since its creation, however, no State Commissioner of Health ever failed or refused to file any of the council's recommendations, and no court has ever overruled any of its acts.

tation laws, health education, hospitals, public health nursing, and the like. New scientific discoveries, improved services by private medical practitioners, better social and economic conditions, free school lunches and better diet, and numerous other developments related elsewhere all contributed to the saving of lives. Nevertheless, a large share of the extraordinary progress may be credited to the organized public health movement of the late nineteenth and early twentieth centuries.

Social workers and other laymen whose devotion to public service was great, played an important part in that movement. They left as a permanent legacy to the nation not so much the principle that a great many lives could be saved through the prevention of communicable diseases, but that it was practical to do so. Their technical skill, political resourcefulness, and executive abilities helped transform scientific knowledge into legislation, ideas into public policy, that not only saved many lives and prolonged countless others but also improved the quality of life for all Americans.

Another element, and perhaps these citizens' greatest contribution to the struggle for health and welfare at this time, was their recognition of the vital importance of mobilizing the entire community—public officials and private citizens, health officers and social workers, physicians and ordinary citizens—in the war against illness and insecurity. And, as a result of their ability to do so, to fuse all these elements into a working team—to engage in successful community organization long before it became an important method among professional social workers—they helped to make the fruits of scientific advance the common knowledge of all, to bring preventive medicine into the organized social welfare crusade of the era, and to extend the scope of social work, thereby making it a more valuable and welcome addition to organized efforts for the improvement of the community.

Unfortunately, by the 1980s many of the older lessons were forgotten or ignored, and some new, as well as some older, epidemics once again penetrated and ravaged nearly every community in the nation. The first of these was the illicit drug, especially "crack" cocaine, epidemic, which reached alarming dimensions by the late 1980s and which, in turn, helped to spawn rapidly rising crime (including homicide) rates throughout America. While by that time the nation had launched several "wars on drugs," such conflicts had little funding and for the most part concentrated on the symptoms rather than the causes of the problem. Thus, they had very little success, especially in poor urban neighborhoods, where substance abuse, and increased crime and violence, were doing their most severe damage.

The drug epidemic was directly related to another scourge of the cities in the 1980s—the epidemic spread by a new and lethal disease first documented in 1981 and soon thereafter named Acquired Immune Deficiency Syndrome, or AIDS. The product of a new virus, HIV, transmitted by the exchange of bodily fluids—blood or semen—AIDS destroyed the body's immune system and made its victims highly vulnerable to other deadly, or potentially deadly, diseases to which they otherwise would have had a natural resistance, including some forms of cancer, pneumonia, and tuberculosis.

The first victims of AIDS—and in the early 1990s those who still constituted the most cases—were homosexual men. By that time, however, as the gay male community began to take preventive measures, the disease was spreading rapidly to others, especially to drug users of both sexes, many of whom were heterosexual but who spread the virus by sharing contaminated hypodermic needles or by trading sex, often unprotected, for the illegal substances, or to young children, who inherited the virus at birth from their AIDS-infected mothers. By the end of 1992, one million Americans possessed the HIV virus and at least 250,000 AIDS cases had been reported in the United States, about 150,000 of whom had died—and the numbers were rising rapidly. Although by that time researchers had discovered several drugs that appeared to delay or limit the effects of AIDS, and in February 1993 a Harvard University medical student apparently discovered a way to stop the growth of the HIV virus *in a test tube* (by using three of those drugs simultaneously—AZT, ddl, and pyridinone), neither a cure nor a vaccine was imminent. Indeed, even that development proved to be false when, several months later, the medical student and others discovered a flaw in his research. So, although not everybody infected with the HIV virus necessarily developed AIDS, a large percentage of them did, and would for the foreseeable future—and they were likely to die from the disease.

Indeed, the best estimate was that the number would climb to 350,000 by 1995.[7]

Meanwhile, tuberculosis made an alarming reappearance, kindled by the drug and AIDS epidemics as well as by a growth in poverty and homelessness. While tuberculosis was not easy for healthy people to contract, those whose immune systems had broken down due to AIDS were very susceptible to the disease.[8] So, too, were many of the nation's poor, rundown homeless citizens, many of whom were drug addicts or alcoholics who often shared cigarette butts or wine bottles and who huddled together on outdoor heating grates or in poorly ventilated, overcrowded shelters—terrible breeding grounds for the airborne disease.

As a result, all across America the number of tuberculosis cases climbed relentlessly, especially among poor, unhealthy (and uninsured) children. Thus, for example, in 1991–92, the incidence of tuberculosis among children increased 40 percent over the prior half-decade, and one New York City Health Department survey found that 22 percent of the adolescents living in impoverished areas of Brooklyn, Queens, and Manhattan were infected with the germ, a higher percentage than in many poor African nations.[9]

---

[7]At first, little money was appropriated for research into the problem and what might be done, if anything, to prevent and/or cure it. By 1985 and 1986, however, that began to change, partly because of gay activists who charged that President Ronald Reagan, many physicians, and other health workers harbored prejudice against homosexuals and minorities (especially African-Americans and Hispanics, who accounted for close to 50 percent of the nation's AIDS cases despite the fact that they constituted only about 21 percent of the population). Still, most sufferers, and many others, believe that the federal government has not appropriated enough money for research and public health measures to stop the spread of the disease.

[8]Interestingly, and ironically, another factor that hindered the fight against tuberculosis was the fact that since it had been virtually extinguished earlier, many physicians were not trained to recognize the disease, and thus they often (again) misdiagnosed it as pneuminia or bronchitis, a potentially lethal mistake. Also, many of those who suffered from the disease failed to complete the full course of drug treatment (which lasts from six months to two years) and thus spread it to others; as a result, there was talk once again of forcibly quarantining "carriers" in hospitals or other long-term facilities, although since most states had not revised or updated their antituberculosis statutes enacted early in the century, there was some question concerning their legality today.

[9]It should be mentioned that the 1980s also witnessed a resurgence of measles, one of the most contagious of all diseases but one that is preventable by a vaccine (developed in 1963), and

Thus, by the early 1990s, a sinister combination of drug abuse, AIDS, and tuberculosis ran loose throughout the United States and showed no signs of abating. It was evident that Americans needed to undertake a massive new public health crusade to put an end to the staggering human and financial waste. Again, however, whether or not they had the will and the resources to do so, remained to be seen. Meanwhile, to go back to the early twentieth century, other developments, including the appearance of settlement houses in America's larger cities, were helping to improve the nation's urban areas—and the lives of their many inhabitants.

Bibliography

ADAMS, SAMUEL HOPKINS. "Guardians of the Public Health," *McClure's Magazine* 31 (July 1908): 241–52.

———. "Tuberculosis: The Real Race Suicide," *McClure's Magazine* 24 (January 1905): 234–49.

BARTLETT, HARRIET M. *Fifty Years of Social Work in the Medical Setting.* New York: National Association of Social Workers, 1957.

———. "Ida M. Cannon: Pioneer in Medical Social Work," *Social Service Review* 49 (June 1975): 208–29.

———. *Social Work Practice in the Health Field.* New York: National Association of Social Workers, 1961.

BOAS, ERNST. "The Contribution of Medical Social Work to Medical Care," *Social Service Review* 13 (December 1939): 626–33.

hence one that had been all but eliminated. It, too, proved difficult for physicians to diagnose promptly, because many of them had not been exposed to such cases during their medical training. While measles certainly was not the rampant scourge it once was—wiping out hundreds of people at a time in colonial America, for example—it was a very serious problem once again, especially among children who never were inoculated against the disease. In fact, in recent surveys of major cities around the United States—the only industrialized country in the world that did not guarantee free vaccine against measles and other childhood diseases for all of its youngsters, and one that had close to the lowest immunization rate in the Western Hemisphere—the federal Centers for Disease Control and Prevention found that the immunization level among two-year-olds often ranged from only 45 to 60 percent, especially in major cities, particularly those with large African-American and Hispanic populations. Six urban counties encompassing Chicago, Los Angeles, Houston, Milwaukee, Brooklyn, and San Diego had the lowest measles immunization levels and the highest rates of infection.

BRAINARD, ANNIE M. *The Evolution of Public Health Nursing.* Philadelphia: Saunders, 1922.

CANNON, IDA. *On the Social Frontier of Medicine: Pioneering in Medical Social Service.* Cambridge, Mass.: Harvard University Press, 1952.

———. *Social Work in Hospitals: A Contribution to Progressive Medicine.* New York: Russell Sage Foundation, 1913.

CANNON, M. A. "History and Development of Hospital Social Work," *The Family* 4 (February 1924): 250–55.

CASSEDY, JAMES H. *Charles V. Chapin and the Public Health Movement.* Cambridge, Mass.: Harvard University Press, 1962.

———. "The Roots of American Sanitary Reform, 1843–47: Seven Letters from John R. Griscom to Lemuel Shattuck," *Journal of the History of Medicine and Allied Sciences* 30 (April 1975): 136–41.

CHADWICK, EDWIN. *The Sanitary Condition of the Labouring Population of Great Britain,* in Roy Lubove, ed., *Social Welfare in Transition.* Pittsburgh: University of Pittsburgh Press, 1966.

CHADWICK, H. D., AND A. S. POPE. *The Modern Attack on Tuberculosis.* New York: Commonwealth Fund, 1946.

DUBLIN, LOUIS I. *Twenty-five Years of Health Progress.* New York: Metropolitan Life Insurance, 1937.

DUFFY, JOHN. *A History of Public Health in New York City, 1625–1966,* 2 Vols. New York: Russell Sage Foundation, 1968–74.

———. *The Sanitarians: A History of American Public Health.* Urbana: University of Illinois Press, 1992.

ELIOT, MARTHA M. "New Frontiers of Health and Welfare," *Social Service Review* 15 (December 1941): 636–50.

FLEMING, DONALD H. *William H. Welch and the Rise of Modern Medicine.* Boston: Little, Brown, 1954.

FOX, DANIEL. "Social Policy and City Politics: Tuberculosis Reporting in New York, 1889–1900," *Bulletin of the History of Medicine* 49 (Summer 1975): 169–95.

GALISHOFF, STUART. *Safeguarding the Public Health: Newark, 1895–1918.* Westport, Conn.: Greenwood Press, 1975.

GUNN, S., AND P. PLATT. *Voluntary Health Agencies.* New York: Ronald Press, 1945.

Handbook on the Prevention of Tuberculosis. New York: Charity Organization Society, 1903.

KRAMER, HOWARD D. "The Beginnings of the Public Health Movement in the United States," *Bulletin of the History of Medicine* 21 (May–June 1947): 352–76.

———. "Early Municipal and State Boards of Health," *Bulletin of the History of Medicine* 24 (November–December 1950): 503–29.

———. "The Germ Theory and the Early Public Health Program in the United States," *Bulletin of the History of Medicine* 22 (May–June 1948): 233–47.

LARSEN, LAWRENCE H. "Nineteenth-Century Street Sanitation: A Study of Filth and Frustration," *Wisconsin Magazine of History* 52 (Spring 1969): 239–47.

MEEKER, EDWARD. "The Improving Health of the United States, 1850–1915," *Explorations in Economic History* 9 (Summer 1972): 353–73.

PUMPHREY, RALPH. "Michael Davis and the Transformation of the Boston Dispensary, 1910–1920," *Bulletin of the History of Medicine* 49 (Winter 1975): 451–65.

RAVENEL, MAZYCK P., ed. *A Half Century of Public Health.* New York: American Public Health Association, 1921.

ROSENBERG, CHARLES. "Social Class and Medical Care in Nineteenth-Century America: The Rise and Fall of the Dispensary," *Journal of the History of Medicine and Allied Sciences* 29 (January 1974): 32–54.

ROSENKRANTZ, BARBARA GUTMANN. *Public Health and the State: Changing Views in Massachusetts, 1842–1936.* Cambridge, Mass.: Harvard University Press, 1972.

RUGGIE, MARY. "The Paradox of Liberal Intervention: Health Policy and the American Welfare State," *American Journal of Sociology* 97 (January 1992): 919–44.

SEARS, ALAN. "To Teach Them How to Live: The Politics of Public Health from Tuberculosis to Aids," *Journal of Historical Sociology* 5 (March 1992): 61–83.

SHATTUCK, LEMUEL. *Report of a General Plan for the Promotion of Public and Personal Health . . . Relating to a Sanitary Survey of the State.* Boston, 1850; facsimile edition, Cambridge, Mass.: Harvard University Press, 1948.

SHRYOCK, RICHARD H. *The Development of Modern Medicine.* New York: Knopf, 1947.

———. *National Tuberculosis Association, 1904–1954.* New York: National Tuberculosis Association, 1957.

———. "The Origins and Significance of the Public Health Movement in the United States," *Annals of Medical History* 1 (November 1929): 645–65.

SMILLIE, WILSON G. *Public Health: Its Promise for the Future.* New York: Macmillan, 1955.

TELLER, MICHAEL E. *The Tuberculosis Movement: A Public Health Campaign in the Progressive Era.* Westport, Conn.: Greenwood, 1988.

TERRIS, MILTON. "Concepts of Social Medicine," *Social Service Review* 31 (June
     1957): 164–78.

TOBEY, JAMES A. *Public Health Law.* New York: Commonwealth Fund, 1947.

TORCHIA, MARION. "The Tuberculosis Movement and the Race Question,
     1890–1950," *Bulletin of the History of Medicine* 49 (Summer 1975):
     152–68.

TRATTNER, WALTER I. "Homer Folks and the Public Health Movement," *Social
     Service Review* 40 (December 1966): 410–28.

WASSERMAN, MANFRED. "The Quest for a National Health Department in the
     Progressive Era," *Bulletin of the History of Medicine* 49 (Fall 1975):
     353–80.

WINSLOW, C. E. A. *The Conquest of Epidemic Disease.* Princeton, N.J.: Princeton
     University Press, 1943.

———. *The Evolution and Significance of the Modern Public Health Campaign.*
     New Haven, Conn.: Yale University Press, 1935.

———. *The Life of Hermann M. Biggs.* Philadelphia: Lea and Febiger, 1929.

The Settlement House Movement

■ Until late in the nineteenth century, most social welfare efforts were aimed at alleviating distress. Poor law officials and charity workers administered public assistance and private philanthropy, moral or material, to the destitute. For the most part, they overlooked the actual causes of need. In the late 1880s, however, a new approach developed—the settlement ideal. Largely a reaction to organized charity work, which for a long time did little to improve urban living and working conditions, settlement house residents regarded themselves as social reformers rather than charity workers.[1] They were not interested in doling out relief, either financial or verbal. Rather, their goal was to bridge the gap between the classes and races, to eliminate the sources of distress, and to improve urban living and working conditions. Like the public health reformers, with whom they frequently cooperated, theirs was the preventive approach.

American cities, which contained a bewildering number of people—mainly immigrants who lived crowded together in wretched tenements—needed improving. They had grown enormously in the late nineteenth and early twentieth cen-

---

[1]In fact, settlement workers tried desperately to disassociate themselves from the charity organization societies in the public mind, and there was a great deal of antagonism between the two movements. A typical encounter occurred at a meeting in the 1890s, when a charity organization society speaker made the usual allusions to the failings of the urban poor and the need for "moral force" to lift them up. The next speaker, a settlement house resident, said she could not bring herself to criticize a filthy tenement apartment when she knew that smoke and soot were pouring into it from unregulated factories nearby. Only in the twentieth century did they come together and cooperate.

turies. In 1860, one-sixth of the American people lived in cities; by 1900, the proportion of city dwellers had grown to one-third; and by 1920, it was one-half. New York City's population increased by four times between 1860 and 1910, rising from 1,174,779 to 4,766,883. Philadelphia's population increased threefold between 1870 and 1910, and the same was true for Boston. Yet the most dramatic growth occurred in the Midwest. Chicago was eighth among American cities with 109,260 inhabitants in 1860; by 1910, it was the nation's second largest city with a population of 2,185,283, a twentyfold increase. Growing almost as rapidly were St. Louis, Cleveland, Detroit, and other midwestern cities.

While a large proportion of the urban population came from Americans leaving farms, the major share of it came from Europeans migrating to the United States. Between 1860 and 1900, some four- teen million immigrants came to America, and about another nine million, mainly from southern and eastern Europe—Austrians, Hungarians, Bohemians, Poles, Serbs, Italians, Russians, and so on— arrived between 1900 and 1910. Too poor to buy a farm or invest in the machinery and stock necessary for agriculture, and lacking the skill needed to strike out for themselves in a new country in farming or in any other occupation in the modern age, most of the immi- grants settled in cities where they became unskilled laborers in the nation's factories.

Thus, in America's eight largest cities in 1910—all having 500,000 inhabitants or more—more than one-third of the population was for- eign born, and considerably more than another third was of second- generation immigrant stock. By 1900, three-fourths of Chicago's pop- ulation was foreign born, and the proportion in New York City was even higher. The number of Italians living in New York in the 1890s, even before the wave of "new immigrants" engulfed the nation in the following decade, equaled that of Naples, while the number of Germans equaled that of Hamburg. Twice as many Irish lived in New York as in Dublin, and so it went.

Nowhere in the world were people as crowded as in the poorer quarters of America's larger cities. By 1893, 1.5 million human beings, of whom five out of every six huddled together in cramped tene- ments, lived in the congested neighborhood of New York's Lower East Side, described by observers as the home of pushcarts, paupers, and consumptives. While the densest crowding in London never got beyond 175,000 people per square mile, New York's Lower East Side contained 330,000 inhabitants per square mile. And although New York's conditions were the worst in the nation, similar conditions existed elsewhere, creating all sorts of problems.

Housing, already desperate by the time of the Civil War, was among the most serious of those problems. Most of the newcomers were forced to live in the cluttered, filth-ridden tenements described so well by Jacob Riis—breeding places for vice, crime, and disease. Life in the sordid, dark, damp structures, in which the inhabitants underwent a process of decay which they themselves termed "tenant house rot," was made worse by overcrowding. Within the two or three rooms which each of the so-called dwellings comprised, there often lived a household composed not only of man, wife, and several children, but of other relatives and lodgers as well.

Sanitary facilities were scarcely endurable. Several families used a common sink and a common toilet, rarely cleaned by anyone. Bathtubs were luxuries most tenement dwellers never enjoyed. Even drinking water was scarce, for the pressure often was too low to lift the water above the first floor of the buildings which, like the streets they were on, were covered with mounds of matted debris. "Look up, look down," wrote one observer, "turn this way, turn that way—here is no prospect but the unkempt and disorderly, the slovenly and the grim; filth everywhere, trampled on the sidewalks, lying in the windows, collected in the eddies of doorsteps."

Another serious problem was that of wages, which were abysmal for many of the immigrants. Whereas $15 per week was needed for survival by families living in Pittsburgh in 1909, two-thirds of the immigrants working in that city at the time earned less than $12.50—and half of them made less than $10 per week. The same was true elsewhere. In fact, only about one-half of the immigrant families throughout America could survive on one paycheck—and many could not even do so on two.

While most immigrants found life in the New World, even under these conditions, sweeter than what they had known in the Old, many nevertheless realized that the famed American entrepreneurial ethic—the notion that with hard work, morality, and perhaps a bit of luck, anyone could prosper—was becoming less a realistic ideal than a fantasy. Thus, they sometimes concluded, as did one Rumanian immigrant: "This was the boasted American freedom and opportunity—the freedom for respectable citizens to sell cabbages from hideous carts, the opportunity to live in those monstrous dirty caves [tenements] that shut out the sunshine."

Settlement house residents sought to improve these conditions, to promote social and economic reform so that those who had dreams about getting ahead would have the opportunity to do so. Where their predecessors had emphasized the individual and moral causes of destitution, drawing distinctions between the worthy and unworthy poor, settlement house workers looked upon all the indigent alike, stressing the social and economic conditions that made and kept them poor. While the charity workers were interested in dependency, settlement house residents were concerned with poverty. Whereas the philosophy of the charity organization movement led to private charity and spiritual uplift, the philosophy of the settlement house movement led to social and economic change. While charity organization society agents constantly said "don't, don't," settlement house residents would say "do, do."

There were some similarities between the two movements. Both believed that the urban poor had been hurt by the circumstances of city life, including the separation of the classes, and both relied heavily on the use of volunteers, especially well-motivated people of the privileged classes who, for one reason or another, felt impelled to do something about the class divisiveness. Friendly visitors and settlement house residents, in other words, had similar conceptions of individual duty and class relationships; both Josephine Shaw Lowell, spokeswoman for the organized charities, and Jane Addams, leader and philosopher of the settlement house movement in America, emphasized sacrifice and human fellowship, the need to bring the rich and the poor together, to reduce social disintegration and class divisiveness. The question was not whether they had a commitment to the poor, but how that commitment could best be discharged.

In addition, both movements were "romantic" in that they were as interested in people's "spiritual" conditions as in their material conditions; that both had a religious tone to them is not surprising. And finally, both the organized charities and the settlement houses believed in the scientific approach to problems. However unscientific their efforts were, friendly visitors no less than settlement house residents emphasized the need for investigation; each demanded the facts before acting.

On the other hand, the settlement and charity organization movements were in many ways the very antithesis of each other. While not all social settlements were alike, most exemplified the democratic ideal in principle and in action, while the organized charities were the very opposite—the embodiment of inequality in theory and in practice. It should be pointed out, however, that some scholars would take issue with this statement. In their opinion, concentration by historians on such nationally known settlements as Hull-House "has created a distorted picture of the entire movement." While it is true that such people as Jane Addams, Graham Taylor (of Chicago Commons), Lillian Wald (of the Henry Street Settlement), and others "were genuinely progressive or even radical in their political and social orientation," accepting "the immigrants on their own terms" and practicing "some degree of cultural pluralism," these people and their institutions were not typical of the movement, according to these critics. Rather, in the words of Raymond Mohl and Neil Betten, "most settlements were religious missions" that "reflected, acted upon, and transmitted the values and attitudes of the larger society; beyond their proselytizing activities, they adopted a derogatory view of ethnic traditions and assumed that their proper role was that of Americanizing the immigrant with all possible speed," a sentiment shared by Ruth Crocker, a more recent student of the subject. Settlement house residents also equated human betterment with middle-class values and supported voluntarism and anti-radicalism as well as Americanization, according to Paul Boyer, but they did so by more subtle means than their predecessors had used; they tended to mute "their negative . . . judgments [of their working class neighbors] or place them within a larger framework of positive comment," as opposed to the louder, more "aggressive[ly] moralistic" pronouncements of C.O.S. members. Also, more responsive than the older C.O.S. leaders to the newer social thought, with its emphasis on the role of the environment in shaping behavior and morals, settlement house residents relied on technical skills and social "reform"—such as tenement house legislation and the building of parks—to regulate the poor, while friendly visitors utilized the older class dominance and moral uplift. In any case, settlement houses, no less than charity organization societies, were conservative responses to cultural diversity and social fragmentation. Both were more interested in order and efficiency than in justice and equality, and each, in its own way, helped to rationalize and stabilize the social and economic order of the day.[2]

It is possible, then, that the settlement house movement may not have been quite as democratic and progressive a force for social change as I have portrayed it here. Yet even their most ardent critics would agree that, despite some similarities, the settlements were significantly different from the organized charities and that many were mechanisms for reform that made invaluable contributions to the movement for social welfare and justice in late-nineteenth- and early twentieth-century America. To the extent that settlement house residents advocated or practiced social control, it was because they realized (as did public health crusaders and others as well) that social cohesion and justice in modern society depended upon purposeful planning and the curtailment of some individual liberty. The two were neither contradictory nor antagonistic; rather, they were entwined and inseparable, appropriate and perhaps even obligatory. Suffering could be alleviated and justice achieved only through some measure of social control, as E. A. Ross, the famed sociologist who coined the term (and used it benevolently), pointed out in his classic study, *Social Control* (1901). Was it not possible, therefore, or perhaps even unavoidable, that the settlements reinforced the social order and, at the same time, served as staging grounds for social and

---

[2]For the revisionist view, see Raymond A. Mohl and Neil Betten, "Paternalism and Pluralism: Immigrants and Social Welfare in Gary, Indiana, 1906–1940," *American Studies* 15 (Spring 1974): 5–30; Paul Boyer, *Urban Masses and Moral Order in America*, 1820–1920 (Cambridge, Mass.: Harvard University Press, 1978), pp. 156–58; Edward A. Shapiro, "Robert A. Woods and the Settlement House Impulse," *Social Service Review* 52 (June 1978): 215–26; Dominick Cavello, *Muscles and Morals: Organized Playgrounds and Urban Reform*, 1880–1920 (Philadelphia: University of Pennsylvania Press, 1981); John F. McClymer, *War and Welfare: Social Engineering in America* (Westport, Conn.: Greenwood Press, 1980); Rivka Lissak, "Myth and Reality: The Pattern of Relationships Between the Hull House Circle and the 'New Immigrants' on Chicago's West Side, 1890–1919," *Journal of American Ethnic History* 2 (Spring 1983): 21–50; Mina Carson, *Settlement Folk: Social Thought and the American Settlement Movement, 1885–1930* (Chicago: University of Chicago Press, 1990); Ruth Crocker, *Social Work and Social Order: The Settlement Movement in Two Industrial Cities, 1889–1930* (Urbana: University of Illinois Press, 1991).

economic change, or that they were somewhat intrusive but served their clients' interests rather than their own—or, at worst, that they "engaged in social work with a conscience," to use Eileen Boris's words?

Whatever, many settlement house residents surely regarded themselves, and were regarded by others, as friends and neighbors of the poor, not as dispensers of charity; they were more fraternalistic than paternalistic, more objective than judgmental. For the most part, their work was based upon the needs and desires of those with whom they were working, not upon a pattern of behavior prescribed by donors of moral enlightenment. Rather than look down upon the poor or seek to impose their way of life upon them, they preserved and bolstered their self-respect and accepted them for who they were. Among the first social workers to realize that cultural differences were important for welfare work and the nation, an idea in sharp contrast to prevailing views during the period, many, if not all, even encouraged immigrants to retain and be proud of their Old World heritage. They also taught second-generation immigrants to be proud of their parents' traditional ways and values—"gifts" they brought to America, as Jane Addams put it in her autobiography, *Twenty Years at Hull-House.*

Too, while charity workers were concerned only with paupers—those dependent upon others for their livelihood—settlement house residents felt that their task included all people, the employed as well as the unemployed, those above the poverty line as well as those below it. The settlements, explained Jane Addams, were designed "to aid in the solution of the social and industrial problems which are engendered by the modern conditions of life," which affect all people. Their services, therefore, were directed toward others besides the antisocial, the ill, the dependent, or the like. They believed in the concept that later came to be known as "social engineering," the notion that constructive workers (reformers) or "engineers" were needed all the time, not just when there was something wrong.

And finally, while settlement house residents did not lose sight of the individual, they saw him or her as a member of a group and not as an isolated human being. Thus, they worked for group rather than individual improvement; they concentrated on the problems of an entire area and neighborhood. In the words of Stanton Coit, who in 1886 opened America's first settlement house, Neighborhood Guild:

> The fundamental idea which the settlement embodies is this: that, irrespective of religious belief or non-belief, all the people, men, women, and children, in any one street, on any small number of streets in every working-class district . . . shall be organized into a set of clubs which are by themselves, or in alliance with those of other neighborhoods, to carry out, or induce others to carry out, the reforms—domestic, industrial, educational, provident or recreative—which the social ideal demands. It is an expression of the family idea of cooperation.

The settlements, then, embodied the neighborhood ideal—the desire to create an organic community among the people and institutions of a specific location. Rejecting the prevalent idea that society would benefit while all men and women pursued their own self-interest, they stressed instead the interdependence of social groups (and the state) in an organically structured society.

This view of society, in turn, led to the conclusion that action to help some would in the end help all. It was a misfortune for all people, the well-to-do as well as the needy, if the different classes lived in complete isolation from each other—physically and intellectually. Settlement house residents sought to bridge the gap between the classes: "What a blessing it would be to the residents of Fifth Avenue to have a settlement of mechanics there," pioneer resident Robert Woods said in all seriousness. "Living among the poor," said another, "my sense of values changed, for the better. Whereas I was brought up to cherish frugality and thrift, I learned from the needy that other things were more important—patience, amiability, sharing, and the like."

The gulf between the classes, however, was usually bridged the other way—by members of the middle or upper classes moving into the nation's poorest neighborhoods for the purpose of getting to know local living and working conditions at first hand, and then helping to improve those conditions. The settlements, therefore, had no well-defined method or specific goal. In fact, the residents took great pride in being opportunistic and pragmatic—in program and in philosophy—something for which they were criticized by charity organization society leaders.

Ironically, agents of the organized charities dismissed settlement house residents—who, in Donna Franklin's words, represented a shift in social work's approach from "moral certainty to rational inquiry"— as too vague, too sentimental, and too unscientific to be useful. One friendly visitor compared the settlement house worker to a man who found a drunkard lying in the gutter and said to him, "I can't help you, my friend, but I will sit down in the gutter beside you." Another told of the elderly society matron who inspected a settlement house from top to bottom and when finished said, "Well, I do think you people down here are doing magnificent work—whatever it is you are doing."

What the organized charities people did not understand was that the settlements did not seek to do any one thing but, rather, to be neighbors and to help provide an atmosphere for ties of understanding and sympathy between people of different backgrounds and positions in life. Full of optimism and zeal, the settlement house residents were confident that if the more fortunate members of society were to live among the less fortunate they would learn to know the real problems of the poor and how, together, they could meet them.

Interested in people rather than doctrine, in action rather than theory, Residence, Research, and Reform were the "3 Rs" of the movement. And in attaining their goals, the settlements had an enviable record. Accepting the forces of urbanization and industrialization, they went about their task of eliminating the causes of poverty and making the city a better place in which to live. Because they had a realistic understanding of the social forces and the political structure of the city, and nation, and because they battled in legislative halls as well as in urban slums, they became successful initiators and organizers of reform.

Who were these idealistic men and women, conscious of real problems in urban-industrial America, confident that they could be solved, and certain that the settlement ideal was the key to the solution? As a group they were quite young, averaging only about twenty-five years of age. They were single and fairly well-to-do native-born Americans who had graduated from college. Most had been born and brought up in the Northeast or Midwest in an environment far removed from the slums.

What was it, then, that impelled them to postpone or abandon a comfortable way of life for one of social reform in some of America's most wretched neighborhoods? For one thing, they were members of the first sizable generation of American college graduates, men and women, who came to maturity in an industrial or commercial society in which there was no clearly defined place for them. With big business at the top and organized labor at the bottom, many felt alienated from the society into which they had been born.[3] The complexity and challenge of the large city, however, offered them opportunities to create meaningful careers for themselves and, at the same time, to rescue society from the social ills resulting from rapid industrial and urban change. Instead of pulling up stakes and heading west, as they might have done a half-century earlier, these young people became "settlers" in the slums in order to help discover solutions to the social and economic problems of the new frontier—the wilderness of the modern city, or perhaps "the jungle," as Upton Sinclair would call it. This was especially true for many young women, who, if they wished to embark upon a career, had few other useful activities open to them.

By the late nineteenth century, the higher education of American women was an established fact; as early as 1880, about one-third of all students enrolled in institutions of higher learning were women, and the percentage would increase over the next few decades. The chief difficulty facing American women, then, was not securing a college degree but using it. Those graduates who were unwilling or unable either to return home, get married, and settle down as wives and mothers or to perform work for which they were vastly overqualified had difficulty finding suitable employment, especially in the professions. Either the difficulties and social disapproval facing them were sufficient to keep many from seeking such work, or most professions barred their admission. Nursing, which by now had been elevated to a profession, was open to women, as was teaching, especially at the lower grades. Most of the other professions, however, including law and medicine, were still largely closed to them. As a result, America had a sizable group of educated women searching for self-satisfaction and a way to play a more important role in society than custom permitted. For many of these women, social service, especially settlement house work, proved to be an acceptable solution to the problem. Not

---

[3]Basically, this is the so-called Hofstadter or status thesis, the idea that the reform spirit derived less from external changes or conditions in American society than from the alienation of the professional classes, those with learning and skills; their security and status threatened by industrialists at the top and political bosses and labor union leaders at the bottom, they became reformers. See Richard Hofstadter, *The Age of Reform* (New York: Knopf, 1956), esp. pp. 131–72.

only was it a socially viable alternative to married family life that provided opportunities for them to utilize their college educations and to influence public policy, but it also furnished a supportive atmosphere in an often otherwise hostile environment, one that allowed them to develop their talents and enjoy ties of companionship and sociability like those they had nurtured and come to cherish while at college, especially at female institutions. As Dr. Alice Hamilton, the well-known social activist who remained single and who specialized in industrial medicine, said of Hull-House, where she resided for many years, "The life there satisfied every longing—for companionship, for the excitement of new experiences, for constant intellectual stimulation and for the sense of being caught up in a big movement. . . ."

Many of these people, men and women alike, had discovered the city and its problems firsthand, either while at college or during the depression of 1893. Others read about it in the muckraking magazines and books that came from the nation's presses at the time, works that depicted in lurid detail many of the nation's urban problems and social injustices. But it was more than a loss in status and hostile feelings toward those who possessed power, or the discovery and challenge of the city, or the desire for some avenue of satisfaction or advancement, that made many settlement workers want to serve. As Allen Davis, the historian of the movement, has demonstrated, most residents took their religion seriously, and religious feeling was an important factor in the conversion to settlement work and social reform. Jane Addams, in describing her own motivating "impulse to share the lives of the poor," spoke for many when she indicated that it came from a desire "to make social service . . . express the spirit of Christ." Influenced by the militant Social Gospel movement of the day, an attempt by liberal Protestant ministers in the late nineteenth century to revitalize the Church and recapture the militant spirit of Christ by concerning it with matters of poverty and social justice and by aligning it with the working rather than the employing classes, these neophytes found in settlement work a sense of mission to God and to mankind that had been aroused and nurtured by the religion of their youth. Instead of entering the ministry, which for the most part was closed to women (or becoming teachers as so many of their parents had done and as they might have done otherwise), they chose a life of practical helpfulness to the poor, one that was devoid of theological doctrines and ritualistic practices, one that would give them more satisfaction than was afforded by the cloth (or the classroom). Settlement house work, then, was for many a practical substitute for a religious (or educational) vocation, one that allowed them to translate theory into action, to practice rather than preach (or teach).

In addition, many of the women who became residents—well over 40 percent—had fathers or other male family members who were, or had been, active in some way in "politics," another field that was closed to women at the time. Settlement house work, then, no doubt was for many of these women an alternative to that form of service as well.[4]

Others—journalists, novelists, and graduate students in sociology, political science, economics, and the other social sciences—were attracted to settlement house work for different reasons. For journalists writing muckraking articles, novelists in the new naturalistic school, or graduate students in search of material for doctoral dissertations, the settlements offered the perfect vantage point from which to observe and study the teeming city and to collect the necessary data for studies on child labor, crowded tenements, workers' strikes, racial strife, and other topics of human interest. The settlements, then, not only carried on the struggle for social justice and a more tolerable and humane urban environment, but they were intellectually stimulating places in which to live. An early Russian revolutionist who had escaped from Siberia and gone to Hull-House testified that she enjoyed her stay there, especially because of the interesting conversations and discussions; she had not felt so much at home, she declared, since joining the Terrorists.

Like the charity organization societies, the American social settlements had English predecessors. In fact, the movement originated in England among British intellectuals such as John Ruskin and Thomas Carlyle, and among Christian Socialists such as Frederic Maurice and Charles Kingsley. And while they may have drawn some inspiration from Reconstruction era missions to the former slaves, clearly settlements in the United States were patterned after Toynbee Hall, estab-

---

[4]For that insight, I am indebted to Kathryn Kish Sklar, who is writing a biography of Florence Kelley and who, on May 2, 1983, delivered a paper at the University of Wisconsin-Milwaukee on Kelley and the Chicago settlement house workers in which she stressed that point.

lished in 1884 in East London, which many pioneer residents knew firsthand.

Stanton Coit, a young Amherst graduate engaged in further study in Europe, visited Toynbee Hall and then served as a resident there for several months. In 1889, two of Coit's assistants, both Smith College graduates, joined a Wellesley College instructor, Vida Scudder, who also had visited Toynbee Hall, in opening America's second settlement house—the College Settlement. In Chicago, Hull-House, which would become the most famous, was founded that same year by yet another visitor to Toynbee Hall, Jane Addams. Although only four settlements were founded before 1890, their number increased rapidly thereafter; by 1900 there were about 100 in existence (already far more than in England), and by 1910 roughly 400 were in operation.

Needless to say, these highly educated, well-dressed young men and women were at first quite conspicuous in their new surroundings. Soon after Graham Taylor opened his settlement house, Chicago Commons (in 1894), a friend who visited him pointed out that "a missionary in the heart of Africa could hardly present a greater contrast with his surroundings" than did the cultured and refined Dr. Taylor among the many poor immigrants on the city's West Side. So striking was the contrast between the new residents and their surroundings that neighbors questioned their motives. For instance, shortly after opening her University of Chicago Settlement, Mary McDowell, who had come from Hull-House, was confronted by a suspicious citizen who asked: "Why should you come here, why should you want such a place? Does Mr. Rockefeller furnish the money?"

At most settlements, then, the residents' first task was to establish good relations with their neighbors so that, together, they could work to improve the neighborhood. The initial step in the program usually called for a kindergarten, in large part to gain rapport with the parents, but also because of the desperate need for play space in the slums. (Perhaps, too, it was a consequence of the preponderance of women staff members.) Soon, nurseries and day care centers were created, so that working mothers had a safe place to leave their children.

As mutual understanding and trust were gained, the settlements broadened their activities. They added such things as men's clubs, courses in arts and crafts, libraries, gymnasiums, penny savings banks, employment bureaus, kitchens, music halls with orchestras, art galleries, and other services, such as dispensaries in which low-cost medicines could be purchased. When Mary McDowell, the first kindergarten teacher at Hull-House, opened the University of Chicago Settlement she developed not only these programs but also a school in citizenship for recent immigrants. Lillian Wald made a visiting nurse service a major feature of the settlement house she opened on Henry Street in New York's Lower East Side.

In addition to the programs and services offered by the residents, the facilities were made available to various groups and clubs in the neighborhood. Ethnic and religious groups, trade unions, and others partook of the hospitality of these new social centers. Certainly, the problems did not disappear, nor did easy long-lasting solutions usually emerge, but by providing these and other everyday needs of slum dwellers at least a spirit of helpful cooperation and warm friendliness developed. And, if nothing else, that spirit helped to restore a sense of neighborliness and community in many of the nation's most depressed urban areas.

But the settlements did more than that. Most residents did not merely want to live in the city and work with its people. They wished to understand, explain, and write about the slum dwellers and their needs. By means of speeches, magazine articles, and books full of human interest, they produced a whole body of literature on urban ills and tenement life.[5] As a result, many citizens not identified with the movement, and perhaps unaware of the seamy side of life, were made cognizant of how the other half lived. Long before the discovery (or

---

[5]They wrote not only about the problems of the city but about their hopes as well. Thus, as one settlement house worker phrased it: "The city historically and inherently is the most important and permanent political unit," the source of civilization's highest achievements. "From the city," he predicted, "will come the humanity, opportunity, and justice that will bless the individual . . . and make more glorious the nation." Settlement house residents, then, while appalled at the estrangement between the classes and the poverty and corruption they saw all around them, certainly did not reject the city and urban life; rather, they sought to "reestablish . . . those social relations which modern city life has thrown into confusion, and to develop [in cities] such new forms of cooperation and public action as the situation may demand." See Robert Woods, *The City Wilderness* (Boston: Houghton Mifflin, 1918), p. 273.

rediscovery) of the "other America" in the 1960s, settlement house residents were concerned about the invisibility of the poor—and they did something about it.

Too, residents were convinced from the very beginning that research was an integral part of their work; many had gone to the settlements for that very reason. This, along with their personal relationships with their neighbors, with whose problems and needs they became well acquainted, enabled them to lay bare the true causes of poverty. They did not visit tenement families only in times of trouble but, living among them as they did, they saw all sides of slum life and did not consider their neighbors as miserable wretches in need of moral uplift, but as underprivileged or oppressed human beings.

Never losing sight of the fact that research should lead to action— even a rough count of bathtubs in a neighborhood was translated into petitions demanding public bathhouses—the settlements became, in Allen Davis's words, "spearheads for reform." Whereas the agents of the organized charities felt that poverty could be obliterated by moral virtue alone, settlement house residents turned to social change. Through their clubs, lectures, and other activities, they sought to encourage cooperative efforts toward community betterment. And while they did not initiate the widespread reform movement that swept through America in the late nineteenth and early twentieth centuries, they did contribute significantly to it. By providing meeting places, discussion centers, and clearing houses for urban reform, and by wrestling with the social and economic problems facing many Americans, they played a vital part in what historians have called the Progressive or "social justice" movement.

It should be pointed out, however, that here, too, there is some disagreement among students of the movement. Thus in his 1987 study of the subject, *The Sentinels of Order: A Study of Social Control and the Minneapolis Settlement House Movement, 1915–1970*, Howard J. Karger alleged that the major concern of most settlement houses was "to better the daily lives of people within their neighborhoods, not to effect significant social change activities." The reform impulse, in other words, was not all that strong. Residents did not seek to change the world, but merely to improve a small piece of it.

One other area of contention concerns the matter of race. The traditional view is that, in the struggle for black freedom, as in their effort to preserve the cultural heritage that foreigners were bringing to America, settlement house residents stood far above most other so-called Progressives. As indicated earlier, as a group blacks received little or no attention from the public or private sector in the late nineteenth century. In the South, where the overwhelming majority of the nation's blacks resided and where their lot was extremely difficult, they were excluded from the welfare system. In the North, where black poverty was as pervasive, racial discrimination and neglect also prevailed. It was easier to ignore the plight of northern blacks because, until they migrated from the South in large numbers during the era of World War I, they were relatively few in number.[6] In any event, since charity workers stressed the individual-moral causes of poverty, they could be of little assistance to destitute blacks, even had they chosen not to be indifferent to their problems.

Settlement house workers, however—Jane Addams, Lillian Wald, Frances Kellor, Florence Kelley, Mary White Ovington, Louise de Koven Bowen, Sophonisba Breckinridge, William E. Walling, Henry Moskowitz, and many others—were exceptions to the rule. In an age of widespread racism and bigotry, many—although certainly not all—advocated the unpopular cause of equality for all Americans, blacks included; they were among the few outstanding pioneers in the fight against racial discrimination. Just as they understood the problems many immigrants faced in adjusting to life in a new country (apart from their problems as industrial workers), so, too, settlement house residents, one of the few groups that had at least some direct contact with urban blacks, were aware of the unique problems

---

[6]In New York City, blacks constituted only 2 percent of the population in 1900 while members of various foreign-born white groups made up about 40 percent of the city's inhabitants. Likewise, in Chicago at the turn of the century, there were fewer than 100,000 Negroes in a population of close to two million, or less than 5 percent of the total; blacks ranked tenth among the city's various racial or ethnic groups. The same thing was true throughout the North at this time. It was easy, therefore, to argue that blacks should receive no special attention. For an excellent brief discussion of the widespread oppression against, and suffering of, blacks in northern cities during the Progressive era, see Bruce S. Jansson, *The Reluctant Welfare State* (Belmont, Cal.: Wadsworth, 1988), pp. 105–6.

blacks faced as a result of racial discrimination (apart from their problems as members of the lower class). They understood the stresses and strains to which blacks were exposed in a hostile environment and were aware of the deep gulf that separated most blacks from the larger society in which they lived but to which they did not belong. Thus, they not only had greater sympathy for their lot than did most Americans, but by their many efforts to improve the nation's living and working conditions and by engaging in careful research and speaking out on the problem, they sought to combat prejudice and do battle against Jim Crowism.[7] Long before it was popular to do so, at least some settlement house workers helped foster black pride and Afro-American culture. They played an important part (in 1909) in the creation of the National Association for the Advancement of Colored People and in the establishment, two years later, of the National Urban League, the nation's leading black welfare agency. They also served as delegates to the 1921 Pan-African Congress held in London, Brussels, and Paris, under the leadership of the noted black American educator and writer, William E.B. DuBois. In these and in yet other ways, they sought to aid blacks in their struggle for a better life.

While conceding much of the above, critics, however, argue that the movement *as a whole* was more racist than previously thought; that many (if not all) of the residents shared the prevailing belief that blacks were inferior; and certainly that most (again if not all) of the nation's settlement houses were for whites only, although, of course, there were others for African-Americans, created and staffed, however, largely by black women, such as Victoria Earle Matthews's White Rose Mission (New York City), Margaret Murray Washington's Elizabeth Russell Settlement (Tuskegee, Alabama), Janie Porter

---

[7]Thus, in 1913 Louise de Koven Bowen and some fellow settlement house workers published the well researched *The Colored People of Chicago*, which in no uncertain terms documented wholesale discrimination against blacks in business, employment, labor unions, the criminal justice system, education, housing, and recreational facilities. Two years earlier, Mary White Ovington authored *Half a Man*, a study of the New York City Negro, which also documented widespread discrimination against blacks and the massive difficulties they faced as a result. She also was one of the major organizers of the National Association for the Advancement of Colored People.

Barrett's Locust Street Settlement (Hampton, Virginia), Lugenia Burns Hope's Neighborhood Union (Atlanta), and so on.[8]

Regardless of where the emphasis is placed, clearly these years produced little social or economic progress for the oppressed minority. The general public did not share the "committed" white (or black) settlement house workers' perceptions of and concern for the problem, and racism continued to permeate American society. Most blacks were unaffected by the reform activities and social advances that characterized the era, for these benefits applied largely to those who lived in white rather than black ghettos and worked in industries in which Negro participation was minimal. As the authors of a recent study on the subject have indicated, in "an era marked by economic progress and social mobility, this group [the nation's black citizens] remained poor and powerless."

In any event, whether working with blacks, with whites, or with both, settlement house residents first sought to improve the neighborhood by means of building more public parks and playgrounds, establishing more and better public health facilities and services, and supporting improved garbage collection. Better tenement house laws and their strict enforcement, a more practical curriculum in the schools, and political reform through the election of honest and more responsive local officials were also matters of prime concern.

---

[8]While quite a few black women, many of them well educated and relatively well off, thus were involved in settlement house work, most were more interested in other things; they joined and worked for the National Association of Colored Women (created in 1895), which, for the most part, reinforced the social welfare activities of black churches, fraternal orders, other women's clubs, and mutual benefit societies. Thus, they mainly established and maintained homes for the aged and the young, various health institutions (including hospitals and other public health facilities), and above all, schools; education was the single most important area of activism for black women. In these and in other ways, there apparently were significant differences between black and white women "welfare" activists: Blacks worked largely to uplift members of their own race while whites worked, on the whole, to promote "the general welfare"; black women worked for the establishment of "broad" programs while white women worked for more restricted and closely supervised ones; black women had a much higher regard than did their white counterparts for paid employment and achieving economic independence; and finally, as might be expected, black females were more concerned than white females with devising strategies to protect women from sexual exploitation. See Linda Gordon, "Black and White Visions of Welfare: Women's Welfare Activism, 1890–1915," *Journal of American History* 78 (September 1991): 559–90.

Soon, settlement workers became active in broader fields. Beginning their drive for reform in the neighborhood, they soon found that they had to get involved in municipal, state, and even national affairs. Thus, Jane Addams and other settlement house residents played a prominent role in the Chicago Civic Federation, an influential citywide political reform group. Julia Lathrop, a Hull-House resident, led the fight for the founding of the Cook County Juvenile Court, the first of its kind in the world. She and others also campaigned for a progressive state child labor law, which was enacted in 1903.

Beginning to see the connection between justice and the struggling labor movement, concerned residents toiled not only for improved working conditions but also for recognition of trade unions and the opportunity to organize, for women as well as for men. Thus, some, including "Fighting Mary" McDowell, cooperated with nonsettlement house reformers in helping to create the National Consumers' League in 1899, the National Women's Trade Union League in 1903, and similar groups later on.

Their research and the support of others' also had wide ramifications. Jane Addams and other residents were influential in persuading President Theodore Roosevelt and Congress to launch the important federal investigation of women and child laborers in America which ultimately resulted in the enactment of federal child labor legislation. Equally important was the creation, in 1905, by settlement workers and others, of the Charities Publication Committee. Organized specifically to sponsor social investigations, the committee immediately began two studies, one on the lot of blacks in northern cities, the other on the conditions of life, labor, and education in Washington, D.C. The success of these investigations and financial support from the newly founded Russell Sage Foundation (which made the project its first extensive investment in social research) inspired a much larger endeavor—the Pittsburgh Survey.

The Pittsburgh Survey, directed by Paul Kellogg (a young man who came to New York from a small town in Michigan to edit various publications for the New York C.O.S.), was designed to study the entire life of one industrial city as carefully and as exhaustively as possible—the first major attempt to do so by team research. Published in six volumes between 1909 and 1914, the survey revealed the cost and consequences of low wages, preventable diseases, industrial accidents, ramshackle housing, and lack of urban planning. With page after page of statistics and other factual material, the investigators documented the appalling human waste and misery, driving home the need for reform, regulation, and planning. The Pittsburgh Survey, which was read, summarized, and discussed around the country, inspired many similar investigations. Thus, the Russell Sage Foundation immediately sponsored similar surveys in six other cities from Atlanta, Georgia, to Topeka, Kansas, and numerous other communities organized their own self-study programs, all of which fed the fires of reform.

In addition, Lillian Wald and Florence Kelley (avowed socialists, or "slowcialists," who put aside their radicalism to push for social reform) worked with James West and others interested in child welfare to prepare the way for the historic White House Conference on Dependent Children in 1909, and were primarily responsible for the creation, three years later, of the U.S. Children's Bureau. Also in 1912, a number of settlement house residents participated in the drafting of a program of "national minimums" for well-being in an industrial society—an eight-hour workday and a six-day workweek, the abolition of tenement homework, the prohibition of child labor, and so on—that became part of the Progressive Party's 1912 presidential platform—one of the most advanced major party platforms in American history.

Sometimes the lessons learned in the settlement neighborhood led even farther afield—to the international scene. The involvement of Jane Addams and other residents in the organized peace movement stemmed in part from the realization that men and women of different backgrounds got along well on Chicago's Halsted Street, New York's Henry Street, and numerous other American working-class neighborhoods.

By the early twentieth century, then, as the settlements and the organized charities were beginning to cooperate, indeed merge, into "social work" (vividly symbolized in 1905 when Graham Taylor's settlement house journal, *The Commons*, merged with the New York Charity Organization Society's *Charities* into *Charities and The Commons*, and four years later, Jane Addams was elected president of the National Conference of Charities and Correction, the first woman and settlement house resident to be accorded that honor), the theory that if an individual depended upon others for his or her maintenance it was due to some inherent personal defect or weakness was being reexamined. Settlement house residents and others, including charity organization society agents, did not deny that personal frailties and shortcomings contributed materially to want and insecurity, but they considered a poor environment or other adverse social or economic factors the basic causes of poverty. Actually, some went even further, such as Edward T. Devine, who declared: "Personal depravity is as foreign to any sound theory of the hardships of our modern poor as witchcraft or demonic possession . . . these hardships are economic, social, transitional, measurable, [and] manageable."

Since in most cases need resulted from circumstances outside and beyond the control of the individual, he or she, therefore, ought not be held responsible for dependency—or locked up in an institution because of it. Unemployment, low wages and high living costs, overwork, unsanitary and unhealthful living conditions, dangerous working conditions and industrial accidents, poor health, lack of security in old age, child labor, and other shortcomings in the social and economic order took precedence over the idleness, improvidence, and intemperance considered primary by earlier advocates of the moralistic view of poverty. ("Many, many thousand families," wrote Robert Hunter in *Poverty*, "receive wages so inadequate that no care in spending . . . will make them suffice for the family needs.") Poor people were no longer considered a social burden, but an oppressed lot. Social reform was more important than the elevation of personal morality; anything short of that was only a "down payment" toward justice.

In view of the business at hand, reformers turned to two solutions to the problem as they saw it—preventive legislation and social insurance, or replacing charity with social justice. As for the first, their research and experience convinced them that the social evils had to be eradicated, that the forces breeding poverty and degrading living and working conditions had to be, and could be, eliminated. To discover the evils, to draft bills aimed at eliminating them, and then to arouse the public to support the proposed measures comprised the basic task. State intervention was not only permissible but essential. As Jane Addams phrased it: since the "very existence of the State depends upon the character of its citizens, . . . if certain industrial conditions are forcing the workers below the standard of decency, it becomes . . . [necessary to have] State regulation."

Specifically, legislation to establish and maintain fair standards of wages, hours, and housing, to prohibit child labor and regulate the dangerous trades, to establish more vigorous and effective public health programs, and to institute a more practical system of public education was proposed. And, in respect to the passage of this protective legislation, the reformers were highly successful.

They were far less successful, however, in achieving their second proposal—the enactment of a comprehensive system of compulsory social insurance against the hazards of sickness, unemployment, physical disability, old age, and the death of the family breadwinner. If dependency was primarily a problem of the social system rather than one of personal fault for which the needy should be blamed, to spread its burden more rationally, to regularize financing, and to assure recipients (or eligible recipients) of their benefits on the basis of objective qualifications, rather than official discretion, made sense. Despite that logic and the many European precedents for such action, the reformers were ahead of their time; at best, they only were partially successful in their efforts to substitute social cooperation for individual provision of losses and thus make life more secure for all. While they succeeded in getting widows' pensions, workmen's compensation, and some old-age pension programs, they were rebuffed in their attempts to secure health insurance and unemployment compensation; those efforts— the successful and the unsuccessful ones—will be discussed in Chapter 10.

Still, the reformers should be applauded for their efforts. Taken separately, the proposals for preventive legislation or those for distributing the costs of uncontrollable social and economic hazards were neither novel nor drastic. Taken together, however, they did imply a new attitude in America toward politics and economics. Nearly all the proposals involved, in one way or another and in varying degrees, limitations on private property rights and the extension of public authority into areas previously regarded as the exclusive preserve of the individual. Collectively, they demonstrated a strong tendency to substitute public benefit for private profit, to place human rights above property rights, and to create a strong positive and compassionate government.

At the time they were formulated, supporters of the measures referred to them as "preventive social work."[9] Since the Great Depression and the New Deal, when most of them were adopted, we have referred to them as the "welfare state."[10]

In the meantime, the settlements had declined in importance. They had been doing so since World War I, which had an adverse effect on them. While many residents supported the war, looking upon it as an opportunity to unite the nation in reform and reconstruction, many others—including Jane Addams, Grace Abbott, Lillian Wald, and other leaders—opposed the conflict and became preoccupied with efforts to keep America out of the struggle, and then, after its entrance, with attempts to bring a halt to the fighting. The less-than-enthusiastic support by these people of America's decision to enter the war and the efforts to bring the conflict to a quick end through negotiations were not particularly appreciated by a people intent upon destroying the "Hun." Public suspicion and distrust grew, and the settlements suffered, especially during the so-called Red Scare of 1919–20; financial support was more difficult to obtain and people began to look elsewhere for leadership.

The immediate postwar recession made matters worse, as did the conservative reaction that set in with the return of prosperity. As Grace Abbott remarked, reform and social justice lost their appeal in

---

[9]Perhaps it should be noted that the same developments were occurring in England, where for some time there had been a great deal of dissatisfaction with the Poor Law Reform Act of 1834. In December 1905, a Royal Commission on the Poor Laws and the Relief of Distress was appointed to study the situation. After thirty-eight months of investigation and deliberation and the writing of fifty volumes, the commission completed its work and returned a report that departed drastically from the principles of 1834 and the idea of "less eligibility," namely, that the needy should be provided only bare maintenance under deterrent conditions. While there were majority and minority reports, members of both groups agreed on the need for more administrative centralization of the public welfare system, a public assistance program geared to prevention and rehabilitation, and creation of a compulsory universal tax-supported system of social services, including health care; in short, a positive rather than a negative approach, a constructive rather than an ameliorative one.

[10]It has been argued that these reformers laid the basis for the New Deal and the welfare state not only through their ideas and programs but through their organizations as well—"protobureaucratic associations" that were vital for the modern era. See Robert L. Buroker, "From Voluntary Association to Welfare State," *Journal of American History* 58 (December 1971): 643–60.

the Jazz Age: it was "a long, hard struggle . . . uphill all the way," she noted. The general public, keeping cool with Coolidge or relishing Herbert Hoover's "two chickens in every pot," became indifferent to the plight of the poor—or denied their existence.

Furthermore, there seemed to be less need for social settlements in the 1920s and thereafter. The growth of night and summer school programs, neighborhood youth centers, the Y.M.C.A., summer camps, and so on seemed to make their presence less imperative.

Of importance, too, were the population changes that occurred at the time. Not only did many members of the professional classes (including social workers) move out of the cities and into the suburbs, but so did the newly rich. The central city increasingly became the home of various minority groups that few people really cared about—Latin Americans, Puerto Ricans, Indians, and especially African-Americans migrating in large numbers from the rural South to northern cities. It was very difficult to raise money or to sustain interest in programs aimed at helping these people.

The settlements were also hurt by their inability to continue to attract the dedicated young reformers who had done so much to make them "spearheads for reform" early in the century. Aside from the changing nature of the urban population and the increased opportunities for women to enter the male work world, living in the slums of New York City was no longer as attractive as previously when compared to teaching school in Africa, working with the Red Cross in warravaged Europe, or even just living in Greenwich Village. In any event, for the most part, the postwar charity workers were not reformers; rather, they were professional social workers, graduates of training schools, experts in casework which, perhaps more than anything else, hastened the decline of the settlement movement.

Beginning in the second decade of the twentieth century, social workers became preoccupied with professionalization, resulting in an emphasis on specialization, technique, and expertise, especially in casework, including psychiatric casework. Casework, with its concern for the individual and emotional and personality problems, became not only fashionable but virtually synonymous with "social work." Settlement house residents, generalists without a well-defined method who engaged in reform rather than in personality adjustment and who looked upon the poor as their equals, were not only regarded as "old fashioned" but as a threat to their "professional" colleagues who spoke of clients rather than of neighbors in need and who (like earlier C.O.S. "friendly visitors") operated from an ideal that emphasized an unequal relationship between the providers and the recipients of services. Thus, while not completely dead, the settlement house movement was seriously injured in the postwar years. In addition, those settlements that survived into the 1920s and after became, for the most part, institutions to serve the neighborhood rather than to alter it. Concentrating on "group work," they engaged largely in educational and recreational programs. While on occasion they cooperated with others in agitating for reform, they no longer led or initiated it. In 1928, Paul Kellogg referred to them as "convents and monasteries" rather than the "missionary outposts of yesteryear."

In the long run, these developments had many drawbacks. Among other things, participation by untrained volunteers was curtailed almost completely. Thus, social workers lost potential allies, interpreters, and sources of revenue, all of which they needed.

Too, social workers lost interest in research and reform. As a result, badly needed social legislation was either ignored or drafted by politicians who usually knew little and cared less about the needy than about creating the jobs and contracts on which the spoils system and staying in office rested.

The decline of the settlements also brought the demise of the principle of residence. Few social workers continued to communicate with the poor and the public as earlier residents had done. The new breed of social workers talked to their colleagues in their own jargon, at annual meetings or through professional journals. They lost touch with neighborhood leaders, local politicians, union organizers, and others speaking for the poor, especially for the new groups rapidly moving into the inner city.[11] As events in the 1960s all too clearly demonstrated, social workers isolated themselves from the mainstream of American reform and were no longer friends of the poor.

The interest in casework and psychological, emotional, and mental

---

[11]Because these groups often had no indigenous leaders and, for a variety of reasons, did not develop the array of voluntary associations—social, cultural, and philanthropic—which other immigrant groups had, they were really at the mercy of unconcerned politicians and were in a poorer position than their predecessors to meet hardship.

problems was not entirely new to the "prosperity decade." Since that which affects a part, or parts, of the physical body also affects the mind, and vice versa, social workers and others realized long before that it was essential to concern themselves with mental as well as physical health.

Bibliography

ABBOTT, EDITH. "The Hull House of Jane Addams," *Social Service Review* 26 (September 1952): 334–38.

ADDAMS, JANE. "Charity and Social Justice," *North American Review* 192 (July 1910): 68–81.

———. "Function of the Social Settlements and the Labor Movement," *Annals of the American Academy of Political and Social Science* 13 (May 1899): 323–45.

———. *The Second Twenty Years at Hull-House.* New York: Macmillan, 1930.

———. *Twenty Years at Hull-House.* New York: Macmillan, 1910.

AMSTERDAM, SUSAN. "The National Women's Trade Union League," *Social Service Review* 56 (June 1982): 259–72.

APTHEKER, HERBERT. "DuBois on Florence Kelley," *Social Work* 11 (October 1966): 98–100.

ATHEY, LOUIS L. "Florence Kelley and the Quest for Negro Equality," *Journal of Negro History* 54 (October 1971): 249–61.

BORIS, EILEEN. "The Settlement Movement Revisited: Social Control With a Conscience," *Reviews in American History* 20 (June 1992): 216–21.

BUROKER, ROBERT L. "From Voluntary Association to Welfare State: The Illinois Immigrants' Protective League, 1908–1926," *Journal of American History* 58 (December 1971): 643–60.

CARSON, MINA. *Settlement Folk: Social Thought and the American Settlement Movement, 1885–1930.* Chicago: University of Chicago Press, 1990.

CASH, FLORIS B. "Radicals or Realists? African-American Women and the Settlement House Spirit in New York City," *Afro-Americans in New York Life and History* 15 (January 1991): 7–17.

CHAMBERS, CLARKE A., AND ANDREA HINDING. "Charity Workers, the Settlements, and the Poor," *Social Casework* 49 (February 1968): 96–101.

COIT, STANTON. *Neighborhood Guilds, an Instrument of Social Reform.* London: Sonnenschein, 1891.

CROCKER, RUTH H. *Social Work and Social Order: The Settlement Movement in Two Industrial Cities, 1889–1930*. Urbana: University of Illinois Press, 1991.

DAVIS, ALLEN F. *American Heroine: The Life and Legend of Jane Addams*. New York: Oxford University Press, 1973.

———. "The Social Workers and the Progressive Party, 1912–1916," *American Historical Review* 69 (April 1964): 671–88.

———. *Spearheads for Reform: The Social Settlements and the Progressive Movement, 1890–1914*. New York: Oxford University Press, 1967.

DEVINE, EDWARD T. *Misery and Its Causes*. New York: Macmillan, 1924.

———. *The Spirit of Social Work*. New York: Macmillan, 1911.

———. *When Social Work Was Young*. New York: Macmillan, 1939.

DINER, STEVEN J. "Chicago Social Workers and Blacks in the Progressive Era," *Social Service Review* 44 (December 1970): 393–410.

DUFFUS, ROBERT. *Lillian Wald, Neighbor and Crusader*. New York: Macmillan, 1938.

FISHER, ROBERT. *Let the People Decide: Neighborhood Organizing in America*. Boston: Twayne, 1984.

FRANKLIN, DONNA L. "Mary Richmond and Jane Addams: From Moral Certainty to Rational Inquiry in Social Work Practice," *Social Service Review* 60 (December 1986): 504–25.

GORDON, LINDA. "Black and White Visions of Welfare: Women's Welfare Activism, 1890–1915," *Journal of American History* 78 (September 1991): 559–90.

HAMILTON, ALICE. *Exploring the Dangerous Trades*. Boston: Little, Brown, 1943.

HANDEU, ELLA. "Social Service Stations: New Jersey Settlement Houses Founded in the Progressive Era," *New Jersey History* 108 (Spring–Summer 1990): 1–29.

HARMON, SANDAR D. "Florence Kelley in Illinois," *Journal of the Illinois State Historical Society* 74 (Autumn 1981): 163–78.

HOPKINS, CHARLES H. *The Rise of the Social Gospel in American Protestantism, 1865–1915*. New Haven: Yale University Press, 1940.

HUNTER, ROBERT. "The Relation Between Social Settlements and Charity Organization," *Proceedings* of the National Conference of Charities and Correction (Boston: Ellis, 1902): 302–14.

JACKSON, PHILIP. "Black Charity in Progressive Era Chicago," *Social Service Review* 52 (September 1978): 400–417.

JANSSON, BRUCE S. *The Reluctant Welfare State*. Belmont, Cal.: Wadsworth, 1988.

KALBERG, STEPHEN. "The Commitment to Career Reform: The Settlement

Movement Leaders," *Social Service Review* 49 (December 1975): 608–28.

KARGER, HOWARD J. *The Sentinels of Order: A Study of Social Control and the Minneapolis Settlement House Movement, 1915–1950.* New York: University Press of America, 1987.

KIRSCHNER, DON S. "The Ambiguous Legacy: Social Justice and Social Control in the Progressive Era," *Historical Reflections* 2 (June 1975): 69–88.

KOGUT, ALVIN. "The Settlements and Ethnicity, 1890–1914," *Social Work* 17 (May 1972): 22–31.

LEIBY, JAMES. "How Social Workers Viewed the Immigration Problem— 1880–1930," in *Current Issues in Social Work Seen in Historical Perspective.* New York: Council on Social Work Education, 1962.

———. "Social Welfare Institutions and the Poor," *Social Casework* 49 (February 1968): 90–95.

LEIGHNINGER, LESLIE. "Social Workers, Immigrants, and Historians: A ReExamination," *Journal of Sociology and Social Welfare* 2 (Spring 1975): 326–44.

LEVINE, DANIEL. *Jane Addams and the Liberal Tradition.* Madison, Wis.: State Historical Society, 1971.

LISSAK, RIVKA. "Myth and Reality: The Pattern of Relationships Between the Hull House Circle and the 'New Immigrants' on Chicago's West Side, 1890–1919," *Journal of American Ethnic History* 2 (Spring 1983): 21–50.

LUBOVE, ROY. *The Progressives and the Slums.* Pittsburgh: University of Pittsburgh Press, 1962.

MCCLYMER, JOHN F. *War and Welfare: Social Engineering in America.* Westport, Conn.: Greenwood, 1980.

MAY, HENRY F. *Protestant Churches and Industrial America.* New York: Harper, 1949.

MOHL, RAYMOND, AND NEIL BETTEN. "Paternalism and Pluralism: Immigrants and Social Welfare in Gary, Indiana, 1906–1940," *American Studies* 15 (Spring 1974): 5–30.

NATHAN, MAUD. *The Story of an Epoch Making Movement.* Garden City, N.Y.: Doubleday, 1926.

OVINGTON, MARY W. *The Walls Came Tumbling Down.* New York: Harcourt, Brace, 1947.

PACEY, LORENE M., ed. *Readings in the Development of Settlement Work.* New York: Association Press, 1950.

PICHT, WERNER. *Toynbee Hall and the English Settlement Movement.* New York: Macmillan, 1914.

REAMER, FREDERIC G. "The Concept of Paternalism in Social Work, *Social Service Review* 57 (June 1983): 254–71.

REINDERS, ROBERT C. "Toynbee Hall and the American Settlement Movement," *Social Service Review* 56 (March 1982): 39–54.

REYNOLDS, JAMES B. "The Settlement and Municipal Reform," *Proceedings* of the National Conference of Charities and Correction (Boston: Ellis, 1896): 138–42.

RIIS, JACOB. *How the Other Half Lives.* New York: Scribner's, 1890.

ROSS, EDWARD A. *Social Control: A Survey of the Foundation of Social Order.* New York: Macmillan, 1901.

ROUSMANIERE, JOHN P. "Cultural Hybrid in the Slums: The College Woman and the Settlement House, 1889–1894," *American Quarterly* 22 (Spring 1970): 45–66.

SCOTT, ANNE F. "Jane Addams and the City," *Virginia Quarterly Review* 43 (Winter 1967): 53–60.

SCUDDER, VIDA. *On Journey.* New York: Dutton, 1937.

SHAPIRO, EDWARD A. "Robert A. Woods and the Settlement House Impulse," *Social Service Review* 52 (June 1978): 215–26.

SHERRICK, REBECCA. "Their Fathers' Daughters: The Autobiographies of Jane Addams and Florence Kelley," *American Studies* 27 (Spring 1986): 39–53.

SIMKHOVITCH, MARY K. *Neighborhood: My Story of Greenwich House.* New York: Norton, 1938.

———. *Twenty-Five Years of Greenwich House, 1902–1927.* New York: Greenwich House, 1927.

TAYLOR, GRAHAM. *Chicago Commons Through Forty Years.* Chicago: University of Chicago Press, 1936.

———. *Pioneering on Social Frontiers.* Chicago: University of Chicago Press, 1930.

TAYLOR, LEA D. "The Social Settlement and Civic Responsibility—The Life Work of Mary McDowell and Graham Taylor," *Social Service Review* 28 (March 1954): 31–40.

TROLANDER, JUDITH. "Hull-House and the Settlement Movement," *Journal of Urban History* 17 (August 1991): 410–20.

TURNER, JAMES C. "How the Other Half Lived: Jane Addams's Hull-House," *Humanitas* 10 (September–October 1989): 15–18.

WADE, LOUISE C. *Graham Taylor: Pioneer for Social Justice.* Chicago: University of Chicago Press, 1964.

———. "The Heritage from Chicago's Early Settlement Houses," *Journal of the Illinois State Historical Society* 60 (Winter 1967): 411–41.

WALD, LILLIAN D. *The House on Henry Street.* New York: Holt, 1915.

————. *Windows on Henry Street.* Boston: Little, Brown, 1934.

WHITE, GEORGE C. "Social Settlements and Immigrant Neighbors, 1886–1914," *Social Service Review* 33 (March 1959): 55–66.

WILSON, HOWARD E. *Mary McDowell: Neighbor.* Chicago: University of Chicago Press, 1928.

WOODS, ELEANOR. *Robert A. Woods: Champion of Democracy.* Boston: Houghton Mifflin, 1929.

WOODS, ROBERT. *The City Wilderness.* Boston: Houghton Mifflin, 1918.

————. *The Neighborhood in Nation-Building.* Boston: Houghton Mifflin, 1923.

————, AND ALBERT J. KENNEDY. *The Settlement Horizon: A National Estimate.* New York: Russell Sage Foundation, 1922.

CHAPTER 9

The Mental Health Movement

■ Because mental health is an aspect of total health, it was essential that Americans develop a sound mental as well as public health program. The development of such a program resulted from a combination of public and private activities.

As we have seen, in the nineteenth century the state began to assume responsibility for the care and treatment of the mentally ill, mainly by building and maintaining mental institutions. That trend, which Dorothea Dix furthered in the 1840s, continued for the next half-century, culminating in 1890 with passage of the historic New York State Care Act. Under its provisions, New York State assumed complete care of all its insane poor—chronic and acute cases alike. A milestone in the history of the care and treatment of the insane in America, the statute reached beyond the boundaries of New York in that it prompted similar action in other states.[1]

---

[1]Among the fundamental provisions of the act, which swept away all local responsibility for the indigent insane, were the following: The mentally ill in all county institutions (with the exception of three) were to be removed to state hospitals as rapidly as accommodations could be accorded them; the state was to be districted, each state hospital receiving the patients in its district; the entire cost of the system was to be borne by the state (which was prohibited from requiring relatives to reimburse it for the expenses incurred in maintaining their poor kin).

It should be pointed out that there are some critics of the act who argue that mental patients were better off in smaller county institutions located close to their homes. Most students of the subject, however, agree that the measure was a significant step forward—that patients received more advanced and much better treatment in state hospitals than county ones, many of which, from the outset, tended to be underfinanced and understaffed custodial institutions. For both sides of the argument, see Michael Katz, *In the Shadow of the Poorhouse* (New York: Basic Books, 1986), p. 101, and Gerald Grob, *Mental Illness and American Society, 1875–1940* (Princeton, N.J.: Princeton University Press, 1983), pp. 90–92.

While for the most part the federal government adhered to the principles of the Pierce veto and thus, throughout the nineteenth century, did little in this as in other fields of social welfare in the way of providing direct services, indirectly it took at least one significant action. Due largely to prompting by the state boards of charities, the U.S. Congress enacted legislation in 1882 making it unlawful for the mentally ill to enter the country; and over the next several years it revised and strengthened that legislation.

By the turn of the century, then, the federal and state governments were participating, in one way or another, in the field of mental hygiene, still largely centered, however, in "asylums." Over the next forty or fifty years, however, private citizens—physicians and members of the laity, including social workers—led the way in developing a new mental health program, one designed to replace custodial institutions with what one analyst has called "civic medicine"—a variety of individualized community-based programs, one of which was "aftercare" work.

Aftercare of the insane, or providing temporary assistance for people discharged from mental institutions, was not a new idea when in 1905 it was mentioned for the first time at the National Conference of Charities and Correction. Although widely used in Europe, especially in London and Paris, the plan had never been tried in America. Yet within a few years it became one of the most important features of work with the mentally ill.

After hearing of the idea at the National Conference, Alexander Johnson, long-time secretary of that organization who was then head of the New York School of Philanthropy, and Homer Folks of the New York State Charities Aid Association, hired two young social work students to investigate the condition of the patients discharged from the Manhattan State (Mental) Hospital during the previous three months. To their amazement, they discovered that about one-third of the patients could not be found, although so short a time had elapsed since their discharge. Of the remaining ones, it was discovered that some were doing well, some were in danger of relapse, and some were once again seriously disturbed. It appeared certain that some of the former patients would have benefited from suitable aftercare work at the time they were discharged.

On the basis of this study and the belief that the social environment of patients could contribute to the prevention and cure of mental problems, a voluntary statewide aftercare system for the insane was launched in New York. Working under the direction and control of the New York State Charities Aid Association's central office in New York City (and in the tradition of the more knowledgeable, experienced "friendly visitor"), volunteer aftercare committees for each of the state's mental hospitals were organized to provide "temporary [financial] assistance, employment, friendly aid and counsel for needy persons discharged recovered" from mental institutions.

Aftercare work—which looked not to the chronic patient and dependence but to the cured indigent person and independence—was a manifestation of the larger progressive social reform movement of the period, which emphasized the underprivileged individual and his or her social environment. Its essence was the recognition of a mental patient as a human being, not simply a case, and, like the juvenile court and probation, it was based on the conviction that an individual's behavior was determined to a large extent by his or her surroundings. "The process of cure is not completed when the hospital doors open and the patient leaves," explained one proponent of the system. "The opportunity and the need for treatment, advice, aid, and counsel," he continued, "are only [a] little less in the period immediately following release from the hospital than they were in the period preceding such release."

In large part, then, aftercare work was a formal recognition of the medical value of a constructive intellectual and emotional environment in the treatment of what are now called neurotic diseases. It was no accident that it paralleled not only the rise of reform in social welfare but psychotherapy in psychiatry, behaviorism in psychology, and public health work in medicine. As James V. May, an eminent New York psychiatrist, phrased it early in the century: "If the mental habits and surroundings of an individual are largely responsible for the onset [or recurrence] of a psychosis, we can look forward to accomplishments which may rival the success achieved in the crusade against tuberculosis." Science and reformism went hand in hand in this as in other areas.

In any event, by the end of the aftercare program's first year of operation in New York State (1907), interest in the subject, which received widespread publicity, was aroused and organizations in other states began to take up the work. Within a few years—beginning in 1911 in New York, by which times less emphasis was placed on economic assistance and more on psychological adjustment—trained social workers were placed on the payrolls of mental hospitals (giving birth, in effect, to psychiatric social work) and aftercare work became (and still is) an integral part of the services of all such institutions throughout the United States.[2]

Early aftercare work in New York had much broader consequences. In New Haven, Connecticut, on May 6, 1908, Clifford Beers, a former mental patient interested in and influenced by the aftercare work being carried on in New York State, organized the Connecticut Society for Mental Hygiene, the first committee of its kind, thus initiating the organized mental health movement in America.

Let us consider its background. In 1900, three years after graduating from Yale University, Clifford Beers lapsed into severe mental illness, which ran a course from mute depression to extreme excitement. After an unsuccessful suicide attempt, he was confined. During his three years in public and private institutions, he suffered not only from deprivation but from severe cruelty on the part of incompetent, callous, and even sadistic attendants and members of medical staffs. Upon his discharge, he was determined to expose the evils of the system, hoping to bring relief to the other victims of such harsh treatment in the nation's insane asylums, retreats, and sanatoriums.

Five years later, in 1908, with the help of others, including William James, the noted Harvard psychologist, and Adolf Meyer, the Swiss immigrant who became America's most influential psychiatrist, Clifford Beers published his famous *A Mind That Found Itself*, a graphic description of his mental collapse, the inhuman treatment to which he was subjected, his recovery, and his determination to effect

---

[2]Actually, it could be argued that psychiatric social work began in 1905 (the same year in which medical social work began) when for the first time a social worker was employed to work with mental patients in a hospital—in the neurological clinic of the Massachusetts General Hospital under the direction of Dr. James J. Putnam. The following year, a social worker was employed in the psychopathic wards of Bellevue Hospital.

radical changes in the system. While the book did not immediately alter the care of the mentally ill, it did stimulate interest in the subject. Beers then formed the Connecticut Society and began his lifelong crusade.

According to his plan (one that eventually came to fruition), the Connecticut Society was to be the first in a growing network of societies extending across the United States and around the world; it was to serve as a pilot effort to provide experience in organizing. As soon as feasible, he proposed to found a national society, a plan he carried out to the letter when, on February 19, 1909, he invited about a dozen people to come to New York City's Manhattan Hotel for the purpose of creating the National Committee for Mental Hygiene (later the National Association for Mental Health), a group instrumental in improving mental hospitals, in arousing public concern over the nation's unfortunate victims of mental illness, and in furthering prevention of the disease.

Most fundamental for mental health work was a knowledge of the disease and its causes, and a movement for its prevention. Despite the nineteenth-century work of physicians and lay reformers such as Dorothea Dix and others, these were still lacking, for the most part— even at the time the National Committee for Mental Hygiene was organized. The early twentieth century, however, which witnessed the transformation of psychiatry from its asylum-based origins into an extensive mental health "industry" located in the community (as well as in institutions), presaged hopeful developments, including an increasing concern with the causes, treatment, and, especially, prevention of mental illness.

Among the few who comprehended, or at least wrestled with, the true nature of mental disease, there was some agreement as to its major causes. As byproducts of such diseases as typhoid, diphtheria, and influenza, the body was sometimes so weakened that interference with the nervous system occurred and mental breakdown followed. Also, concussions, falls, and other accidents were said to cause insanity at times. There were, then, physical or somatic causes of the disease which, generally speaking (with the exception of maintaining a sound body), could not be prevented—by the patient or by the doctor; in such cases medical treatment by kind, concerned physicians was the answer.

Doctors, however, were most interested in what were considered to be the moral and psychological causes of insanity, such things as intemperance, domestic difficulties, marital problems, jealousy, pride, excessive ambitions, personal disappointments, daydreaming, brooding, fears and anxieties, and especially the pressures of an urban, industrial, and commercial civilization. These not only seemed to account for the largest number of mental cases but appeared to be preventable.

The question of heredity and mental illness was controversial. Many felt it was an important, if not the main, cause of insanity. Foremost among those stressing the woeful results of heredity were physicians connected with the nation's institutions for the feebleminded. Others gave it only secondary importance at best. One did not inherit insanity, they claimed, although mental instability was another matter. This, though, was no cause for alarm. An unstable person, whether he or she came from a family with a history of mental illness or not, could escape the dread consequences through proper training (especially during childhood), good surroundings, healthful and temperate activities, and a suitable mental and physical regime. The most important fact with regard to heredity and insanity, they pointed out, was that most ancestors of each individual were normal. Therefore, heredity tended strongly toward mental health rather than illness.

On the basis of what facts were known, or believed (and the experience of the early aftercare work), the National Committee for Mental Hygiene, in conjunction with state and local groups—as well as some physicians, social workers, and other interested citizens—began to fill the obvious need for a widespread educational campaign on the causes, early diagnosis, prevention, and treatment of mental illness. Attempting to mold a sympathetic public opinion and convince the public that insanity could be prevented or cured—if, after all, the disease resulted from either individual shortcomings or physical breakdown, it followed that a healthy social and medical environment could reverse the tendency (providing it had not yet reached a chronic stage)—they distributed hundreds of thousands of leaflets endorsed by knowledgeable physicians, supplied newspapers and periodicals with news and information, sponsored lectures in the larger cities, and prepared exhibits for conferences and other large meetings.

Sympathy and knowledge were not enough. The reformers saw the vital importance of having resources in the community for detecting and treating the illness, especially in rural areas where such facilities were almost totally lacking; it availed little to understand the needs of the mentally ill if treatment was impossible because of a lack of facilities. For this reason, their chief goal was the founding, wherever needed, of free child guidance clinics, dispensaries, outpatient centers, and hospitals for the early detection, diagnosis, and treatment of mental disorders.

Social workers, as individuals and in their official capacities, helped develop and strengthen not only the therapeutic model but also mental health work itself through these outreach programs and facilities. They realized that efficient social services were a necessary corollary to successful clinical work. Moreover, a reduction in mental illness would not only lessen suffering, but because as much as one-sixth of the entire budget in many states went for caring for the insane, it would also release a large sum of money that might be expended on more constructive measures for social betterment. Crusaders for mental health, then, just as those working for the prevention of tuberculosis and other physical ailments, courted two natural instincts—self-interest and altruism; by helping to prevent (and cure) insanity, they served both the sick and themselves.

While the mental hygiene movement never entirely fulfilled its promise—as David Rothman has shown in *Conscience and Convenience*, many patients remained confined to overcrowded institutions, where they were ignored or mistreated, and others never were identified and helped—progress did occur. By the 1920s and 1930s, free clinics for mental patients could be found, if not in rural areas, at least in most large cities around the nation. There, the ailing could receive expert medical consultation and treatment as well as social services from field agents, trained nurses, and social workers attached to the clinics as well as to staffs of state hospitals.

In broad terms, through its efforts to create a wholesome physical and social environment as a key to mental hygiene (as well as its new way of looking at mental illness, especially the notion that it was susceptible to research and could be prevented), the mental health crusade may be interpreted as part of the larger struggle after 1900 to conserve the nation's human as well as physical resources. Like other reforms that sought to improve the social conditions of men, women, and children, the campaign to prevent mental illness represented an effort to liberate the human personality from a repressive burden—a mental rather than a physical one.

In addition to the crusade to prevent insanity, another important early twentieth-century campaign—one in which social workers again played a crucial role—was the movement for the identification, custodial care, special education, and social supervision of higher-grade defectives, the feebleminded, or retarded, as they are now called.[3] The ugly aspects of neglected feeblemindedness had been revealed many times to social workers, especially to child welfare workers who, in the course of their work, discovered entire families and even groups of families that were feebleminded.

Most early studies of the feebleminded, such as Robert Dugdale's *The Jukes* (1877) and the Reverend Oscar C. McCulloch's "The Tribe of Ishmael" (1888), supposedly supplied data to support the thesis that the feebleminded tended almost invariably to reproduce and multiply their kind in increasing number. The studies also showed, or seemed to show, an undue amount of disease, incapacity, pauperism, alcoholism, crime, and vice among the descendants of certain family groups, indicating the inheritance of mental retardation and these other "traits."[4]

---

[3]Earlier, they had been called idiots. There is no generally accepted definition of feeblemindedness (or idiocy). However, there is agreement that the term contains three essential and interrelated concepts: (1) marked limitation or deficiency of intelligence, frequently associated with other shortcomings of personality, due to (2) lack of normal development, rather than to mental disease or deterioration, which manifests itself in (3) social and economic incompetence.

[4]The work of some Europeans in related fields seemed to verify these findings, especially the research of the influential criminologist, Cesare Lombroso. After a series of detailed studies, Lombroso concluded that criminal behavior resulted from atavistic heredity; criminals displayed the marks of savagery—oddly shaped heads, hooked noses, cleft palates, etc. The message was clear: deviant behavior was hereditary and, therefore, not susceptible to social reform. For an excellent analysis of the earlier concern about and treatment of idiots/the feebleminded, especially during the middle decades of the nineteenth century, see Russell Hollander, "Mental Retardation and American Society: The Era of Hope [1840–1880]," *Social Service Review* 60 (September 1986): 395–420.

The first large-scale systematic survey of the care and control of the feebleminded was undertaken by the British Royal Commission in 1904. In 1908, the commission published an eight-volume report that reaffirmed most of the stereotypes, including the hereditary nature of feeblemindedness. As a result, the mentally deficient, like the diseased and the defective, were for the most part tucked away in custodial institutions and forgotten.

Concern about the problem of feeblemindedness in this country was heightened as a result of the British study. A series of further studies, investigations, and reports on the subject by American investigators followed (including H. H. Goddard's *The Kallikak Family*, 1912), all of which agreed with the earlier findings—that the mentally retarded were habitually criminal, immoral, anti-social, and incapable of self-support, a grave menace who had to be dealt with for their own good as well as for the welfare of the nation.

Concerned citizens who saw the need to act pointed out the differences between the insane and the feebleminded, for, while both groups were mentally defective, they differed in significant ways. In general, feeblemindedness occurred earlier in life than insanity. Insanity was seen to arise largely from external factors while feeblemindedness appeared to be congenital. More important, much insanity seemed preventable through hygienic measures, whereas feeblemindedness appeared to be controllable only through death, sterilization, or segregation during the reproductive years.

To a few alarmists (primarily physicians not involved in providing direct services to the feebleminded), euthanasia, or even genocide, was the solution. Wiser counsel, however, advocated eugenics, the science of improving the human race by better breeding through the use of sterilization or segregation—another import from England. Despite its frightful implications and possible uses, eugenics actually reflected the rise of the preventive ideal among reformers. The prevention of feeblemindedness seemed to be a key in the fight against crime, pauperism, and prostitution; by preventing the birth of children condemned by defective heredity to lives of sinfulness, squalor, and vice, its advocates thought of themselves as humanitarians seeking the improvement of society. They were convinced that eugenics was a reform of major value, and no doubt many people believed them since it became public policy during the era—one usually referred to as the era of Progressivism. Beginning with Indiana in 1907, fifteen states enacted sterilization laws within a few years.

This is not to say that the matter was not controversial. Proponents of sterilization met with a great deal of opposition not only from people whose response was moral and emotional, but also from scholars and in many cases from social workers, who argued that the research behind the movement was inadequate. While they acknowledged that the problem was a serious one and a matter of public concern, they also felt that the hereditary transmission of mental and moral characteristics according to known genetic laws had not been conclusively proved. For them, the most practical and acceptable means of controlling the reproduction of the feebleminded was not with a scalpel, but through incarceration and segregation during the childbearing years. It was a less radical and a more morally, religiously, and scientifically defensible means of achieving the desired goal; it was, as one well-known reformer put it, "kindly elimination."

Unfortunately, there were not enough facilities to go around. Studies of the problem demonstrated both the evils that resulted from allowing the feebleminded to remain at large, and the overcrowded conditions at existing institutions. Hence, social workers throughout the country, either individually or through the National Committee on Provision for the Feebleminded and similar groups, carried on major campaigns to remedy the situation. In response to their efforts, state after state provided funds for more institutions to care for and segregate the feebleminded.[5]

This response failed to solve the problem. During the 1920s, it was estimated that only a fraction of the feebleminded who, most experts agreed, comprised about 3 percent of the total population, were in institutions. In New York, one of the nation's most progressive states, only about 8 percent of its feebleminded were in institutions in 1923.

---

[5]Eugenists, of course, could not ignore the birth control movement launched by Margaret Sanger in the second decade of the twentieth century. A minority opposed the movement out of conviction that, on the whole, persons who were prudent and farsighted would make most use of birth control; hence, those who had qualities that made them desirable parents would be influenced to refrain from parenthood. A majority of eugenists, however, supported birth control. Indeed, by the 1920s, they led the movement in the hope that proper education would lead the indigent and others, including blacks, to practice restraint in producing offspring, an argument Margaret Sanger frequently used at the time.

There simply were not enough custodial facilities to provide places for all who needed them.

As it turned out, infatuation with heredity proved to be relatively short-lived; by the 1920s, it was fading rapidly. The decline stemmed in part from an awareness of the unsavory uses to which extreme hereditarian ideas might be put, and in part from a growing knowledge of the complex relationship between heredity and environment. More meaningful experiments were conducted, both on animals and on human beings, which cast doubt on the simple assumption that mental defects (and illness) stemmed directly and inevitably from the genes. Other studies called into question the earlier findings that the feebleminded were extremely prolific and outrunning "normal stocks," that they were dangerous, and that they could not manage their own affairs.

Concurrently, the introduction of Freudian ideas and of behaviorism turned psychologists and others to the study of early childhood experiences to explain the apparently inexplicable traits that earlier had been attributed to heredity. As a result, new devices for the care of the feebleminded emerged. Such measures were constructive rather than repressive in that, through training, those mentally deficient who were capable of adjustment would be restored to society.

Along these lines, the parole and colony plans, long used in caring for the feebleminded in Scotland, Belgium, and Germany, were developed in America. Under the parole plan, those retarded persons deemed suitable for normal life were permitted to return to the community on a trial basis while they remained under the continuing supervision of the institution's field agent or social worker. Dr. Walter E. Fernald (of Waverly, Massachusetts) was the first in this country to prepare certain mentally deficient charges for the more normal life in the community.

The colony idea rested on the principle that it was both inhumane and uneconomical to confine to the wards of an institution many strong, able-bodied persons simply because of a mental deficiency. Dr. Charles Bernstein, superintendent of the State School for Mental Defectives at Rome, New York, was the first to establish in an extensive and practical way a colony for the feebleminded in America.

Social workers—who, as a result of their child care work had experience with both parole and placing-out—became leading advocates in a campaign to utilize these plans for the mentally deficient. They had become convinced that it was both possible and desirable to remove some inmates from institutions and to place them in a more normal environment. Living and working where they could help care for and support themselves, they could still be supervised for their own and the public's safety. Placing-out also offered the further advantage of releasing institutional beds for more serious cases, especially for those from whom society needed protection.

The wisdom and usefulness of these plans, wrote the author of *Social Control of the Mentally Deficient*, published in 1930, "have been amply demonstrated." For the patients, they provided an outlet for energies through practical vocational training and actual development, as well as an opportunity to prove their ability to return to community life. For the public at large, the parole and colony systems offered a means of segregating and training large numbers of subnormal individuals without heavy tax burdens. (And for employers, these plans provided lots of low-wage, menial laborers.)

Still, not all of the mentally deficient were brought under state or medical supervision; many could not be located, and others would not "surrender." Therefore, many remained at large, where they apparently were living law-abiding and self-supporting lives in their communities without professional supervision. Others, however, attended public schools. Consequently, reformers and service providers turned their attention to helping to organize special classes for these handicapped youngsters.

The first special class for the mentally deficient in an American public school was established in Providence, Rhode Island, in 1896. Few other school systems followed suit, however, even when Alfred Binet's famous psychiatric testing techniques, which suggested that intelligence could be scientifically measured and classes established on that basis, reached America in 1906. Those school systems that did set up such classes usually made them voluntary. As a result, there were few in existence when in 1917 New York (and subsequently other states) made such classes mandatory. State aid, which social workers helped to obtain, was effective in increasing their number and quality since, in order to be eligible for the aid, school systems usually required that teachers meet exacting qualifications.

In the meantime, the movement to prevent insanity continued, with disappointing results. In a sequel to his earlier study on the nineteenth-century origins of institutions for the deviant and dependent, David Rothman has told the story of their twentieth-century alternatives—the mental hygiene programs, psychopathic hospitals, and outpatient clinics discussed earlier. In that work, *Conscience and Convenience*, he argued that those measures, designed to replace earlier insane asylums, most of which had begun as relatively good therapeutic and curative hospitals but, by the late nineteenth century, had become repressive, dehumanizing custodial institutions, also fell far short of their goals. According to Rothman, they failed chiefly because personnel in the field, primarily superintendents of the older institutions, "conveniently" used the reforms (including expanded state authority) to their own advantage and succeeded in more or less perpetuating the status quo.

Whatever the reason, the number of mentally ill in need of institutional treatment continued to rise. In most states, the number of mental patients equaled that of all other state dependents combined. Overcrowding in hospitals was extremely serious and interfered with proper care and treatment. Furthermore, many of the aged buildings were firetraps and in dangerous states of disrepair. Throughout the 1920s and 1930s, concerned citizens labored with some success to finance programs to repair old and to build new mental institutions.

Such programs, however, could not keep pace with the high annual increase in mental illness. New developments in the field, though, finally began to have some impact. The use of "extrainstitutional" methods of care (parole and boarding-out) for selected mental patients (as well as for retardates), the discovery of insulin shock treatment as a cure for some forms of mental illness, and the appearance (in the 1940s) of other cheaper and more easily administered forms of shock therapy—Metrazol and electric—at least slowed the rate of growth of the nation's mental institutions, for the first time in American history.

About then, one of the most outstanding examples of a private agency's contributions to mental health and national welfare was conceived of and initiated by Katharine Ecob of the New York State Charities Aid Association's Committee on Mental Hygiene. During the early stages of World War II, as during World War I, because of the large number of men drafted, the speed with which they had to be examined, and the limited number of available psychiatrists, eliminating the mentally unfit from the draft was an enormous and basically impossible task. In the hasty procedures at draft boards and induction centers, draftees took five-minute psychiatric tests to determine their mental fitness for service in the armed forces. Mistakes were costly to the military, the taxpayers, and the individuals involved.[6]

In March 1941, it became evident to Miss Ecob that voluntary mental health agencies could assist the Selective Service boards in dealing with the problem. It appeared that the screening of drafted men would be vastly more effective if, among other things, social histories of the registrants were available to the medical and psychiatric examiners at induction centers. Therefore, she prepared a program designed to implement the idea which—after a hurried trip to the nation's capital—was approved on a trial basis by Dr. L. G. Rowntree, chief of the Medical Division, National Headquarters, Selective Service System.

The plan included a six-point program whereby the State Charities Aid Association's Committee on Mental Hygiene would act as an intermediary between those in need of psychiatric service and those willing to provide it, ranging from offering psychiatric review courses to a followup program for men found unfit for military service. Of more immediate importance was the social service for securing and providing social histories of all men called up for the draft.

All available information about registrants was obtained by volunteer, trained social workers attached to local boards as field agents. They canvassed the communities in which the selectees lived, including employers, welfare agencies, school reports, court and hospital records, and the like; any history indicating unfitness for military service was summarized and presented to the local draft boards and to the examining psychiatrists at induction centers.

By the close of 1942, the committee had enlisted the volunteer services of over 700 social workers, attached to every draft board in New York State. At the peak of the work, some 19,000 names were being

---

[6]During World War I, General Pershing, American military chief overseas, cabled: "Prevalence of mental disorders in replacement troops received suggests urgent importance of intensive efforts in eliminating the mentally unfit from organizations in new draft prior to departure from the United States."

investigated monthly by these workers. Selective Service officials found the program, first planned for the army, so helpful that it was extended to all the armed forces. In the spring of 1943, the service was made mandatory throughout the state. And in October 1943, the War Manpower Commission announced the adoption of the plan on a comprehensive nationwide scale. Before the end of the conflict, the services of several thousand social workers were utilized to obtain the personal histories of more than a million men.

In the meantime, a federal program to provide psychiatric treatment to members and former members of the armed forces, established two decades earlier, had collapsed. Immediately after World War I, the United States government initiated a program of medical care, including psychiatric services, for soldiers and veterans who needed them. The services were rendered at local and state facilities at federal expense. The arrangement proved unsatisfactory, though, as the service was costly and usually not very good.

The problem appeared to be solved when in 1920 the newly created federal Veterans Bureau (which brought together five federal agencies serving the needs of veterans and members of the armed forces and which, in turn, in 1930 merged with the Bureau of Pensions and a number of other federal agencies into the Veterans Administration) established a chain of veterans' hospitals.

While during the interwar years these hospitals did some creative work in treating "battle fatigue," or what was then called "shell shock," on the whole they proved disappointing. They, too, were very costly, and for the most part rather backward, mainly because they took little part in psychiatric research and training and, as a result of political decisions, were located in remote places. As a result, by the time World War II broke out, they had virtually collapsed.

Therefore, when World War II came to an end, there were still several important needs for future progress in the field of mental health. More and better trained psychiatrists and hospitals were badly needed, as were new methods of treatment, greater knowledge of the causes of insanity, and stronger efforts for its prevention. Through a revamping of the Veterans Administration and passage of the National Mental Health Act, signed into law by President Harry S. Truman on July 3, 1946, Congress took giant steps toward fulfilling these needs.

Both of these developments resulted from World War II, which, like previous wars, brought some major advances along with the death and destruction. When the nation sifted through its manpower to raise a fighting force for the war, some very interesting, but unpleasant, national health statistics came to light—none more startling than those on mental illness and nervous diseases. Some 1,100,000 out of 4,800,000 men—almost 25 percent—were rejected for military duty because of mental or neurological disorders, by far the largest single group deemed unfit for service. Furthermore, of those inducted into the armed forces and subsequently given medical discharges, about 40 percent, close to 400,000 men, were dismissed for psychiatric disorders. On the other hand, a substantial number of service personnel suffering from "stress" were successfully treated close to battle zones, suggesting not only that human intervention could alter psychological outcomes but that such treatment could be provided—perhaps even be best provided—in a community setting rather than in a remote or isolated institution. In any event, clearly mental illness was one of the nation's major social problems. A revitalized Veterans Administration and the National Mental Health Act were the responses of the American people and the U.S. Congress to these conditions.[7]

Under the aegis of a reinvigorated Veterans Administration, a nationwide program of services for veterans was established, including a wide distribution of mental hospitals and community clinics, many of which were located near medical schools, from whose counsel and cooperation they profited. In addition to providing a high quality of inpatient care, the facilities extended outpatient services, demonstrating the value and practicability of psychiatric services at the community level. And finally, as part of its total service to all veterans, the V.A. committed the facilities to training programs in psychiatry, clinical psychology, and psychiatric social work.

The National Mental Health Act, which created a Mental Hygiene Division within the United States Public Health Service, and a center for information and research that later became the National Institute of Mental Health, was designed mainly to develop preventive health

---

[7]Concurrently, President Truman signed into law the Hill-Burton Act, which promised huge federal sums for the construction of hospitals and the expansion of available hospital beds across the nation, a reaction to the large number of citizens rejected for military service because of physical (as well as mental) problems.

measures. It provided for an extensive mental health program by enabling the states and private institutions to obtain federal funds for research, professional training, and community mental health programs. In short, it authorized a broad national program to combat mental illness and, more than any other development, represented a repudiation of the position taken by President Pierce in his veto message of 1854. The campaign to improve the care of the mentally ill and to build more institutions in which to treat them, begun in the first half of the nineteenth century by Dorothea Dix and others, had by the mid-twentieth century developed into a broad movement for mental health under the aegis of the federal government.

Still, conditions did not improve dramatically after passage of the National Mental Health Act. Mental illness remained a serious problem and state institutions continued to be overcrowded and understaffed, in bad repair, and costly to operate. However, a number of major intellectual, scientific, and social developments occurred which stimulated sweeping changes in national policy and a reshaping of the nation's entire mental health system.

To begin with, as in the area of juvenile corrections and elsewhere, a diverse group of critics—journalists, politicians, members of various lay and professional organizations, psychiatrists such as Thomas Szasz and R. D. Laing, and others—were claiming that professional services and facilities, especially "institutions," tended to worsen rather than improve the condition of their patients. Thus, for example, in 1948 Albert Deutsch, the investigative reporter, published *The Shame of the States*, which described the terrible conditions in state mental hospitals and the devastating effects they had on many of their patients. Six years later Alfred Stanton and Morris Schwartz completed their detailed, carefully prepared study, *The Mental Hospital: A Study of Institutional Participation in Psychiatric Illness and Treatment*, which argued that the organization and milieu of the traditional state mental hospital made patients worse rather than better. Then came the discovery of tranquilizing drugs, especially reserpine and chlorpromazine, and their use in the treatment of mental patients. Introduced on a large scale that same year, they not only improved life on the wards but also, and perhaps more important, made it possible to discharge many patients who, with the help of such drugs (which decrease emotional agitation without impairing alertness), and sometimes with other assistance, could function in the community.[8] As a result, by 1957 most states already had stabilized or reduced their mental hospital populations despite a continued rise in first admissions.

Meanwhile, not only did continued research in the field narrow the distinction between "normal" and "abnormal" behavior, but also groundbreaking work in psychiatric epidemiology highlighted the importance of socioeconomic factors in the origins as well as the cure of mental illness, further suggesting that treatment could best occur in socially supportive, community-based programs rather than in institutions—and implying that serious mental illness could be prevented by the early detection of its symptoms in the community.

It was no surprise, therefore, when, in 1961, a congressional committee created six years earlier issued a report on *Action for Mental Health* that recommended large-scale federal funding for community-based services. Two years later, President John F. Kennedy (sensitive to the issue, in part, because of a mentally ill, institutionalized sister) secured enactment of the Community Mental Health Centers Act, which, in David Rochefort's words, "touched off one of the most dynamic revolutions in the history of the mental health movement," one that ushered in an era of community mental health and deinstitutionalization practices that continued to shape the public mental health system well into the 1980s.[9] The measure allocated federal funds for the construction of a network of mental health centers throughout the United States that were to provide a range of both

---

[8]Important in this regard was passage in 1955 of the New York State Community Mental Health Services Act, which other states quickly copied. The measure offered state aid to localities for the establishment of mental hygiene clinics, which stimulated the construction of such facilities. The state could afford to do that since it derived savings from not having to construct, repair, and operate as many mental hospitals and since it could place ex-patients on categorical assistance—Aid to the Permanently and Totally Disabled—and thereby have the federal government share the cost of their maintenance.

[9]Included among those practices were changes by most states in their commitment statutes which made it virtually impossible to confine anyone over eighteen years of age in a mental institution without his or her consent; only if it could be proven in a court of law that a person was an imminent danger to him- or herself, or to the community, could an adult be institutionalized without his or her consent. Thus it is not surprising that the number of patients in mental hospitals went from around 500,000 in the early 1960s to approximately 125,000 in the early 1980s.

outpatient treatment services and preventive mental health programs—and after some hasty amendments, increased staff as well.

Deinstitutionalization—supported both by liberals who were anxious to get mental patients out of what they believed were oppressive
institutions and by conservatives who believed that doing so would
save a great deal of money—however, did not prove to be a panacea;
indeed, serious problems remained, and in some ways worsened. To
begin with, the infusion of large amounts of federal dollars necessary
to address the magnitude of the problem never materialized. As a
result, few community mental health centers were created, and the
performance of those that were was dubious. Thus support for it
already was waning when, in the late 1970s, a report by a Ralph
Nader study group that undertook to represent the "consumer interest" was very negative, to say the least: "The centers," it declared,
"have neither been accountable backwards to the National Institute of
Mental Health . . . nor forward to the consumers and citizens in the
community they allegedly serve. They have often become . . . wind-
falls for psychiatrists who have systematically ignored the program's
directives to serve poor and . . . blue collar workers" and have treated
the relatively minor problems of middle-class patients instead. Then
came significant cuts in the program from the Reagan administration,
which came into office in 1981. As a result, most of the nation's mental patients were left to the resources of the states and local communities, "with far from salutary effects," to use Gerald Grob's understated
words. Most states and localities were not very responsive to the needs
of these disturbed citizens, many of whom had no families to care for
them. As a result, many, if not most, of them were reinstitutionalized,
not in mental hospitals under the care of physicians, but in substandard and poorly run nursing and old-age homes or in wretched boarding houses, skid-row tenements, local jails, overcrowded municipal
shelters, and especially on the nation's streets, which had become its
new mental wards.[10] Consequently, concerned citizens, including
many former supporters of the change, now view it as a self-serving,

[10]It has been estimated that the mentally ill comprise about one-half of the nation's homeless
population. For an excellent, but depressing, account of the results of deinstitutionalization on
the mentally ill, see Michael Harrington, *The New American Poverty* (New York: Penguin,
1985), pp. 102–9.

fiscally motivated move on the part of the states to rid themselves of an unrewarding and expensive public burden. The future of the program and, more important, the fate of these unfortunate victims of mental illness, remains up in the air. In the meantime, however, some notable advances in public welfare occurred.

Bibliography

ACKERKNECHT, ERWIN H. *A Short History of Psychiatry*. New York: Hafner, 1959.

BASSETT, CLARA. *The School and Mental Health*. New York: Macmillan, 1931.

BEERS, CLIFFORD. *A Mind That Found Itself*. New York: Longmans, Green, 1909.

BROMBERG, WALTER. *The Mind of Man: A History of Psychotherapy and Psychoanalysis*. New York: Harper, 1959.

BURNHAM, JOHN C. "Psychiatry, Psychology, and the Progressive Movement," *American Quarterly* 12 (Winter 1960): 457–65.

CRUTCHER, HESTER B. *Foster Home Care for Mental Patients*. New York: Commonwealth Fund, 1944.

DAIN, NORMAN. *Clifford Beers: Advocate for the Insane*. Pittsburgh: University of Pittsburgh Press, 1980.

———. *Concepts of Insanity in the United States*. New Brunswick, N.J.: Rutgers University Press, 1964.

DAVIES, STANLEY P. *The Mentally Retarded in Society*. New York: Columbia University Press, 1959.

———. *Social Control of the Mentally Deficient*. New York: Crowell, 1930.

DEUTSCH, ALBERT. *The Mentally Ill in America*. New York: Doubleday, 1937.

———. *One Hundred Years of American Psychiatry*. New York: Columbia University Press, 1944.

DUGDALE, ROBERT. *The Jukes*. New York: Putnam, 1877.

DWYER, ELLEN. *Homes for the Mad: Life Inside Two Nineteenth-Century Asylums*. New Brunswick, N.J.: Rutgers University Press, 1987.

FOX, RICHARD W. *So Far Disordered in Mind: Insanity in California, 1870–1930*. Los Angeles: University of California Press, 1978.

GISH, LOWELL. *Reform at Osawatomie State Hospital: Treatment of the Mentally Ill, 1866–1970*. Lawrence: University of Kansas Press, 1972.

GODDARD, H. H. *The Kallikak Family*. New York: Macmillan, 1912.

GREENBLATT, MILTON. *From Custodial to Therapeutic Patient Care in Mental Hospitals*. New York: Russell Sage Foundation, 1955.

GROB, GERALD N. "The Forging of Mental Health Policy in America: World War II to the New Frontier," *Journal of the History of Medicine and Allied Sciences* 42 (October 1987): 410–46.

———. *From Asylum to Community: Mental Health Policy in Modern America.* Princeton, N.J.: Princeton University Press, 1991.

———. "Mental Illness, Indigency, and Welfare: The Mental Hospital in Nineteenth-Century America," in Tamara K. Harevan, ed., *Anonymous Americans.* Englewood Cliffs, N.J.: Prentice-Hall, 1971.

———. *The State and the Mentally Ill.* Chapel Hill: University of North Carolina Press, 1966.

HALLER, MARK H. *Eugenics: Hereditarian Attitudes in American Thought.* New Brunswick, N.J.: Rutgers University Press, 1963.

———. "Heredity in Progressive Thought," *Social Service Review* 37 (June 1963): 166–76.

HEALY, WILLIAM. "The Bearings of Psychology on Social Case Work," *Proceedings* of the National Conference of Social Work (Chicago: Hildmann, 1917): 104–12.

HOLLANDER, RUSSELL. "Euthanasia and Mental Retardation: Suggesting the Unthinkable," *Mental Retardation* 27 (April 1989): 53–61.

———. "Life at the Washington Asylum for the Insane, 1871–1880," *Historian* 44 (February 1982): 229–41.

———. "Mental Retardation and American Society: The Era of Hope," *Social Service Review* 60 (September 1986): 395–420.

JIMENEZ, MARY ANN. "Community Mental Health: A View from American History," *Journal of Sociology and Social Welfare* 15 (December 1988): 121–37.

JOHNSON, ALEXANDER. *Adventures in Social Welfare.* Fort Wayne, Ind.: Fort Wayne Printing, 1923.

LEE, PORTER, AND MARION KENWORTHY. *Mental Hygiene and Social Work.* New York: Commonwealth Fund, 1931.

LERMAN, PAUL. *Deinstitutionalization and the Welfare State.* New Brunswick, N.J.: Rutgers University Press, 1982.

McCULLOCH, OSCAR C. "The Tribe of Ishmael: A Study in Social Degradation," *Proceedings* of the National Conference of Charities and Correction (Boston: Ellis, 1888): 154–59.

McGOVERN, CONSTANCE M. "The Isane, the Asylum, and the State in Nineteenth-Century Vermont," *Vermont History* 52 (Fall 1984): 205–24.

———. "The Myths of Social Control and Custodial Oppression: Patterns of Psychiatric Medicine in Late Nineteenth-Century Institutions," *Journal of Social History* 20 (Fall 1986): 3–24.

MECHANIC, DAVID. "Correcting Misconceptions in Mental Health Policy: Strategies for Improved Care of the Seriously Mentally Ill," *Milbank Memorial Fund Quarterly* 65 (Spring, 1987): 203–30.

———. *Mental Health and Social Policy*. Englewood Cliffs, N.J.: Prentice-Hall, 1969.

NOLL, STEVEN. "Care and Control of the Feeble-Minded: Florida Farm Colony, 1920–1925," *Florida Historical Quarterly* 69 (July 1990): 57–80.

OWINGS, C. "What Social Hygiene Problems Confront the Social Worker?," *Journal of Social Hygiene* 17 (November 1931): 468–77.

PICKENS, DONALD K. *Eugenics and the Progressives*. Nashville, Tenn.: Vanderbilt University Press, 1969.

POLLACK, HORATIO, ed. *Family Care of Mental Patients: A Review of Family Care in America and Europe*. Utica, N.Y.: State Hospitals' Press, 1936.

PRATT, GEORGE. "Twenty Years of the National Committee for Mental Hygiene," *Mental Hygiene* 14 (April 1930): 399–428.

RIDENOUR, NINA. *Mental Health in the United States*. Cambridge, Mass.: Harvard University Press, 1961.

RUSSELL, WILLIAM. *The New York Hospital: A History of the Psychiatric Service, 1771–1936*. New York: Columbia University Press, 1945.

SICHERMAN, BARBARA. "The Paradox of Prudence: Mental Health in the Gilded Age," *Journal of American History* 62 (March 1976): 890–912.

STANTON, ALFRED, AND MORRIS SCHWARTZ. *The Mental Hospital: A Study of Institutional Participation in Psychiatric Illness and Treatment*. New York: Basic Books, 1954.

THOMPSON, TOMMY R. "Feeble-Mindedness, Criminal Behavior, and Women: A Turn-of-the-Century Case Study," *Palimpsest* 71 (Fall 1990): 132–44.

VECOLI, RUDOLPH J. "Sterilization: A Progressive Measure?," *Wisconsin Magazine of History* 43 (Spring 1960): 190–202.

WINTERS, EUNICE. "Adolf Meyer and Clifford Beers, 1907–1910," *Bulletin of the History of Medicine* 43 (September–October 1969): 414–43.

Renaissance of Public Welfare

■ From the start, care of the needy in America was a public responsibility. As we have seen, however, over the years, private citizens, either individually or in groups, undertook the providing of aid and services to the dependent. While such assistance became more and more popular, it remained a voluntary assumption by private individuals of a public task; the government's legal responsibility to aid those in need stood unchanged. Nevertheless, by the late nineteenth century, welfare work had become more of a private or voluntary matter than a public one; save for placing the destitute elderly and the permanently disabled in public institutions, public assistance had been substantially curtailed or in many cases even abolished.

In the early years of the twentieth century, however, as the complex of problems associated with rapid industrialization, a market economy, urbanization, and immigration intensified—especially economic insecurity and deprivation—a growing number of reformers saw the need for more public assistance. The magnitude of the task, they felt, called for greater monetary support (and authority) than agencies controlled by volunteers could command. Moreover, since poverty was a social rather than an individual matter, one endemic to a modern industrial society, more public intervention and aid was not only necessary but just. There was room for public welfare and private charity work. The best results could be obtained by the two working in harmony rather than by one outdoing or assuming superiority over the other. After two decades of activity, the advocates of more public assistance succeeded in redressing the balance, at least to an extent. At the same time, they laid the foundation for many of the important public welfare developments of the 1930s.

An early success was the historic 1909 White House Conference on Dependent Children. The idea to call a White House conference on dependent children came from James E. West, a Washington lawyer and close friend of President Theodore Roosevelt who later became head of the Boy Scouts of America. An orphan who was reared in an institution, West was interested in the problem of caring for dependent youngsters. He thought that a national conference on the subject would attract attention and be useful, especially if called by the President and held at the White House. Accordingly, West broached the idea to Roosevelt, urging him to "cooperate in an effort to bring the problem of the nation's unfortunate children before the American people." After West got the support of a number of prominent welfare workers—Homer Folks, Lillian Wald, Jane Addams, Florence Kelley, and others—the President agreed, and invited some 200 prominent men and women from all parts of the country to a two-day meeting held late in January 1909.

The conference, which for the first time brought the subject of dependent children before the entire nation, gave to social work, especially child welfare work, a place in the national life that it had never had before. More important, it represented another, and much earlier, about-face from the concept elaborated more than a half-century earlier by President Franklin Pierce—that the federal government had no responsibility in matters of social welfare.

The gathering was designed to perform two functions: to provide an interchange of ideas and experiences among leaders in the work for dependent children, and to recommend a general plan for their care. Through a report adopted unanimously by conference members, the meeting served both of these functions. As its keynote, the report proclaimed: "Home life is the highest and finest product of civilization," and "children should not be deprived of it except for urgent and compelling reasons." For those children "who for sufficient reasons must be removed from their own homes, or who have no homes," the report went on to state, "it is desirable that they should be cared for in families whenever practicable. The carefully selected foster home is for the normal child the best substitute for the natural home."

The meeting had far-reaching practical effects. Its strong recommendation in favor of family care strengthened the movement for home rather than institutional care for dependent and delinquent children. It contributed greatly both to the development of adoption agencies and to the increased use of the boarding-out system for children unsuitable or unavailable for adoption. Increased use of the cottage-type rather than the congregate institution—one of the report's recommendations—was another outcome of the conference.

Other recommendations on the subject of state incorporation and inspection of children's institutions and agencies also resulted in attaining higher standards of child care. Furthermore, the conference set a precedent still followed—every ten years since 1909, there has been a White House conference on child problems and needs, each of which, in turn, has had a far-reaching effect on concepts of child care and progressive child welfare programs.

One of the most immediate and important effects of the first White House Conference was the creation (three years later) of the U.S. Children's Bureau, another and perhaps even more important break with the Pierce doctrine. The idea of creating a federal children's bureau was not new in 1909. As early as 1900, in speeches at colleges across the nation, Florence Kelley had called for the creation of some sort of central agency to collect and exchange ideas and information on child welfare. Four years later, Lillian Wald of the Henry Street Settlement House, incensed over a news item announcing a large-scale federal campaign against the boll weevil (which was damaging the southern cotton crop) at a time when Washington took no notice at all of the decimation of the nation's crop of young children, outlined a plan for a federal children's bureau which she, Kelley, and Edward T. Devine took to the White House. President Roosevelt like the idea and agreed to support it.

Next, Lillian Wald and Florence Kelley, both board members of the National Child Labor Committee, induced that organization to draft a bill for the proposed bureau which was introduced in Congress in 1906. The National Child Labor Committee marshaled support for the measure throughout the nation; prominent citizens, welfare groups, educational associations, newspapers, and others came out in its favor. Opposition to the proposal, however, was violent, especially from business interests fearful that creation of the bureau would lead to the end of child labor, a practice they had a vested interest in preserving. As a result, the bill was never even debated; for several years, it merely languished in committee.

Then came the 1909 White House Conference, which recommended not only that the bill be passed, but that the President send Congress a special message on its behalf. Roosevelt readily complied. "It is not only discreditable to us as a people that there is no recognized and authoritative source of information upon . . . subjects related to child life," the Chief Executive told the nation's lawmakers, "but in the absence of such information as should be supplied by the Federal Government many abuses have gone unchecked. . . ."

The recommendations of the White House Conference and the publicity they received, along with President Roosevelt's support and special message, forced Congress into finally acting. Unable to continue to ignore the matter, lawmakers reluctantly called for public hearings on the bill. Many of those who had attended the White House Conference returned to Washington to appear before Congress and testify on behalf of the measure. The main theme of their testimony was the fact that, through the Bureau of Animal Husbandry within the Department of Agriculture, which had a staff of more than 1000 and an annual appropriation of nearly $1,250,000, the federal government spent far more money each year on animal research than on research into the problems of childhood—and, as a result, the mortality rate of young animals was lower than that of young children.

Still, three more years were to pass before the measure, which called for an appropriation of $50,000 and a staff of fourteen, won approval. In the meantime, numerous individuals, parent-teacher groups, labor unions, and public health, social work, and civic organizations continued to support it. Then there were five days of bitter floor debate in which it was charged that those who favored creation of the children's bureau were working under orders from European socialists and communists who intended to use the agency to regulate the nation's youth. Finally, the bill passed the Senate on January 31, 1912. Two months later, it went through the House, and on April 9 it was signed into law by President William Howard Taft.

The U.S. Children's Bureau received an initial appropriation of $25,640 and was placed within the Department of Commerce and Labor from which, a year later, it was transferred to the newly created Department of Labor. (In 1953, it was placed in another newly created federal department, the Department of Health, Education, and Welfare.) Charged with the duty of investigating and reporting upon "all matters pertaining to the welfare of children and child life among all classes of our people," the bureau had no administrative power, nor was it to perform any services, strictly speaking. Rather, it was a research agency. It would establish the facts concerning the condition and treatment of the nation's children, and then call attention to those facts.

Despite its limited function and modest initial appropriation, the Children's Bureau was extremely significant; it soon became the central, and in some cases the sole, source of authoritative information about the welfare of children and their families throughout the United States. More important, its creation marked a significant departure in public policy. It was the first time the federal government recognized not merely the rights of children, but also the need to create a permanent agency at least to study if not yet to protect them.

President Taft appointed Julia Lathrop, former Hull-House resident and member of the Illinois State Board of Charities, to head the bureau. This was an excellent choice. Lathrop, the first female to head a federal agency, believed fervently in the importance of public welfare and in the need to rejuvenate services set up by the taxpayers to help those in need. She also knew how to use the potent constituency network she had at her disposal and, at the same time, recognized the need to avoid controversy and to divorce politics from social welfare in order to gain and retain congressional support for the new bureau. At the outset, she thus subordinated studies of child labor in favor of less controversial ones, such as the problem of infant mortality. She thereby quickly won confidence in the new agency and additional resources for it; by 1915, for example, its funds had achieved a sixfold increase and its staff had multiplied by a factor of five.

Meanwhile, a "baby-saving" campaign had been initiated in America in 1908 when the New York City Department of Health set up a Division of Child Hygiene—the first official admission by a large American city that child health was worthy of special attention from a public health department. Another landmark in the movement to lower the infant mortality rate was a 1909 Conference on the Prevention of Infant Mortality held at Yale University. Called at the request of the America Academy of Medicine, the conference attracted a number of prominent physicians, social workers, sociologists, and educators. The American Association for the Study and Prevention of Infant Mortality, which proved to be instrumental in reducing the infant mortality rate, had its inception at this gathering.

There was, then, some precedent for engaging in infant hygiene work when, in 1913, the newly created Children's Bureau undertook as its initial major project a study to determine, first, how many babies died each year, and second, why. To the dismay of many—members of the general public as well as those who worked as in the field—the bureau's investigators found not only a shockingly high infant mortality rate—caused, as earlier studies had indicated, by deficient family income as well as by a lack of adequate medical facilities—but they discovered an exceedingly high death rate for mothers as well. That more women died unnecessarily each year during childbirth (or lived on afterward in chronic invalidism) than from any other cause except tuberculosis, was a startling revelation. Moreover, the maternal death rate was higher in America than in any other leading nation in the world; hence, the large number of orphans in the nation.

Uncovering this information was not enough for Julia Lathrop, who in 1917 drew up a plan for the "public protection of maternity and infancy" and published it in her *Annual Report* to Congress. Her idea was that the federal government should aid the states to improve their maternal and child health facilities and services, especially in rural areas, where such provisions were especially lacking or poor. The government would offer grants-in-aid, on a matching basis, to those states promising to establish facilities and services such as public health nursing and education, outpatient clinics, hospitals, better inspection of maternity homes, and the like, in accordance with specifications established by the Children's Bureau. State health departments would administer the grants.[1]

---

[1]Two things should be noted in this connection. First, impetus for the proposal came from America's World War I experience as well as from Children's Bureau studies. As noted earlier, during the war, thousands of men were rejected from the military draft because of medical problems, many of which could have been averted through suitable health care during infancy and childhood. And second, while rural areas throughout the nation had few such facilities, this was especially true of the South where, because (among other things) of the relatively low per capita income, public services in general were scarce. It should be mentioned that here, perhaps even more than elsewhere, there was a great deal of racial discrimination; thus, the black population in southern rural areas would find it very difficult to reap the benefits of the program.

Julia Lathrop embodied her ideas and program into a bill which, when introduced in Congress in 1918 (by Jeanette Rankin, the first woman to serve in that body), became known as the Infancy and Maternity or Sheppard-Towner Bill. During the campaign for its enactment, the epithets of socialism, communism, and nationalization of the nation's youth, hurled earlier against the Children's Bureau and other pieces of social legislation, were again heard, this time even more often because of the recent Bolshevik Revolution. Moreover, proponents of the measure had to meet a highly organized and well financed propaganda campaign initiated by leaders of the nation's medical profession, who invoked against it the bugaboos of "state medicine," "interference with private practice," and other such charges.

Typical of the attacks on the bill was a pamphlet entitled *Shall the Children of America Become the Property of the State?*, written and circulated by the Legislative Committee of the Illinois State Medical Society. Attacking both the bill and the Children's Bureau, whose members were referred to as "endocrine perverts [and] derailed menopausics," authors of the pamphlet charged that those who supported the "iniquitous" and "menacing" measure were "masquerading as humanity" while "battening upon the incredulous imagination of the citizens who feel that by this legislation they might evade some of their civic responsibilities." The Children's Bureau, they continued, "will by this bill be the ruling power in the United States. This Bureau, headed by one woman, will become the most despotic influence in the country imposing a yoke that will annually become more unbearable in its crushing burdens."

Such absurd charges reached the floor of the U.S. Senate, where Senator Thomas Reed of Missouri, a staunch opponent of the measure, stated that, if the Sheppard-Towner Bill passed, "female celibates would instruct mothers on how to bring up their babies"; they would "look over the nation's birth lists, check some off, and say 'let's take charge of this or that baby.'" Despite these attacks, after three years of agitation and days of bitter floor debate—and ratification of the Nineteenth Amendment, granting women the right to vote—the bill emerged successfully from Congress on November 19, 1921, and was signed into law four days later by President Warren G. Harding.

As passed, the act authorized an annual appropriation of

$1,252,000 for a five-year period, later extended to seven. Each year, the Children's Bureau would have $50,000 to administer the program and to engage in further research on the problems of maternal and infant care; the remainder was to be divided among the states participating in the program.

The Sheppard-Towner Act proved to be a great success. Between 1921 and 1929, when, owing to several factors—Herbert Hoover's opposition to the measure, the collapse of the economy, the weakened clout of female voters, and, above all, a virulent campaign against the measure by the medical profession which sought (successfully) to wrest control of infant and maternal health from female-run public clinics and place it, instead, in the hands of private, male physicians— Congress refused to renew its funds, nearly 3000 child and maternal health centers were established in forty-five states, chiefly in rural areas. In addition, the act strengthened state health departments and helped foster the development of county health units, which in turn led to the better administration of local services. The nation's infant and maternal mortality rates dropped significantly during its limited life.

The Sheppard-Towner Act was important for other reasons as well. It brought the federal government into the field of child welfare through the area of health and was another measure that aroused the lay public's interest and activity in a subject long considered the exclusive domain of the medical profession. And finally, its influence was long-lasting. On the foundation laid by the Infancy and Maternity Act—the first statute to provide federal grants-in-aid to the states for a welfare program other than education—were reared many of the cooperative federal-state programs established under the Social Security Act of 1935. Title V of the Social Security Act, for example, provided for federal grants-in-aid to the states (to be administered by the Children's Bureau) for work in maternal and child health. Yet, all did not end well. As Sheila Rothman, Joseph Hawes, and others have pointed out, defeat of the Sheppard-Towner Act "was one of the most grievous blows American [women and] children have ever received." The long-term consequences of its destruction were the demise of significant female input in the delivery of preventive health services for women and children—and one of the highest infant mortality rates in the entire industrialized world. (Incidentally, Americans still invest more money in animals than they do in children, and as a recent article in *Time Magazine* on "The Child Care Dilemma" pointed out, they pay animal caretakers higher wages than they do those who care for their children.)

The Sheppard-Towner Act resulted in large part from creation of the Children's Bureau, which, in turn, sprang from the 1909 White House Conference on Dependent Children. From that conference also came another highly significant development in public welfare— the widows' pension or mothers' aid movement, now referred to as Aid to Families with Dependent Children (A.F.D.C.).

Delegates attending the White House Conference reaffirmed the idea that, whenever possible, needy children should be provided for in their own homes. Still fearing home relief, however, especially public outdoor assistance, administered by untrained personnel, they went on to say that the financial aid necessary to keep families together should be furnished by private rather than by public agencies: the "home should not be broken up for reasons of poverty," the report stated, and added that the aid necessary to keep families intact "should be given by such methods and from such sources as may be determined by the general relief policy of each community, preferably in the form of private charity rather than public relief." Public relief, Frederic Almy, the renowned secretary of the Buffalo C.O.S. (which was in the midst of becoming a charity-granting agency) declared, is "like undoctored drugs . . . poisonous to the poor."

Unfortunately, private agencies, even when present (and often they were not, especially in rural areas), were poorly equipped or lacked the funds to do this. Moreover, agencies with funds usually refused to help women deemed capable of working. Many widows therefore were forced to give up their children solely because they could not make ends meet.

Some women placed their youngsters in institutions or foster homes; some gave them up for adoption. Others attempted to keep them at home while they went to work in an effort to support themselves and their brood, often as prostitutes. But low wages—in beds or in factories—forced women to work long hours, which not only was exhausting and dangerous but also meant that they could not provide adequate supervision over their young ones. The result, then, of taking jobs while trying to raise a family, of being both breadwinner and homemaker, was that many of the women broke down and many of the children became demoralized and delinquent. In the end, both required further aid—in institutions or hospitals. In 1913, in New York State alone, some 1000 children were committed to public institutions because their widowed mothers had become ill, usually due to overwork and worry (while almost 3000 others were placed in such institutions because their parents could not support them); many of the women were also institutionalized.

For many, widows' pensions, or public aid to women with dependent children, was the answer. Such assistance would end the separation of mother and child for reasons of poverty alone. Furthermore, it would be as much a preventive as an ameliorative device, for it would tend to prevent juvenile delinquency and adult illness by insuring the kind of home surroundings that children needed for proper development and mothers needed for physical well-being. Moreover, to assist dependent mothers so that they could remain at home and care properly for their children would require less expense, it was demonstrated, than to maintain them and their youngsters in public institutions or in foster homes. As a result, social reformers and other interested citizens threw their support behind a campaign to provide public allowances for women with dependent children—persons in need through no fault of their own.[2]

Some people, including a number of social workers, especially those working for private agencies, opposed the idea. Fearful of widows' pensions lest they become the entering wedge in the transformation of charity into entitlement, they continued to argue that public authorities should maintain public institutions and private agencies, with their precariousness and their personal touch, should provide home or outdoor relief. Mothers' pensions, of course, questioned this

---

[2]As Julian Mack, the highly regarded judge who presided over Chicago's juvenile court from 1904 to 1907, phrased it: "If we take a child away from the mother we willingly pay an asylum [or foster home] to care for him; the public funds pay for his support. Why should not the public funds be paid to the mother herself and keep the family together?" It is not surprising that many children's court judges and probation officers also worked hard for the enactment of widows' pension laws. They were as interested in the economic as in the emotional well-being of their charges: the former was as likely to be the source of difficulty as the latter. Yet personality problems could be dealt with through counseling, friendship, advice, or psychiatric treatment, while often there was no acceptable agency in the community to deal with economic problems.

informal division of labor; they aimed at returning to public authorities a welfare function that had been assumed voluntarily by private agencies—and certainty and impersonality were their greatest virtues, in the minds of their supporters.

Proponents of the idea argued that changes in the family and in the economic system required greater government or public intervention on a "regular" basis. The family's survival was contingent upon uninterrupted earnings, yet because of a variety of impersonal matters—forced unemployment, illness, death of the family breadwinner, and so on—that was not always possible. There was a need, then, for a new, impersonal mechanism that would assure income flow in the event of a decline in an individual's or a family's earnings. Furthermore, mothers' pensions were based on the idea that married women who stayed home (where they "belonged") and raised their children were performing an ongoing service to society, and that they should be rewarded for such service. Clearly, then, widows' pensions were gender-specific; whether or not they were designed to keep women out of the workplace or to remove those already in it, *in order to benefit male wage earners,* or to subsidize low wages for females who continued to work, *and thus profit employers* (as opponents of Speenhamland earlier had charged and critics of widows' pensions now maintain), are matters of debate.

Whatever, these arguments eventually prevailed. In fact, synthesizing the era's concerns about children, widows, the family and the home, and just rewards for work well done, mothers' pensions achieved remarkable legislative success. In April 1911, Missouri enacted America's first widows' pension law, a permissive statute allowing the counties to provide cash assistance to "full-time" mothers with dependent children (although evidence suggests that many women who received such aid, in Missouri and elsewhere, also worked for wages). Two months later, Illinois followed suit, and so rapidly did the idea spread that within two years seventeen other states did the same. By 1919, similar statutes had been enacted in thirty-nine states, and by 1935 all but two—South Carolina and Georgia—were extending aid to widows with children.

While the specific provisions of the statutes differed, they were similar in that they were compromise measures. Patterned on the nineteenth-century concept of relief, they were based upon behavioral considerations as well as economic need. All the statutes contained "suitable home" provisions; that is, they applied only to needy widows who, in the opinion of the authorities, were "fit" or worthy parents, exposing them, of course, to administrative discretion and possible abuses—and thus were not as impersonal as some would have liked. Nevertheless, the statutes represented a major step forward in that they enabled many families to remain intact who otherwise would not have been able to do so.

Moreover, while at the outset, most of the statutes were restrictive in that they were not mandatory, were financed by local or county units, and applied only to dependent widows, before long they were improved. Most became mandatory; they were paid for, in whole or in part, by the state, and their coverage was extended to all needy mothers—women with illegitimate children as well as those whose husbands were sick or incapacitated, in prison, or for any other reason unable to support their families.[3]

Widows' pension laws marked a definite turning point in the welfare policies of many states. In theory at least, they removed the stigma of charity for a large number of welfare recipients. They also broke down the nineteenth-century tradition against public home relief. Their enactment constituted public recognition of the facts that poverty did not necessarily reflect moral weakness, that long-time care must be provided for children whose fathers were dead or incapacitated or who had deserted them, that security at home was an essential part of such care, and that such security could be gained only through public aid.

And finally, like the Sheppard-Towner Act, widows' pension laws laid the foundation for what proved to be one of the more important parts of the federal Social Security Act of 1935. Title IV of that act, Aid to Dependent Children, established a federal program of cash payments to mothers deprived of their husbands' support. Known now as Aid to Families with Dependent Children, or A.F.D.C., it is the cornerstone of today's welfare system. Thus, with federal aid, the

---

[3]Also, many widows' pension laws established a new principle in public assistance in that they were not only to provide aid, but *adequate* aid, so that the mother could stay at home and devote herself to housekeeping and the care of her children, a far cry from the nineteenth-century concept of "less eligibility."

widows' pension movement was carried to its logical conclusion and one of the chief recommendations of the 1909 White House Conference—that needy children be cared for in their own homes whenever possible—came close to reality.

The drive for widows' pensions was part of a broader movement, during and after the so-called Progressive era, designed to increase the social and economic security of all citizens living in a modern industrial society. That movement also included efforts to enact workmen's compensation legislation, health and unemployment insurance schemes, and old-age pensions.

As the advocates of mothers' pensions indicated, the traditional methods of insuring against the vicissitudes of life were totally unsuited to the new conditions of an impersonal, wage centered, competitive industrial order. The wage earner was in a precarious position: any interruption of income flow destroyed his or her, and the family's, ability to purchase the goods and services necessary for survival. Yet such interruptions occurred frequently, through no fault of the individual. The only way to restore a measure of security to the working man or woman was by instituting compulsory social insurance—a rational means of minimizing the financial losses from the ordinary contingencies of life in the modern era.

Germany had established a comprehensive system of social insurance as early as 1884 and, by the turn of the century, all the countries of continental Europe had some form of social insurance. In the United States, federal and state labor bureaus had shown interest in these European plans as early as the 1890s. However, it was the American Association for Labor Legislation, founded in 1906 by a group of labor union leaders, economists, political scientists, and social reformers, that led the drive for social insurance.[4] Heading the movement was I. M. Rubinow, chief statistician for the Metropolitan Life Insurance Company, whose 500-page book, *Social Insurance* (1913), became the bible for the cause.

At every turn, the proponents of social insurance were constrained

---

[4]The American Association for Labor Legislation was assisted by many settlement house residents, under whose leadership the National Conference of Charities and Correction in 1912 drafted its platform of "minimum standards" for well-being in industrial society, which included a federal system of accident, old-age, and unemployment insurance.

by the ideology of voluntarism, with its credo of self-reliance and the notion that private institutions—"welfare capitalism," industrial establishment funds, trade union benefits, fraternal, mutual, and commercial insurance, and the like—were adequate for the task. However, advocates of social insurance argued that such voluntary programs were full of shortcomings and thus did not preclude the need for government action. In their opinion, welfare capitalism—efforts by astute corporate executives to nurture a pliable work force and check the growth of labor unionism and radicalism by providing employees with a variety of "benefits," including company homes and stores, libraries, recreational facilities, profit-sharing schemes, group life and health insurance policies, and retirement pensions[5]—was particularly reprehensible. Dubbed "industrial feudalism" by its critics, welfare capitalism denied workers vested rights to their benefits; those accused of "unsatisfactory conduct" could be dismissed from their jobs and thus lose all their protection. The scheme, then, was coercive, an obvious effort at social control that failed to provide the protection that industrial wage earners needed.

Other forms of private insurance were very expensive and inefficient and reached only a small percentage of the working population; more often than not, those who most needed protection were not covered by such programs. Security and justice, then, could be achieved only by transferring responsibility from the voluntary to the public sector; compulsory social insurance was the only mechanism that could respond predictably and adequately to the needs of all wage earners (and their families) suffering from income deprivation.

This, however, is not to say that those "private" measures were unimportant or entirely negative in their impact. Aside from providing some benefits to some workers prior to the appearance of public programs, they influenced later public activities, as Edward

---

[5]In the first full-length study of the subject, *A History of Retirement* (New Haven, Conn.: Yale University Press, 1980), William Graebner argued that retirement (through pensioning off older workers) developed to serve not the needs of the elderly but rather those of the marketplace; it was designed, in other words, not for the purposes of social justice but for the demands of a capitalist economy for efficiency and social control.

Berkowitz and Kim McQuaid have more than adequately demonstrated.[6] Indeed, whatever their motivations, businessmen's initiatives
clearly affected the ways in which reformers and public officials
established their own priorities and programs, and in the process they
contributed to the political economy of twentieth-century reform
and the creation of the welfare state. Whether that contribution was
as significant, and as positive, as Berkowitz and McQuaid contend, is
arguable.

In any event, optimism pervaded the social insurance forces as a
result of the rapidity with which states passed both mothers' pensions and workmen's compensation laws, which automatically paid
injured workers according to a uniform scale of benefits on the
assumption that "industrial accidents are not accidents at all, but
normal results of modern industry." Between 1909 and 1920,
forty-three states enacted workmen's compensation, mainly, however, the record indicates, because such measures had a good deal of
appeal to employers, who thus pushed for their enactment.
Compensation programs (which avoided the large payments the
courts occasionally awarded in injury cases) made it easier for businessmen to insure against losses resulting from industrial accidents,
the cost of which easily could be added to the price of production
and passed on to the consumer. Furthermore, most compensation
statutes omitted many workers, did not include occupational diseases, provided fairly low benefits to disabled laborers, and in other
ways were quite weak.

Still, these statutes were important. Whatever their limitations,
they at least established the principle that workers injured on the job
had a right to compensation. Thus, like widows' pensions, they represented a small but irreversible step from charity toward entitlement,
and social insurance advocates confidently turned next to health
insurance. Their confidence, however, was short-lived: the opposition
proved overwhelming. The strenuous and costly campaign against
health insurance was waged by a strange alliance—the medical profession, insurance companies, employers, Christian Scientists, some

---

[6]See Edward Berkowitz and Kim McQuaid, *Creating the Welfare State* (New York: Praeger,
1988).

labor unions,[7] and a host of superpatriotic groups that during World War I labeled the proposal as "Made in Germany" and later charged that it was "Made in Russia." By 1920, after health insurance bills had been defeated in New York and California (the two states that seemed most likely to enact such legislation), the reform forces acknowledged defeat.

The setback in the drive for health insurance seemed to take the remaining steam out of the social insurance movement, although the fight continued in the fields of old-age pensions and unemployment compensation. A number of states passed old-age pension laws in the 1920s, but the statutes were weak and for the most part they remained inoperative.[8] Not until 1929 was an effective statute enacted (in New York State).

The drive for unemployment compensation moved even more slowly. Although bills were introduced in a number of states between 1916 and 1931, none was enacted during that time. Wisconsin became the first state to place such a law on its books when, in January 1932, in the midst of the nation's most severe depression, it enacted such a statute, to become effective two years later. It was not until passage of the Social Security Act in 1935 that Americans awakened to the problem of unemployment.

Despite the failure to secure some social insurance programs and the faulty provisions of others, American social welfare had come a long way since the late nineteenth century. Beginning with efforts to remove dependent children from institutions and to place them in privates homes, reformers had come to see the elemental importance of preserving the family. They had moved to the larger concern for

---

[7]Actually, organized labor, striving for recognition against heavy opposition and generally suspicious of a government that often had helped to crush strikes, was divided on the issue of compulsory social insurance, especially health insurance. Many labor leaders, including Samuel Gompers, opposed the idea, especially since they remembered that Bismarck had introduced social insurance in Germany in part to remove issues of contention on which unions might be able to recruit members. Still, others favored health insurance, as did a number of state federations of labor and individual unions.

[8]Once again, as with widows' pensions, some social workers, especially "professional" caseworkers, who came into ascendency in the 1920s, opposed old age pensions, primarily because they implied a "right" to such funds without any determination of need by a trained social worker.

preventive health and other social welfare measures, including the provision of adequate financial resources through state and even federal assistance and the adoption of a comprehensive system of compulsory social insurance, to conserve childhood and the established home. Meanwhile, other important developments included the emergence of a social work profession.

Bibliography

ABBOTT, EDITH. "Grace Abbott: A Sister's Memories," *Social Service Review* 13 (September 1939): 351–408.

ABBOTT, GRACE. "Recent Trends in Mothers' Aid," *Social Service Review* 8 (June 1934): 191–220.

ADDAMS, JANE. *My Friend Julia Lathrop*. New York: Macmillan, 1935.

ALMY, FREDERIC. "Public Pensions to Widows," *Proceedings* of the National Conference of Charities and Correction (Fort Wayne, Ind.: Fort Wayne Printing, 1912): 481–85.

ASHER, ROBERT. "Failure and Fulfillment: Agitation for Employers' Liability and the Origin of Workmen's Compensation in New York State, 1876–1910," *Labor History* 24 (Spring 1983): 198–222.

BARKER, SIR ERNEST. *The Development of Public Services in Western Europe, 1660–1930*. New York: Oxford University Press, 1944.

BELL, WINIFRED. *Aid to Dependent Children*. New York: Columbia University Press, 1965.

BERKOWITZ, EDWARD, AND KIM MCQUAID. *Creating the Welfare State*. New York: Praeger, 1988.

BLUMBERG, DOROTHY M. *Florence Kelley: The Making of a Social Pioneer*. New York: Kelley, 1967.

BRADBURY, DOROTHY E. *Five Decades of Action: A History of the Children's Bureau*. Washington, D.C.: U.S. Children's Bureau, 1962.

BRANDES, STUART D. *American Welfare Capitalism, 1880–1940*. Chicago: University of Chicago Press, 1976.

BRECKENRIDGE, SOPHONISBA. *Public Welfare Administration in the United States*. Chicago: University of Chicago Press, 1938.

CANDELA, JOSEPH L. "The Struggle to Limit the Hours and Raise the Wages of Working Women in Illinois," *Social Service Review* 53 (March 1979): 15–34.

CHEPAITIS, JOSEPH B. "Federal Social Welfare Progressivism in the 1920s," *Social Service Review* 46 (June 1972): 213–29.

Conference on the Care of Dependent Children. *Proceedings*. Washington, D.C.: Government Printing Office, 1909.

COSTIN, LELA B. *Two Sisters for Social Justice: A Biography of Grace and Edith Abbott*. Urbana: University of Illinois Press, 1983.

DAVIS, ADA J. "The Evolution of the Institution of Mothers' Pensions in the United States," *American Journal of Sociology* 35 (January 1930): 573–87.

GEDDES, ANNE E. *Trends in Relief Expenditures, 1910–1935*. Washington, D.C.: Government Printing Office, 1937.

GOLDMARK, JOSEPHINE. *Impatient Crusader: Florence Kelley's Life Story*. Urbana: University of Illinois Press, 1953.

GRATTON, BRIAN. "Social Workers and Old Age Pensions," *Social Service Review* 57 (September 1983): 403–15.

HAMOVITCH, MAURICE B. "History of the Movement for Compulsory Health Insurance in the United States," *Social Service Review* 27 (September 1953): 281–99.

HARRIS, REBA F. *Mothers' Pensions in Michigan*. Lansing: Michigan State Welfare Department, 1934.

JAMBOR, HAROLD. "Theodore Dreiser, the *Delineator Magazine*, and Dependent Children: A Background Note on the Calling of the 1909 White House Conference," *Social Service Review* 32 (March 1978): 33–40.

JOHNSON, ARLIEN. *Public Policy and Private Charities*. Chicago: University of Chicago Press, 1931.

———. "The Transition from Charities and Correction to Public Welfare," *Annals of the American Academy of Political and Social Science* 105 (January 1923): 21–25.

KELLEY, FLORENCE. *Some Ethical Gains Through Legislation*. New York: Macmillan, 1905.

LEFF, MARK. "Consensus for Reform: The Mothers' Pension Movement in the Progressive Era," *Social Service Review* 47 (September 1973): 397–417.

LEMMONS, J. STANLEY. "The Sheppard-Towner Act: Progressivism in the 1920's," *Journal of American History* 55 (March 1969): 776–86.

LENROOT, KATHARINE F. "Friend of Children and the Children's Bureau," *Social Service Review* 22 (December 1948): 427–30.

LUBOVE, ROY, "Economic Security and Social Conflict in America," Part I, *Journal of Social History* 1 (Fall 1967): 61–87; Part II, *ibid.* 1 (Summer 1968): 325–50.

———. *The Struggle for Social Security, 1900–1935*. Cambridge, Mass.: Harvard University Press, 1968.

MACDOUGALL, A. W. "Trend Toward Public Social Service," *Survey* 34 (May 15, 1915): 163.

NELSON, BARBARA J. "The Origins of the Two-Channel Welfare State: Workmen's Compensation and Mothers' Aid," in Linda Gordon, ed., *Women, the State, and Welfare*. Madison: University of Wisconsin Press, 1990.

NELSON, DANIEL. *Unemployment Insurance: The American Experience, 1915–1935*. Madison: University of Wisconsin Press, 1969.

NUMBERS, RONALD L. *Almost Persuaded: American Physicians and Compulsory Health Insurance, 1912–1920*. Baltimore: Johns Hopkins Press, 1978.

PARKER, JACQUELINE, AND EDWARD CARPENTER. "Julia Lathrop and the Children's Bureau: The Emergence of an Institution," *Social Service Review* 55 (March 1981): 60–77.

QUADAGNO, JILL, AND MADONNA MEYER. "Organized Labor, State Structures, and Social Policy Development: A Case Study of Old Age Assistance in Ohio, 1916–1940," *Social Problems* 36 (April 1989): 181–96.

REAGAN, PATRICK D. "The Ideology of Social Harmony and Efficiency: Workmen's Compensation in Ohio, 1904–1919," *Ohio History* 90 (Autumn 1981): 317–31.

ROMANOFSKY, PETER. "Infant Mortality, Dr. Henry Dwight Chapin and the Speedwell Society," *Journal of Medical Society of New Jersey* 73 (January 1976): 33–38.

———. "Saving the Lives of the City's Foundlings: The Joint Committee and New York City Child Care Methods, 1860–1907," *New-York Historical Society Quarterly* 61 (January–April 1977): 49–68.

ROTHMAN, SHEILA M. "Women's Clinics or Doctors' Offices?: The Sheppard-Towner Act and the Promotion of Preventive Health Care," in David J. Rothman, and Stanton Wheeler, eds., *Social History and Social Policy*. New York: Academic Press, 1981.

RUBINOW, ISAAC M. *Social Insurance*. New York: Holt, 1913.

STADUM, BEVERLY. *Poor Women and Their Families*. Albany: State University of New York Press, 1991.

TOBEY, JAMES A. *The Children's Bureau*. Baltimore: Johns Hopkins Press, 1925.

WEINSTEIN, JAMES. "Big Business and the Origins of Workmen's Compensation," *Labor History* 8 (Spring 1967): 156–74.

WEISS, NANCY. "Save the Children: A History of the Children's Bureau, 1903–1918," Ph.D. dissertation, University of California, Los Angeles, 1974.

YELLOWITZ, IRWIN. "The Origins of Unemployment Reform in the United States," *Labor History* 9 (Fall 1968): 338–60.

CHAPTER 11

The Quest for Professionalization

At one time, the word "profession" was a generic term that embraced the ministry, law, and medicine. Over the years, especially in the late nineteenth century, as the day of the generalist was beginning to fade before the mounting complexities of modern existence, other groups—teachers, engineers, geologists, chemists, economists, political scientists, and so on—experienced a formative growth toward self-consciousness and efficient organization that resulted in their becoming professions. Before they could do so, they had to have exclusive possession of a systematic body of knowledge, a monopoly of skill obtained from higher education and training, and a subculture whose members shared a group identity and common values.

During the early twentieth century, charity workers also sought professional status. As in so many other areas of American life, the need for professional education and procedures in social service had become clear if some rational control was to be asserted over the drift of life. The complex problems resulting from rapid industrialization (and the shift of most economic activity from the small personal setting of the home to the large impersonal setting of the factory), the advent of capitalism (with wage labor and other elements controlled by the marketplace), widespread immigration (from the far reaches of southern and eastern Europe as well as from American farms and small towns), and the crowding together of citizens in ugly, sprawling centers of population, demanded the creation of a group of social experts trained to alleviate, and hopefully resolve, them. As Charles P. Neill, the federal Commissioner of Labor, put it in 1914:

The need for trained workers is obvious to anyone at all familiar with the many complex, subtle, and baffling problems growing out of the mere fact of poverty and destitution in all our great congested centers of population. . . . Zeal for the cause of health or devotion is not accepted as a sufficient basis to turn anyone loose as a healer. But too often zeal in the cause is all that is expected of the charity worker. The unintelligent, untrained charity worker can, in spite of disinterested zeal, often cause . . . havoc [with the needy].

The emergence of a profession of social work, then, was related to what Robert Wiebe has called "the search for order" in a "distended society." Ghettos and slums, the white plague, rising rates of crime, juvenile delinquency, the lack of provision for sanitation and public health, the psychological and economic dependency that arose from uncertain employment, low wages, industrial accidents, premature old age—these and other social hazards constituted problems in American life that good intentions alone could not dispel; the creation of schools for the training of social servants, social research and other highly technical skills, and professional discipline was essential.[1]

Charity workers did not have these tools at the turn of the century, nor, in the eyes of the public, could they ever develop or acquire them. It was commonly felt that social work consisted of little more than providing aid to people in need, and that no person or group could claim a monopoly on benevolence or could create a profession out of it. To the extent that every person had an obligation to help the suffering, social work was everybody's business. Only when social workers succeeded in convincing the public that not everyone with love in his or her heart could do the job, that social work consisted of more than benevolence and well-wishing, that it had a scientific as well as an ethical component, did they achieve professional recognition. By that time—around the third decade of the twentieth century—social workers had not only founded professional schools that transmitted a systematic body of knowledge rooted in scientific theories, but had demonstrated that they utilized unique skills, and they

---

[1]So, too, according to some (as we have seen), was the enactment of a comprehensive system of social insurance—another effort at "rationalizing" the social and economic order, one that paralleled the professionalization of charity work.

had a self-conscious group of practitioners who belonged to a number of newly created professional organizations.[2]

All this did not occur overnight; the road to professionalism was being paved for some time, at least as far back as the 1870s, when the Conference of Charities was created. The Conference of Charities was the child of the American Social Science Association, an organization founded in 1865 to discuss

> questions relating to the sanitary condition of the people, the relief, the employment, and the education of the poor, the prevention of crime, the amelioration of criminal law, the discipline of persons, the remedial treatment of the insane, and those numerous matters of statistical and philanthropic interest which are included under the general head "Social Science."[3]

Nine years later, members of the existing state boards of charities attending the American Social Science Association's annual meeting decided to get together to discuss common problems and compare methods used to solve them. Later that year, the paid secretaries of those boards got together, in what was no doubt the first meeting of persons making a career of charitable work, to round out a program for another meeting of state board members at the next annual convention of the American Social Science Association. Thus, the Conference of Charities (or Conference of State Boards, as it was sometimes called) came into being.

Both of these organizations—the American Social Science Association and the Conference of Charities—were products of the latter nineteenth century's faith in scientific investigation, as were the state boards of charities. Although the movement for state supervision of its charitable and correctional institutions was inspired, in part, by a humanitarian concern for the wards of the state, it also was, as we have seen and as William Brock has pointed out, "sustained by a belief that proper investigation and scientific analysis could lead to efficient

---

[2]The following analysis of the professionalization of social work is based in part on the excellent work by Harold Wilensky and Charles N. Lebeaux, *Industrial Society and Social Welfare* (New York: Free Press, 1958).

[3]The American Social Science Association was itself the child of the British Association for the Promotion of Social Science, established in 1857 by the heirs of those who had sponsored the poor law "reforms" of 1834 and other social welfare and public health legislation.

administration and thus benefit the whole society." No wonder membership in all three bodies overlapped.

In any event, the Conference of Charities continued to meet annually with the American Social Science Association until 1879, when, at the urging of Frederick H. Wines of Illinois and Andrew E. Ellmore of Wisconsin, the group separated from its parent body in order to give more intensive study to its own "practical" work. From the outset, the group, which (in 1884) changed its name to the National Conference of Charities and Correction, opened its doors to others, including those engaged in private charity, both religious and secular.[4] It published the *Proceedings* of its annual meetings, and later a quarterly bulletin as well, and in general it served as a national clearing house for ideas and experiences in the broad field of social welfare.

Actually, the National Conference served a variety of functions. For the young and inexperienced worker, it provided the first opportunity to witness the relationship between different areas of charitable work. The long-time secretary of the organization saw it as "an occasional or post-graduate school of social work where reformers acquired an education in principles and methods of charitable work—one that reduced the tuition fees of the School of Experience." More important, by creating a certain *esprit de corps* among charity workers and by delimiting a specific occupational area over which they and no others could claim expertise, members of the National Conference established charity work as a distinct field within the social sciences and hence took a major step toward laying the foundation for a professional self-identity and awareness. At the same time, however, by stressing more "practical" concerns over scientific inquiry—especially procedures for operating public and private agencies and techniques of administering assistance—charity workers moved away from social

---

[4]This open-door membership policy led to important changes in the organization. Shortly after its creation, the organization was taken over by the representatives of private charitable agencies, especially the charity organization societies. During the early twentieth century, the advocates of preventive social work (social reform), especially settlement house residents, dominated its councils. During and after World War I, professional social workers (mainly caseworkers) assumed control of the organization, as witnessed by its name change in 1917 to the National Conference of Social Work. In 1957, it went through another name change, this time to the National Conference on Social Welfare, and once again began to fall under the general influence of the representatives of public welfare, especially at the state and federal levels.

theory and research to a preoccupation with methods and treatment, a development not only that some later social work leaders would bemoan and seek to rectify but that, in fact, would precipitate an ongoing "fight" among them over the nature and control of their profession.

Meanwhile, another step along the same road was taken by the charity organization societies and their agents who developed what has come to be called casework: "Those processes which develop personality through adjustments consciously affected, individual by individual, between men [and women] and their social environment," according to one widely used definition. In so doing, friendly visitors realized that to be effective they had to be trained in investigation, diagnosis, preparation of case records, and treatment, all of which required guidance, counsel, supervision, and a knowledge of the principles of scientific philanthropy. By the late nineteenth century, then, social work was beginning to pass beyond mere philanthropy to a vocation based upon the assumption that it required specific knowledge, skills, and techniques, as well as good intentions, and that such capabilities could be transmitted from teachers to students. As one C.O.S. agent put it, charity work must become scientific "by the development of professional skill, professional schools, and authoritative standards of entrance and excellence" in the field.

In the meantime, the settlement house movement had appeared on the scene. And, while it stressed social reform rather than individual treatment, residents were keenly aware of the need to acquire more knowledge, especially in the fields of economics, political science, sociology, and the other social sciences, and to develop more skill in research and what has come to be called community organization, some of the very areas and techniques their immediate predecessors had shunned. Both groups—friendly visitors and settlement house residents—however, were concerned with the problem of education and training for social work and both identified with the National Conference.

Both groups knew that formal education was an inherent part of every profession, and that the more highly developed the profession, the stronger, clearer, and closer the relationship between the school and the field, between advanced education and actual practice. Since the concepts, values, standards, and techniques of the profession are rooted in education, vitality in the field depends upon a reciprocal flow of knowledge between the teacher and the practitioner, between theory and practice, between the training school and the agencies in the community. Social work, then, could not become a profession, and practitioners could not enter the field, without professional training, nor could it remain a profession if it broke its ties with educational institutions.

At first, a form of apprenticeship or "on-the-job training" was all that social agencies offered recruits, salaried workers and volunteers alike. By watching older members, by talking to executives, and by attending staff meetings and the National Conference, new workers learned something of the art and science of helping those in need. Then a number of private agencies, beginning in Brooklyn in 1891 and in Boston a year later, started what amounted to training programs for their workers—if they could be called that—by arranging informal lectures and distributing reading lists.

Some of those people who had entered the field after receiving a higher education, especially those going into settlement house work, had taken some courses in sociology, which in the 1890s was beginning to be taught at American colleges and universities. The emergence of sociology at this time as an academic discipline resulted from a variety of factors, including the needs of a rapidly changing society. More important, however, although related, was the decline of social Darwinism. The belief that the evolution of society was a mechanical process determined by fixed natural, or scientific, laws that should not be tampered with came under attack by a number of people in the late nineteenth century. The most important of these critics was Lester Frank Ward, who argued that society's development could and should be studied and even guided, thus formulating what came to be referred to as reform Darwinism.

The philosophical groundwork for Ward's position—the scientific study of society for the sake of guiding its evolution, thus replacing aimless drift with purposive change—was laid with the publication in 1883 of his important two-volume book, *Dynamic Sociology*. That work provided the first elaborate argument for the development of a science of society, or sociology, for the purpose of "artificially" improving its development, especially by abolishing poverty and providing all citizens with a sound education—a far cry from the social Darwinists' laissez-faire and "survival of the fittest."

Whether one agreed with Ward or not, sociology became a popular course of study at colleges and universities throughout America, and many pioneer instructors in the field, including such well known scholars as Franklin Giddings of Columbia University, Albion Small of the University of Chicago, Charles Cooley of the University of Michigan, and E. A. Ross of Stanford and the University of Wisconsin, emphasized the relationship between sociology and social work.

They pointed out that, while each subject was in a field of its own, they dealt largely with the same material—human beings and their social relationships. Each had a contribution to make to the other, sociology to discover the general laws and principles governing human intercourse, and social work to furnish the data necessary for the formulation and testing of those laws and principles. During the 1890s the two disciplines were wed, and it appeared as though the marriage between the teaching of sociology and the practice of social work would be a lasting and happy one.[5]

Yet, before long, the honeymoon came to an end. While no divorce or complete separation occurred, the two disciplines began to part. Sociologists felt a need to disassociate themselves and their research from social workers who, they felt, were too value oriented and thus not objective enough, while social workers felt that sociology was too theoretical or scientifically oriented and not applied or practical enough. More important was the fact that many social workers were beginning to feel that their work was related to many disciplines, not just one; that to be effective they had to know as much about such diverse subjects as biology and economics, psychology and law, as about sociology. Hence the need for broader training.

In the meantime, the quest for professionalism continued, and a number of social workers began to plead for the establishment of

---

[5]In 1892, Albion Small, head of the newly created Sociology Department at the University of Chicago, offered a job to Homer Folks, the well known New York social worker. When Folks declined the offer, Small turned to Charles R. Henderson, a Baptist minister who was known primarily for his work with various charitable organizations. Similarly, Franklin Giddings, the first professor of sociology at Columbia University, was head of the New York Charity Organization Society's Committee on Statistics.

some sort of special social work education. In 1893, Anna L. Dawes of Pittsfield, Massachusetts, read a paper before the National Conference on "The Need for Training Schools for a New Profession"—the first public plea for the founding of formal schools for the education and training of social workers. After lamenting the want of suitable people in charity work, which, she was convinced, was due not to an unwillingness to serve but to a lack of opportunity for training, she raised the question of why those retiring from the field could not be allowed to transmit to their successors much of what they had learned during their years of service. New workers thus schooled could take up where their predecessors left off without repeating all their mistakes. Dawes strongly felt that there was much to be taught and to be learned in the practice of charity work, and that such knowledge could be passed on to those who wished to absorb it.

Not many years later, Mary Richmond of the Baltimore Charity Organization Society read what turned out to be a more important paper on the same subject: "The Need of a Training School in Applied Philanthropy." Richmond also argued that only through some sort of educational opportunity could college graduates and any others of talent be drawn into social work. She went on to define the conditions under which such a school should be established, the sort of curriculum it should have, the personnel needed to staff it, and its probable cost. All this went much farther than Anna Dawes's appeal.

According to Mary Richmond, the training school in applied philanthropy should be located in a large city, possibly affiliated with some institution of higher learning. While classroom instruction was important, the curriculum should emphasize "practical work," especially experience in the field. The school should be in close touch with the public and private charities of the community so that its students could observe and engage in social work training under the supervision of experienced practitioners.

In 1898, one year after Mary Richmond delivered her widely discussed paper, the New York Charity Organization Society founded the first "school" of social work when it organized an annual six-week summer program designed to increase the knowledge and efficiency of those already in the field. Twenty-seven social workers attended the first session of the Summer School of Philanthropy, which comprised lectures, visits to public and private agencies and institutions, and field work.

Some years later, when Edward T. Devine, secretary of the Charity Organization Society, replaced his assistant, Philip W. Ayres, as director of the school, the program was expanded to an academic year. Redesigned primarily for students without experience in social work, it was renamed the New York School of Philanthropy. In the fall of 1910, the program was further expanded, this time to two years, and nine years later it underwent still another name change to the New York School of Social Work. Later, it became the Columbia University Graduate School of Social Work.

In the meantime, other such schools had come into existence. In 1901, Graham Taylor's Chicago Commons settlement house and the University of Chicago (already becoming the center of urban sociology in America) cooperated in offering a special extension course taught by Taylor and Julia Lathrop of Hull-House, which in 1907 led to the founding of an independent institution, the Chicago School of Civics and Philanthropy, perhaps the clearest example of the early union of sociology and social work; in 1920, it became the University of Chicago School of Social Work (now the University of Chicago School of Social Service Administration). In 1904, under the prodding of Zilpha Smith, General Superintendent of Boston's Associated Charities, Simmons College and Harvard University joined in founding the Boston School of Social Work. Similar developments occurred elsewhere, and by 1910 America's five largest cities had schools of social work, all of which, with the exception of Chicago's, were established by charity organization personnel.[6]

The creation of these and other schools of social work hardly solved all of the budding profession's educational problems; indeed, they raised many important ones. The real question was the nature of those schools and their curricula. What kind of schools were they to be, educational institutions or training centers? Were they to provide prospective social workers with knowledge (theory) or experience

---

[6]These early institutions, especially the eastern ones, were in effect graduate schools, although, when it was established in 1915, the Bryn Mawr School of Social Work was the first to limit admission to students with college degrees. Beginning in the same year, first at Ohio State University, then at Indiana University and the University of Minnesota, social work programs were designed for students pursuing the bachelor's degree. Later, post-master's degree study leading to certificates in advanced practice or to the doctorate were added. Now, technical and vocational training at less than the baccalaureate level is in the stage of preliminary development and experimentation.

(field work)? If they concentrated on theory, should it be in subject matter or methods; if they concentrated on field work, under whose supervision should it be carried out, an educator or a practitioner? Was there a need for research at such schools? Should they be autonomous institutions, or should they be attached to or affiliated with a college or a university? Answers to these and other questions did not come overnight.

At first, most schools of social work were like the New York School of Philanthropy; that is, they were adjuncts of private social agencies which supplied the instructors and the opportunities for field work, and which for the most part subordinated theory and research to field work. They produced practitioners (mainly caseworkers) to staff their own agencies rather than administrators, scholars, social theorists, and the like.

Eventually, an attempt was made to change the situation. People like Julia Lathrop, Grace and Edith Abbott, and other midwesterners who had come out of the settlement house movement and were interested in social policy and public welfare (and who would refer to psychiatric social work as "sick-y-atric" social work and, from the start, made the University of Chicago School of Social Work an exception to the rule by stressing research, social policy, and public administration) began a movement to broaden the curricula and bring schools of social work within the mainstream of American higher education—just as the professions of law and medicine had done. In an influential book, *Social Welfare and Professional Education*, published in 1931 during the Great Depression when it was becoming increasingly obvious that individual treatment and private charity had to give way to social reform and public welfare, Edith Abbott outlined the case for an expanded curriculum and university affiliation. The following paragraph (from a chapter entitled "The University and Social Welfare") sets forth the gist of her argument:

> The academic curriculum of most of the professional schools [of social work] is now poor and slight and covers . . . only the various aspects of a single field—casework. None of us will deny the importance of casework. It is as necessary to the social worker as, for example, the study of contracts is to the law student. But casework is very far from being the whole story. There are great reaches of territory, some of them yet unexplored and stretching out to a kind of no man's land—the great fields of public charitable organization, of law and government in relation to social work, of social economics, of social insurance, of modern social politics—all of which are required if the social worker is to be an efficient servant of the state. In these fields the indepen-

dent schools will always be limited. It is in the university where there is well-
organized graduate work not merely in one, but in all, of the social sciences
and where there are cooperative relations with the law and medical schools
that the great schools of social welfare will ultimately be developed. At the
present time, particularly in the non-university schools, the student too often
becomes a routine technician—sometimes a clever technician—but still a
technician and not a scientific person with the love of knowledge and the use
of the tools of learning.

So if the profession was to be more than a mere technique, if it was
to have social workers rather than just caseworkers, training for the
field had to have a foundation in many of the social and biological sciences. A knowledge of the structure and functioning of society was as
indispensable to social workers as physiology was to physicians; therefore, they had to study sociology and anthropology. The same was
true of economics, for society's economic institutions and resources
vitally affected the very nature and scope of social work, as people living through the depression all too readily knew. Psychology, biology,
and other sciences were also essential to social workers, as was law.
Aside from having to know law to be able to recognize legal problems
and advise clients, social workers involved in public assistance had to
digest legislative details and judicial rulings and, when necessary, even
draft new legislation. For these and other reasons (including their
superior library resources), schools of social work had to become integral parts of universities, according to the reformers.

Then there was the question of research which, in one form or
another, became an essential part of the curriculum at all schools of
social work. While settlement house residents and others had for a
long time engaged in research and seen its value for social work and
reform, a 1908 Supreme Court decision highlighted its importance.
The case, *Muller v. Oregon*, involved a law prohibiting the employment of women in factories and laundries for more than ten hours in
any one day. The statute was challenged by some employers, who
argued that it impaired women's freedom of contract and thus violated their rights under the Fourteenth Amendment of the U.S.
Constitution. When the question eventually reached the U.S.
Supreme Court, the state hired Louis Brandeis, the able Massachusetts
lawyer known as the "people's counsel," to argue its case.

Brandeis, in preparing his brief, departed from standard practice—
the arguing of cases on the basis of abstract logic and legal precedents;

in fact, he presented only two pages of conventional legal reasoning and citation of past cases. Instead, he offered the court more than one hundred pages of "facts"—statistics and other empirical evidence—amassed for him by a group of social workers, including Florence Kelley and Josephine Goldmark of the National Consumers' League, engaged for the purpose. By citing the evidence they had gathered from a variety of sources, including case studies and reports of government bureaus, legislative committees, commissions on hygiene, and factory inspectors, Brandeis showed that long hours of work were dangerous to women's health and safety and that a shorter workday had practical benefits for themselves and, if married, for their families as well. When he declared that there "is no logic that is properly applicable to these laws except the logic of facts," the justices, to the surprise of many, agreed unanimously.

Their decision not only upheld the Oregon statute but, in effect, sanctioned what came to be known as "sociological jurisprudence"—the presentation of factual data to establish the reasonableness (or unreasonableness) of social legislation, which quickly became ordinary legal practice. Thus, research was important not only for the development and analysis of new social service programs and policies, but also for all campaigns involving social legislation. Therein lay another reason for social workers to have training in research, and for schools of social work to become integral parts of American universities, primarily research institutions.[7] The proliferation of Ph.D. programs in social welfare indicates continued interest in research among those in the field today.

---

[7]Edith Abbot believed that there was a close relation between practice and research in social work, that social workers' subjective concerns about problems informed rather than distorted their research, and that social research therefore should not be left solely in the hands of "objective" social scientists. As she put it:

> Some of our social science friends are afraid that we cannot be scientific because we really care about what we are doing, and we are even charged with being sentimental. Now this does not frighten me ... the social worker may care very genuinely about what happens to the unfortunate child or the broken family for whom she is temporarily responsible without being less scientific.

Other developments helped to foster social research, especially the spread of social science research facilities at colleges and universities and the growth of foundations, independent research organizations, and federal and state government agencies (many of which have research divisions) devoted to the study of social problems.

Finally, in regard to field work, it was customary for students to get their practical experience by working in an agency while attending school. However, it came to be felt, and this was eventually so stated by the professional accrediting agency, that practice as well as theory should be directed by college faculty members—clinical or field work instructors rather than agency personnel—who would presumably perfect educational methods in field practice, a major step forward in distinguishing professional social work education from apprenticeship training. Thus emerged the curriculum pattern common to all schools of social work—a substantial number of courses in theory (both in subject matter and in methods), some training in social research, plus field work instruction.[8]

In the meantime, as more schools of social work appeared, their directors met annually at the National Conference to discuss common problems, including the maintenance of standards. When it became clear that some accrediting agency was necessary, Porter R. Lee, director of the New York School of Social Work, invited the heads of the seventeen existing schools to discuss the matter. Thus, in 1920, was established the Association of Training Schools of Professional Social Work, which, after undergoing a number of name changes (National Association of Professional Schools of Social Work, American Association of Schools of Social Work), in 1952 became the Council on Social Work Education, an organization that has continued to set the standards of social work education in the United States and Canada.

This accrediting body gave enormous impetus to the movement to bring schools of social work under the aegis of a university—and make a reality of Edith Abbott's model of social work education based largely on social science theory and research—when, in 1935, it decreed that any school desiring membership had to be part of an institution approved by the Association of American Universities.

---

[8]This helped to overcome long-standing opposition to university affiliation by leaders of the private charities, who feared that such institutions would not place enough value on field work for students. In any case, at the outset, especially during the period of social reform, most schools offered such courses as political science, sociology, labor, economics, child welfare, and, above all, "charities and corrections." As we shall see, however, after World War I, almost all schools became obsessed with the teaching of casework, especially as practiced in private agencies—medical and psychiatric casework. Later, courses in group work, community organization, and social policy became quite popular.

Interestingly, the New York School of Social Work, the nation's first such school, was the last to give up its independent status when it affiliated with Columbia University in 1940. By the early 1990s there were approximately 110 accredited graduate schools of social work in the United States (and some 377 undergraduate programs).

Another important, although much more informal, development in the emerging profession was the appearance of specialized magazines and journals. In the late nineteenth century, there were no means of providing continuity for persons engaged in health and welfare work between the meetings of the National Conference, whose official *Proceedings* contained the best of the papers and addresses delivered each year. In response to this need, concerned persons caught up in charitable and reform work in Boston, New York, and Chicago founded journals to carry news of welfare activities to the executives and board members of agencies which provided services, to volunteers and paid employees in the field, and to others interested in the work.

In Boston, the journal *Lend-A-Hand* was established in 1886 under the editorship of Edward Everett Hale. Five years later, the New York Charity Organization Society began publishing *Charities Review* which, according to Edward T. Devine, its editor and one of the most prominent men in the field, was a "dignified, scholarly, educational, and provocative journal," one that for the next ten years spoke for the social work of the day. Then a review for settlement house workers, which quickly became the national organ for that movement, *The Commons*, was launched in 1896 by Graham Taylor, founder of Chicago Commons.

To meet the demand for a more practical journal, in December 1897, the New York C.O.S. launched a second official publication, *Charities*, a kind of house organ which promoted the work of the agency. In March 1901, in the first of a series of mergers, *Charities* absorbed its predecessor, *Charities Review*. Then, in 1905, the journal (which went by its original name) was joined by Graham Taylor's *The Commons*, and a year later by *Jewish Charity*, the official paper of the United Hebrew Charities of New York, becoming *Charities and The Commons*. After four years of publication, *Charities and The Commons* became *Survey*, taking its name from the monumental study of Pittsburgh initiated in 1907.

During all these years, the publications had been under the wing of the New York C.O.S., but in 1912 *Survey* was incorporated separately and placed under the editorship of Paul Kellogg. From that time until it ceased publication in 1952, *Survey* (and its child, *Survey Graphic*, conceived as an independent journal in 1923 to reach a broader audience than its parent), under Kellogg's command, was unequaled in the field of social work publications; not only did it stand at the heart of the evolution of social work as a profession, but it also had a profound influence in the shaping of social welfare policy, both public and private.

Meanwhile, numerous other specialized and general practice journals appeared—*Social Casework* in 1920, *Child Welfare* in 1922, *Social Service Review* in 1927, *Social Work Today* and *Public Welfare* in the mid-1930s, and so on—all of which were exceedingly important; not only did they provide an outlet for the publication of the results of research, but they allowed students and practitioners to keep abreast of such research and of other technical and nontechnical professional developments, in general providing education, guidance, and a means of communication for those in and out of the field.

Before it could be considered a profession, however, social work needed some other things, including agencies of control other than schools—professional associations. Professional associations are important, for they help to raise standards and to determine the relationship between the profession and the society they serve. Also, if paid professionals could be linked to their colleagues through a network of such organizations, it would be easier to view amateurs, volunteers who could not join such bodies, as nonprofessionals or "outsiders." Perhaps more important is the fact that professional organizations serve as the main channel of reciprocity between schools and practitioners. While there are other channels of communication, it is at meetings of professional associations (and through their journals) that faculty members and practitioners get together regularly and exchange views. Through these experiences, the nature and "character" of the profession are created and progress is achieved.

Traditionally, there have been two types of national associations in social work—groups concerned with extending and improving the quality of work of member agencies (such as the National Federation of Settlements, the Family Welfare Association, the Council on Social Work Education), and associations of individual social workers which seek to further professional development and improve working conditions (such as the American Association of Medical Social Workers and the American Association of Psychiatric Social Workers). Since space does not permit discussion of all such associations, perhaps it would be useful to look at one of the earliest and most important of these—the National Association of Social Workers.

The National Conference offered the first opportunity for charity workers across the country to meet together to exchange ideas and experiences. It was not composed exclusively of paid workers, nor did it have vocational criteria for selection of membership. As a result, it largely ignored vocational questions, considering, instead, social ones. As schools of social work emerged, faculty members and graduates felt the need for a new kind of organization, one that brought together paid personnel in the field for the discussion of "bread-and-butter" issues.

The so-called Monday Club of Boston was the first such group, and by the second decade of the twentieth century, New York, Detroit, Pittsburgh, Minneapolis, San Francisco, and other cities had similar gatherings with such revealing names as the Hungry Club, the S.O.S. Club, and so on. Social workers employed by different agencies met to try to understand each other's work better and to discuss mutual problems. However, since there was no formal communication between these clubs, they were not the direct precursors of the national professional association, although their members did influence its development, especially the organization of local chapters, something that, when founded in 1921, the professional association had not anticipated doing.

The unwitting parent of the first national professional association was the Intercollegiate Bureau of Occupations, organized in 1911 by the New York City alumnae of several eastern women's colleges to serve as an employment agency. Soon after the bureau began to operate, its members discovered that the demand for social work positions was so great, and that the field was so loosely defined, that a special department was needed for social work applicants. Such a department was established, but it soon ceased functioning solely as an employment agency; among other things, it maintained a registry of all social workers who wished to affiliate with it, laying the foundation for a national organization.

In 1917, the department separated from its parent body, the

Intercollegiate Bureau of Occupations, and established the National Social Workers' Exchange which, although basically an employment bureau, from the outset assumed supervision over a variety of other areas, including recruitment, working conditions, salaries, ethics, standards, and means of better communication between various branches of the field. Members of the exchange obviously felt a need for a national organization with a wider scope of activities than mere job placement.

The matter of defining requirements for membership proved difficult. After a year of study, the exchange, with branches in several cities, decided not to restrict membership to employed workers, but to open its ranks to anyone engaged in social work either on a paid or on a volunteer basis, and to others interested in the work. Thus, it took in all those who felt, or wanted themselves, included under the term social worker.

On June 27, 1921, at a meeting held in Milwaukee, Wisconsin, in conjunction with the National Conference, members of the exchange voted to change its name to the American Association of Social Workers, a name retained for the next quarter-century. After merging with a number of other bodies in 1955 and deciding that graduation from an accredited school of social work was necessary for membership, the organization again changed its name, this time to the National Association of Social Workers. N.A.S.W. is currently the social workers' major professional association with some 140,000 members.[9] Through it all, its purpose, as outlined in its constitution, has remained the same:

> To serve as an organization whose members, acting together, shall endeavor through investigation and conference 1) to develop professional standards in social work; 2) to encourage adequate preparation and professional training; 3) to recruit new workers; and 4) to develop a better adjustment between workers and positions in social work.

In the meantime, social workers in hospitals and clinics, aware of a professional society's advantages for doctors and its contribution to

---

[9]A degree from an accredited school of social work (or welfare) meant graduate education; recently, however, that was changed. Now, one can gain membership after securing a bachelor's degree in social work, and there is talk of extending membership to people with a bachelor's degree in other areas who have some experience in the field of social welfare.

medical progress, organized, in 1918, the American Association of Hospital Social Workers, which later became the American Association of Medical Social Workers. In 1926 the American Association of Psychiatric Social Workers was launched, and other organizations were created similarly. While all of these groups grappled with such questions as professional education and job analysis, prerequisites for admission, financing, and effective practice, they tended to raise the level of professional worth and to promote the delivery of more adequate and efficient social services.

By the time of World War I, then, charity workers were making rapid headway in becoming professional "social workers," as indicated by the change in name, in 1917, from National Conference of Charities and Correction to National Conference of Social Work. Schools of social work abounded, in and out of universities. The volunteer friendly visitor had yielded to the paid, trained caseworker. The pragmatic, reform-oriented settlement house resident was beginning to decline in importance and prestige. And new professional groups were forming. All that remained for professionalization was popular acceptance of the fact that social work had a well-defined body of knowledge and unique techniques capable of transmission through a formal educational process.

Bibliography

ABBOTT, EDITH. *Social Welfare and Professional Education*. Chicago: University of Chicago Press, 1931.

———. "Twenty Years of University Education for the Social Services," *Social Service Review* 15 (December 1941): 670–705.

American Association of Social Workers. *Vocational Aspects of Family Social Work*. New York: American Association of Social Workers, 1925.

———. *Vocational Aspects of Medical Social Work*. New York: American Association of Social Workers, 1927.

———. *Vocational Aspects of Psychiatric Social Work*. New York: American Association of Social Workers, 1925.

BRECKINRIDGE, SOPHONISBA. "The New Horizons of Professional Education for Social Work," *Social Service Review* 10 (September 1936): 437–49.

BROWN, ESTHER L. *Social Work as a Profession*. New York: Russell Sage Foundation, 1935.

BRUNO, FRANK J. *Trends in Social Work, 1874–1956*. New York: Columbia University Press, 1957.

————. "Twenty-Five Years of Schools of Social Work," *Social Service Review* 18 (June 1944): 152–64.

CABOT, RICHARD C. *Social Service and the Art of Healing*. New York: Dodd, Mead, 1928.

CHAMBERS, CLARKE A. *Paul U. Kellogg and the Survey*. Minneapolis: University of Minnesota Press, 1972.

COSTIN, LELA B. "Edith Abbott and the Chicago Influence on Social Work Education," *Social Service Review* 57 (March 1983): 94–111.

DAWES, ANNA. "The Need of Training Schools for a New Profession," *Lend-A-Hand* 11 (1893): 90–97.

DINER, STEVEN J. "Department and Discipline: The Department of Sociology at the University of Chicago, 1892–1920," *Minerva* 13 (Winter 1975): 514–53.

GETTLEMAN, MARVIN. "John H. Finley and the Academic Origins of American Social Work, 1887–1892," *Studies in History and Society* 2 (Fall 1969 and Spring 1970): 13–26.

GLASSER, MELVIN A. "The Story of the Movement for a Single Professional Association," *Social Work Journal* 36 (July 1955): 115–22.

GREENWOOD, ERNEST. "Attributes of a Profession," *Social Work* 2 (July 1957): 45–55.

HARRISON, FRANCIS N. *The Growth of a Professional Association*. New York: American Association of Social Workers, 1935.

HENDERSON, CHARLES R. *Modern Methods of Charity*. New York: Macmillan, 1904.

HILLMAN, ARTHUR. *Sociology and Social Work*. Washington, D.C.: Public Affairs Press, 1956.

JOHNSON, ARLIEN. *School Social Work: Its Contribution to Professional Education*. New York: National Association of Social Workers, 1962.

LUBOVE, ROY. *The Professional Altruist: The Emergence of Social Work as a Career, 1880–1930*. Cambridge, Mass.: Harvard University Press, 1965.

MEIER, ELIZABETH G. *A History of the New York School of Social Work*. New York: Columbia University Press, 1954.

NATHAN, MAUD. *The Story of an Epoch-Making Movement*. Garden City, N.Y.: Doubleday, 1926.

PIVEN, FRANCES F., AND RICHARD A. CLOWARD. "Notes Toward a Radical Social Work," in Roy Bailey and Mike Brake, eds., *Radical Social Work*. New York: Pantheon Books, 1976.

RICHMOND, MARY. "The Need of a Training School in Applied Philanthropy," *Proceedings* of the National Conference of Charities and Correction (Boston: Ellis, 1897): 181–86.

STEINER, JESSE. *Education for Social Work.* Chicago: University of Chicago Press, 1921.

STITES, MARY A. *History of the American Association of Medical Social Workers.* Washington, D.C.: American Association of Medical Social Workers, 1955.

TUFTS, JAMES H. *Education and Training for Social Work.* New York: Holt, 1923.

TYLER, RALPH W. "Distinctive Attributes of Education for the Professions," *Social Work Journal* 33 (April 1952): 55–62.

WALKER, SYDNOR H. *Social Work and the Training of Social Workers.* Chapel Hill: University of North Carolina Press, 1928.

WARD, LESTER FRANK. *Dynamic Sociology,* 2 Vols. New York: Appleton, 1883.

WENCOUR, STANLEY, AND MICHAEL REISCH. *From Charity to Enterprise: The Development of American Social Work in a Market Economy.* Urbana: University of Illinois Press, 1989.

WIEBE, ROBERT H. *The Search for Order, 1877–1920.* New York: Hill and Wang, 1967.

WITTE, ERNEST F. "Social Work Education in the United States: A Review," *Child Welfare* 31 (June 1952): 6–9.

WRIGHT, HELEN R. "Research and the Social Services," *Social Service Review* 15 (December 1941): 625–35.

Social Work and Welfare in the 1920s

In their drive toward professionalization, social workers underwent changes in outlook and in practice. To paraphrase two students of the subject, in outlook, from viewing the needy person as largely a product of impersonal social and economic forces, social workers came to see him or her as primarily a product of personal impulses. In practice, they went from concern with social reform and preventive legislation to preoccupation with individuals and with methods and techniques to help them become adjusted to their environment.[1] Thus, at the turn of the century, the spirit of social work had been described in this way: "Other tasks for other ages. This be the glory of ours, that the social causes of dependency shall be destroyed." Twenty-five years later, with the push for professionalism and the evolution of social and psychiatric casework, it was described otherwise: "The concern of social work is the individual, . . . the understanding of his needs, . . . and his adjustment to his environment."

Absorbed in the technical aspects of their work (such as more competent use of their new skills and training so that they could be deemed worthy of professional recognition), most social workers in the 1920s no longer had the time or inclination for social reform. Instead, they operated on the premise that an individual in need had the strength and inner resources which, if freed from the shackles of fear, inhibition,

---

[1]The author wishes once again to acknowledge his debt to Harold L. Wilensky and Charles N. Lebeaux, *Industrial Society and Social Welfare* (New York: Free Press, 1958), as a source of many of his ideas on the professionalization of social work, including the developments in the 1920s.

and other psychological impediments, could overcome his or her diffi-culty. They frequently discussed ego strengths and weaknesses and tried to help clients help themselves by clarifying their problems. Men out of work were no longer regarded as able, healthy people willing to work if given a chance; rather, they were viewed as abnormal or mal-adjusted individuals whose mental or emotional deficiencies were the causes of their unemployment. Hence, they were not supplied with jobs; instead, they were helped to understand why they had lost their jobs or why they were having difficulty finding new ones.

This method of dealing with needy people on a personal basis in an attempt to reconstruct their lives, rather than the social and eco-nomic conditions under which they lived and worked, was, of course, not novel. The charity organization societies and their friendly visitors had a personalized approach to social welfare. But because they knew little about the human personality—psychology was still in its infancy and there was a paucity of knowledge about emotional problems—and because they had a moralistic approach to the needy—they made decisions on the basis of judgmental attitudes and middle-class values and sought to distinguish between the "worthy" and "unworthy" poor—friendly visitors provided little or no real treatment. They merely investigated the needy and on occasion attempted to manipu-late them, to get them to change their way of life or rid themselves of "bad" influences (especially alcohol or bad associates), in the long run relying upon the shaping power of the environment. In their hands, "casework," as it came to be called, was basically a device for snoop-ing, refusing appeals for help, or attempting to control the needy. No wonder it came under heavy attack.

Despite the attacks, casework did not disappear; it was utilized in a number of institutional settings—in the court (probation work), in the school (truancy work), in the hospital (medical social work), and in the mental facility (aftercare work). As a way of dealing with pover-ty, however, it was pushed into the background. Settlement house resi-dents focused on social and economic problems rather than on needy people, being more interested in reform and preventive legislation than in individual treatment. By the early 1920s, however, thanks largely to Mary Richmond, publication of her classic book, *Social Diagnosis*, and a number of other factors, casework once again became dominant.

Miss Richmond, a frail woman who spent most of her life over-coming chronic invalidism in order to help others, was born in Belleville, Illinois, in 1861. Orphaned when young and frequently ill, she spent a lonely, unhappy childhood in Baltimore. Starting in 1878, she held a variety of jobs, but in 1889 she began her life's work by becoming assistant treasurer of Baltimore's Charity Organization Society. Two years later, she became its general secretary, a position she held until 1899 when, after moving to Philadelphia, she headed that city's Society for Organizing Charity. In 1909, she became direc-tor of the Charity Organization Department of the newly formed Russell Sage Foundation in New York City.

Influenced by the organized charity movement at home and abroad and by such European figures as Thomas Chalmers and Octavia Hill, both of whom believed in the individual causes of poverty and the self-help concept, Mary Richmond came naturally to the casework approach. Unhappy, however, because it had no logical-ly conceived theoretical base, she spent years on the tedious and sometimes painful task of systematically probing the entire proce-dure. Eventually, she applied the medical model to social work and conceived of investigation, diagnosis, prognosis, and treatment as entities in a chain-like series; the treatment of individuals, then, was an extended, logical process, the techniques of which could be ordered, described, analyzed, and transmitted from one generation of social workers to another. She embodied her ideas in *Social Diagnosis* (which of course implied a pathology, or disease), the first definitive treatise in book form of social casework theory and method. The work not only won immediate widespread acclaim, but almost overnight helped raise casework from one of several instruments of the charity worker—one clearly overshadowed at the time by research and reform—to a method and philosophy that was preeminent in the profession.

Three things are worth noting. First, Mary Richmond's book, orig-inally published in 1917, was not influenced by the writings or thought of Sigmund Freud, the brilliant psychoanalyst. Freud had paid a visit to the United States—his only one—in 1909 to deliver a significant series of lectures at Clark University in Worcester, Massachusetts. At the time, he was still a relatively obscure Viennese neurologist. And although his progress as a celebrity was fairly rapid thereafter, and Freudianism and psychoanalysis became more and more popular between 1909 and 1917, as Nathan Hale, Jr., has shown, most of the literature on the man and the subject was confined to periodicals read mainly by physicians, psychologists, and a few young intellectuals. Freud was still not widely known to the general public. In any event, *Social Diagnosis* bore the impress of the preceding sociological rather than the oncoming psychoanalytical era; it described the caseworker as an artificer in social relations and emphasized the social environment and financial distress rather than psychological factors and intrapsychic conflict. As a result, it soon would be outdated, as "Mary Richmond's 1922 defeat as a candidate for the presidency of the National Conference of Social Work may have symbolized," to use the words of Stanley Wencour and Michael Reisch (although it should be added that, in a book published five years later, *What Is Social Case Work?*, Mary Richmond talked about personality rather than character, indicating that she embraced the path casework would take).

Second, while Mary Richmond was not enthusiastic about social reform, she was not hostile toward it or toward other social work methods. In fact, she deplored the "socially mischievous" antagonism between the social worker and social reformer, and tried desperately to show her associates how casework was related to other forms of social work, including research and reform: "This topic of the interplay of different forms of social work deserves fuller treatment than I have been able to give it," she pointed out, "but that all forms are inextricably woven in the great task of furthering social advance should be evident." On another occasion she exclaimed in exasperation: "I have spent twenty-five years of my life in an attempt to get social casework accepted as a valid process in social work" and now "I shall spend the rest of my life trying to demonstrate to social caseworkers that there is more to social work than . . . casework."

Still, in her opinion, social reform had failed. Despite the rise of preventive social work and the enactment of a great deal of social legislation, poverty and need had not been eliminated—nor could they be. The need for individual treatment would always persist. As one of her colleagues put it, social action and reform dealt with need in wholesale, casework dealt with need in retail; both were essential. Mary Richmond employed the retail method. Handling individuals in need, she used the step-by-step process of helping them, a process that once again became widely accepted by social workers.

Third, casework, for Mary Richmond, consisted of both diagnosis and treatment, and she was as concerned with the latter as with the former. *Social Diagnosis*, however, dealt only with the first of these matters—the investigation of clients' problems. She intended to deal with the second at a later date, something she never did.

In any event, one reason for the enormous enthusiasm casework received after publication of *Social Diagnosis*, was the negative approach that had been taken in a widely publicized paper read at the 1915 National Conference by Dr. Abraham Flexner, assistant secretary of the General Education Board and the foremost authority in America on graduate professional education. In his paper "Is Social Work a Profession?" Flexner, to the dismay of his audience, concluded that social work was not a profession since it had no unique method. Rather, it was a function of conscripting the resources of the community and placing them at the disposal of the needy. Social workers, he said, were kindhearted, resourceful people engaged in good work— work, he contended, that almost anyone could do. They were mediators rather than originators of action; the "very variety of the situations the social worker encounters compels him to be not a professional agent so much as the mediator invoking this or that professional agency." Hence, if a man is sick, the social worker gets a doctor; he does not utilize any technical skill of his own. Lacking its own "technique which is communicable by an educational process," social work was no profession!

Flexner's paper had a profound effect upon the social worker and his or her world. While not all social workers accepted his criteria, or his analysis, most did, including four leaders in the field chosen to "respond" to Flexner's assessment, all of whom agreed that social work had to narrow its focus and develop an educationally communicable technique in order to become a profession. So, accepting the verdict as pronounced by this expert on the subject, social workers (whose slogan, according to John Ehrenreich, had become "neither alms nor a friend nor a neighbor but 'a professional service'") desperately began trying to define and perfect techniques they could call their own.[2]

Then came Mary Richmond's *Social Diagnosis*, a 500-page work that guided the reader—the beginning caseworker—through every conceivable circumstance to be found in the lives and attitudes of prospective clients, and described in minute detail how to secure the necessary data in each instance, why such data were basic, what weight should be given each item in determining the final assessment, and the like, thus seemingly meeting the most exacting requirements of professional and scholarly standards, the very criteria specified by Flexner.[3] Perhaps more important, because the work codified activities social workers previously thought of as "investigation" but referred to them as "diagnosis," it further signified to many social work's professionalism. As a result, the effect of the work was dramatic. Almost overnight, social diagnosis or casework became the method of social work and the badge of professionalism, overshadowing even to this day all other techniques in the field.

This trend toward casework was reinforced by America's entrance into World War I. First of all, shortly after the United States entered the war, the American Red Cross set up a Home Service Division to provide casework services to uprooted soldiers and their families—of all classes. Existing schools and well-known social workers collaborated with the agency in developing training "sessions" to prepare people for such work. In fact, the American Red Cross provided funds to fifteen colleges and universities, some of which came from the United States Public Health Service, to finance the creation and teaching of

---

[2]They did so with such a singleness of purpose that they virtually blinded themselves to the fact that method was only *one* test of a profession. And while method is important, indeed essential, for a profession, the practitioner whose sole objective is facility in a method becomes a technician and fails to realize to the fullest his or her professional responsibilities; that is, to examine his and the profession's place in society and continuously interpret to himself and to his contemporaries the social problems he and his colleagues are attempting to solve, something most social workers failed to do in the 1920s.

[3]Unfortunately, *Social Diagnosis*, the first edition of which sold out in a month, was more concerned with process than with person, with means rather than with ends, and continued to blind many social workers to the fact that methods were not the raison d'être of social work.

such courses, and Mary Richmond prepared a special casework manual for use in them. Welcoming the opportunity to expand their practice and theory in casework, social workers eagerly registered for those
courses and then worked with the Red Cross in providing such services to some 3,700 chapters that reached into 15,000 communities
all across the United States.

More important, dealing with people "above the poverty line"
demonstrated that successful casework did not have to depend on
relief funds to hold its clients and made it easier to construe casework
as a technical service analogous to that performed by a lawyer or even
a doctor. At the same time, however, it raised challenging problems
for the social worker. Since much casework dealt with maladies formerly outside the social worker's experience—war neuroses, for example—the necessity of linking hands with psychologists and psychiatrists in order to become well versed in their revelations of the human
psyche was seen. Psychologists and psychiatrists, for their part,
encouraged such an alliance.

Psychologists, psychiatrists, and physicians who examined the men
called into military service, or who treated those rejected or dismissed
because of mental or emotional problems, saw in caseworkers, specialists in the field of social adjustment, just the assisting personnel they
needed. Enamored by the opportunity to work with doctors and flat-
tered by the offer, many social workers seized the opportunity. World
War I thus helped facilitate the social workers' shift from a social-eco-
nomic to an individual-psychological base. Then, in July 1918, thanks
to the initiative of Dr. E. E. Southard, director of Boston's
Psychopathic Hospital, and Mary Jarrett, chief of its Social Services
Department, Smith College established a School of Psychiatric Social
Work to train personnel for work with mental patients—the first of
its kind in America which, interestingly, began by offering a six-
month course for psychiatric aides attached to the Army Medical
Service. This not only symbolized the growing importance of psychiatric theory for social work, but by training psychiatric social workers
the school furthered its use as well.

Creation of the school symbolized another, related matter—two
different reactions to World War I among "social workers." Many settlement house residents and social reformers opposed the war and
America's involvement in it, while most caseworkers supported the

conflict. Thus, while Jane Addams and many of her colleagues were actively involved in the peace movement, Mary Richmond and many of her colleagues were actively involved in the Home Service Division of the American Red Cross. And revealingly, although Jane Addams would receive a number of honorary degrees during her lifetime, not one came from a school of social work; in 1921 Smith College conferred such an honor on Mary Richmond.

Meanwhile, the need for new knowledge, which wartime social workers had felt, was further satisfied in the 1920s by the mental hygiene movement and the work of the National Committee for Mental Hygiene, and especially by psychoanalytic thought, which by that time had become almost a national mania. The casework emphasis upon the individual and upon an introspective view of problems made social workers naturally receptive to Freud. More important, enthusiastic acceptance of his ideas resulted from the fact that much of what Freud said found responsive echoes in caseworkers' experiences and at the same time provided them with both a theoretical base and a scientific method of treatment that until that time had been lacking.

Social workers already knew that some individual afflictions (of the flesh as well as of the spirit) were not amenable to programs of social betterment; they remained untouched by social engineering. They could not predict which persons would respond successfully to such an approach and which would not. Moreover, they did not have a systematic way to proceed when personality *was* the resistant factor. They acted intuitively and used "common sense"; success depended more on chance than on any logically conceived process. Therefore, they were ready to accept and utilize the new concept of psychoanalysis, with its relatively coherent theory of personality, focusing upon the importance of childhood experiences and emotions in shaping personality and behavior.[4]

In other words, Freud's ideas placed caseworker's relationships with clients in a new light; psychoanalytic theory was a body of knowledge that provided them with a scientific understanding and a way of deal-

---

[4]Psychoanalysis is both a systematic structure of theories concerning the relation of conscious and unconscious psychological processes to human behavior and a technical procedure for investigating those processes and treating psychoneuroses.

ing with psychological factors in human behavior that they had long observed but could not explain—facets of human behavior hitherto ignored as irrelevant or dismissed as irrational. It was obvious that a close relationship existed between the method of evaluating social data, as developed by the caseworker, and the psychiatrist's method of probing the inner recesses of the mentally ill. Each dealt with people in difficult situations but only the latter had developed a method designed to explain the nature of the trouble and how to aid the patients or clients to overcome it by themselves. It was inevitable, or certainly likely, that an intellectual mating of the two would occur, and that they would work together to achieve their respective goals.

Elated, many social workers set about adapting Freud's major discoveries in the language and practice of psychoanalysis to the language and practice of casework. They naturally identified themselves with the psychiatric clinical team rather than with social reformers or even social caseworkers, who seemed old fashioned if not passé. (Once alerted to the effects of the unconscious on motivation, psychiatric caseworkers felt that environmentalism, based upon the assumption that people are rational, had no relation to the dynamic factors in human behavior.) They developed a fresh concept of casework, based on Freud, the mysteries of the psyche, personality, and the emotions. As one historian has written, "The psychiatric social worker emerged as the queen of the caseworkers," for if her point of view was relevant to all casework, no group was better qualified by training and experience to speak for the profession.

Most important, psychiatry promised to eliminate one of the most serious obstacles to the attainment of professional status by the social worker—the historic link with charity and humanitarianism, the belief that social work required nothing more than a warm heart and a cheerful outlook. The new preoccupation with psychological rather than with economic factors allowed social workers to see and portray themselves in a new light. No longer were they dispensers of charity interested primarily in the poor. Rather, shorn of old-time moralism and armed with a vocabulary strewn with psychological and medical terms, they were social physicians concerned with problems of emotional maladjustment—problems that occurred as frequently among the upper classes as among the lower—and this was worthy of professional status. To no one's surprise, then, when in 1925 William

Hodson, president of the American Association of Social Workers, gave the keynote address at the National Conference of Social Work, entitled, "Is Social Work Professional? A Re-Examination of the Question," he and most others attending the session answered resoundingly in the affirmative. So too, apparently, did the general public, for five years later social workers were included for the first time in the federal census as a distinct occupational group.

The new professionalism, however, may not have been as far removed from the old moralism as many social workers would have liked to believe. As David and Sheila Rothman have pointed out, the net result of the new approach "was to couch in modern terminology some very traditional ideas." Once again, the poor were responsible for their difficulties, only now rationalized in updated language. The unworthy poor had become the emotionally disturbed or deprived poor. Or, as an equally perceptive student of the subject put it: "Substituting expertise for moral superiority as the basis of the relationship, social workers [in the 1920s] perpetuated the charity organization ideal of personal contact and influence in place of material relief, but avoided the fiction that such contact was one of friends and peers bound in neighborhood association." Or finally, in the words of John Ehrenreich, yet another commentator on this return to a theory of client culpability in a new guise, "It was a matter of St. Sigmund rather than St. Peter. . . . it was certainly not a matter of St. Karl."

Nevertheless, this surrender to Freud and the clinical orientation contributed further to the shift already taking place in social workers' orientation from the social environment to the individual emotional environment, from poverty and economic problems to personality and emotional problems, from social reform to individual adjustment. Other forces within the field—forces not peculiar to social work but typical features of an urban-industrial society that affected most aspects of American life at the time—tended to further reinforce this development. The growing size of agency operations and the demand for specialization, for example, meant that social workers were caught up in bureaucratic routines that usually afforded little opportunity for observing or dealing with anything more than their clients; limited by regulations, procedures, and systems of hierarchical structure and forced to abide by various agency as well as professional standards, practitioners did not have the time or the incentive to become involved in social policy, theory, or reform. Increasingly, policies were determined by executives and committees (often comprised of conservative lay men and women) over which the practitioner had little or no control.

With this growth in the size of operations, social work leaders became administrators rather than professional colleagues. Gertrude Vaile, in her presidential address before the National Conference in 1926, lamented the decreasing zeal in the field, attributing it in large part to the decline in crusading leadership and the emergence of a new kind of institutional head, more an organizer and an executive absorbed in administrative duties than someone likely to possess the penetrating insight, broad social vision, or humanity of the great social work leaders of the Progressive era.

Related was the problem of money raising. With more and more and larger and larger agencies, raising funds became a greater problem, not only for organizations but for potential donors as well. Many causes and appeals compelled a degree of selectivity that givers often found difficult to make. Eventually, united giving, or the community chest, the ultimate in bureaucracy—an anonymous public supporting anonymous machinery supporting anonymous clients—was utilized.

Federated fund raising began much earlier, like so many other developments in American social welfare, in England, where it was tried for the first time in Liverpool in 1873. Its inception in America came in 1887 with the creation of the Associated Charities of Denver. While a few other localities followed suit, most community chests were not created until during, and especially after, World War I. During the conflict, "war chests" sprang up almost overnight and thousands of people who never before had known what it was to give to charity, gave generously. After the war, the war chests were converted into community chests. So rapidly did the idea grow, that by the mid-1920s about 200 cities had adopted the plan and the movement was still spreading.

While in theory federated fund raising offered innovative programs and agencies with little popular support an opportunity to get started, in practice just the opposite occurred. Community chests proved to be conservative forces in social welfare, formalizing the somewhat uneasy but long-standing alliance between private agencies and wealthy donors. A throwback to C.O.S. days, in that they sought to streamline, coordinate, and control the financing and administration of private charity (and a reflection of the consolidation of big business that took place in the 1920s, just as the organized charities reflected the monopolization of big business in the late nineteenth century), the chests requested support not for individual agencies but for an organized pattern of welfare services that was tied to the social structure of the community. This, in turn, contested the independence and distinctiveness (and even the leadership of the heads) of the participating agencies, for the power of their purses, and thus their very existence, was in the hands of outsiders—usually the community's business and financial leaders—to whom they had to be accountable.[5] To be funded, agencies were forced to play it safe, to stress service to the community, to refurbish established practice rather than to encourage social reform and change from the existing order—and to "buddy up" to the funding organizations.

Thus, in her study on *Settlement Houses and the Great Depression*, Judith Trolander found not only that the National Consumers' League and other reform groups could not get financial support from community chests but that the programs of various settlement houses, especially the degree to which they sought to alter prevailing social and economic conditions, were related directly to whether or not those institutions were financed by such agencies: "Although settlement boards retained control over personnel, the ultimate decisions as to the programs of the individual houses [in any given city] were made by the chests which controlled their finances." And, she wrote, the "more dependent a settlement house was on a community chest, the more conservative it was on social issues," whatever they happened to be. "Those settlements that functioned meaningfully as community organizers [in the 1920s and 1930s] were those which remained relatively independent of the business-dominated chests." This would help explain the loss of reformist zeal among those settlement houses that managed to survive the so-called prosperity decade.

There were still other external factors that help to explain the shift in social work away from reform and back toward individual service. As Mary Richmond and others had pointed out, despite the reforms of the early twentieth century, many of the problems that had plagued

---

[5]This was especially true since in most cases member agencies were required to give up their own fund raising efforts (in order, theoretically, to avoid duplication of appeal), thus making them almost totally dependent on the community chest, now usually known as the United Way.

the organized charities and the settlement houses persisted. In some ways, the entire Progressive movement had been a failure. In many respects, American society in the 1920s was no different than it had been two or three decades earlier; big business dominated society, racism and bigotry were growing, political corruption was widespread, mass conformity prevailed, and, with the suppression of civil liberties during the war and the enactment of Prohibition after it, even the federal government had become an instrument of repression and social control. Many Americans, not just social workers, were disillusioned with the progressive crusade and with social reform in general.

Then, too, there was the widespread belief that social reform was unnecessary, for this was the "prosperity decade," or so it was believed. There was no need to improve the social environment, to eliminate poverty, to raise the standard of living; for all practical purposes, those tasks had already been accomplished, as Herbert Hoover told Americans in October 1928. Congratulating his countrymen on being born into a land from which poverty had been banished, the G.O.P. presidential candidate declared: "Our American experiment in human welfare has yielded a degree of wellbeing unparalleled in all the world. It has come nearer to the abolition of poverty, to the abolition of fear of want, than humanity has ever reached before." And it got there, Hoover and many others believed, not through state intervention (or social reform) but through individualism and voluntarism— through science and technology, big business, industrial relations, welfare capitalism, and the like. So, emphasis upon the individual and the consequent refusal to face harsh social and economic facts reflected not only the social worker's preoccupation with the three "Ps"—professionalism, psychiatry, and psychoanalysis—but also the conservative social and economic climate of the postwar years.

This is not to say, however, that psychoanalytic theory completely dominated social work thought and practice in the 1920s—that there was a "Freudian deluge" during the prosperity decade.[6] Casework clearly became the nuclear skill of the emerging profession and "coun-

---

[6]To social reformers, though, it may have seemed like such a deluge; social reform, one activist bitterly declared, had given way to "individual psychology, social psychology, psychiatry, and social psychiatry, psychometry, mental testing, mental hygiene, psychoanalysis, child guidance, and what not."

seling," especially family counseling provided by private agencies, often to middle- and upper-class families for a fee, certainly had its roots in this period—and became the major professional ideal. In addition, public welfare departments now hired caseworkers to provide "services" to their clients, as did "habit clinics," psychiatrically oriented, hospital-based facilities designed to treat behavior problems among young children; schools, to provide assistance to families whose children were having adjustment problems; the Commonwealth Fund, to staff its child guidance clinics which now experimented with the psychiatric casework model; and the U.S. Veterans Bureau, to treat maladjusted veterans. However, the psychiatric caseworker still remained a member of an elite (although growing) minority, and psychodynamic formulations did not come to pervade agency practice until later.[7] Actually, most social workers and welfare agencies at this time sought to bring the insights of the new psychology into line with the older practice, based upon rational assumptions and environmental manipulation. If the two could be combined, the best efforts of both approaches could be achieved.

Nor is it correct to suggest that the development of casework as the professional method and of family counseling as the professional function brought an end to all relief giving. Some caseworkers and family service agencies still provided clients with financial aid but reconciled doing so with psychiatry and professionalism. They argued that they had to deal with the reality of clients' obsession with money, the key to both their physical and their emotional survival. Financial dependency in America—a competitive capitalistic society that equated wealth with status—implied personal inadequacy and unworthiness. Needy clients, therefore, carried the burdens of guilt and inferiority, psychological liabilities that financial relief could help rectify. The social worker could not permit clients' concerns with money to go

---

[7]Particularly important in that regard was the publication, in 1930, of Virginia Robinson's *A Changing Psychology in Social Case Work*, a book that sharply contrasted with Mary Richmond's *Social Diagnosis*. To use Roy Lubove's words, Robinson "abstracted casework almost entirely from its roots in the client's social environment and cultural milieu and placed it squarely in the camp of the psychiatrists and psychologists." In other words, she made casework synonymous with psychotherapy, and publication of her work opened the gates much wider to the teachings of Freud in the schools of social work.

unattended. Moreover, the skilled caseworker could use financial relief to promote therapeutic objectives: such assistance provided an excellent entrée into the confidence and good will of clients and, by insuring physical survival, permitted them to divert their attention to non-material matters.

Finally, it also would be incorrect to say that the 1920s were totally devoid of social reform. Clarke Chambers and others have amply demonstrated that, thanks to the efforts of some social workers and others, the decade was not a complete wasteland for constructive social change. In Chambers's words, although they at times suffered from confusion and disunity and were often frustrated and rebuffed, "social workers kept alive and vital the crusade for social action, and thus formed a viable link between prewar progressivism and the New Deal; they sparked many social action crusades that anticipated the reform programs of the following decade." However, while some social workers remained reformers and worked for important social changes, including the abolition of child labor and the improvement of public and mental health services and facilities, most did not.[8] Those who continued the reform tradition were not professional social workers, graduates of training schools, but basically the same people who had led the progressive crusade earlier in the century, including some aging settlement house residents. On the whole, the profession, including its schools and organizations, embodied the spirit herein described.

By the time of the Great Depression, then, social work had undergone or was undergoing a profound change, from "cause" to "function," to use Porter Lee's terms, from advocating reform to efficiently rendering technical services. "I am inclined to think," Lee told his colleagues at the National Conference in 1929, "that in the capacity of the social worker . . . to administer routine functional responsibility in the spirit of the servant in the cause lies the explanation of the great service of social work."

Most social workers attended training schools which had already adopted or were in the process of adopting as their main requirement

---

[8] Thus in 1924, when Roger Baldwin, founder of the American Civil Liberties Union, called upon his colleagues at the National Conference of Social Work to create a new political party committed to social reform, he received a frigid reception.

some sort of course on "Human Growth and Development." Designed to present an integrated theory of human personality, it concentrated on such Freudian concepts as defense mechanisms, transference, ego strengths and weaknesses, libidinal attachment, the Oedipus complex, and so on. After graduation, the students became practitioners—a growing number, psychiatric caseworkers—who helped clients to become adjusted to their environment. They saw themselves as technicians with a responsibility to their cases, not as crusaders bent upon curing the maladies of society.

This, however, did not solve all of social work's problems. On the contrary, it left the young profession with some very serious ones. As noted earlier, the changes that occurred in the 1920s seriously affected the profession's leadership and zeal, and thus its effectiveness. Instead of broad-minded, charismatic leaders motivated by a true sense of neighborliness, such as Jane Addams, Florence Kelley, and Julia Lathrop, leadership was assumed by uninspiring and uninspired bureaucrats and executives who merely conducted the business of running various agencies. Then there was the virtual demise of the settlement house movement, which, in turn, had a detrimental effect on the profession.

More significant, was the fact that psychiatry—which at first seemed to be a blessing that would elevate social work to its deeply cherished professional status—created a serious long-range problem for the field. Aside from undermining the capacity and desire for social workers to promote change and deal with mass deprivation in an urban society, psychiatry threatened the very professional identity which social workers were so anxious to attain, for if psychiatric knowledge was fundamental to the profession, what distinguished psychiatric casework from psychotherapy, except for the social worker's inferior education and training? Were psychiatric social workers mere handmaidens to psychiatrists? Indeed, even members of the Milford Conference, an annual meeting of social work executives and board members held to discuss matters related to the promotion of social work as a profession, suggested as much in their 1928 report when they stated, "At the present stage of [social work's] development, no definition of . . . casework can distinguish it sufficiently from other professional fields." As Roy Lubove has pointed out, it was one thing to reject social reform, but quite another to fail to substitute some specific alternative that really differentiated the social worker from others in the helping professions.[9] For this and other reasons, some critics have argued that social work was, and remains, an "incomplete profession," or a "semi-profession."[10]

And finally, while social workers' efforts to increase scientific understanding of personality were legitimate, they swung the pendulum too far. Despite all their professions, the social and economic causes of poverty—illness, injury, low wages, involuntary unemployment, old age, death of the family breadwinner—had not disappeared. And dependency caused by these factors demanded social and economic solutions, not casework, social or psychiatric. A handful of older charity workers, social workers (Karl de Schweinitz and some others), and reformers such as Jane Addams, Florence Kelley, and Isaac Rubinow not only saw this but also warned of the danger of neglecting these matters. So, too, did the National Federation of Settlements, which in 1928 was so worried about growing unemployment that it launched a study on the subject, one that clearly dispelled the myth of "full employment" (even during the "prosperity decade")—the belief that anyone who really wanted to work could find a job. Meanwhile, the stock market crashed and the Great Depression followed, and the reformers' worst fears proved to be true; the nation's social welfare institutions and agencies were unprepared to meet the crisis.

Bibliography

ALEXANDER, LESLIE B. "Social Work's Freudian Deluge: Myth or Reality?" *Social Service Review* 46 (December 1972): 517–38.

AUSTIN, DAVID M. "The Flexner Myth and the History of Social Work," *Social Service Review* 57 (September 1983): 357–77.

---

[9] In most settings, caseworkers practiced on turf controlled by others—in hospitals, schools, courts, departments of public welfare, and the like. No wonder more and more of them were drawn to private practice.

[10] In addition, and through no fault of their own, social work was, and again is, an "unloved profession," in part because its members work (or are perceived to work) with people in society who are despised, rejected, and feared and in part because most of its members (approximately 80 percent in the late 1920s) were, and remain, women, and American society accords little significance, and prestige, to "woman's work."

BERLEMAN, WILLIAM C. "Mary Richmond's *Social Diagnosis* in Retrospect," *Social Casework* 49 (July 1968): 395–402.

BORENZWEIG, HERMAN. "Social Work and Psychoanalytic Theory: A Historical Analysis," *Social Work* 16 (January 1971): 7–16.

CHAMBERS, CLARKE A. *Seedtime of Reform: American Social Service and Social Action, 1918–1933.* Minneapolis: University of Minnesota Press, 1963.

———. "Women in the Creation of the Profession of Social Work," *Social Service Review* 60 (March 1986): 1–33.

CHEPAITIS, JOSEPH B. "Federal Social Welfare Progressivism in the 1920s," *Social Service Review* 46 (June 1972): 213–29.

COLCORD, JOANNA, AND RUTH MANN, eds. *The Long View: Papers and Addresses by Mary E. Richmond.* New York: Russell Sage Foundation, 1930.

DAVIS, ALLEN. "Welfare Reform and World War I," *American Quarterly* 19 (Fall 1967): 516–33.

DRESSEL, PAULA. "Patriarchy and Social Welfare Work," *Social Problems* 34 (June 1987): 294–309.

EHRENREICH, JOHN. *The Altruistic Imagination: A History of Social Work and Social Policy in the United States.* Ithaca: Cornell University Press, 1985.

FIELD, MARTHA H. "Social Casework Practice During the Psychiatric Deluge," *Social Service Review* 54 (December 1980): 482–507.

FLEXNER, ABRAHAM. "Is Social Work a Profession?" *Proceedings* of the National Conference of Charities and Correction (Chicago: Hildmann, 1915): 576–90.

FRIEND, MAURICE R. "The Historical Development of Family Diagnosis," *Social Service Review* 34 (March 1960): 2–16.

GARRET, ANNETTE. "Historical Survey of the Evolution of Casework," *Social Casework* 30 (June 1949): 219–29.

GILBERT, NEIL, AND HARRY SPECHT. "The Incomplete Profession," in *The Emergence of Social Welfare and Social Work.* Itasca, Ill.: Peacock, 1976.

GREEN, A. D. "The Professional Worker in the Bureaucracy," *Social Service Review* 40 (March 1966): 71–83.

GRINKER, R. R., et al. "The Early Years of Psychiatric Social Work," *Social Service Review* 35 (June 1961): 111–26.

HALE, NATHAN G., JR., *Freud and the Americans.* New York: Oxford University Press, 1971.

HEIMAN, MARCEL, ed. *Psychoanalysis and Social Work.* New York: International Universities Press, 1953.

HODSON, WILLIAM. "Is Social Work Professional? A Re-examination of the Question," *Proceedings* of the National Conference of Social Work (Chicago: University of Chicago Press, 1925): 629–36.

LEE, PORTER. "Social Work as Cause and Function," *Proceedings* of the National Conference of Social Work (Chicago: University of Chicago Press, 1929): 3–20.

LEEBRON, HARVEY. *The Financial Federation Movement*. Chicago: American Association for Community Organization, 1924.

LURIE, H. L. "Private Philanthropy and Federated Fund-Raising," *Social Service Review* 29 (March 1955): 64–74.

NEUSTAEDTER, ELEANOR. "The Integration of Economic and Psychological Factors in Family Case Work," *Proceedings* of the National Conference of Social Work (Chicago: University of Chicago Press, 1930): 198–216.

ODENCRANTZ, LOUISE C. *The Social Worker in Family, Medical and Psychiatric Social Work*. New York: Harper, 1929.

ORME, JOHN G. AND PAUL STUART. "The Habit Clinics: Behavioral Social Work and Prevention in the 1920s," *Social Service Review* 55 (June 1981): 242–56.

PERLMAN, HELEN HARRIS. "Freud's Contribution to Social Welfare," *Social Service Review* 31 (June 1957): 192–202.

POPPLE, PHILIP R. "The Social Work Profession: A Reconceptualization," *Social Service Review* 59 (December 1985): 560–77.

POTUCHEK, JEAN L. "The Context of Social Service Funding: The Funding Relationship," *Social Service Review* 60 (September 1986): 421–36.

PUMPHREY, MURIEL. "The 'First Step'—Mary Richmond's Earliest Professional Reading, 1889–91," *Social Service Review* 31 (June 1957): 144–63.

RICH, MARGARET. *A Belief in People: A History of Family Social Work*. New York: Family Service Association of America, 1956.

———. "Mary Richmond: Social Worker, 1861–1928," *Social Casework* 33 (October 1952): 363–70.

RICHAN, WILLARD, C., AND ALLAN R. MENDELSOHN. *Social Work: The Unloved Profession*. New York: New Viewpoints, 1973.

RICHMOND, MARY. *The Good Neighbor in the Modern City*. Philadelphia: Lippincott, 1907.

———. *Social Diagnosis*. New York: Russell Sage Foundation, 1917.

———. *What Is Social Case Work?* New York: Russell Sage Foundation, 1922.

ROBINSON, VIRGINIA P. *A Changing Psychology in Social Case Work*. Chapel Hill, University of North Carolina Press, 1930.

ROSS, AILEEN D. "The Social Control of Philanthropy," *American Journal of Sociology* 58 (March 1953): 451–60.

RUBINOW, I. M. "Can Private Philanthropy Do It?" *Social Service Review* 3 (September 1929): 361–94.

SEELEY, JOHN R. et al. *Community Chest: A Case Study in Philanthropy.* Toronto: University of Toronto Press, 1957.

SMITH, DAVID H. "The Philanthropy Business," *Society* 15 (January–February 1978): 8–15.

TOREN, NINA. *Social Work: The Case of a Semi-Profession.* Beverly Hills: Sage Publications, 1972.

TROLANDER, JUDITH. *Professionalism and Social Change: From the Settlement House Movement to Neighborhood Centers, 1886 to the Present.* New York: Columbia University Press, 1987.

————. *Settlement Houses and the Great Depression.* Detroit: Wayne State University Press, 1975.

VAILE, GERTRUDE. "Some Significant Trends Since Cleveland, 1912," *The Family* 7 (July 1926): 127–33.

WALKOWITZ, DANIEL. "The Making of a Feminine Professional Identity: Social Workers in the 1920s," *American Historical Review* 95 (October 1990): 1051–75.

WATTS, PHYLLIS A. "Casework Above the Poverty Line: The Influence of Home Service in World War I on Social Work," *Social Service Review* 38 (September 1964): 303–15.

WILENSKY, HAROLD L., AND CHARLES N. LEBEAUX. *Industrial Society and Social Welfare.* New York: Free Press, 1965.

WOODROOFE, KATHLEEN. *From Charity to Social Work in England and America.* Toronto: University of Toronto Press, 1962.

Depression and a New Deal

The stock market crash in the fall of 1929, and the long, deep depression that followed, hit the nation with a jarring impact. Some thirteen to fifteen million workers lost their jobs. Banks were closed, some permanently. Many citizens lost their lifelong savings; some took their own lives. Factories lay idle. Stores had few customers. Hundreds of thousands of farmers were forced off their land. Numerous others lost their homes. Huddled figures shuffling despondently in bread lines or at soup kitchens testified to destitution and suffering (in rural areas and in small towns as well as in large cities) to an extent unknown in American history.

The task of relieving the jobless and their families was first undertaken by private local agencies. It quickly became evident, however, that they were unprepared to meet the crisis. To begin with, they were ill suited to the task because the "services" they performed would not feed the hungry or shelter the homeless. Furthermore, the financial needs of so many people—not only the aged, the sick, the disabled, and other members of the lower classes but also the plain, ordinary middle-class people who had worked all their lives but who were now unemployed, penniless, and hungry, the so-called new poor—were clearly beyond their meager means; indeed, between 1929 and 1932, about one-third of the nation's private agencies disappeared for lack of funds, and many others faced the same fate. As one observer aptly remarked, "Trying to turn back this tide of distress through private philanthropic contributions is about as useless as trying to put out a forest fire with a garden hose." For many, then, the depression answered, once and for all, the vexing question of whether private or public agencies should be responsible for relief-giving. Voluntary charity simply could not cope with the situation; only public agencies could deal with the collapse of the economy, mass unemployment, and widespread destitution.

Despite the suffering, public action to meet the emergency did not make itself felt for some time, especially since so many localities had abolished public home relief. Public officials made some effort to encourage reemployment. A few committees were organized by state and federal personnel, but they were advisory in nature, and for the most part they confined themselves to continued encouragement of local enterprise. Other than certain municipal and state public works projects, no public action of consequence was taken until September 1931—almost two years after the crash. Then, under the prodding of Governor Franklin D. Roosevelt, the New York State Legislature acted to provide unemployment relief to jobless citizens of that state.

In the meantime, many social workers saw—were forced to see— that destitution usually resulted from social and economic factors which the needy could not control. As a result, they began to engage in self-criticism—and to call for a renewed commitment to social reform, to the "cause" orientation they largely had abandoned in the 1920s in favor of the "functional" one. Thus Harry Lurie, executive director of the newly created Bureau of Jewish Social Research, and many other social workers argued that they and their colleagues had to "share responsibility with industrial and political leaders for the present catastrophe" because "we did not throw ourselves into the struggle for a . . . reconstruction of our economic society as zealously as we gave ourselves [over] to the perfection of our technique." It was time, they declared, to return to social action! In the same vein, Grace Coyle lashed out at those in the field who "continued to pick up the pieces without ever attempting to stop the breakage." Or as another social worker put it: "The futility of the case by case method of dealing with the problem is increasingly obvious. The flood must be stopped at its source, not mopped up by the bucketful, however scientifically modelled the bucket." Even Bertha Reynolds, associate director of the Smith College School of Psychiatric Social Work, agreed. It would be absurd to deal with emotional problems when there were millions of hungry people to feed; other methods were needed to handle the crisis. And the Milford Conference, which only a few years earlier had concluded that the progress of social work as a profession was tied to the development of more effective, and distinctive, case-work techniques, now proclaimed that "the future of social work is bound up with the coming of a sounder social order."

Most social workers responded accordingly. Aware of the inadequacy of private and even local public resources, as well as the desperate straits to which many Americans were being driven—and obviously feeling a bit guilty for spending too much time on the perfection of techniques and not enough on social reform in the 1920s—they called for public action, even federal aid. Thus, in October 1931, William Hodson, executive director of the New York City Welfare Council, addressed an open letter to President Herbert Hoover urging federal unemployment relief—not as a matter of charity but as a matter of right. Over the next few months, Hodson and others, including the American Association of Social Workers, took an active part in organizing a series of historic U.S. Senate committee hearings on unemployment relief.

Testifying before the LaFollette-Costigan Committee, which held those hearings, a social worker described how families in Philadelphia were forced to manage under the circumstances:

> One woman went along the docks and picked up vegetables that fell from wagons. Sometimes fish vendors gave her fish at the end of the day. On two different occasions the family was without food for a day and a half. Another family did not have food for two days. Then the husband went out and gathered dandelions and the family ate them.

Another social worker appearing before the committee presented an account of a family of ten that had just moved into a three-room apartment that was already occupied by a family of five. "However shocking that may be to members of this Committee," the witness stated, "it is almost an everyday occurrence." Walter West, executive secretary of the American Association of Social Workers, summed up the situation best when he said, "The relief problem has ceased to be a local one. It is national in origin [and] . . . national in scope." It needed a national response!

Despite the gravity of the situation, the pleas of social workers and others, and the LaFollette-Costigan Committee's evidence that federal aid was needed, there was still a great deal of opposition to such action, especially from President Herbert Hoover. Over the past decade or two, a number of historians—Joan Hoff Wilson, David Burner, and others—have reassessed Hoover and his career, including his presidency, and have argued that he was a complex, thoughtful, intelligent, and able leader who led the way into the policies and programs of the New Deal. It is true that in 1921, as Secretary of Commerce, Hoover had convened a conference on unemployment relief to deal with the problems of the postwar recession and in 1927 he had organized a major flood relief effort in the Mississippi Valley. It also is true that as a result of these and other things, including his successful experiences as a relief administrator in Europe during and after World War I and as a food administrator in America after the United States entered the conflict, Hoover had a good deal of support among social workers throughout the nation when he ran for President in 1928. Nevertheless, when he was in the White House and the economy collapsed, Hoover's response to America's deep depression was less than adequate, to put it kindly—and most of the social work community turned away from him.

To begin with, Hoover refused to recognize or admit the seriousness of the problem. He was convinced that the economy was sound and that prosperity was just around the corner—all that was necessary was a restoration of confidence. Thus, the public was reminded time after time that "the fundamental business of the country . . . is on a sound and prosperous basis," that "we now have passed the worst," that "the crisis will be over within sixty days," and so on.

Hoover's miscalculated optimism or blindness was aggravated by his loyalty to the American folklore of self-help (which, Edith Abbott maintained, was not "rugged individualism but Malthusian sophistry"). For him, relief was a moral, not merely an economic, matter; private charity (such as he had distributed in war-ravaged Europe) was fine, but public aid, especially from the national government, was a "dole." Thus, while Hoover approved of relief distributed by the American Red Cross, for example, he rejected all proposals for federal aid.

Hoover opposed federal aid for a wide variety of reasons. In his opinion, it would delay the natural forces at work to restore prosperity, it impaired the credit and solvency of the government, it stifled voluntary giving, it was inflexible and thus could not respond to local needs, it established politicized bureaucracies, it undermined free enterprise, it was illegal—a violation of local responsibility and states' rights—and it ultimately endangered democratic government: "You cannot extend the mastery of government over the daily lives of the people without at the same time making it the master of their souls and thoughts," Hoover declared. Why federal aid for the unemployed and needy necessarily meant government mastery over their lives—or whether neglect and starvation were better—he did not say, even though *The Nation* magazine asked of him, "Shall Americans Starve?" and "Must Americans perish miserably because of your fear that their characters may be sullied by a dole?"

The belief that public assistance would demoralize and enslave its recipients while private charity would not—that somehow private was democratic and public undemocratic—was, of course, an old idea that long since had been outmoded. Among other things, this notion failed to recognize that the imperatives of a modern society had rendered many of the distinctions between private organizations and public agencies meaningless (if they ever had existed), so that the American Red Cross was far from immune to the bureaucratic rigidities, arbitrary methods, and other alleged evils Hoover attributed to large public organizations. Indeed, it had more staff and higher annual expenditures than most government bureaus—and was more bureaucratic than most as well. Far more important, however, was the fact that by 1930 and 1931 the country's economy had collapsed, millions of citizens were unemployed through no fault of their own, states and cities were teetering on the edge of bankruptcy, *and* the nation's private charitable resources had dried up. The jobless and the hungry wanted and needed to eat! It made little difference to them who supplied the food.

Hoover's attitude toward public relief was exemplified in December 1930, when he approved a congressional appropriation of $45 million to feed stricken livestock of Arkansas farmers but opposed an additional $25 million to feed the starving farmers and their families; cattle, obviously, could not get demoralized. A year later, when House Speaker John Garner and Senator Robert F. Wagner of New York jointly sponsored a measure calling for a $2.6 billion federal public works program, arguing that such a project would put people back to work and stimulate the economy, Hoover vetoed the measure, declaring that "never before in the nation's entire history has anyone made so dangerous a suggestion."[1]

Elsewhere, however, bold action was taken. "The country needs, and unless I mistake its temper, the country demands bold, persistent experimentation," New York Governor Franklin D. Roosevelt would declare in accepting the Democratic Party's presidential nomination in 1932. "It is common sense to take a method and try it. If it fails try another. But above all, try something."

Roosevelt had indeed tried something. Less bound by tradition than Hoover and aware (from studies conducted for him by the Joint Committee on Unemployment Relief of the State Board of Welfare and the New York State Charities Aid Association) that unemployment was not only severe but getting worse, in August 1931 he called a special session of the legislature to consider the emergency. Placing unemployment in the same category as old age, widowhood, and industrial accidents—hazards over which the individual had no control, certainly not in the current crisis—the Chief Executive asked the state's lawmakers for funds to help local authorities meet the needs of the unemployed. "Modern society acting through its government owes the definite obligation to prevent the starvation or dire waste of any of its fellow men and women who try to maintain themselves but

---

[1]Hoover was obviously not a good student of history—the only subject he failed while attending college. The idea of federal public works projects during times of involuntary unemployment was an old one, going at least as far back in England to the Poor Laws of 1536 and 1601 and in America to the depression of the 1890s, when "General" Jacob Coxey of Ohio led an army of unemployed on a march to Washington demanding, among other things, a federal public works program. In any event, despite presidential reassurances, prosperity was not around the corner; in fact, conditions continued to grow worse. Finally, after three winters of depression so severe that it had depleted even state, let alone private and local, resources, Hoover consented to (and thus in essence admitted the need for) some federal action. In the summer of 1932, he signed the Emergency Relief and Construction Act, a measure that authorized the Reconstruction Finance Corporation (a federal agency created six months earlier to extend government aid to large corporations and banks) to lend to the states up to $300 million "to be used in furnishing relief and work relief to needy and distressed people and in relieving the hardships resulting from unemployment." Since they were loans rather than grants, however, many states, already heavily in debt, refused to borrow such funds, and by the end of 1932 only one-tenth of the appropriated sum, or $30 million, was sent to the states for relief purposes, while Congress had sent more than three times that amount to a single Chicago bank, the head of which was former Vice President and R.F.C. chairman Charles G. Dawes. Many of the nation's hungry were incensed.

cannot," Roosevelt told them. Aid to jobless citizens, he declared, "must be extended by government, not as a matter of charity, but as a matter of social duty."

Inasmuch as relief funds came from taxation, which was borne by the entire community, most of those who received aid, Roosevelt argued, had contributed to relief costs during their days of self-support; they were not receiving something for nothing. Since relief was financed on the same basis as all other public services, accepting such aid, the Governor maintained, should be no different from sending children to public school or calling the fire department.

In any event, the State Unemployment Relief Act—better known as the Wicks Act—emerged from the special legislative session, making the Empire State the nation's first to provide unemployment relief to its needy citizens. Enacted on September 23, 1931, the measure provided for an emergency period, during which time millions of dollars in aid were extended to localities throughout the state, on a matching basis, for work and for home relief under the direction of a new, independent agency, T.E.R.A.—the Temporary Emergency Relief Administration. Harry Hopkins, an energetic young social worker employed by the New York Tuberculosis and Public Health Association, was made executive director of the program.

The act was of major significance. Among other things, it helped establish the constructive social value of adequate public relief, and thus helped to break down the notion that such aid tended to pauperize and demoralize its recipients. In addition, by treating unemployment as a statewide social problem, the measure went far toward changing the setting within which social work operated. The army of unemployed had to be dealt with en masse, not individually. Social workers, once again, were forced to visualize themselves as something more than the custodians of the individual; they had to deal with the welfare of many people. Furthermore, by bringing many trained social workers into government service, quite a few of whom were borrowed from private agencies, the T.E.R.A. forged significant links between private charity and public welfare.

Equally important, the Wicks Act was widely copied. By the end of the year, twenty-four states had followed New York's example of providing unemployment relief and setting up a new state agency to administer the funds. And finally, it served as a forerunner and prototype for later federal practices, providing not only a model but also personnel for New Deal programs and agencies.

As the name of its administrative agency (T.E.R.A.) indicated, the Wicks Act was conceived of as a temporary device intended to bring the state into the business of providing unemployment relief merely for the duration of the crisis. Still, New York and the states that followed its lead were acting, while, for the most part, Washington did nothing. Instead, one member of the President's cabinet suggested that restaurant owners be urged to collect plate scraps and leftovers and place them in containers to be distributed to the "worthy" unemployed, perhaps a superfluous suggestion, as an item in a Chicago newspaper indicated: "Around the truck which was unloading garbage and other refuse were about thirty-five men, women, and children. As soon as the truck pulled away from the pile, all of them started digging with sticks, some with their hands, grabbing bits of food and vegetables."

As a result of federal inaction, by the fall of 1932, the nation faced a serious threat. Disorder spread and talk of revolution was heard; many destitute and starving citizens had only contempt for the government and the system that was responsible for their plight but that did little to alleviate their distress. Then came the federal election—a decisive popular rejection of many of Hoover's conservative shibboleths, including a fear of anything that resembled a "dole"—and, several months later, the inauguration of Franklin D. Roosevelt as the thirty-second President of the United States.

Roosevelt had been an excellent governor of New York. While in principle he was rather conservative—he favored small government, local responsibility, and balanced budgets, and thus never endorsed Keynesian deficit spending as a matter of economic theory, and he did not like public home relief—as an heir to the progressive social justice movement he was more concerned about the suffering of the unemployed and other needy than about adhering to certain beliefs. He also knew (as Boss Plunkitt had known) that appealing welfare policies were good politics. Thus, he was especially strong in matters of social justice, and during his two terms in office the state's Public Welfare Law was vastly improved, a progressive Old Age Pension Law passed, and the Wicks Act and other social legislation enacted. Under his leadership, New York became the most progressive state in America with regard to taking practical steps to prevent and relieve distress.

As President, Roosevelt acted on the same ideas that had guided his actions as governor—the beliefs that "government was not the master but the creature of the people," that mankind had a responsibility for the well-being of all human beings, that an impersonal and uncontrolled economic system, not the unemployed themselves, usually caused unemployment, that public assistance was not a matter of charity but a matter of justice that rested upon the individual's right to a minimum standard of living in a civilized society, and that liberty and security were synonymous; thus, the very existence of a democratic state depended upon the health and welfare of its citizens. So, although he came into office with a pledge for retrenchment and economy, it was plain he would do what was necessary in order to aid the needy, even if it meant spending federal funds and incurring large deficits—at least for a while. By instituting a large federal relief program and by reviving the economy, however slowly, Roosevelt succeeded in restoring confidence in the nation's basic institutions, thereby preventing further catastrophe.

This, of course, is not to say that Roosevelt was a saint. He certainly had some shortcomings, particularly in the area of civil rights, especially for blacks, where he moved very slowly. Despite having a favorable image among black people and despite his success in weaning most of them away from the Republican Party, Roosevelt's actual commitment to the Negro was slim; he was more a symbol than an activist for the oppressed minority, at least prior to America's entrance into World War II.

Roosevelt sympathized with the black citizen's plight, but his compassion was tempered by many of the decisions which came before him and by the political considerations he had to face. An astute politician, he generally used political weights and measures on a scale to judge the evidence, and blacks were often found wanting. Thus, when Walter White, executive secretary of the N.A.A.C.P., obtained an audience (through the good graces of Eleanor Roosevelt) with the President to plead for his public support of a federal antilynching bill, F.D.R. demurred because he needed southern votes in Congress on other matters. Likewise, the progress of many federal relief measures was dogged by racial discrimination.

Thus, the Civilian Conservation Corps (C.C.C.) not only restricted the enrollment of blacks to 10 percent of the total but also in many instances placed blacks in segregated areas. In addition, black tenant farmers and sharecroppers suffered greatly from government-induced crop reductions under the provisions of the Agricultural Adjustment Act (A.A.A.).[2] So many others suffered the loss of jobs from the closing of small businesses as a result of the National Recovery Administration's (N.R.A.) "codes of fair competition" that blacks referred to the measure that had created the new federal agency as the "Negro Removal Act." Under the Federal Emergency Relief Act (F.E.R.A.), the design of work projects and the allocation of funds were left to local officials, who often discriminated against blacks, especially in southern rural areas, but elsewhere as well. One could cite numerous other examples of racial discrimination during the so-called New Deal (including the Social Security Act, which will be discussed shortly). In sum, just as wealth was inequitably distributed, so too was poverty; blacks and other minority group members, who usually were the first to lose their jobs and the last to be rehired, and who in the interim received the least assistance, felt the crush of the depression even more than did their white counterparts.[3]

In any event, soon after entering the White House, surrounded by signs of despair and social unrest and convinced that the need for federal assistance was so overwhelming that it could no longer be postponed, President Roosevelt plunged the national government into the business of relief. The Civilian Conservation Corps (C.C.C.) took thousands of unemployed young men off the streets and out of rural slums and put them to work on reforestation and flood and fire control. The Public Works Administration (P.W.A.) provided employment for millions of citizens in vast public works programs created to stimulate depressed industries, especially construction. The National

---

[2]Perhaps it should be mentioned that the most deprived members of American society at this time were small farmers and farm laborers, especially sharecroppers and tenants living in the South, white as well as black. Their bleak living and working conditions and their grievous suffering are movingly described by James Patterson in *America's Struggle Against Poverty, 1900-1985* (Cambridge, Mass.: Harvard University Press, 1986), pp. 38-39.

[3]Nevertheless, according to Nancy Weiss, F.D.R. (or his wife and some members of his administration) did more for blacks, especially after 1935, than did most of his predecessors, and thus, in her words, "for the masses of blacks the New Deal made a difference." See her *Farewell to the Party of Lincoln* (Princeton: Princeton University Press, 1983).

Youth Administration (N.Y.A.) provided part-time jobs for high school and college students so that they could earn enough money to complete their education. The Works Progress Administration (W.P.A., later known as the Works Projects Administration) provided jobs for the unemployed, including artists, musicians, and scholars, suited to their skills and experience. These and a host of other measures—the Wagner National Labor Relations Act, which finally gave unions effective guarantees of their right to organize; the Farm Security Administration, which, in a variety of ways, aided small farmers and migratory workers; the Wagner-Steagall Housing Act, which established the U.S. Housing Authority to provide low-interest loans to local officials to build public housing; and so on—indicated Roosevelt's willingness to mobilize the resources of the nation to battle hard times and to assist those in need through no fault of their own.

This is not to say that all these and other alphabet agencies and programs were ideal or that they worked perfectly. On the contrary, as Bonnie Fox Schwartz has amply demonstrated in her article "Social Workers and New Deal Politicians in Conflict," "politics" was not entirely lacking in their design or implementation. Many party regulars—Democrats and Republicans alike—found it difficult to separate opportunities to aid the unfortunate from opportunities to aid themselves through the bountiful flow of dollars and jobs from Washington to their localities and state.

Moreover, federal work relief programs, which were aimed at patching up rather than significantly changing the system, were not designed to put all the unemployed to work or to pay wages that competed with those of private enterprise. At least partial unemployment was considered desirable in order to keep down the salaries of those who were fortunate enough to be at work, and, in fact, at their maximum effectiveness, all the New Deal work relief programs provided employment for only about one-third of the jobless. Likewise, while the income of those on work relief was greater than that of welfare recipients, their wages were considerably lower than those paid to employees doing comparable work in the private sector and their "hours" far fewer—a source of encouragement not only to continue working but to take a job in private industry as soon as one became available. In short, these programs were clearly constructed so as not to threaten private profits: the welfare of the lower classes remained secondary to the welfare of the business classes—and the principle of "less eligibility" had not completely died out. Still, given the conservative nature of American society and what had, or had not, preceded them, these measures were a significant advance. Moreover, whatever their shortcomings, work relief programs were looked upon favorably by most Americans, chiefly because they made public assistance something earned rather than merely granted, whether it be as a right or as a charity. Not only did millions of citizens who otherwise would have had no income receive at least some assistance thanks to these programs, but also they did so in a way that permitted them to retain their dignity and respectability. Interestingly, while much talked about, public work relief programs have been used very rarely since the early 1930s, no doubt because they continue to be viewed by many as a threat to the marketplace; thus they have been replaced by education and job training programs.

At any rate, one of the earliest and most important of the new federal relief measures was the Federal Emergency Relief Act, signed into law in May 1933. A tradition-shattering statute that opened up an era of federal aid that had momentous consequences for social welfare, the measure made available at the outset $500 million of federal funds to be distributed as grants-in-aid to the states (half on a one-for-three matching basis and half simply on the basis of need) to be used for emergency unemployment relief, transferring responsibility for the relief of a large number of citizens from the county (and, in part, state) to the federal government.

The Federal Emergency Relief Act, which of course acknowledged that unemployment was national in scope and that only the federal government had the resources to adequately deal with the problem, was closely patterned after New York State's Wicks Act and, like its model, was conceived of as a temporary emergency measure. It set up the nation's first national relief agency (the Freedmen's Bureau excepted), the Federal Emergency Relief Administration (F.E.R.A.), and the social-minded Harry Hopkins, executive director of New York's T.E.R.A., was appointed its head.

While the authority for determining the extent of the grants-in-aid to the states was vested in the head of F.E.R.A., the responsibility for administering funds remained with the states and localities. Although from the outset the main emphasis was on emergency work programs, federal aid covered all forms of unemployment relief, including home relief, to be paid in cash, and a surplus commodities program to help distressed rural families.

Furthermore, provisions of the statute stipulated that each local relief administrator was to employ at least one experienced social worker on his or her staff, with at least one qualified supervisor for every twenty employees. This not only helped further bridge the gap between social work and public welfare (a process started earlier by Hopkins in New York under the T.E.R.A.) but also had a profound constructive effect on both—it brought social workers and their methods into every county and township in America and, by assuring the public that welfare would be administered by skillful, professional social workers (rather than politicians or appointive officers), it helped to dissipate further the fears of public assistance.

Also important was a directive by Harry Hopkins that all federal grants were to be handled by public agencies. Thus, state bodies were prohibited from turning over federal funds to private agencies, an important matter in light of the widespread use of the subsidy system and the many abuses that resulted from it.

The federal statute did the job assigned to it and did it well. It was one of the largest public relief programs in the world, eventually touching some twenty million lives and expending some $4 billion. Its policies were uniform throughout the nation, it functioned with speed and dispatch, and its program was carried out with little waste or corruption.

Clearly the best of the New Deal welfare measures, however, was the Civil Works Administration (C.W.A.), created by an executive order of the President in November 1933. This crash program was designed to put lots of people to work quickly, not to provide them with "relief." Thus, whereas to qualify for aid under the F.E.R.A. (and the other welfare programs) potential recipients had to appear at a relief station, certify that they were needy, and then undergo a "means test," no such stigmatizing strings were attached to the C.W.A. Furthermore, it offered "regular" hours of work and paid "going" wages, which averaged two and a half times F.E.R.A. benefits. As a result, no New Deal creation was better received than the C.W.A. (despite opposition from a few social workers who were unhappy with the program because it was in the hands of engineers unsympathetic to their professional aspirations)—or created more dismay when it was terminated in March 1934, throwing some four million people out of work or forcing them on to the rolls of the much less desirable F.E.R.A., which itself was phased out a year and a half later, again placing the unemployed at the mercy of the states and localities, neither of which had the financial resources to care adequately for them.

Actually, the C.W.A. debacle, as it was viewed by some, brought to a head some social work discontent with Roosevelt and the New Deal. Whereas most social workers had few reservations about capitalism, even in the midst of the depression, and hence supported the administration and its reform efforts, a radical minority did not. Seeking a fundamental reorganization of society—a planned socialist economy—members of this group, led by Mary van Kleeck of the Russell Sage Foundation and Harry Lurie, now head of the newly created Council of Jewish Federations and Welfare Funds, were unhappy with both the aims and the accomplishments of the New Deal—and their colleagues who supported it. Known as "Rank-and-Filers" (to distinguish themselves from the majority, "professional" social workers centered in the American Association of Social Workers), they were upset at the administration not only for abruptly terminating the C.W.A. but also for its racism, its political expediency, its emphasis on work relief, its ties to big business, and a number of other things. They would be very unhappy with defeat of the so-called Lundeen bill, or the Workers' Unemployment, Old Age, and Social Insurance Bill, which would have provided, without a means test, "flat" benefits equal to prevailing wages for all the unemployed (including farmers) for as long as they were jobless through no fault of their own, from funds derived from general tax revenues—and they were unhappy with passage, instead, of the Social Security Act, with its emphasis on contributory social insurance, its limited coverage, and its relatively meager benefits. They also would be troubled by the administration's failure to enact health insurance legislation, and the decision to end the F.E.R.A. (in December 1935, several months after passage of the S.S.A.) would further infuriate them. In short, to them, Roosevelt's do-something program was not much better than Hoover's do-nothing approach; it merely stabilized poverty and strengthened the structure of a faulty economic order. An absorbing account of these dissidents, some of whom were vigorous allies of the Communist Party and whose chief accomplishment was the forging of some ties between social work and organized labor, can be found in Jacob Fisher's *The Response of Social Work to the Depression*, or in the pages of their journal, *Social Work Today*.

Whatever the merits or demerits of the New Deal or of the left-wingers' evaluation of it, Roosevelt was intent on getting the federal government out of "this business of relief." Surely, he was anxious to save money, but he also never really liked direct federal assistance or envisioned it as a permanent feature of the American welfare system; indeed, he was anxious to prevent it from becoming what he called a "habit with this country." (Roosevelt's decision to discontinue the F.E.R.A. and replace it with the W.P.A., a work relief program, reflected that desire.) He also knew, however, that relief alone, especially on a temporary basis, was not enough to assuage the economic insecurity that grew out of the depression. Something more was needed, something of a lasting nature that would not only include a rescue operation to relieve distress during emergencies, but would comprise a long-range plan for preventing dependency, especially for the nation's aged, many of whom were hard hit by the depression.[4] Aside from humanitarian considerations, a system of security that would help prevent destitution was essential for social and economic stability: "Democracy has disappeared in several other great nations," the President declared on one occasion, "because the people of those nations had grown tired of unemployment and insecurity. . . . In desperation they chose to sacrifice liberty in the hope of getting something to eat. We, in America, know that our democratic institutions can be preserved and made to work," only, however, by proving that "the practical operation of democratic government is equal to the task

---

[4]From 1920 to 1934, the American population increased by 20 percent, while the number of industrial jobs declined by about 25 percent. In addition, the death rate declined considerably. This meant that more and more people, with fewer jobs, were living longer lives. This was reflected in the estimate that three out of every four people in America over the age of sixty-five were dependent, in whole or in part, upon others for their means of support. It is not surprising, then, that there was a great deal of pressure on the administration for some sort of old-age assistance, especially by advocates of the so-called Townsend Plan, a scheme concocted by Dr. Francis Townsend of California. Townsend, who claimed to have more than a million followers, advocated monthly payments of $200 to all persons over sixty years of age on the sole proviso that they retire from work and spend the money.

of protecting the security of the people"—a far cry from Hoover's fears of government "mastery."

With these things in mind, on June 8, 1934, President Roosevelt sent to Congress a special message calling for "some safeguards against misfortunes which cannot be wholly eliminated in this man-made world of ours." He urged creation of a system that would "provide at once security against several of the great disturbing factors of life," and advised the Congress that when it reconvened in January 1935, he would place before it such a program.

Three weeks later, by executive order, Roosevelt created a Committee on Economic Security and charged it with the responsibility of developing a workable social security program, one that he could submit to Congress for action. The committee, which consisted of four cabinet members and Harry Hopkins, and which was headed by Secretary of Labor Frances Perkins, hired a University of Wisconsin economist and expert in the field, Edwin E. Witte, to be its executive director. An excellent choice for the position, Witte was not only knowledgeable, but patient, statesmanlike, and a tireless worker. He received able help from one of his former students, Wilbur J. Cohen, who came with him to Washington as his research assistant. They, in turn, relied upon the services of numerous others (including another former Witte student who would become the first Social Security Board chairman—Assistant Secretary of Labor Arthur J. Altmeyer), anyone who, in Witte's words, "in one way or another . . . had ever written anything touching on social security problems or who claimed to have any special knowledge of any phase of the subject."

By January 17, 1935, the committee and its staff had finished their work. After much study, the hearing of a great deal of testimony, and wrestling with many technical and policy questions, they supplied a set of recommendations for a social security program which Roosevelt then transmitted to Congress. The program was embodied in a federal bill sponsored in the U.S. Senate by Robert F. Wagner of New York, and in the House by David Lewis of Maryland, two legislators who had known firsthand the problems of social insecurity. The bill, which was passed in Congress by a vote of 371 to 33 in the House and 77 to 6 in the Senate, became law on August 14, 1935.

As finally adopted, the Social Security Act was an omnibus measure, which through two lines of defense—contributory social insurance and public assistance—aimed at preventing destitution. It provided for old-age insurance (or pensions) and public assistance for the aged; unemployment insurance (or compensation) for the jobless; public assistance to dependent children in single-parent families, to crippled children, and to the blind; and federal monies for state and local public health work.

First, and most important, the act created a national system of Old-Age Insurance (O.A.I.) in which most employers were compelled to participate. At age sixty-five, workers would receive retirement annuities financed by taxes on their wages and on their employers' payroll; the benefits would vary in proportion to how much they had earned and contributed. Only those with steady employment records, then, would receive such benefits; "social security" would be tied to the labor market. In addition, however, the measure created a program of Old-Age Assistance (O.A.A.) in which the U.S. government would share with the states the cost of the care of persons over sixty-five who were not able to take part in the Old-Age Insurance system or who, after receiving O.A.I., still "needed" such assistance. (Because only a small proportion of older people were eligible for O.A.I. in 1940, when the first "pensions" were paid, it was not until 1953 that more recipients received O.A.I. than O.A.A.)

It has been argued by William Graebner and others that these old-age provisions of the Social Security Act were included less out of humane considerations than out of concern about the marketplace: corporate leaders and businessmen wanted to encourage (force?) older workers to leave the labor force in order to provide jobs to younger, more productive employees. No doubt there is an element of truth to that view. But there are other elements as well, which cannot be ignored, including the aging of the population and the growing organization among older citizens who wanted such pensions and indeed had been working for them for a long time. As Edwin Witte later put it, without pressure from the elderly "I doubt whether anything . . . would have gone through at all." So, these measures, which provided some security, or at least help, to millions of Americans without any fundamental changes in the social or economic order, were politically advantageous to the administration. In the end, then, Old-Age Insurance and Old-Age Assistance served the interests of many—and were very popular.

The act also set up a federal-state system of Unemployment Insurance designed to encourage the states to carry the administrative burden. The law required employers to contribute to the federal treasury a certain percentage of their payroll for insurance purposes, but it also stipulated that 90 percent of that levy would be returned to those states that set up their own unemployment insurance plans in accordance with standards approved by a federal Social Security Board created to administer the program. (Within two years, every state had set up an unemployment insurance system that met the requirements fixed by the board.)

In addition, the act provided federal aid to the states, on a matching basis, to help single-parent families with dependent children ("to assist, broaden, and supervise existing mothers' aid programs"), crippled youngsters, and the blind. While these "categorical relief" programs would come under severe attack later on, especially in the 1960s, '70s, and '80s, when the Aid to Dependent Children (A.D.C.) rolls increased dramatically and contained many unmarried black women (as opposed to "worthy" white widows), at the time they were included with very little discussion and no controversy. And finally, the act also provided federal funds for state and local public health work.

With the exception of unemployment insurance, which by 1934 had been enacted only in the state of Wisconsin, the provisions of the Social Security Act were not novel. They were influenced by or based upon previous or existing federal and state statutes, such as the Sheppard-Towner and Federal Emergency Relief Acts, and numerous state widows' aid and old-age pension laws.[5] The new statute merely strengthened, expanded, and in some cases revived these practices. Furthermore, based primarily on the insurance principle rather than on the public assistance model (which the fiscally conservative F.D.R. favored), it provided "welfare" only to the needy blind, aged, and young—the unemployable, or "deserving poor."

Nevertheless, the Social Security Act became the target of a good deal of criticism—from all sides. There were those, of course, who liked it, such as Secretary of Labor Frances Perkins, chair of the Committee on Economic Security and the first woman to hold a cabi-

---

[5] By 1934, twenty-seven states had old-age pension systems as well as laws providing cash assistance to the blind, and forty-five had widows' pension laws.

net position, who no doubt spoke for the majority when she said that it constituted "a very significant step in grounding a well-rounded, unified, long-range plan for social security." For others, however, including the U.S. Chamber of Commerce and the National Association of Manufacturers, the measure went too far to the left, was too radical—a violation of the traditional American concepts of self-help and individual responsibility—and therefore was a threat to individual liberty and the American way of life. This, of course, is not to say that all big businessmen opposed it; indeed, some, including Gerard Swope of General Electric and Marion Folsom of Eastman Kodak, openly supported the Social Security Act, and there is evidence to suggest that there was considerably less opposition to the program from the business community than the administration had expected.

In fact, some of the most vigorous opposition came from those who attacked the act for not going far enough, not just the 15,000 or so "Rank-and-Filers" but more moderate people, too, including Isaac Rubinow, Abraham Epstein, another longtime crusader for social insurance, Solomon Lowenstein, executive director of the New York Federation of Jewish Philanthropies, and Frank J. Bruno, a noted social work educator. Bruno considered it "a series of miscellaneous provisions in the field of public welfare which altogether do not furnish a logical plan for social security." It can "only be called a measure to furnish such means as do not arouse opposition," he stated.

Actually, these critics were right. At best, the Social Security Act was a compromise framed within the political and fiscal realities of the day, a practical attempt to provide a floor for recipients to stand on. At worst, it was a conservative racist and sexist measure that fell far short of its title, one that clearly would not provide an adequate standard of living for those exclusively dependent on it. In large part financed through individual contributions, it not only tied benefits to stable long-term labor force participation, but it was a deflationary and regressive measure that siphoned off billions of dollars in taxes from the purchasing power of those it was supposed to protect (made worse by the fact that workers started contributing to the system in 1937 but did not start receiving benefits from it until 1940).

Insofar as workers were taxed for the various benefits, the act was like a sales tax, making the poor pay for the poor, especially since the system of financing the measure levied a stiffer tax burden on low-wage earners than on higher ones. And, insofar as employers were taxed (for old-age pensions and unemployment compensation), the cost was passed on to the consumer in the form of higher prices—in both cases, lowering the standard of living. The measure did nothing about fundamental social and economic problems, including the question of income redistribution. And it established the only welfare system in the world in which the state did not bear full responsibility for the care of its senior citizens (through general tax revenues raised, for the most part, from the more well-to-do); only in America did workers contribute directly to a program of old-age security.

There were other shortcomings. The system paid benefits on the basis of past earnings and contributions, not on current needs. Moreover, the payments were minimal. Also, unemployment compensation was limited to a relatively short period, with no provision for coverage beyond that period. It neglected the question of permanent disability. More important, the law, as originally enacted, left millions of people unprotected, covering only "regular workers"; it excluded from its provisions numerous classes of people, including many of those who needed protection most, especially farm laborers; seasonal and migrant workers, many of whom were black men and women; domestic servants, most of whom, of course, were women, black and white alike; and workers' dependents, also, for the most part, women. In addition, the measure did not eliminate "local variation"; that is, even though they received federal funds and had to adhere to federal regulations concerning eligibility, the states remained responsible for setting benefit levels, virtually assuring disparities in the provision of payments (a problem that continues to plague the system today)—and assuring that blacks, most of whom still resided in southern states, would be deprived of adequate assistance. No wonder that certain critics today maintain that the Social Security Act's purpose was to protect some white males from the vagaries of the marketplace.

The most serious criticism of the act, however, was its omission of health insurance, perhaps the most pressing need in the field of social security, the oldest form of compulsory social insurance in the world, and one that was almost universally included in the social insurance programs of other nations.

When the Committee on Economic Security began its work,

health insurance was designated as the principal topic for inquiry. Thus, the matter was not only discussed, but committee members concluded that sickness was the major cause of insecurity and that its prevention and treatment were the most humane and least expensive ways of dealing with the problem. In their report to the President, they advocated a national health insurance program and even included detailed recommendations for its implementation. But there was a great deal of well-organized opposition to health insurance, especially from the medical profession, and, rather than jeopardize the entire Social Security Bill, its sponsors decided to eliminate it from the measure—with the understanding that a separate national health insurance proposal would be introduced in Congress shortly after passage of the first measure. (In later defending that position, Wilbur Cohen put it this way: It was better "to digest one meal at a time rather than eat breakfast, lunch, and dinner all at once and get indigestion.") The failure to enact such a measure is one of the unwritten chapters in American social welfare history.

Still, the Social Security Act—upheld by the U.S. Supreme Court on May 24, 1937, in two separate decisions, *Steward Machine Co.* v. *Davis* (301 U.S. 548) and *Helvering* v. *Davis* (301 U.S. 619)—was a landmark in American history. Without minimizing its shortcomings, one can say that it brought expanded and improved standards of welfare activities throughout the nation and marked a substantial advance in the nation's treatment of its poor.[6] By giving people cash payments in cases of unemployment, old age, and loss of the family breadwinner—some of the leading causes of poverty—it not only helped prevent destitution and dependency but did so in a way that did not threaten individual freedom and human dignity.

As a result of the statute, destitution (as least in theory) was no longer regarded as a question of individual weakness. It was recog-

---

[6]One of the more important advances in that regard was the establishment of public welfare departments in just about every county in America, virtually made mandatory under the public assistance and child health and welfare titles of the act. While mandating such units and requiring approved plans of operation for receipt of federal monies, which had to be administered on the basis of financial need, not "character," the act, however, left to the states many other specifics, not only regarding benefits but eligibility as well, including "means-testing," which again allowed for great variation from state to state and encouraged a number of other shortcomings, including administrative discretion and discrimination.

nized as a fundamental social and economic problem, one that needed to be attacked by society as a whole, hence the need for a national system of social security. For the first time in the modern period, the American people as a whole accepted the assumption that a large number of people had a right (which could be legally enforced) to public benefits, or at least that failure to provide such benefits was socially and economically shortsighted. In either case, the charitable and the temporary gave way to the just and the permanent, and the dominance of private charity over public welfare came to an end. Public welfare emerged from relatively small and often inadequate programs associated with the poor—a gratuity to be given or withheld at the discretion of an administrator—to a great network of activities providing a variety of services to a broad spectrum of society, services protected by the right to equal treatment and a "fair hearing" when so denied.

The Social Security Act also established a new alignment of responsibility in the field of public welfare. It marked the beginning of a policy of federal aid to the states upon a permanent basis for regular, recurring social work, closing the door on three centuries of the poor law and its principle of local responsibility. For the first time in American history, funds to finance all or part of the needs of selected groups in the population became a major permanent item in the federal budget, one that has continued to grow each year. With the S.S.A. (and other New Deal programs), which introduced the idea of *entitlement* into national policy, the federal government assumed responsibility for the welfare of most, if not all, of its citizens; hence, the American welfare state was born—or at least the "semiwelfare" state, to use Michael Katz's term.[7]

During the last few years, a great many scholars—Theda Skocpol, John Inkenberry, Kenneth Finegold, Margaret Weir, Ann Orloff, Jill Quadagno, and others—have tried to determine why the United States lagged behind the rest of the industrialized world in creating a

---

[7]It consisted largely of (1) social insurance (financed by workers and their employers), which provided pensions to retired workers and unemployment compensation to the jobless, (2) categorical public assistance (financed by the federal government and the states) for the needy aged not entitled to "pensions," the blind, and dependent children, (3) work relief (funded by the federal government) for jobless employables, and (4) general assistance (funded by the states and counties) for the needy who did not fall into the other categories.

welfare state. And while there are differences of opinion among them, most agree that it was due to a combination of factors, including opposition from many labor union leaders and big businessmen who wished to retain their virtual monopoly over workers' "benefits" and thus combated federal intrusion in that area; the resistance of politically powerful southern planters to any loss of local control over their low-wage, predominantly black work force; the lack of adequate financial resources by a national government that did not have an income tax until 1913, and other impediments. Most important, however, were a variety of related political and administrative liabilities that inhibited the systematic development of such a structure, especially a federal system of powerful states, a weak national government, a patronage-based rather than a program-based political party system (due to universal suffrage) and the distrust of public officials that accompanied such a system, a small permanent federal bureaucracy, and an underdeveloped national administrative capacity. It was not until the mid-1930s, thanks to the Great Depression and the enactment of the Social Security Act, that enough of these obstacles were overcome and an American welfare state could germinate.

The seed planted by the Social Security Act sprouted in many ways. Not only did subsequent legislation widen the law's coverage and increase its benefits (making it, in Andrew Achenbaum's words, "a central feature of American life" today, one that helps more people—men and women, black and white—escape poverty than all other federal programs combined) but also, from the agency created to implement the act, the Social Security Board, a new cabinet-level department grew—the Department of Health, Education, and Welfare, established in 1953.[8] Thus, 100 years after President Pierce rejected

---

[8]In 1939, the Social Security Board was transferred to the newly created Federal Security Agency; seven years later, that agency was strengthened and partially reorganized, and in 1953 it was succeeded by the Department of Health, Education, and Welfare. Actually, the idea to create a federal cabinet-level Department of Public Welfare predated enactment of the Social Security Act; a bill to that effect was introduced in Congress as early as 1921. With regard to improvement in the S.S.A., among other changes, payments were increased and unemployment compensation benefits extended. In addition, the act was amended to include dependents or survivors as beneficiaries (S.I.), to cover most of the self-employed (including some farmers) and some others left out of the original legislation, to provide benefits to crippled and disabled wage-earners (D.I.), to include needy children of unemployed (along with dead, dis-

Dorothea Dix's plea to make provision for the indigent insane, the federal government established an agency responsible for the health, education, and social welfare of all its citizens, one that spawned its own bureaucracy whose momentum would be difficult to stop.

Such changes did not escape most social workers. To be sure, as already mentioned, some were unhappy with the President and his administration. To them, the New Deal was too timid or conservative, more interested in bolstering the status quo than in bringing about a just society. They were further embittered by the so-called Roosevelt recession of 1937, when approximately four million workers returned to the unemployment rolls because the President, encouraged by the business advance, called for additional reductions in federal expenditures, especially on relief programs. The critics, however, remained in the minority. Most social workers were quite pleased with the administration's actions, which they felt had had a constructive impact not only on society as a whole but on their own particular activities.

The Great Depression and the New Deal did have a profound effect on social workers and their profession. First of all, many new jobs were created, especially for women, in the public social services. However widespread unemployment was for others during the crisis, qualified social workers were in constant demand; their number— approximately 30,000 in 1930—more than doubled during the decade. This, in turn, made unprecedented demands on training schools, especially on their curricula and resources for field experience, expediting the changes in social work education that people like Julia Lathrop, the Abbott sisters, and others interested in social policy and public welfare had been urging for some time.[9] (Reflective of social workers growing interest, and involvement, in *public* agencies at this time, was the creation in the early 1930s of the American Public Welfare Association, a national organization of social workers con-

---

abled, or absent from home) parents (A.F.D.C.-UP), and to provide hospitalization and limited medical services to the aged (Medicare) and to the poor and near poor (Medicaid). Perhaps it should be added that, with inclusion of Survivors' Insurance in 1939, the principle of "adequacy," as opposed to "equity," was introduced in the program for the first time.

[9]On the other hand, the mushrooming demand for social workers in public agencies tended to drain many social work schools and private agencies of their (few) social reform-oriented personnel, leaving behind psychiatrically oriented faculty and staffs, which would have an important effect on the postdepression years.

cerned with issues of public welfare, which by the end of the decade had several thousand members.)

In addition, the depression made many social workers, as never before, aware of the nature and depth of rural poverty—and suffering. Dramatic accounts of severe destitution in rural areas, home and land foreclosures, and even violence between displaced farmers and local authorities attracted widespread attention and concern among many Americans, including social workers, who were dispatched to rural areas to administer various public relief and resettlement programs. Thanks to the depression and the New Deal, social work no longer would be solely an urban occupation.

The depression also prompted a resurgence of interest among many social workers in social reform as well as old-fashioned relief. What good was psychiatric treatment when millions of citizens were unemployed and whole families were starving? As Paul Kellogg put it: "You cannot deal effectively with an inferiority complex on an empty stomach." The immediate task was to meet material needs—food, clothing, and shelter. The searing experience was proof, at least for the time being, that economic forces were at the root of the problems with which social work dealt. As Grace Coyle stated in her presidential address before the National Conference at the end of the depression decade: "There is no reasonable doubt that poverty itself is responsible for increased illness [physical and mental], that unemployment breeds unemployability, that crowded housing undermines family life, that undernourished children will grow into incompetent" adults. The message was clear: Social workers could best make their contributions by allying themselves with those groups in society working for political, social, and economic change. This, in turn, of course, tended to politicize social workers once again, a sharp contrast to their nonpartisanship of the prior decade.

For others, however, the experiences of the decade had no such effect. By bringing the federal government into the field of social welfare and by getting public agencies to take over the job of maintaining incomes and providing financial aid to the needy, the New Deal seemed to free some social workers and private agencies from feeling an obligation to concern themselves with such matters, giving them the opportunity to return to their work with problems of emotional adjustment and individual development—problems, it was argued, that were compounded by the depression, for those above as well as below the poverty line. So, "direct services" and private social work— concern for the individual and the superego, child and family coun- selling, and the like—did not give way entirely to the economic del- uge and concern for the trade cycle in the 1930s.[10]

Perhaps more important, social work assumed an unprecedented prestige in American life as a result of the depression and the New Deal. Social workers, such as Harry Hopkins, Frances Perkins, "Molly" Dewson (of the Women's Division of the Democratic National Committee), Aubrey Williams (director of N.Y.A.), Katharine Lenroot and Martha Eliot (of the U.S. Children's Bureau), Jane Hoey (of the Social Security Administration), Ellen Woodward (of the F.E.R.A. and W.P.A.), and numerous others were listened to, in Washington and elsewhere, as never before. They were no longer on the outside crying in the wilderness; now they were on the inside, in high positions, shaping policy and making all sorts of other basic deci- sions.

There was good reason for this. The New Deal drew heavily upon the knowledge, assistance, and heritage of social workers. Without minimizing their significance, many New Deal measures were, in Robert Bremner's words, "largely implementations, amplifications, and—in some instances—but partial fulfillments of the program of preventive social work formulated before World War I." No less an authority than Senator Robert F. Wagner, perhaps the New Deal's leading architect, stated that "one could not overestimate the central importance played by social workers" in laying the legislative ground- work for, and then administering, the statutes designed to meet the crisis of the 1930s.

Finally, by the end of the decade, social work was not only an acknowledged obligation of the federal government and every city, vil-

---

[10]In 1935 Grace Marcus protested the low esteem into which casework had fallen among social workers, who, in her opinion, had become obsessed with economic matters. She referred caus- tically to those who had "retreated entirely from any acknowledgment of personal factors in maladjustment . . . into economic dogmas that caricature Marxian theory." She must have had some listeners because whereas earlier in the decade members of the National Conference had confined their discussions to such things as unemployment, health insurance, and social legis- lation, by 1936 and 1937 such topics as social work education and methodology and agency administration again were on the agenda.

lage, and hamlet in the nation, but its scope had greatly expanded. It no longer meant providing financial relief to the destitute, or even casework to the emotionally disturbed, but both of these and much more. Social workers were now involved in social insurance schemes, park and recreational programs, agricultural resettlement projects, slum clearance and relocation plans, and numerous other activities; all efforts to make America a better and more secure place in which to live. Social work was no longer viewed as an emergency profession, but as an accepted part of the machinery of the state, an important everyday function in a modern industrial society. It was operating, in other words, both as a "cause" and as a "function"—and on a scale never envisaged even by its most ardent supporters.

Still, the developments of the 1930s left social workers with many problems. They had to face the question of how to forge links between the fields of private and public welfare—a difficult task, for private social work remained local and was concerned mainly with the problems of individuals and families, relying upon the use of case-work, while public welfare was largely a state and federal matter in which the problem of maintaining the economic and social security of the American people demanded the use of such skills as group work, community organization, and social reform. Also, social workers had to face the related issue of how much of their attention should be devoted to the welfare of society and how much to the welfare of the individual—in other words, whether or not to continue to take an active part in politics and, if so, in which field and by what means.

Bibliography

ABBOTT, EDITH. *Public Assistance*. Chicago: University of Chicago Press, 1940.

————. "Social Insurance and Social Security," *Social Service Review* 8 (September 1934): 537–40.

ACHENBAUM, W. ANDREW. *Social Security: Visions and Revisions*. New York: Cambridge University Press, 1986.

ALTMEYER, ARTHUR J. *The Formative Years of Social Security*. Madison: University of Wisconsin Press, 1966.

————. "The Wisconsin Idea and Social Security," *Wisconsin Magazine of History* 42 (Autumn 1958): 19–25.

AMENTA, EDWIN, AND BRUCE CARRUTHERS. "The Formative Years of U.S.

Social Spending Policies: Theories of the Welfare State and the American States During the Great Depression. *American Sociological Review* 53 (October 1988): 661–78.

ARMSTRONG, BARBARA N. *Insuring the Essentials*. New York: Macmillan, 1932.

BELLUSH, BERNARD. *Franklin D. Roosevelt as Governor of New York*. New York: Columbia University Press, 1955.

BERKOWITZ, EDWARD D. "The First Social Security Crisis," *Prologue* 15 (Fall 1983): 133–49.

———. "How to Think About the Welfare State." *Labor History* 32 (Fall 1991): 489–502.

BRANDT, LILIAN, et al. *The Impressionistic View of the Winter of 1930–31 in New York City*. New York: Welfare Council, 1932.

BREMER, WILLIAM W. "Along the Way: The New Deal's Work Relief Programs for the Unemployed," *Journal of American History* 62 (December 1975): 636–52.

———. *Depression Winters: New York Social Workers and the New Deal*. Philadelphia: Temple University Press, 1984.

BROCK, WILLIAM. *Welfare, Democracy, and the New Deal*. New York: Cambridge University Press, 1988.

BROWN, JOSEPHINE C. *Public Relief, 1929–1939*. New York: Holt, 1940.

BURNER, DAVID. *Herbert Hoover: A Public Life*. New York: Knopf, 1979.

BURNS, EVELINE M. *The American Social Security System*. Boston: Houghton Mifflin, 1949.

———. *Social Security and Public Policy*. New York: McGraw-Hill, 1956.

CHAMBERS, CLARKE A. "Social Security, The Welfare Consensus of the New Deal," in Wilbur J. Cohen, ed., *The Roosevelt New Deal*. Austin: University of Texas, 1986.

CHARLES, SEARLE F. *Minister of Relief, Harry Hopkins and the Depression*. Syracuse, N.Y.: Syracuse University Press, 1963.

CLEMENT, PRISCILLA F. "The Works Progress Administration in Pennsylvania, 1935–1940," *Pennsylvania Magazine of History and Biography* 95 (April 1971): 244–60.

COHEN, MIRIAM, AND MICHAEL HANAGAN. "The Politics of Gender and the Making of the Welfare State, 1900–1940: A Comparative Perspective." *Journal of Social History* 24 (Spring 1991): 469–84.

COHEN, WILBUR J. "The First Twenty-Five Years of the Social Security Act, 1935–1960," *Social Work Year Book* (New York: National Association of Social Workers, 1960): 49–61.

———. "FDR and the New Deal: A Personal Reminiscence," *Milwaukee History* 6 (Autumn 1983): 70–82.

CORSON, JOHN T. "Social Security and the Welfare State," *Social Service Review* 24 (March 1954): 8–12.

EPSTEIN, ABRAHAM. *Insecurity: A Challenge to America.* New York: Smith and Haas, 1933.

FEDER, LEAH. *Unemployment Relief in Periods of Depression.* New York: Russell Sage Foundation, 1936.

FISHEL, LESLIE H. "The Negro in the New Deal Era," *Wisconsin Magazine of History* 48 (Winter 1964–65): 111–26.

FISHER, JACOB. *The Response of Social Work to the Depression.* Boston: Hall, 1980.

FOX, BONNIE. "Unemployment Relief in Philadelphia, 1930–32: A Study of the Depression's Impact on Voluntarism," *Pennsylvania Magazine of History and Biography 93 (January 1963): 86–108.*

FRASER, STEVE, AND GARY GERSTLE, eds. *The Rise and Fall of the New Deal Order, 1930–1980.* Princeton, N.J.: Princeton University Press, 1989.

GRAEBNER, WILLIAM. *A History of Retirement: The Meaning and Function of an American Institution.* New Haven, Conn.: Yale University Press, 1980.

HAMILTON, DONA COOPER. "The National Urban League and New Deal Programs," *Social Service Review* 58 (June 1984): 227–43.

HANLAN, ARCHIE. "From Social Reform to Social Security: The Separation of ADC and Child Welfare," *Child Welfare* 45 (November 1966): 493–500.

HARRIS, JOSEPH P. "Federal Financial Participation in Social Work as a Permanent Policy," *Social Service Review* 9 (September 1935): 445–57.

HENDRIKSON, KENNETH E. "Relief for Youth: The Civilian Conservation Corps and the National Youth Administration in North Dakota," *North Dakota History* 48 (Fall 1981): 17–27.

HIRSHFELD, DANIEL S. *Last Reform: Campaign for Compulsory Health Insurance from 1932–1943.* Cambridge, Mass.: Harvard University Press, 1970.

HOPKINS, HARRY L. *Spending to Save.* New York: Norton, 1936.

KIMBERLY, CHARLES M. "The Depression in Maryland: The Failure of Voluntarism," *Maryland Historical Magazine* 70 (Summer 1975): 189–202.

KRIEGER, LEONARD. "The Idea of the Welfare State in Europe and in the United States," *Journal of the History of Ideas* 24 (October–December 1963): 553–68.

KURZMAN, PAUL. *Harry Hopkins and the New Deal.* Fairlawn, N.J.: Burdick, 1974.

KUTZA, ELIZABETH ANN. "The Promise of Certainty," *Social Service Review* 60 (March 1986): 132–44.

LEFF, MARK H. "Taxing the Forgotten Man: The Politics of Social Security Finance in the New Deal," *Journal of American History* 70 (September 1983): 359–81.

LEIGHNINGER, LESLIE, AND ROBERT KNICKMEYER. "The Rank and File Movement: The Relevance of Radical Social Work Traditions to Modern Social Work Practice," *Journal of Sociology and Social Welfare* 4 (November 1976): 166–77.

LEUCHTENBURG, WILLIAM E. *Franklin D. Roosevelt and the New Deal, 1932–1940.* New York: Harper, 1963.

MCJIMSEY, GEORGE. *Harry Hopkins: Ally of the Poor and Defender of Democracy.* Cambridge, Mass.: Harvard University Press, 1987.

MERIAM, LEWIS. *Relief and Social Security.* Washington, D.C.: Brookings Institute, 1946.

MERTZ, PAUL E. *New Deal Policy and Southern Rural Poverty.* Baton Rouge: Louisiana State University Press, 1978.

NELSON, DANIEL. *Unemployment Insurance: The American Experience, 1915–1935.* Madison: University of Wisconsin Press, 1969.

QUADAGNO, JILL. *The Transformation of Old Age Security.* Chicago: University of Chicago Press, 1988.

RAMSDELL, LEROY A. "The New Deal in Social Work," *The Family* 14 (October 1933): 191–92.

ROMASCO, ALBERT. *The Poverty of Abundance: Hoover, the Nation, the Depression.* New York: Oxford University Press, 1965.

ROPER, ARTHUR F. "The Southern Negro and the NRA," *Georgia Historical Quarterly* 64 (Summer 1980): 128–45.

ROSE, NANCY E. "Work Relief in the 1930s and the Origins of the Social Security Act." *Social Service Review* 63 (March 1989): 63–91.

RUBINOW, ISAAC. *The Quest for Security.* New York: Holt, 1934.

SAUTTER, UDO. *Three Cheers for the Unemployed: Government and Unemployment Before the New Deal.* New York: Cambridge University Press, 1991.

SCHLABACH, THERON F. *Edwin E. Witte, Cautious Reformer.* Madison, Wis.: State Historical Society, 1969.

————. "Rationality and Welfare: Public Discussion of Poverty and Social Insurance in the United States, 1875–1934," Report on a research project entitled "Ideas on Economic Security in America, 1874–1935" (1969).

SCHNEIDER, DAVID M., AND ALBERT DEUTSCH. *The History of Public Welfare in New York State, 1876–1940.* Chicago: University of Chicago Press, 1941.

SCHWARTZ, BONNIE FOX. *The Civil Works Administration, 1933–34.* Princeton, N.J.: Princeton University Press, 1984.

———. "Social Workers and New Deal Politicians in Conflict," *Pacific Historical Review* 42 (February 1973): 53–73.

SEEBER, FRANCES M. "Eleanor Roosevelt and Women in the New Deal," *Presidential Studies Quarterly* 20 (Fall 1990): 707–17.

SHANNON, DAVID. *The Great Depression.* Englewood Cliffs, N.J.: Prentice-Hall, 1960.

SKOCPOL, THEDA. "Thinking Big: Can National Values Explain the Development of Social Provision in the United States? A Review Essay." *Journal of Policy History* 2 (1990): 425–38.

———, AND JOHN INKENBERRY. "The Political Formation of the American Welfare State in Historical and Comparative Perspective," in Richard Tomasson, ed., *Comparative Social Research: The Welfare State, 1883–1983.* Greenwich, Conn.: JAI Press, 1983.

———, AND KENNETH FINEGOLD. "State Capacity and Economic Intervention in the Early New Deal." *Political Science Quarterly* 97 (Summer 1982): 255–78.

SPANO, RICK. *The Rank and File Movement in Social Work.* Washington, D.C.: University Press of America, 1982.

SWAIN, MARTHA. "The Forgotten Woman: Ellen S. Woodward and Women's Relief in the New Deal," *Prologue* 15 (Winter 1983): 201–14.

SYDENSTRICKER, EDGAR. "Health Under the Social Security Act," *Social Service Review* 10 (March 1936): 12–22.

WEIR, MARGARET; ANN ORLOFF, AND THEDA SKOCPOL, eds. *The Politics of Social Policy in the United States.* Princeton, N.J.: Princeton University Press, 1988.

WEISS, NANCY. *Farewell to the Party of Lincoln: Black Politics in the Age of FDR.* Princeton, N.J.: Princeton University Press, 1983.

WILSON, JOAN HOFF. *Herbert Hoover: Forgotten Progressive.* Boston: Little, Brown, 1975.

WITTE, EDWIN E. *The Development of the Social Security Act.* Madison: University of Wisconsin Press, 1962.

CHAPTER 14

From World War to Great Society

■ While the United States still had a long way to go to provide adequately for its impoverished and handicapped citizens, it had taken giant strides in that direction in the half-century from 1890 to 1940, summed up in the title of Grace Abbott's book, *From Relief* to *Social Security*, published in 1941.

In the late nineteenth century, public assistance, still referred to as poor relief, was the responsibility of the locality. For the most part, it was confined to institutional care for the young, the old, and the physically or mentally infirm. Outdoor relief, or cash assistance to the needy in their own homes, if provided at all, was usually given by private agencies, and then only sparingly. The obligation to provide care for the mentally ill, the defective, and the delinquent had been accepted by the states, but they had undertaken almost no preventive work. The juvenile court and probation movements, as well as widespread use of home placement for dependent children, were just beginning. The public health movement was in its infancy, and the mental health movement had not even been thought of as yet. A partnership of federal, state, and local governments in anything resembling a national system of social welfare was unknown.

By 1940, the situation had greatly changed. As a result of certain developments, including passage of the Social Security Act (and its 1939 Amendments) and other legislation, the states and the federal government were linked in their public assistance to the aged, the blind, and crippled and dependent children, in the expansion of public (and soon mental) health programs, and in the administration of unemployment compensation. In addition, the federal government had instituted

305

a national system of old-age and survivors' insurance and such other programs as low-cost housing, public works, and agricultural resettlement—advances that social workers helped bring about.[1]

Still, all was not clear sailing, especially since many social workers were beginning to revert to individual service. While the depression and destitution of the 1930s had returned many members of the profession to social action and reform, by the end of the crisis, and then in the 1940s and 1950s, most social workers again became concerned with casework and technique rather than with the further expansion of public social services and the improvement of living conditions; once again, they lost touch with the larger social problems of which maladjustment of the individual was only a small part.

How can one account for this rapid flight from reform and return to casework? As indicated, some social workers felt that, as a result of the many reforms of the 1930s, the provision of financial assistance and the betterment of "living conditions" were being taken cared of by those in political office. This was especially true with the enactment of the Social Security Act, which, despite its limitations, many people felt provided most citizens with a foundation of income maintenance, thus protecting them from poverty and want. There was no need for social workers to concern themselves with all that; instead, they could return to providing aid to individuals in need of psychological assistance.

Then there was World War II, which brought full employment and rising incomes for most Americans, blacks and (with the exception of Japanese-Americans living on the West Coast who were sent to miserable internment camps in rural areas, where they were kept behind barbed wire under armed guard) members of other oppressed groups included. The wartime gains in jobs and incomes were not achieved easily. There was a great deal of opposition to the employ-

---

[1] These changes can readily be seen in a few simple statistics. Annual expenditures for public welfare went from $40 million and less than one-tenth of 1 percent of the national income in 1890, to more than $6 billion and 8 percent of the national income in 1940. Another important trend was the marked centralization of such expenditures. In 1890, 65 percent of the total expenditures for public welfare came from local revenues and the rest came from the states; the federal government made no significant contribution. In 1940, local contributions had declined to 20 percent of the total, state funds had increased to 39 percent, and federal funds had jumped to 41 percent. Also, outdoor relief declined from 85 percent of total expenditures for public welfare in 1890 to 10 percent in 1940.

ment of African-Americans in the nation's factories and shops, resulting in numerous race riots throughout 1940 and 1941. Still, the administration realized that in time of dire need blacks (and women, too) were a source of untapped and underutilized labor. Moreover, the administration was alarmed by the prospect of a march on the nation's capital by 100,000 African-Americans designed primarily to open up opportunities for Negro labor in the burgeoning defense industries, which was planned for July 1941 under the leadership of A. Philip Randolph, president of the Brotherhood of Sleeping Car Porters. Such a demonstration would be a major embarrassment to a government about to enter a war for the defense of democracy and human equality. As a result, on June 25, 1941, President Roosevelt issued his famous Executive Order 8802, which forbade "discrimination in the employment of workers in defense industries or Government because of race, creed, or national origin" and established a Fair Employment Practices Committee (F.E.P.C.) to administer the measure. And although the committee lacked the necessary power to effectively punish offenders of the directive, and there was some defiance of its provisions, blacks and members of other disadvantaged groups did make gains unprecedented in American history.[2]

Also during the war years, social workers again helped meet the needs of members of the armed forces having difficulty adjusting to the military, and the needs of their families, often middle- and upper-class families, troubled by the absence of husbands and fathers who were in the service and of mothers who were in the labor force.[3] This

---

[2]Thus, thanks to F.E.P.C.'s activities and the critical labor shortage, African-Americans' share of wartime jobs in the defense industries increased from 3 to 8 percent, and the number of black employees in the federal government jumped from approximately 40,000 to more than 300,000. It is worth mentioning that due to these advances and a variety of other reasons, especially the Fascist threat abroad and the Popular Front at home, the Rank-and-File movement virtually disappeared during World War II.

[3]Perhaps it should be mentioned that World War II and military conscription again provided a rough yardstick for measuring the health of the nation or, rather, of its healthiest and most vigorous citizens, those between the ages of eighteen and forty—with the same shocking results as previously. Although the government adopted the most minimal physical and mental requirements for military service, the overall rejection rate was exceedingly high—above 50 percent (and as high as 70 percent in some areas)—largely due to malnutrition and an acute shortage of basic medical care. The military draft demonstrated a critical national health problem.

trend continued into the postwar years, as more and more self-sup-porting individuals and families turned to social workers for help. And while at first such help (casework services), paid for by private fees, was provided under the auspices of social work agencies, before long many social workers exchanged their low salaries in public and private agencies for the far more lucrative rewards of private practice, built largely on referrals from doctors and other professional person-nel and shared with various other counselors. Ironically, social workers seemed to receive a better reception from many of these clients than from those of the poorer classes whom they had helped in the past. Perhaps casework was most appealing to clients more or less like social workers themselves, with whom they could identify; psychoanalytic methods certainly were geared to, and worked best with, those who were relatively verbal and had the time for extensive treatment. Whatever the reason, this "better" clientele enamored many social workers, made their work more financially rewarding, and helped divert their attention from social issues.

Then there was the demise of *Survey* magazine, for nearly a half-century the major organ in the field of social policy and reform. When *Survey* ceased publication in 1952 it left a void that no other journal could fill and, in the words of its official biographer, Clarke Chambers, "the attachment of the profession as a whole to broad social action was irrevocably weakened."

Not surprisingly, then, the settlement house movement, which had declined significantly after the first World War, reached its nadir after World War II—and once again social workers returned to Abraham Flexner's question, "Is social work a profession?" When, in 1957, Ernest Greenwood, a University of California social work professor, answered that old but familiar query with a resounding "yes," most of his colleagues happily agreed. And when he told them that they "might have to scuttle their social action heritage as a price of . . . [maintaining] the public acceptance accorded a profession," the vast majority, caseworkers with little interest in social reform, hardly cared. Social work, after all, was in harmony with the dominant currents of the era.

"Benign neglect" of the poor was furthered in the post-World War II years by the enhanced power of corporate groups, the military, and a conservative coalition in Congress determined to scuttle New Deal relief agencies. Then there was the Cold War, the brandishing of atomic weapons, and the other anxieties of the postwar era. Sheer survival of the human race became a real concern, before which advances in the field of social welfare seemed insignificant.

Related was the problem of McCarthyism. A nation shaken by fears and suspicions, by vague rumors and charges of disloyalty and Communist conspiracies, by government campaigns to ferret out radicals and to impose tests of loyalty based not upon people's actions but upon their intentions, ideas, associations, and other criteria so vague as to guarantee confusion and error, hardly offered a climate hospitable to social criticism and reform.

Of importance, too, was the fact that many of the poor—those who had not shared in the war-born prosperity or who suffered during the postwar years, in part because of increased longevity and mobility, including the suburbanization of the nation, which left many older citizens without the help of friends and relatives who used to live nearby—were scattered and, as the social critic Michael Harrington would say, "invisible"; they were isolated in dark pockets of Appalachia and Harlem, and in other rural and urban ghettos where the nonpoor rarely ventured. Moreover, the poor comprised those who were least articulate, and who were unable to make their plight known or their power felt—the young, the old, the unskilled, and members of minority and culturally distinct groups.

Concern with poverty seemed remote and almost antiquarian during the war and postwar years, which leads to the most important factor responsible for the decline of social reform during the period—widespread belief in mass prosperity. Just as in the 1920s, most Americans thought that prosperity existed and that there was little or no poverty. Despite a series of recessions (in 1948–49, 1953–54, and 1957–58), the general image of the nation, once again, was that of an affluent society with the highest standard of living in the world, which gave everyone its fair share. Why engage in reform? For all practical purposes, the task had already been accomplished. Almost everyone had a television set and a car, didn't they?

While the theme of prosperity, and the idea that poverty and insecurity no longer existed, affected virtually every aspect of

American life—from President Eisenhower's news conferences to publication of David Potter's *People of Plenty* (1954)—it was given its fullest statement by the liberal economist, John Kenneth Galbraith, whose influential book *The Affluent Society* led the best-seller list in the late 1950s. In this work, Galbraith stated that American civilization had essentially solved the age-old problems of scarcity and poverty. He did not say there was absolutely no poverty in America. In fact, he said there was some, and that its survival in so affluent a society was "remarkable" and a "disgrace." Still, he stressed affluence, and defined poverty as a uniquely "minority problem," one confined to Appalachia and a few other depressed areas. Poverty in America, the well-known and highly regarded economist concluded, was "no longer a massive affliction [but] more nearly an afterthought."

Galbraith's statement, although highly inaccurate, was widely accepted—so much so that Walter Lippmann, the syndicated journalist, scornfully observed: "We talk about ourselves as if we were a completed society, one which has achieved its purposes and has no further business to transact." It was an era of complacency: contain the Communists, balance the budget, cut taxes, and don't rock the boat, these were the goals.

One of the ways to achieve those goals, or at least some of them, was to get the needy off the welfare rolls, which, despite the claims of Galbraith and others, actually were increasing at this time. They also were changing, dramatically: Whereas between 1935 and the early 1950s, the elderly received the bulk of federal and state welfare funds, by the middle of the decade recipients of A.D.C. (or A.F.D.C., Aid to Families with Dependent Children, as the program was now called) outnumbered all others receiving such assistance. Furthermore, whereas earlier most recipients of A.D.C. were dependent white children with widowed mothers, an increasing number of those who received such funds now were single black women with illegitimate children—a trend that would increase significantly in the following years. Thus, in the late 1950s state after state began instituting punitive administrative policies designed to reduce the number of such welfare recipients and to deter new applicants. State residency requirements were strictly enforced so that migrants (especially blacks moving from the South to the North) would not receive assistance, and all sorts of new eligibility investigations were initiated, including "suitable home" and "man-in-the-house" policies.[4]

The most publicized of such efforts—one that was symbolic of all others—occurred in Newburgh, New York, where Joseph Mitchell, the reactionary city manager, promulgated a thirteen-point code of regulations intended to uncover alleged welfare fraud, reduce the assistance rolls, encourage the work ethic, and cut public expenditures. Since the new rules—including the loss of benefits for all able-bodied adult males who refused municipal work, the denial of relief to anyone who voluntarily left a job, the substitution of vouchers for cash payments, and the termination of relief to unwed mothers who had another illegitimate child—did not comply with federal grant-in-aid regulations and thus jeopardized New York's receipt of federal welfare funds, the state's Social Welfare Board ordered Newburgh officials to refrain from administering the regulations and they never were implemented.

Meanwhile, however, the flight from social reform in the 1940s and 1950s and the attack on public welfare and its recipients did not proceed without uneasy words of warning from at least some people inside as well as outside the social work profession—scholars, reporters, politicians, and others. Ernest Hollis and Alice Taylor, the authors of *Social Work Education in the United States* (1951), a widely discussed study prepared for the Council on Social Work Education, maintained that for the last quarter-century "the profession has accepted too little of a unified responsibility for appraising and improving social welfare institutions" and urged readers to take a stand on the major social issues of the day.

Whitney Young, the social worker who later headed the National Urban League, told the National Conference on Social Welfare that "social work was born in an atmosphere of righteous indignation," but

---

[4]Under these policies, widely adopted at the time, the presence of a man automatically made a home "unsuitable" and was considered evidence that financial need did not exist, regardless of who the man was, his economic situation, or his relationship to the family. "Midnight raids" by welfare department personnel to uncover men in the homes of A.F.D.C. recipients were common until March 1967, when the California Supreme Court in effect ruled that they were illegal invasions of privacy. A year later, man-in-the-house rules were held unconstitutional by the U.S. Supreme Court in *King* v. *Smith*, 329 U.S. 309 (1968). As mentioned earlier, the following year the U.S. Supreme Court also invalidated residency requirements.

that "somewhere along the line 'the urge to become professional' had overcome the initial crusading impulse." He called upon the profession to reclaim the "lost heritage" of its founders. So did Marion Craine, who, speaking at a University of Chicago symposium on "Pioneers and Professionals" in social welfare, chastised her colleagues for being "too timid" to engage in reform, blaming it on the fear of being labeled "unprofessional."

Benjamin Youngdahl, when retiring as president of the American Association of Social Workers in 1953, concluded his farewell address with the rhetorical question: "Is our function as social workers limited to the treatment of pathologies, or do we have a positive or preventive function to perform as well?" There was little doubt where he stood on the issue.

The 1956 Alumni Day address at the Columbia University Graduate School of Social Work, given by Agnes E. Meyer, was another forthright and militant plea for a return to social action. She exhorted social workers as, in her words, "the conscience of American society," to assume the task of "community reorganization." Observing that the older professions—law, medicine, and teaching— "have become encrusted in bureaucracy, respectability, and economic rewards," she argued that social work "is still free—to some extent— from this lockstep towards success which most Americans worship." Now was the time to act, before it was too late!

In addition, throughout the 1950s, Saul Alinsky, the well-known community organizer who stressed conflict and giving the poor the power to speak for themselves, talked about the existence of poverty and the need to abolish it. Also, Senators Paul Douglas (Dem.-Ill.) and John Sparkman (Dem.-Ala.) chaired congressional committees during the decade that conducted studies and hearings on the health of the economy. Many low-income families "had been left behind in the progress of America," they concluded, and only a "vigorous attack" on poverty would overcome their distress. In 1956, Adlai E. Stevenson, the Democratic presidential candidate, echoed that theme.

These critics were not totally ignored. As Edward Berkowitz, Kim McQuaid, and others have pointed out, neither welfare expansion nor welfare reform disappeared in the 1950s, at least not completely. Few reversals occurred—and, in fact, some modest gains were recorded. To begin with, thanks in part to the pressure of labor unions, which had grown quite strong during the war, many private businesses either began to provide or increased their provision of employee benefits— life insurance, health insurance, retirement programs, and the like. Such private measures constituted an important secondary layer of assistance above the benefits offered by Social Security and other public programs.

Moreover, many public programs, including Social Security, were broadened during the "affluent decade." Thus, in 1950, Congress amended the S.S.A. to provide "caretaker" grants to mothers of dependent children (changing the name of the program from A.D.C. to A.F.D.C.) and added a new category of public assistance—Aid to the Permanently and Totally Disabled. In 1956, Disability Insurance was added to the system, and shortly thereafter several groups omitted from the original legislation were brought into the program, including farm workers and the self-employed. Meanwhile, "social services" were added to the A.F.D.C. program, child welfare services were extended from rural to urban areas, a partial sliding scale for assistance grants to the states was adopted in an effort to equalize welfare payments in poor and wealthy states, at least in part, and the Department of Health, Education, and Welfare was created.

Finally, some new welfare programs were enacted during these years, including the Servicemen's Readjustment Act, or the so-called G.I. Bill of Rights (1944), the National Mental Health Act (1946), the National School Lunch Program (1946), the Full Employment Act (1946), the Housing Act (1949), the School Milk Program (1954), and the Vocational Rehabilitation Act (1954). The postwar era, then, was not a complete wasteland for welfare reform.

Despite these advances, many Americans continued to suffer throughout this period, especially those who were marginally employed or who were not in the labor force at all—the old, the sick, the disabled, women with children whose husbands had deserted them or who had no husbands, and so on. For the most part, they were ignored; most Americans knew little and cared less about them and the other needy. The prevailing belief was that prosperity and economic growth had conquered or soon would conquer the remaining poverty problem, that it would "wither away," to use James Patterson's words, or that it was "more nearly an afterthought," to use Galbraith's.

Before long, however, the situation would change. Indeed, by the early 1960s, when some of the optimism of the postwar years had begun to fade, a change already was evident. Before long, few subjects would be as fashionable—at least to talk about. President Johnson's declaration of war on poverty in 1964 only put the highest official sanction on what had already become a vogue, or at least a significant national issue.

This rather sudden turnabout resulted from a variety of factors. The running debate in the 1950s on American foreign policy, especially the question of foreign aid, may have had some effect; no doubt it awakened many Americans to the discrepancies between the affluent and the poorer nations of the world and this, in turn, may have awakened some citizens to the existence of similar discrepancies at home. Also, poverty was an embarrassment that gave the Soviet Union ammunition to use against the United States in the Cold War.

More important was the coming into office of President John F. Kennedy, who not only made poverty, unemployment, and hunger major themes in the bid for his party's nomination but also was elected to the presidency after a campaign that was highly critical of the 1950s, one that conveyed a sense of vitality and urgency in the approach to social problems neglected by his predecessor. Setting the tone in his inaugural address of 1961, Kennedy asked the nation to "bear the burden of a long twilight struggle against the common enemies of man: tyranny, poverty, disease, and war. . . ." "The hand of hope," he said, "must be extended to the poor and the depressed." Such statements aroused many citizens, especially the nation's young people, and helped to revive faith in purposeful social action.

Even more important was the staggering relief explosion that accompanied the mass migration to the nation's cities of people who belonged to groups for whom poverty was endemic but who, for the most part, had been left out of the mainstream of American life: displaced and unemployed southern blacks and mountain whites, Mexican Americans and American Indians leaving their hovels and reservations in the West and Southwest, and Puerto Ricans moving to the mainland in search of a better life. While this massive urban movement by members of these "fringe" groups resulted from a variety of factors, the major cause was the agricultural revolution that occurred between the 1940s and 1960s, especially modernization and mechanization, which lessened the need for farm labor. Thus, a Presidential Commission on Rural Poverty found that between 1950 and 1965 new machines and new agricultural methods increased farm output in the United States by 45 percent, and at the same time reduced farm employment by the same percentage. Between 1940 and 1970, well over twenty million people (a great many of whom were black) were forced off the land, especially in the South, where these forces had their greatest impact.

This tremendous upheaval caused a good deal of suffering, especially since, as these displaced citizens migrated to the nation's cities, mainly in the North and West, the need for unskilled labor was declining. They were unable to secure adequate employment (or employment at all) and were forced to live in wretched, crowded ghettos, swelling the relief rolls. The number of persons receiving public assistance more than doubled from 1960 to 1970, from approximately six to twelve million as did the amount of money distributed to them, which increased from about $3.1 billion to well over $6 billion.[5]

Was this relief explosion mainly the result of the migration of large numbers of displaced farm workers and others to the nation's cities where, in numerous instances, relief was available to them for the first time, as many maintain? Or did it result from other (although related) factors? Frances Piven and Richard Cloward, in their widely read book *Regulating the Poor*, take issue with the premise that relief rolls automatically grow when the pool of people eligible for assistance increases, arguing that the outpouring of relief payments at that time was not solely, or even principally, the result of the urban migration and an increase in poverty. The expansion of the relief rolls in the 1960s, they contend, "was a political response to political disorder," a response to both the urban violence of the decade and the increased political power (and demands) of the mass of black poor, who now had to be contended with in the nation's voting booths as well as on its city streets. Rather than deal with the real poverty-producing factors—

---

[5]Two other things should be noted in this connection: (1) The enormous increase in the number of recipients during the 1960s was in marked contrast to the previous decade, when about 800,000 citizens were added to the welfare rolls; and (2) of the six million new recipients between 1960 and 1970, about five million were in various Aid to Families with Dependent Children (A.F.D.C.) programs.

racial discrimination and structural unemployment—the administration chose to give these people money in an effort to pacify them.[6] Whether Piven and Cloward or their critics are correct, the staggering increase in the number of people applying for and receiving public assistance and the enormous growth of welfare expenditures during these years helped make the problem a major topic of public concern rather than merely a marginal affair.

The civil rights movement, which centered attention on the desperate economic condition of millions of black citizens, also played a prominent role in the changes that occurred during the decade. Again, Americans who had regarded poverty as somehow an exception in an otherwise affluent nation were confronted with a militant reform movement that arose precisely because that was not the case. It was demonstrated that social and legal discrimination against African-Americans—the last to be hired, the first to be fired, the lowest paid, and so on—had induced and prolonged their poverty. It was clear that American Negroes were both class and race, for whatever criteria were used—income, employment, education, skill, health, dependency— they constituted a disproportionate number at the bottom of society.

There was, then, an obvious relationship between civil rights, or the lack of them, and poverty; to be made aware of the injustice of racial discrimination was inevitably to be made aware of want, and this could no longer be ignored when blacks and then other minority

---

[6]Those who differ with Piven and Cloward argue that, in addition to the movement of many needy Americans from poor rural areas to the nation's cities, other factors responsible for the relief explosion of the 1960s were: a rapidly increasing divorce rate; a growing feeling that low-paying jobs are demeaning and exploitive, which encouraged many marginally employed citizens to stop working and "go on welfare"; increasing "advocacy" by social workers—that is, efforts to encourage and mobilize the poor to exercise their right to public assistance; and the invalidation by the courts of restrictive administrative and investigative features of the welfare system, including "man-in-the-house" rules and "midnight raids," arbitrary terminations without hearings, residency laws, and the like. But it is precisely this relaxation of regulations for the receipt of public assistance that Piven and Cloward argue was the political response to the urban disorder and new political realities of the decade. For an extended criticism of *Regulating the Poor* and the authors' response to it, see Eugene Durman, "Have the Poor Been Regulated? Toward a Multivariate Understanding of Welfare Growth," *Social Service Review* 47 (September 1973): 339–59, and Frances F. Piven and Richard A. Cloward, "Reaffirming the Regulation of the Poor," *Ibid.* 48 (June 1974): 147–69. Also see Walter I. Trattner, ed., *Social Welfare or Social Control?* (Knoxville: University of Tennessee Press, 1983), pp. 152–57.

groups became demonstrative and began to press their claims for equality and the full rights of citizenship. Those who had overlooked the unskilled, the migrant laborer, the tenant farmer, the victim of regional depression, black and white alike, were forced to come to grips with a blight that they had tried to forget, or pretend did not exist; they were forced to describe American society more accurately— to "tell it as it was."

The 1960 census figures provided scholars and writers with the raw material to do just that, to factually discover or rediscover what the civil rights movement and the rising relief rolls already were beginning to indicate—that the New Deal and World War II had not eradicated poverty and it had not withered away—and they took great advantage of the opportunity. The literature on poverty grew large as it was demonstrated that, beneath the layers of American affluence, there were strata of deprivation, and that the deprived were not merely those who lived in Harlem or other black ghettos, or even those who lived in the depressed areas of the rural South. Rather, the poor were ubiquitous; they could be found in all sections of the country, in all parts of the population, in all age groups.

Gabriel Kolko, the historian, in his *Wealth and Power in America*, showed that income statistics failed to tell all there was to say about the poor. James Morgan and his team of University of Michigan social scientists provided further data exposing the poverty syndrome in *Income and Welfare in the United States*. Dwight Macdonald, the social critic, summed it up well in a *New Yorker* article entitled "Our Invisible Poor."

Above all, Michael Harrington, the journalist and social activist— whose book, *The Other America: Poverty in the United States*, which was the focus of the Macdonald article and which challenged complacent assumptions about American affluence and focused movingly on poverty, quickly became a classic—successfully evoked the peculiar state of being poor and analyzed the reasons for the persistence of mass poverty amidst abundance. Harrington demonstrated that the poor, black and white alike, were subjected to a chronic suppression of their living standards, something that escaped most citizens. The average American could not view the rundown company towns from the highways he traveled, and there were no shacks in the national parks where he roamed. Nor did he really see the urban slums as he commuted to and from his suburban home and downtown office on new freeways or rapid transit. Therefore, the poor continued as a hidden subculture, one that was beyond the reach of the contemporary welfare state, one that was perpetuated by an endless cycle of neglect and injustice.[7]

The poor were unemployed laborers haunting employment agencies; displaced miners, loitering on street corners or in bars; former midwestern meat-packers shoved aside by automation; misfits on New York's Bowery; the aged stored away to die in institutions and roominghouses. All were not necessarily unemployed; some were poorly paid dishwashers whose small earnings had to be supplemented by public aid; some were farmers unable to subsist off their poor land; many were African-Americans, at work (if lucky enough to be employed) in the worst-paying jobs.

Then there were others who, for a long time, had been mired in poverty, such as Mexican Americans, or Chicanos, whose plight was as bad and who now were being spurred to action by black activism and other forces encouraging increased racial and ethnic pride. The nation's second largest disadvantaged minority, most of the four million persons of Mexican ancestry were still gathered in various barrios throughout the Southwest and West. Handicapped by lack of job skills, inadequate schooling, language problems, and discrimination, they had been generally ignored, even by those seeking to improve the lot of the other impoverished. Similarly, efforts to help those in need had failed to reach the American Indian, perhaps the nation's most desperate and deprived minority group—the poorest of the poor. Some 450,000 Indians lived in squalor in twenty-five states, not

---

[7]Just as later critics would do, Harrington and others argued that the American welfare system created and perpetuated the poverty it was intended to prevent and alleviate. Thus according to Richard Elman, author of *The Poorhouse State* (1966), just as the nineteenth-century county almshouse collected the dependent of that era, current public assistance programs collected the poor "into stagnant pools of dependent people who become increasingly separated from the mainstream of economic life." The system eroded the poor's psychic energy and self-image so that they became "steadily more crystallized as a residue from the normal economic and social life of the nation." Until we "vest dependency itself with decency, and provide assistance without the implication that the recipient of such assistance is maladjusted or sick," wrote Kermit Wiltse in reviewing that book, "we will perpetuate the Poorhouse State." So, whereas later critics would call for an end to welfare, these commentators called for *more* welfare, *without strings (or a stigma) attached.*

always in obscure rural areas.[8] As Harrington and others demonstrated, poverty was one of the nation's gravest social problems, one that was not disappearing but growing worse, a way of life that had become permanent for some forty to fifty million Americans.

As if to bear out what these writers were saying, America's cities exploded in the mid-sixties. Riots erupted not only in the slums of New York, Los Angeles, Detroit, and Newark, but also in hundreds of other black communities around the nation. And while the various outbreaks differed in their origin and development, all resulted from long-festering wounds—unemployment, poverty, poor housing, crowded living conditions, economic exploitation, widespread desperation, frustration, hopelessness, and a profound disillusionment with urban conditions; clearly, the city was not the promised land full of economic opportunity and free of institutionalized oppression, as many Americans had been led to believe. Feeling that the power structure militated against them and that the channels of social redress were closed, the have-nots in society expressed themselves by bombing, sniping, burning, looting, harassing, and striking against the symbols of the establishment—namely, the police and the businessmen who had long exploited them. Once again, the issue was joined; the blacks of America's urban slums were no longer "invisible." Their violent expressions of bitterness and frustration forced all Americans (including most social workers who, thanks to their retreat from social reform, once again were caught unprepared for the widespread disor-

---

[8]During the 1960s both of these groups, affected by the black revolt and the various nationalist movements of the decade, took on a new militancy; "Uncle Taco," the stereotype of the servile Mexican American, gave way to the "Sons of Zapata," while the Indians bid farewell to "Uncle Tom-Tom" and joined movements for "Red Power." Their increased aggressiveness and sense of unity began to create an awareness in the nation of their organizations, their leaders, and their demands: civil and legal rights, better educational opportunities, dignified treatment, and a voice in their own and the nation's affairs. The best known Mexican-American movement was led by Cesar Chavez and the National Farm Workers Association, whose successful strike and boycott of the grape growers in Delano, California, demonstrated the benefits of organization. Other new and dynamic alliances included the Political Association of Spanish-Speaking Organizations (P.A.S.O.) and the Mexican-American Political Association (M.A.P.A.). Perhaps the largest and best-known Indian groups were the National Congress of American Indians (N.C.A.I.) and the National Indian Youth Council (N.I.Y.C.), although more recently the militant American Indian Movement, under the leadership of Russell Means, had emerged as an important organization, especially for the young urban Indian.

der and suffering) to confront unpleasant realities they had largely managed to avoid until the "troubled decade."[9]

Following the 1967 riots, President Lyndon B. Johnson created a National Advisory Commission on Civil Disorders, the so-called Kerner Commission, to determine the cause of the disturbances and to recommend ways to prevent their future occurrence. After intensive study, the commission placed most of the blame for the riots on "white racism." Its report stated that the civil rights gains of the previous fifteen years had done very little to improve the quality of life in the black ghetto, where millions of citizens continued to be denied an equal chance in American society. In fact, "our nation is moving toward two societies, one black, one white—separate and unequal," the commission concluded, and then went on to make a series of modest proposals for social change, including the creation, or recreation, of a federal jobs program for the poor unemployed, few of which were implemented; the principal response to the riots was greater expenditures for police and weaponry.

Still, the urban violence and wide variety of other developments throughout the decade—social, political, economic, and demographic—which clearly shattered the prevailing belief that America was a classless and relatively homogeneous society, led to a new look at poverty and new attempts to prevent it or at least to alleviate its effects. Those attempts began early in the Kennedy administration, long before the eruptions in the nation's ghettos. Among the more important of the early measures was the extension, in 1961, of A.F.D.C. to needy two-parent families whose heads of household were out of work and had exhausted their unemployment benefits. Not only would such a change help families in need but also it would keep them together by discouraging desertion by unemployed fathers in order to get wives and children off general relief and onto the more generous federally aided categorical assistance program, for which they were ineligible with a "man" present in the home. Although the change was not made mandatory and many states, especially poorer

---

[9]Adding to the turmoil of the period and at the same time arousing concern for the underprivileged was the anti-Vietnam War movement. Among many other things, the antiwar movement was a protest against the nation's draft policies, which clearly militated against the poor and especially against African-Americans.

rural ones, refused to participate in it, Aid to Families with Dependent Children-Unemployed Parent (A.F.D.C.-UP) was an important step forward.

The Kennedy administration also turned to the areas of juvenile delinquency and mental health. Shortly after taking office in the spring of 1961, Kennedy created the President's Committee on Juvenile Delinquency and Youth Crime, which led to the passage, that same year, of the Juvenile Delinquency and Youth Offenses Control Act, a measure that, among other things, helped fund and operate projects for the prevention and treatment of delinquency in inner-city neighborhoods, including Mobilization for Youth. Two years later, after receiving a message from the President on the subject, Congress enacted the Mental Retardation Facilities and Community Mental Health Centers Act, which provided federal funds for research, training, and the construction and staffing of community mental health centers throughout the United States.

The most widely heralded of the Kennedy administration's responses to the growing welfare crisis, however, were the 1962 Public Welfare Amendments to the Social Security Act, signed into law by the President on July 25, 1962.[10] These measures, more familiarly known as the Social Service Amendments, greatly increased federal support (from 50 to 75 percent of the cost) to the states for the provision by local welfare departments of casework, job training, job placement, and other direct services to public assistance recipients. The amendments grew out of lengthy study and extensive advice from social workers and other experts who promised the President, the Congress, and the nation that their new approach would rehabilitate and bring financial independence to the needy and, hence, a reduction in the relief rolls and in public welfare expenditures.

Actually, the amendments were the product of several forces, including the fact that "social services" were added to the A.F.D.C. program in 1956 but, for various reasons, went unfunded. Basically they reflected social workers' renewed concern with casework—the belief that the poor needed not just, or even primarily, financial aid

---

[10]Earlier, on February 1, 1962, President Kennedy had delivered a message to Congress on "Public Welfare," the first presidential message in American history devoted entirely to the subject.

but rather psychological assistance and other forms of counseling; they had to "adjust" to being single parents or to life in the city; they needed instruction on how to keep house and manage their meager resources in order to make ends meet; they needed to learn how to make friendships and develop self-esteem; above all, of course, they had to be taught how to secure and retain jobs. In reality, then, the new approach was an old one: attributing the needy's problems to personal shortcomings and providing "counseling," or advice, in order to promote participation in the labor force. (Moreover, by once again linking relief granting to the provision of "services" and placing both functions in the hands of the same person, it was a further throwback to charity organization society days.)

Nevertheless, by putting the power of the White House and the federal bureaucracy behind the drive for welfare reform—or at least the notion that the federal government had the responsibility to help poor Americans to help themselves—Kennedy shattered the relative complacency that characterized the previous decade, and his successor, Lyndon B. Johnson, followed suit. Under their administrations, dubbed the New Frontier and the Great Society, respectively, the poor obviously were moved from a state of benign neglect to a prominent place on the public agenda. Most of the measures enacted at the time, however, were based on the idea that the economic well-being of the period could lead to the abolition of poverty if only the poor would take advantage of the opportunities before them; hence they were designed to do the same thing as the Social Service Amendments—to reinforce commitment to the work ethic by those who were economically marginal, a clear shift away from the many cash and public works programs of the New Deal. Thus, the Area Redevelopment Act of 1961 and the Economic Development Act of 1965 were designed to focus on regional unemployment by inducing new industries to move into depressed areas of the nation; the 1962 Manpower Development and Training Act was intended to provide training or retraining for workers displaced by economic or technological change; Title VII of the 1964 Civil Rights Act prohibited racial, sexual, or ethnic discrimination in employment and established an enforcement mechanism—the Equal Employment Opportunity Commission—to implement the provision; and, above all, there was the so-called War on Poverty, conceived by Kennedy before his death—or, more accurately, by Walter Heller, his chief economic adviser—but carried out by his successor.

In his State of the Union Message in January 1964—a time when the President's Council on Economic Advisors concluded that about one-fifth of the American people, including nearly half of the nation's blacks, were poor—Lyndon Johnson, a Roosevelt protégé who wanted to start his own New Deal, called upon Congress to enact a thirteen-point program that would declare "unconditional war on poverty," a "domestic enemy which threatens the strength of our Nation and the welfare of our people." Seven months later, the Economic Opportunity Act (E.O.A.), or the antipoverty bill, was passed, establishing the Office of Economic Opportunity (O.E.O.), an independent federal agency headed by a director (Sargent Shriver, a man of "infectious energy") responsible to the President. The measure also called for the creation of Volunteers in Service to America or V.I.S.T.A., a domestic peace corps; a Job Corps for school dropouts; an Upward Bound program to encourage bright slum children to go to college; a Neighborhood Youth Corps for jobless teenagers; Operation Head Start, a project to give preschool training to children; special programs of grants and loans to low-income rural families and migrant workers; a very controversial and never fully agreed upon comprehensive Community Action Program designed, in theory to empower the poor by securing their "maximum feasible participation" in the creation and operation of community action agencies (or CAAs) to combat poverty in their communities; and a number of other programs designed to "pursue victory over the most ancient of mankind's enemies."

The Economic Opportunity Act, planned by a task force of experts, including some of the nation's leading academics and social scientists, was a make-do, crash program that left a good deal to be desired. However well intentioned, it was badly conceived, never really fully understood by many of its commanders, including the Chief Executive, and, in the opinion of many, bound to fail, primarily because it was designed not to change society but to change its victims. Like the Public Welfare Amendments of 1962 and most of the other legislation of the period, it emphasized not adequate income and job creation—indeed, it gave no money or jobs to the poor—but rather education, manpower training, and various social services that were supposed to enhance the productive ability of the needy and facilitate their transition from welfare to work. (In that sense, it was perfectly in tune with the widely held, but misguided, notion that economic growth would continue and that it would lead to the elimination of poverty.) Even on its own terms, however, the statute did not live up to expectations. Less a war on poverty than a minor skirmish—or "a sitzkrieg, a phony war of stalemate and standstill," according to one scholar, and "a war that was declared but never fought," according to another—it was scantily financed. In fact, Congress appropriated less money each year to combat poverty across the country than was necessary to finance an adequate welfare program in any one of the nation's leading cities. During the first year of the act's operation, when Mayor John Lindsay said that New York City needed $10 billion annually for five years to solve its welfare problems, Congress allocated around $750 million (or approximately $30 for each needy citizen) for the entire nation—and the figure never even reached $2 billion a year during the life of the program. (The act also did virtually nothing to alleviate destitution in the countryside, where a sizable proportion of the nation's poor still resided.)

Moreover, much of what little money was appropriated was squandered or caught in bureaucratic red tape, delaying tactics, and political imbroglios. Throughout the United States, power struggles occurred in deciding who was to control the programs—and reap the rewards. For the most part, mayors (aghast at the prospect of money being placed in the hands of people outside of and often hostile to their administrations) came out on top. By keeping the funds in City Hall, they were able to create high-paying jobs for faithful political supporters and thus strengthen their hold on office, at the same time preventing meaningful political and social action by the needy, who might otherwise have jeopardized the status quo. No wonder radicals like Saul Alinsky attacked the program as a "huge political pork barrel," a "macabre masquerade," and a "prize piece of political pornography," while conservatives called it a "Madison Avenue deal," a "poverty grab bag," and "the Santa Claus of the free lunch." In the meantime, those who were supposed to be helped by the measure continued their miserable existence in urban and rural slums.[11] Then, late in 1966, by which time President Johnson had become increasingly disenchanted with the program, as well as obsessed with the Vietnam War (which, ironically, as John Ehrenreich has pointed out, provided lots of "jobs" for the poor, although often fatal ones), dismemberment of the O.E.O. began, a process continued by Richard M. Nixon when he came into office in 1969 and completed in 1974.

Meanwhile, however, some unintended and rather unfortunate results occurred. The disastrous affair, especially the cruel contrast between promise and performance, infuriated the poor and punctured their inflated aspirations, which, in turn, contributed (ironically) to the urban rioting of the period, Piven and Cloward notwithstanding. And, as James Patterson has pointed out, the war's failure also "chastened theorists," congressional activists, and others, who began to question the potential of "social engineering," including such academics as Edward Banfield, Nathan Glazer, and Daniel Moynihan, one of the program's designers, whose book *Maximum Feasible Misunderstanding* (1969) summed up his and others' disenchantment with the entire affair. "More than any other program of Johnson's so-called Great Society," Patterson wrote, "the war on poverty accentuated doubts about the capacity of social science to plan, and government to deliver, ambitious programs for social betterment"—and no doubt helped provoke the surge of neo-conservative developments that would follow.

---

[11]As June Axinn and Herman Levin, to whom I am indebted for some of the ideas in this chapter, have indicated in their book on *Social Welfare*, while some of the education programs had some success, perhaps the most important feature of the E.O.A. was the development of community legal services. Such services were not specifically mentioned in the original act. Once they began, their importance for testing older rights and securing new ones for the poor (through various class action suits) became so obvious that later amendments to the statute spelled out their inclusion. Ironically, these services then helped to terminate the whole program, for the President and members of Congress were not pleased by having legal actions against various public programs supported by government-funded legal services. Another contribution of the program, however, was its tendency to move at least some social workers, once again, from a therapeutic to a reform approach; as social workers were brought into community action programs, some of them began to reevaluate their views regarding the profession and its function in society, even going so far as to become "advocates" of the poor.

Before that, however, there were some exceptions to the rule, including passage by Congress in 1964 of the Food Stamp Act, a considerable improvement over an existing food distribution program. At the time the nation had a commodity scheme that was designed primarily to promote the interests of commercial farmers rather than those of poor consumers; economic, rather than social welfare, policy determined its operation. Under its provisions, which were embodied in the Agriculture Act of 1949, the Secretary of Agriculture, in order to reduce surpluses and prevent waste, was directed to distribute commodities acquired through federal price supports to low-income families. The level of program activity, then, as well as the type of items provided, depended entirely on the availability of surplus foods rather than on the nutritional needs or desires of those participating in the program.

The Food Stamp Program was aimed at overcoming these deficiencies, largely by expanding the purchasing power of the needy and by separating operation of the program from the concerns of agricultural producers and the condition of their markets. Certified low-income families could purchase stamps at substantial savings—a family of four with a monthly income of $100, for example, could buy $78 worth of stamps for $44—which in effect replaced cash in food stores, allowing their users the freedom to purchase what they wished and needed. And while the scheme was by no means perfect—it was optional rather than mandatory, and many communities chose not to participate in it; each state set its own eligibility requirements and hence there was a good deal of variation within the program; the cost of the stamps was too high for some, who could not take advantage of the arrangement and, in fact, when the program began the number of participants dropped considerably from those who had been receiving federal "commodities," especially in the South—it was an important welfare-oriented program that served the needs of many low-income families, one that would grow and be improved later. Thus, in March 1993 food stamps were helping to feed close to 27 million Americans, or about 10.5 percent of the population.

An advance for the nation's aged—considered by most to be both especially needy and deserving—was also scored at that time with the adoption of Title XVIII, or the "medicare" amendments to the Social

Security Act, approved by President Johnson on July 30, 1965.[12] A victory over the American Medical Association and its allies, who relentlessly lobbied against it, the measure represented the nation's first major stride toward some sort of *national* health insurance scheme, at least for more than twenty million of its older citizens.

Actually, Medicare was an outgrowth of an older, existing program established under the provisions of the Kerr-Mills Act of 1960, named after Senator Robert Kerr of Oklahoma and Representative Wilbur Mills of Arkansas, two powerful Democrats who overcame a great deal of opposition to get the measure enacted into law. Kerr-Mills established a health insurance plan for the nation's senior citizens which followed a welfare, or public assistance, format; that is, it provided federal grants to the states on a matching basis to help pay for the medical care of elderly welfare recipients, or for the "medically indigent"—those who did not qualify for welfare but who could not afford to pay for medical care. The measure, however, had all sorts of deficiencies, which had become increasingly obvious. To begin with, it did not include anyone under the age of sixty-five. In addition, it was optional, and thus some states participated in the program and others did not; by 1963 only thirty-six had "joined" the system. And finally, among those states that did participate in the program, the coverage varied greatly; while all paid for hospital care, only some paid physicians' fees, whether for services performed in or outside of hospitals. By 1965, then, it was clear that the states were not the answer to the nation's health care problem, even for the elderly, and the program was replaced by Medicare.

In brief, Medicare provided hospital and medical insurance (as well as coverage for some posthospital care) for virtually all Americans on reaching age sixty-five. The hospital insurance (HI) was compulsory and financed by an increase in Social Security taxes, while enrollment in the medical plan (SMI) was voluntary and paid for by a monthly

---

[12]Another program to aid the elderly was enacted in 1965—the Older Americans Act, which, among other things, subsidized a variety of programs and services for older citizens at the state level, including those who were homebound, and established a national network of Area Agencies on Aging (A.A.A.s), which served as a foundation on which could be (and were) built other programs and services for senior citizens.

premium of three dollars (and general tax revenues). While this measure also had its shortcomings—it, too, covered only the aged, it was relatively costly, it did not cover all medical and hospital expenses, it was curative rather then preventive, and so on—the fact is that a large number of older people received medical and hospital care that previously they could not have obtained, or that otherwise would have exhausted their savings—and did so "free" from the stigma of relief.

A mixed blessing, too, were the "medicaid" amendments to the Social Security Act, usually referred to as Title XIX, another (and in some ways truer) outgrowth of Kerr-Mills signed into law by President Johnson on July 30, 1965. Under their provisions, the federal government provided grants to the states to assist them in helping needy citizens receive improved medical and hospital services. While the plan was established primarily for recipients of federally aided public assistance programs, if funds were available coverage could be extended to citizens who were not on welfare but who otherwise could not afford medical treatment (the "medically indigent", in other words). The program was designed to end "charity medical care" by giving the needy the money and, presumably, access to the entire health care system: whereas previously most of the poor were forced to depend on overcrowded and sometimes distant public hospitals and clinics, where they frequently received inadequate care, Medicaid recipients could now visit any doctor or hospital willing to treat them.

While an excellent idea in theory, in practice the program proved to be full of shortcomings. To begin with, whereas Medicare was given the dignity of Social Security, Medicaid was burdened with the stigma of public assistance. Also, as with Kerr-Mills (and A.F.D.C.), conservative and poorer states covered fewer services and had more restrictive eligibility criteria than the more progressive and wealthier ones. More important, many doctors and hospitals refused to treat such patients, often citing excessive paperwork, inadequate compensation, and government interference in medicine as their reasons. In the early 1970s, only 17 percent of New York's physicians accepted such patients, and the situation was similar elsewhere. In addition, the care given to those who were treated by private physicians and hospitals frequently tended to be less than ideal; all too often they were run through offices and wards as if through a mill, given unnecessary treatment and drugs, overcharged, and forced to put up with a number of other abuses that the system was devised to eliminate. Again, however, despite these and other shortcomings, the program grew—to the point, in fact, where now many feel it has gotten out of hand and has created serious new problems[13]—and delivered health care over the years to millions who otherwise would not have been able to afford it.

Meanwhile, the welfare crisis continued. Neither the Public Welfare Amendments of 1962 nor the Economic Opportunity Act of 1964—or the spate of other measures enacted during the Kennedy-Johnson administrations, including a rent supplement program (1965), the Elementary and Secondary Education Act of 1965, the Higher Education Act of the same year, and the 1966 Demonstration (Model) Cities and Metropolitan Development Act—succeeded in getting people off the relief rolls and onto the tax rolls, as had been hoped. Indeed, the number of recipients and total expenditures continued to climb: despite the fact that between 1963 and 1966 federal grants to the states for social services more than doubled, approximately one million new public assistance cases were added to the welfare rolls, especially in A.F.D.C. programs—and another 3.3 million would be added before the end of the decade. While the poor had become a major topic of public concern instead of a marginal affair—indeed, the national mood had gone from complacency to urgency, perhaps even hysteria, in about a decade—and the scope of the welfare state had expanded considerably, poverty certainly had not disappeared. As one student of the subject put it, the New Frontier and the Great Society had promised the moon and had gotten it; they had not solved the welfare problem, however. As a result, the belief that poverty, and the need for welfare, would "wither away" tended to disappear,

---

[13]While at first many physicians refused to treat Title XIX patients, before long they and their colleagues began to take advantage of the program—and the costs of Medicaid, and health care in general, soared. This, in turn, led many people to call for cutbacks and the imposition of cost containment measures in the program. Meanwhile, thanks to those skyrocketing costs, millions of Americans, too "rich" for Medicaid but too "poor" to purchase private medical insurance or adequate health care, were squeezed out of the medical market altogether. In the end, many commentators have suggested that the principal beneficiaries of Medicaid (and Medicare as well) have been doctors, pharmacists, nursing home operators, and other health care professionals who, ironically, were among the first to object to cuts in the program by a later administration.

and the image of A.F.D.C. recipients as members of some sort of self-perpetuating, deviant underclass was reinforced.

Intellectually, these ideas were embodied in the "culture of poverty" theory, one that "echoed old ideas and prefigured future debates," to use Michael Katz's words. Formulated by Oscar Lewis, an anthropologist who worked with poor families in the slums of Puerto Rico and New York City; Daniel Moynihan, the sociologist whose controversial study *The Negro Family* (published in 1965 while he was Assistant Secretary of Labor in the Johnson administration) caused something of an uproar; and others, the theory posited the existence of a subculture with patterns of behavior that distinguished it from the larger social structure and prevented its members—who exhibited such aberrant psychological and moral traits and vaules as feelings of fatalism, helplessness, inferiority, dependence, and present-mindedness—from taking advantage of the opportunities available to better their lives. While Lewis and Moynihan did not intend to label those caught in this situation as unworthy—indeed, according to Moynihan their problems stemmed from slavery (which, he maintained, had weakened the traditional husband–wife family structure among African-Americans) and involuntary black male unemployment since that time—others with a more conservative agenda did; accordingly, those stranded in this so-called culture of poverty quickly became the undeserving poor. They allegedly lacked the will to be, or to become, self-supporting and tended to transmit their characteristics from one generation to another through socialization. Simply giving them money, or even casework services, then, would not improve their lot. They needed to be forced to change their outlook and their lifestyle.

Meanwhile, social workers and their services had become increasingly subject to scrutiny, and in 1967 Congress responded with further amendments to the Social Security Act, which tended to denigrate or downplay casework and other "soft" social services in favor of such "hard" or more tangible programs as day care, housing, vocational rehabilitation, and drug treatment centers—and permitted the states to "purchase" such services from nongovernmental, or private (profit-making), agencies, many of which did not always have the best interests of their clients at heart.

More important, using January 1967 as a base, Congress imposed a freeze on the number of children under age twenty-one who would be allowed to receive A.F.D.C. payments because of the absence of a parent from the home. Since the measure was aimed at pressuring the states to crack down on welfare payments due to desertion and illegitimacy, it exempted cases resulting from either the death of a father or a parent's unemployment.[14] Next, it established a Work Incentive Program, or W.I.P., a carefully chosen acronym that would later be changed to W.I.N. The Work Incentive Program—which was based on "the pathological idea of poverty," the old but again popular notion that deprivation and dependency were products not of the political economy but of the individual, and that welfare compounds rather than helps to solve the problem—disqualified adults and older out-of-school children from A.F.D.C. payments if they refused to accept employment or participate in training programs—females and males alike, mothers as well as fathers, even in single-parent, female-headed families. This was a far cry from the approach to public assistance and child welfare that had been taken throughout the twentieth century. Whereas mothers' pensions and the Social Security Act had stressed the needy child's right to public support and to a mother's care, this measure affirmed the right to remove that child from the welfare rolls and to force his or her mother to work outside the home for such support.[15] Here again, however, the states had some discretion in requiring participation in the program, and since some excluded mothers with young children, and many others never established an adequate number of costly job-training schemes, the full effects of the program were delayed. Still, the punitive nature of the measure (which affected primarily weak and abandoned women and helpless children and was referred to by one observer as the "first [piece of] purposively

---

[14] It should be noted that the measure was hotly resisted by some, especially officials in hard-pressed states. As a result, President Johnson, and then Nixon after him, delayed implementation of the freeze, which Congress repealed in 1969. Its spirit lived on, however, as we shall see in the next chapter.

[15] It should be pointed out, however, that today some feminists see this as a gain for women. See the Virginia Sapiro article cited in the bibliography.

punitive welfare legislation" in American history), which was a dismal failure, was clear and signaled what was to come.[16]

As the welfare explosion continued and the stereotype of the "reliefer" hardened into the image of the black woman with hordes of illegitimate children—adding racism to the traditional prejudice against the poor, a potent combination—the reaction progressed. A growing number of citizens and leading politicians denounced the "welfare mess," including the newly elected governor of California, Ronald Reagan, who in his first inaugural address in 1967 asserted: "We are not going to perpetuate poverty by substituting a permanent dole for a paycheck." Meanwhile, the riots in the black ghettos, the civil rights demonstrations, the anti-war protests, the student upheavals, and other developments—women's liberation, new lifestyles, the drug culture, inflation and high taxes, etc.—were also causing a great deal of resentment, especially among members of the working class, or the so-called Silent Majority, who in 1968 turned to Richard Nixon to end the social turmoil and, in the words of the new President, make sure that "social workers would be looking for honest work."

Bibliography

ABBOTT, GRACE. *From Relief to Social Security.* Chicago: University of Chicago Press, 1941.

ALINSKY, SAUL. *Reveille for Radicals.* New York: Random House, 1946.

ALTMEYER, ARTHUR J. "The Future of Social Security in America," *Social Service Review* 27 (September 1953): 251–68.

---

[16]W.I.N. was a simplistic device that failed to get at the real problem—poverty itself, caused not by welfare but by a variety of deep social and economic causes, including the lack of decent-paying, steady jobs for all able-bodied workers and the need for adequate income for the unemployable poor. It was especially inappropriate for A.F.D.C. recipients, mothers who were ill, untrainable, without access to day care for their young children, or already working at menial, low-paying jobs. As a result, only a small percentage were enrolled in the program and, of those, only about one-fourth completed the training; only a handful of the latter could find or were placed in jobs, almost always low-wage work with little or no opportunity for advancement. All studies indicate that the program cost more to operate than it saved in reduced welfare expenditures.

AXINN, JUNE, AND HERMAN LEVIN. *Social Welfare: A History of the American Response to Need*, 2d Edition. New York: Harper and Row, 1982.

BALL, ROBERT M. "Is Poverty Necessary?" *Social Security Bulletin* 28 (August 1965): 18–24.

BANFIELD, EDWARD. *The Unheavenly City Revisited*. Boston: Little, Brown, 1970.

BERKOWITZ, EDWARD D. *Disabled Policy*. New York: Cambridge University Press, 1987.

———. "Welfare Reform in the 1950s," *Social Service Review* 54 (March 1980): 45–58.

———, AND KIM MCQUAID. *Creating the Welfare State: The Political Economy of Twentieth-Century Reform*. New York: Praeger, 1980.

BRAUER, CARL M. "Kennedy, Johnson, and the War on Poverty," *Journal of American History* 69 (June 1982): 98–119.

BREMNER, ROBERT H., et al., eds. *American Choices: Social Dilemmas and Public Policy Since 1960*. Columbus: Ohio State University Press, 1986.

BRIAR, SCOTT. "Welfare from Below: Recipients' Views of the Welfare System," *California Law Review* 54 (May 1966): 370–85.

BURNS, EVELINE M. "Further Needs in Social Security Legislation in the Field of the Social Insurances," *Social Service Review* 25 (September 1951): 283–88.

CHAMBERS, CLARKE A. "Social Service and Social Reform: A Historical Essay," *Social Service Review* 37 (March 1963): 76–90.

COHEN, HENRY. "Poverty and Welfare: A Review Essay," *Political Science Quarterly* 87 (December 1972): 631–52.

COHEN, WILBUR J. "A Ten-Point Program to Abolish Poverty," *Social Security Bulletin* 31 (December 1968): 3–13.

Council on Social Work Education. *Current Issues in Social Work Seen in Historical Perspective*. New York: Council on Social Work Education, 1962.

DONOVAN, JOHN C. *The Politics of Poverty*. New York: Pegasus, 1967.

DURMAN, EUGENE. "Have the Poor Been Regulated? Toward a Multivariate Understanding of Welfare Growth," *Social Service Review* 47 (September 1973): 339–59.

ELMAN, RICHARD M. *The Poorhouse State*. New York: Pantheon Books, 1966.

FISHMAN, LEO, ed. *Poverty amid Affluence*. New Haven, Conn.: Yale University Press, 1966.

GALBRAITH, JOHN KENNETH. *The Affluent Society*. Boston: Houghton Mifflin, 1958.

GANS, HERBERT J. "Redefining the Settlement's Function for the War on Poverty," *Social Work* 9 (October 1964): 3–12.

GARVIN, CHARLES D., AUDREY D. SMITH, AND WILLIAM J. REID, eds. *The Work Incentive Experience.* Montclair, N.J.: Allanheld, Osmun, 1979.

GILBERT, CHARLES E. "Policy-Making in Public Welfare: The 1962 Amendments," *Political Science Quarterly* 81 (June 1966): 196–224.

GLAZER, NATHAN. "The Limits of Social Policy," *Commentary* 52 (September 1971): 51–58.

GORDON, MARGARET, ed. *Poverty in America.* San Francisco: Chandler, 1965.

HARPHAM, EDWARD J., AND RICHARD K. SCOTCH. "Rethinking the War on Poverty: The Ideology of Social Welfare Reform," *Western Political Quarterly* 41 (March 1988): 193–207.

HARRINGTON, MICHAEL. *The Other America: Poverty in the United States.* New York: Penguin Books, 1962.

HOLLIS, ERNEST, AND ALICE TAYLOR. *Social Work Education in the United States.* New York: Columbia University Press, 1951.

KAHN, ALFRED. *Issues in American Social Work.* New York: Columbia University Press, 1959.

———. "Social Services in Relation to Income Security," *Social Service Review* 39 (December 1965): 381–89.

KEYSERLING, LEON. *Progress or Poverty: The United States at the Crossroads.* Washington, D.C.: Conference on Economic Progress, 1964.

KLARMAN, HERBERT. *The Economics of Health.* New York: Columbia University Press, 1965.

KOLKO, GABRIEL. *Wealth and Power in America.* London: Thames and Hudson, 1962.

LEMANN, NICHOLAS. *The Promised Land.* New York: Knopf, 1991.

———. "The Unfinished War [on Poverty]," *The Atlantic* 262 (December 1988): 37–56, and 263 (January 1989): 53–68.

LEVITAN, SAR A. *The Great Society's Poor Law: A New Approach to Poverty.* Baltimore: Johns Hopkins Press, 1969.

———, AND ROBERT TAGGART. *The Promise of Greatness.* Cambridge, Mass.: Harvard University Press, 1975.

LEWIS, MICHAEL. "The Negro Protest in Urban America," in J. R. Gusfield, ed., *Protest, Reform, and Revolt.* New York: Wiley, 1970.

LEWIS, OSCAR. *The Children of Sanchez.* New York: Random House, 1961.

———. *Five Families.* New York: Basic Books, 1959.

———. *La Vida.* New York: Random House, 1966.

LOVE, JOSEPH L. "La Raza: Mexican-Americans in Rebellion," *Transaction* 6 (February 1969): 35–41.

LUBOVE, ROY. "The Welfare Industry: Social Work and the Life of the Poor," *The Nation* 202 (May 23, 1966): 609–11.

MacDonald, Dwight. "Our Invisible Poor," *New Yorker* 38 (January 19, 1963): 82–132.

MacDonald, Maurice. "Food Stamps: An Analytical History," *Social Service Review* 51 (December 1977): 642–58.

Matusow, Allen J. *The Unravelling of America: A History of Liberalism in the 1960s.* New York: Harper and Row, 1984.

May, Edgar. *The Wasted Americans.* New York: Harper and Row, 1964.

Mencher, Samuel. "Perspectives on Recent Welfare Legislation, Fore and Aft," *Social Work* 8 (July 1963): 59–65.

Meriam, Ida C. "Social Welfare in the United States, 1934–1954," *Social Security Bulletin* 18 (October 1955): 3–14.

Merrifield, Aleanor. "Implications of the Poverty Program: The Caseworker's View," *Social Service Review* 39 (September 1965): 294–99.

Miles, Rufus E. *The Department of Health, Education, and Welfare.* New York: Praeger, 1974.

Miller, Herman P. *Rich Man, Poor Man.* New York: Crowell, 1964.

Morgan, James, et al. *Income and Welfare in the United States.* New York: McGraw-Hill, 1962.

Moynihan, Daniel P. "The Crisis in Welfare," *Public Interest* 10 (Winter 1968): 3–29.

———. *Maximum Feasible Misunderstanding: Community Action in the War on Poverty.* New York: Free Press, 1969.

———. *The Negro Family: The Case for National Action.* Washington D.C.: Government Printing Office, 1965.

———. "The Professionalization of Reform," *Public Interest* 1 (Fall 1965): 6–16.

Murray, Charles. "The War on Poverty, 1965–1980," *The Wilson Quarterly* 8 (Autumn 1984): 94–139.

Naples, Nancy. "Contradictions in the Gender Subtext of the War on Poverty," *Social Problems* 38 (August 1991): 316–32.

Newcomer, Mabel. "Fifty Years of Public Support of Welfare Functions in the United States," *Social Service Review* 15 (December 1941): 651–60.

Patterson, James T. *America's Struggle Against Poverty, 1900–1985.* Cambridge, Mass.: Harvard University Press, 1986.

Pearce, Diana. "Welfare Is Not for Women: Why the War on Poverty Cannot Conquer the Feminization of Poverty," in Linda Gordon, ed., *Women, the State, and Welfare.* Madison: University of Wisconsin Press, 1990.

Pechman, Joseph A., et al. *Social Security: Perspectives for Reform.* Washington, D.C.: Brookings Institute, 1968.

Perlman, Helen Harris. "Social Work Method—A Review of the Past Decade," *Social Work* 10 (October 1965): 166–78.

PIOUS, RICHARD M. "The Phony War on Poverty in the Great Society," *Current History* 61 (November 1971): 266–72.

PIVEN, FRANCES F., AND RICHARD A. CLOWARD. "Reaffirming the Regulation of the Poor," *Social Service Review* 48 (June 1974): 147–69.

———. *Regulating the Poor: The Functions of Public Welfare*. New York: Random House, 1971.

President's National Advisory Commission on Rural Poverty. *The People Left Behind*. Washington, D.C.: Government Printing Office, 1967.

RAINWATER, LEE, AND WILLIAM L. YANCY. *The Moynihan Report: The Politics of Controversy*. Cambridge: Massachusetts Institute of Technology Press, 1967.

RAPPAPORT, LYDIA. "In Defense of Social Work: An Examination of Stress in the Profession," *Social Service Review* 34 (March 1960): 62–74.

Report of the National Advisory Commission on Civil Disorders. Washington, D.C.: Government Printing Office, 1968.

RITZ, JOSEPH P. *The Despised Poor: Newburgh's War on Welfare*. Boston: Beacon Press, 1966.

ROHRLICH, GEORGE. "Guaranteed Minimum Income Proposals and the Unfinished Business of Social Security." *Social Service Review* 41 (June 1967): 166–78.

SAPIRO, VIRGINIA. "The Gender Basis of American Social Policy," in Linda Gordon, ed., *Women, the State, and Welfare*. Madison: University of Wisconsin Press, 1990.

SELIGMAN, BEN B., ed. *Poverty as a Public Issue*. New York: Free Press, 1965.

STEINER, STANLEY. *La Raza: The Mexican Americans*. New York: Harper and Row, 1970.

STEVENS, ROBERT AND ROSEMARY. *Welfare Medicine in America: A Case Study of Medicaid*. New York: Free Press, 1974.

STEWART, PAUL. "United States Indian Policy: From the Dawes Act to the American Indian Policy Review Commission," *Social Service Review* 51 (September 1951): 451–63.

THEOBALD, ROBERT. *The Challenge of Abundance*. New York: Mentor Books, 1962.

———, ed. *The Guaranteed Income: Next Step in Economic Evolution?* Garden City, N.Y.: Doubleday, 1966.

TOBIN, JAMES. "The Case for an Income Guarantee," *Public Interest* 4 (Summer 1966): 31–41.

TRATTNER, WALTER I., ed. *Social Welfare or Social Control?* Knoxville: University of Tennessee Press, 1983.

WEEKS, PHILIP, AND JAMES B. GIDNEY. *Subjugation and Dishonor: A Brief History of the Travail of the Native Americans*. New York: Krueger, 1981.

WEISBROT, ROBERT. *Freedom Bound: A History of America's Civil Rights Movement*. New York: Penguin Books, 1991.

WICKENDEN, ELIZABETH. "The '67 Amendments: A Giant Step Backward for Child Welfare," *Child Welfare* 48 (July 1969): 388–94.

WILL, R. E., AND H. G. VATTER, eds. *Poverty and Affluence*. New York: Harcourt, Brace, and World, 1965.

YOUNGDAHL, BENJAMIN E. *Social Action and Social Work*. New York: Association Press, 1966.

ZAREFSKY, DAVID. *President Johnson's War on Poverty: Rhetoric and History*. University: University of Alabama Press, 1986.

CHAPTER 15

A Transitional Era

■ Richard Nixon's election in 1968 was the result of many factors, including the growing unpopularity of Johnson's Vietnam policies and the divisions within the Democratic Party over the war and other matters. In large part, however, it was the product of a changing national mood—a distinct turn to the right. After four decades of activity, the yearning for social change and increased federal involvement in social welfare (and other areas) had faded—and the transition to a new era had commenced.

By the late 1960s, an increasing number of Americans were tired of the decade's social turmoil and resentful of the attention directed toward minorities and the poor. In their view, the middle-class values of thrift, hard work, and self-reliance had been assaulted. Federal social programs had funneled billions of dollars into the inner cities to help the poor and unemployed, at the expense of "hard-working citizens" and of local and state government, all in vain, no less, as the "welfare mess" continued. In their opinion, it was time for a change.[1]

In Richard Nixon, these unhappy middle-class Americans found a person who mirrored their mood. A product of an

---

[1]As James Leiby has pointed out in his excellent *History of Social Welfare and Social Work in the United States*, it was not only conservatives who were affirming solicitude for state and local government; so, too, were members of the New Left and other radicals, who were preaching "participatory democracy" and community control and criticizing bureaucrats, "experts," and other managers of society. Even Common Cause, a liberal consumer organization, stated that the "reason the United States cannot solve the urgent problems that are plaguing our country, is because *the government is the problem*," a sentiment President Reagan would repeat.

industrious middle-class family, Nixon had risen to prominence as a result of his own efforts. He was sternly dedicated to traditional values and the conservative approach, or so it appeared. He constantly spoke about the need for "law and order" and for the reestablishment of authority over young people and the turbulent masses in the nation's cities. He constantly criticized federal involvement in services to individuals and communities, preferring self-help, individual responsibility, and private action or local and state efforts. He voiced suspicions of "welfare fraud" and tended to be moralistic and punitive toward recipients of public assistance. He disliked government bureaucrats (especially since most tended to be Democrats who favored social welfare) and what he referred to as the elitist, liberal intellectual establishment. No wonder *Newsweek* called Nixon "the champion of the good God-fearing burghers of Heartland, U.S.A."

In fact, however, the Nixon presidency was full of surprises. To begin with, he initiated a series of programs, dubbed the "New Federalism," to "reverse the flow of power and resources from the states and communities to Washington and start power and resources flowing back . . . to the people all across America." That effort, designed to make the national government smaller, to stop it from meddling in social reform, and to liberate capitalism from the alleged restraints imposed by prior administrations, was to be accomplished primarily through "revenue sharing"—the return of funds from the federal government to the states and localities for their use with virtually no conditions attached (but which, it was understood, were to be used for such social programs as improved schools, better hospitals, new drug programs, and the like.)[2]

In the area of social welfare, though, Nixon began by advocating a major alteration in the nation's welfare system—a bold plan grounded

---

[2]Actually, there were two parts to revenue sharing: (1) general revenue sharing, whereby monies were distributed to the states without any strings attached, and (2) special revenue sharing, which was used by the federal government to consolidate 130 conditional grants-in-aid to the states into six areas to deal with urban community development, rural community development, education, law enforcement, transportation, and manpower training. In general, however, communities devoted the vast majority of their "returned" funds to such things as street and road repairs, fire protection, parks and other recreational areas, and the like. In fact, one early survey found that only 2.7 percent of such funds were applied to social programs (including health care).

in an income strategy as opposed to a services strategy and designed, ironically, to shift the burden of payments *from* the states and localities *to* the federal government and to equalize such payments throughout the country. However, the plan's key feature, establishment of a federally guaranteed minimum annual income, was coupled with an elaborate system of penalties and incentives designed to force recipients to work—a theme the President mentioned sixty times in his thirty-five-minute speech proposing the measure.

Nixon's Family Assistance Plan (F.A.P.)—conceived largely by Daniel Moynihan (a liberal social scientist who, remember, had become disenchanted with Lyndon Johnson's "war on poverty" and who now was a counselor to President Nixon) and announced in August 1969—was motivated, in part at least, by a desire to destroy the network of bureaucrats and social workers (as well as community organizers, political activists, and civil rights leaders) established by the E.O.A. and other welfare programs of the decade, and in part by a fear that the Democrats, who controlled the Congress, would pre-empt the issue and propose a more liberal program. Under the F.A.P., limited to families with children, every unemployed family of four would receive at least $1600 (subsequently raised to $2400) a year from the federal government. Since the program was designed, in part, to provide the difference between marginal wages and the money needed to live above the poverty line, the working poor would receive the $1600 minimum and would be allowed to keep their pay until their earned income reached close to $4000, at which time the benefits would be discontinued.[3] To be eligible for such assistance, the able-bodied—including women with children over three years of age—would be required to work (or be placed in a job training program). The administration of the program would eventually be turned over to the states under a principle that Nixon labeled the "new federalism."

The President's welfare recommendations provoked immediate controversy. While some people hailed them as a great step forward in helping the poor, most experts denounced the proposals as inadequate and even retrogressive. To begin with, the minimum figure was

---

[3]A family of four with no regular income would be permitted to retain the first $720 of earned income without any reduction in the proposed minimum grant of $1600. Thereafter, it could keep one-half of all additional income, with the cutoff point for a family of four at $3920 (or $5720 for a family of seven). It was assumed that the application of this 50 percent marginal

approximately $2000 less than the federal government's own official poverty line and some $4500 below the Bureau of Labor Statistics' adequate income level for a family of four. Also, while the program would have increased welfare payments in some parts of the country, especially in the rural South where approximately 10 percent of the nation's welfare recipients lived, it would have added little or nothing elsewhere, where the remaining 90 percent of the nation's public dependents resided. Indeed, there were fears that it would lead the more progressive areas to cut back their welfare payments in order to conform to the federal standard.

In addition, the notion that women with young dependent children should leave home and go to work—at any type of job, often at substandard wages—was anathema to many, which led to the proposal's most glaring shortcoming: its emphasis on job training and work when a majority of the poor were "either too young, too old, or too sick to work," were "already employed at below subsistence wages," or were women with young children. Moreover, the plan was work oriented at a time when absorption of all Americans into the labor market (even those with normally marketable skills) was hardly possible. Despite tax cuts, the war in Vietnam, general prosperity, and other factors making for increased job opportunities, unemployment hovered at about 6 percent of the labor force and was rising. Jobs were not available for many Americans, especially for semiskilled and unskilled workers. The administration, however, bound by old stereo-

---

tax on nonexempt earnings, instead of the 100 percent tax which for the most part prevailed in public assistance, would provide the incentive to work.

Proposed Family Assistance Plan Payment Schedule for Family of Four
(Assuming $720 Income Exemption and 50 Percent "Tax" on Nonexempt Income)

Earnings	Nonexempt Earnings	"Tax" at 50 Percent	Net Payment	Net Income
$ 0	$ 0	$ 0	$1600	$1600
720	0	0	1600	2320
1000	280	140	1460	2460
1500	780	390	1210	2710
2000	1280	640	960	2960
2500	1780	890	710	3210
3000	2280	1140	460	3460
3500	2780	1390	210	3710
3920	3200	1600	—	3920

types and myths, continued to set up complex and costly work and training programs for a client population unable to utilize them.

Still, the proposed F.A.P. had virtues, especially in theory. The principle of a federal welfare system (which would eliminate state variations in eligibility requirements and in payments) and what amounted to a guaranteed annual income, however inadequate to begin with, constituted a major step forward in meeting current and especially future needs, one, in fact, as *Newsweek* reported, that left Nixon's cabinet members "gasping for [their] conservative breath." As a result, at least some social workers and welfare groups supported it, as did some local and state officials, who welcomed the financial relief the program would provide their welfare budgets. Most of those concerned, however, did not, including the National Welfare Rights Organization and its leader, George Wiley, who set out to "zap F.A.P."—the "Family Annihilation Plan," which, in Wiley's opinion, would "fuck America's poor." Meanwhile, Nixon lost interest in the proposal and never really exerted much pressure to secure its passage. Thus, several years after it was submitted, the F.A.P. was still bogged down in committee, where it eventually expired.

In the meantime, the welfare problem grew as two distinct economies emerged in America. One, the economy of affluence, included most Americans—well trained, holding steady jobs, in relatively good health, living in reasonably comfortable homes. The other, the economy of poverty, was inhabited by the poorly trained, unable to find or hold jobs, suffering from low incomes, bad health, and poor housing. Born to the wrong parents, in the wrong part of town, or in the wrong racial group, they were trapped in a cycle of poverty and degradation.

Despite various welfare programs and expenditures, it appeared as though poverty, even in an affluent society, had congealed and hardened into a kind of subculture that represented a social syndrome, an ineradicable condition, not, however, because of the needy's personal shortcomings, passed on from generation to generation, as some critics contended, but rather because of the political economy (and racism), over which they had no control. Perhaps Ben Seligman, the author of *Permanent Poverty*, was right when he stated that America would always have its outcasts:

In an industrial society where large segments of the population must suffer joblessness because they are unskilled, low wages when they are employed, a distorted family structure and inadequate services in such areas as education and health [due to discrimination and other factors] there are many who [always] will find themselves rejected.

Yet, few Americans were willing to concede this point—or deal with its implications. Most echoed the sentiments of Senator Russell Long of Louisiana, chairperson of the influential Finance Committee, who charged that the "welfare system . . . is being manipulated and abused by malingerers, cheaters, and . . . frauds."

Still, all was not bleak; there were a few rays of hope. Notwithstanding the lack of significant social welfare reform and a novel attack on the problem (apart from Nixon's stillborn F.A.P.), some progress toward conquering poverty had been made. In 1960, the number of poor—not of welfare recipients—was officially estimated to be around forty million, or 20 percent of the population; in 1969, the number had declined to about twenty-five million, or 12 percent of the population (thanks largely to urban migration, to Medicare, to increased welfare expenditures—Medicaid, food stamps, rent subsidies, etc.—and especially to vast increases in old-age insurance). While not the total victory L.B.J. had talked about in 1964, it was nevertheless a large step in the right direction. Then, too, the war in Vietnam was winding down and even showed signs of coming to an end, and when it did, presumably more funds would be available for badly needed domestic social services.

Also, more Americans were beginning to accept the idea that since automation had broken the traditional link between jobs and income—some citizens could not work, or find jobs, or earn living wages in the labor market—there was a need to set up a truly sound system of social security, including some sort of federal income maintenance program, especially a guaranteed annual income, as Nixon had proposed. Only in this way, they argued, by meeting immediate need with the instrument best designed to overcome that need—money—would the rejects of society, most of whom were not maladjusted or ill, be brought into the mainstream of American life. Even Milton Friedman, the famed conservative University of Chicago economist, favored such a plan, although for different reasons. Believing that it would abolish the welfare bureaucracy and cut welfare costs, he had worked out such a plan—in this case a "negative income tax"— and explained it as early as 1962 in his widely read *Capitalism and Freedom*.

It was not totally surprising, therefore, that when President Johnson's Commission on Income Maintenance Programs, better known as the Heineman Commission, appointed in January 1968 and composed of political activists, leading economists, and above all big businessmen, including such stalwart capitalists as IBM's Thomas Watson and the Rand Corporation's Henry Rowen, released its report in November 1969, it recommended the "creation of a universal income supplement program [a negative income tax] . . . for all members of the population in need," one far more generous than that proposed by Nixon four months earlier. The commission's report stated that unemployment and underemployment "were basic facts of American life" and that the nation's social and economic structure "virtually guaranteed" poverty for millions of citizens. "The simple fact is," members of the commission concluded, "that most of the poor remain poor because access to income through work is currently beyond their reach." As a result, while Nixon's F.A.P. stressed work— indeed, required it as a condition for receiving aid—the commission's proposal discounted it entirely; only a negative income tax without any strings attached could deal with the situation, in its opinion.

Meanwhile, the expectations of the poor had been aroused, and it appeared that they no longer were willing to return to their urban and rural slums and sit by in quiet desperation. Influenced by the mass protest programs and techniques of the civil rights movement and faulting the system rather than themselves for their condition, they demanded adequate assistance as a right, not as a privilege.

Mass welfare rights demonstrations began in June 1966, with thousands of people in sixteen cities across the nation participating. Then, in August 1966, 100 representatives from twenty-three cities met in Chicago to form the National Coordinating Committee of Welfare Rights Groups and to formulate goals and strategies for a nationwide organizing campaign. By 1969, the movement had expanded to more than 22,000 dues-paying members in 523 identifiable groups in states all across America, and it was still growing.

Among the movement's chief aims were: an adequate guaranteed annual income; curtailed investigatory practices, especially with regard to "man-in-the-house" rules, violations of privacy, and "midnight raids"; the right to earn additional income without reduction in assistance payments until an adequate minimum was reached; more respect for recipients' legal rights; improved day care for children of working mothers; higher clothing and furniture allowances; more adequate medical care; and elimination of all residency requirements. The demonstrations, with their picket lines, protest marches and meetings, sit-ins, and school and rent boycotts—which were aimed as much at social workers, those who administered social services, as at welfare departments and the general public—promised to end only when those demands were met, when the stigma of poverty was gone and the promise of American life was fulfilled for all citizens.

And finally, by the late 1960s and the start of the 1970s, there was considerable evidence that social work was again beginning to carry the banner of reform, that it was identifying once more with the "cause" (rather than just the "function" or service) aspects of its historic tradition. While most social workers still trod a narrow path, acknowledging the importance of social reform but seeing themselves primarily as clinicians whose first responsibility was to their clients, the profession appeared to be changing once again.

A growing number of younger social workers, as well as members of the radical student-based Social Welfare Workers Movement, declared that casework was not effective, that it had little impact on those it was supposed to help, that, in fact, it was often more harmful than helpful, and that social workers should be "advocates" for the poor, or "social brokers," not therapists. These dissidents, who charged that M.S.W. stood for "Maintaining Social Wrongs," aided the organizing efforts of the new welfare rights groups. Also, schools of social work were recruiting students from among traditionally disadvantaged segments of society and revising their curricula, placing more emphasis on such things as group work and community organization, public administration, and social policy, and even opening up new field placements in militant community groups. In addition, the Council on Social Work Education demanded that its members shape their curricula on the assumption that their graduates would be called upon to participate in the making of social policy. Even Helen Harris Perlman, the well known educator and author of several casework textbooks, forthrightly enjoined her fellow social workers to become more interested in social reform: "The great federal programs for poverty prevention and for education and training call for versatile social workers," she wrote. "Our present-day articulated repertoire of actions is a limited one. It needs expansion, experiment, ranging. . . ."

Professional associations—such as the National Conference on Social Welfare, which during its 1969 meeting in New York City had been seized by dissidents, including members of the newly formed Association of Black Social Workers, who demanded that the organization open its leadership to minority members and that it deal with the issues of poverty and racism in society—began placing social problems on the public agenda and pressing to keep them there until the American people and their political leaders grappled creatively and effectively with them. The National Association of Social Workers (which changed its bylaws to state that the profession had a dual obligation to use "both social work methods and . . . social action" to prevent and alleviate "deprivation, distress, and strain") stationed a paid lobbyist in Washington, D.C., for the purpose. It also appointed a committee to devise a method of translating data from practice into social policy, and began stressing its members' responsibility for social action.

Then there was the announcement by the Community Service Society of New York (the forerunner of the Association for Improving the Condition of the Poor and the nation's oldest, largest, and wealthiest family service agency) that it was discontinuing casework. "If you don't deal with the pathology of the ghetto, all the individual counseling you do with a person is not going to help," said Dr. James G. Emerson, the agency's executive secretary. "The situation," he added in words that could have come out of the settlement house movement sixty years earlier,

> is not just a matter of persons with problems, but rather of whole areas afflicted with social ills. If the individual is to be helped, someone has to deal with the complex of social ills that bears on the individual, not just on the individual himself. We are convinced that an approach that focuses primarily on individuals may help some people, but will not really alleviate the basic

problem of a sick community. Instead of starting out by saying that the individual is the client, we're going to say the community is the client.

The rays of hope occasioned by these developments, however, quickly dimmed. Poverty did not disappear, nor was the welfare problem legislated out of existence—and the plight of many of its victims remained problematical. The darkening situation resulted from a variety of factors. First of all, it soon became evident that social work activism would not be self-sustaining; indeed, before long the social policy and social action drives within the profession collapsed and confusion reigned, and a growing number of social workers once again viewed their function as helping individuals of all classes to adapt to their environment. Also, various income maintenance proposals continued to be ignored, including those recommended by President Johnson's Commission on Income Maintenance Programs. If anything, the enactment of these and other pieces of social legislation appeared less likely than a half-decade earlier; a more conservative President and Congress and other developments did not bode well for the future.

One such development, which appeared to foreshadow what was likely to follow, was a measure Congress enacted into law in December 1971. Rather than pass legislation designed to deal with the causes of the problem or meet the needs of the poor, Congress strengthened the more coercive features of the Work Incentive Program (and the now dead Family Assistance Plan). The measure, known as the Talmadge Amendments, or W.I.N. II, repealed that section of the 1967 Public Welfare Amendments that allowed the states to determine who was to be referred to job and training programs. Now *all* A.F.D.C. recipients had to register for work or training programs, with the exception of mothers with children under six years of age, and those states which did not somehow place (in jobs or such training programs) at least 15 percent of those so registered faced the loss of federal funds. The administration and Congress continued to reject the idea that the poor always would be with us and that some sort of guaranteed minimum income therefore was essential; few wanted to spend time or money on the "undeserving poor." Instead, they ignored the "facts"—including the severe job shortage and other factors that rendered most welfare recipients either unable to find work or unsuitable for it—and thus the obvious failure of the original program, continuing to fantasize about "workfare" as the cure for dependency.[4]

To its credit, though, Congress at least passed the Comprehensive Child Care Act, a measure that would have provided billions of federal dollars to fund preschool, day care, nutritional, and other programs for children whose mothers now would be forced to leave home and enter the work force. President Nixon, however, vetoed the measure, declaring that if enacted it would encourage parents to abdicate their responsibilities and thus take the family from "its rightful position as the keystone of our civilization." What the President meant to say, no doubt, was that "ladies," or professional women, should stay at home and stop competing with men for jobs, but that it was all right, indeed essential, for lower-class women to enter—be forced to enter—the labor market to perform menial work at substandard wages (even if they had no place to leave their young children).

Meanwhile, in 1970 the unpredictable Nixon had signed into law the Occupational Safety and Health Act (O.S.H.A.), an important statute that increased, significantly, federal oversight of safety and health standards in industry at a time when toxic chemicals and advanced technology demanded such new protection. And two years later the President gave his signature to the Local Fiscal Assistance Act, or so-called revenue sharing, which provided federal block grants to the localities for various social programs, including, among other things, low-income housing and job training (see footnote 2 earlier in this chapter).

In 1972 he also approved the decision by Congress to raise Social Security benefits by 20 percent and to expand and improve, dramatically, the funding for the Food Stamp Program, especially by establishing national eligibility standards; by making the program mandatory on the states; by allowing recipients with no earned income to receive stamps without having to make cash payments for them, thereby giving millions of impoverished families the resources to purchase food in quantities not possible with their meager welfare

---

[4]The results of W.I.N. II were about the same as those of W.I.N. I: the program put few people to work, those who did go to work were employed in unskilled, low-paying jobs, and the real problem of welfare dependency remained unresolved.

checks; and by establishing a revised benefit schedule that allowed larger families with inadequate income to receive additional stamps, thus transforming the program from a stigmatizing "welfare" measure to one that served the needs of a large number of low-income working families.

Another significant advance for many of the nation's needy citizens occurred in the fall of 1972 when the federal government combined all three of the categorical assistance provisions of the Social Security Act—Old Age Assistance (O.A.A.), Aid to the Blind (A.B.), and Aid to the Permanently and Totally Disabled (A.P.T.D.), all of which were financed by shared costs with the states and which gave to the states the authority to determine their own eligibility requirements and support levels—and assumed complete responsibility for them, establishing uniform eligibility standards and a relatively adequate uniform federal income guarantee (without any work requirements) for all recipients. Adoption of the Supplemental Security Income Program, or S.S.I., as it was called, which was to become effective on January 1, 1974, and which thus federalized all public assistance for the adult poor who clearly were considered unemployable, was a landmark in American social welfare history in that it created the nation's first guaranteed annual income program: The needy elderly, blind, and disabled were "entitled" to such assistance; it no longer was a gratuity to be doled out at the discretion of some administrator.

At the same time, of course, the measure symbolized the strength of America's work ethic—and the low regard its citizens had for poor children and their parents. While the unemployable, or "deserving poor," would be relatively well treated, some eleven million other people on welfare, mainly A.F.D.C. recipients (women and children) and the unemployed receiving general assistance at the county level (mainly males and childless couples who were not elderly or permanently disabled) remained under an inadequate and punitive system. The states and localities continued to avoid federal regulations aimed at humanizing their welfare systems, equalizing the amount of aid they provided recipients, and improving administration. Thus, administrators attempted to keep eligible people off the rolls and to stigmatize and humiliate those receiving such assistance, and variations from state to state and from county to county continued to plague these systems. Above all, payments remained low, falling further and further below the inflation rate and the poverty level, making the plight of these people increasingly dire.

Meanwhile, Nixon continued to lambaste the Great Society, "big spenders," and liberals, especially federal civil servants, who he said were undermining conservative programs, and social workers, who in his opinion coddled the poor. After his landslide re-election victory in 1972, he promised to cut back many of the welfare programs enacted by his predecessors, as many of his supporters—blue-collar workers plagued by their own problems of inadequate wages, soaring prices, and rising taxes[5]—called for reductions in government services and expenditures. Thus, when American troops were withdrawn from Vietnam early in 1973, the President announced that none of the "saved" defense funds would be diverted to domestic social programs, as many earlier had hoped.

Once again, however, Nixon confounded the experts. While he placed in office many anti-welfare conservatives and often impounded funds appropriated by Congress for various social programs, he also approved passage of another slew of costly measures designed to help needy citizens; that is, "deserving" needy citizens, or the permanently disabled, the elderly, or the working poor. Thus, for example, he signed into law the Rehabilitation Act of 1973, according physically disabled persons protection from discrimination; legislation establishing the Earned Income Tax Credit (E.I.T.C.), or a negative income tax of sorts, which provided families with dependent children who earned $4000 a year or less a refundable tax credit of 10 percent of their earnings (up to $400), to be administered through the Internal Revenue Service as part of the annual tax collection process, thereby for the first time in American history using the tax system as a mechanism to provide resources to the needy; the Comprehensive Employment and Training Act, or CETA, which subsidized hundreds of thousands of public service jobs (in both public and private nonprofit agencies) for

---

[5]With regard to rising taxes, the Social Security tax, one of the most regressive of all, was a major case in point. It rose from 4.8 percent of the first $7800 earned in 1970 to 5.85 percent of $15,300 in 1976 (and 5.85 percent of $16,500 a year later), hitting hardest the lowest paid in the working class. Today it stands at 7.65 percent of the first $57,600 in wages (and an additional 1.45 percent of all wages between $57,600 and $135,000 for Medicare). In addition, however, inflation pushed many citizens into higher federal income tax brackets despite the fact that, in "real" dollars, they were earning less.

the unemployed (without a means test and thus was reminiscent of the best of the public works programs of the 1930s); and the Social Service Amendments (to the Social Security Act) of 1974, or Title XX, which allocated $2.5 billion annually to the states to be used by them with broad latitude for programs they deemed best to meet the needs of their welfare recipients and, on a fee-for-service basis, others as well, which marked the first time the federal government funded (or at least subsidized) "social services" for those above the poverty line (senior citizens excepted). Nixon also approved further changes and improvements in the Food Stamp Program, additional increases in Social Security (11 percent in 1974), and perhaps most important, the indexing of Social Security (or O.A.I.) and S.S.I.—that is, the decision to make an automatic "cost-of-living adjustment" (COLA) in such benefits, and hence to increase them annually whenever the rate of inflation rose by 3 percent or more.

For all of his conservatism and harsh rhetoric, then, Nixon supported, and in some cases even initiated, many important social policy measures—and in hindsight most commentators agree with Sar Levitan, the noted policy analyst, that, whatever his motives, whether it be political opportunism—an attempt to broaden the base of the Republican Party in the face of pressure from a Democratic Congress and an increasingly powerful group of needy citizens—dislike of social workers, growing destitution, or whatever, "the greatest extensions of the modern welfare system were enacted under the conservative Presidency of Richard Nixon . . . dwarfing in size and scope the initiatives of [John Kennedy's New Frontier and] Lyndon Johnson's Great Society." Indeed, while spending for various poverty programs had increased by $27 billion (in 1986 dollars) during the Kennedy-Johnson administrations, it nearly doubled that during Nixon's years in the White House.

As Bruce Jansson has suggested in *The Reluctant Welfare State*, perhaps the nature of Nixon's welfare reforms obscured their reality. Whereas his predecessors had sought new measures, many of Nixon's were procedural and administrative changes in existing programs, such as increasing and indexing Social Security benefits and federalizing food stamps and aid to the elderly, the blind, and the disabled (S.S.I.). Also, whereas the Kennedy-Johnson measures usually utilized the services of federal bureaucrats and professional social workers, many of Nixon's

programs relied on local officials and used private market mechanisms
to achieve their ends, such as revenue sharing and CETA—and thus
had a conservative appearance. Yet, they were substantial additions to
the welfare state, as Ronald Reagan realized when he entered office a
few years later and sought to eliminate most of them.

Meanwhile, the Nixon administration had become mired in one of
the gravest political scandals in American history—Watergate—which
by March 1974 had led to the resignation or firing of more than a
dozen men from high national office and the indictment or conviction of thirty-five people for criminal acts of one kind or another. In
August of that year, faced by almost certain removal from office
through impeachment, Nixon became the only Chief Executive in
American history to resign from the presidency. Many, liberals included, began to question sharply the ability of elected officials to govern
fairly and to control the course of events, especially in a humane and
rational way, and to urge that government involvement in social programs be curtailed. This liberal opposition to the nature of the federal
role in social welfare intersected with conservative opposition to *any*
federal role and, under Nixon's successors, the nation moved away
from the expansive path of the recent past.

First to succeed Nixon was Gerald Ford, the longtime Michigan
congressman and short-term Vice-President, who took the oath of
office on August 9, 1974, while the former President and his family
were flying to their home in California. Amiable, even-tempered,
open, hard-working, and, above all, honest, Ford was, for the most
part, well liked and respected. He destroyed some of his good will,
however, when shortly after entering the White House he granted
Nixon an unconditional pardon for all federal crimes, known or
unknown, he had committed while in office—an act that would come
back to haunt Ford when he sought election in 1976.

While thought to be a moderate, in reality Ford was quite conservative, much more so than his predecessor. At no time while in the
White House did he express any concern for the needy or mention
welfare reform as one of his, or the nation's, legislative priorities. On
the contrary, Ford was committed to restricting welfare funds, as his
vetoes of a wide range of important welfare measures—among them a
federal public works bill, federal aid to education, health care, a school
lunch program—indicate. In addition, he repeatedly cut H.E.W.'s

budget, fulminated against proposed compulsory health insurance schemes, and proved indifferent to civil rights (especially busing) legislation.

Inflation, which Ford called Public Enemy Number 1, and the ailing economy were the President's top priorities, but he approached these matters in a very conservative way. His obsession with inflation at a time of rising unemployment and declining productivity (ills inherited from the Nixon administration) made conditions bad, or worse, for many Americans. Under Ford's efforts to fight inflation with unemployment, joblessness in America had climbed to 9 percent by the spring of 1975, the highest rate since 1941, while the real gross national product had fallen more sharply than at any time since the collapse of the economy in 1929. Meanwhile, the inflation rate remained high, creating a condition termed "stagflation," which continued to baffle the experts and plague the nation. Symptomatic of the situation were the poverty figures; not only had they ceased to decline, but the number of poverty-stricken citizens in the nation increased significantly once again. Whereas at the start of 1975 the number of poor in America was close to twenty-five million, about the same as six years earlier (although, owing to the growth in population, the percentage had dropped from 12 to 11.5), a dramatic reversal occurred that year. Primarily because of long-term unemployment, spiraling inflation, and a decline in purchasing power, some 2.5 million more citizens dropped below the official poverty level—the largest increase in a single year since the federal government began keeping such figures in 1959,[6] and the figure would continue to rise each year, so that by 1980 the total number of people below the poverty line would be greater than in 1969. Proportionally speaking, the greatest gain occurred among those who did not ordinarily dominate such statistics—members of white, male-headed families; as in the 1930s, the "new" joined the "old" poor.

---

[6]While the overall unemployment rate in 1975 was around 9 percent, it was approximately twice that for the nation's blacks and three times that for its youth. Not only had the problem increased significantly, but a total of 4.3 million individuals were out of work for so long in 1975 that they exhausted their unemployment compensation benefits, while two million others had done the same the year before. Furthermore, owing to inflation, there was a decline in real wages for those who were fortunate enough to be working; consumer prices, especially for food, were rising from 10 to 15 percent a year, much more rapidly than wages. As a result, the real purchasing power of the typical American family dropped by about 2.6 percent in 1975.

Still, the distribution of poverty remained, as always, structured by race, ethnicity, sex, family situation, and employment status—lowest for whites, higher for Hispanics, and highest for blacks; higher for women than for men; higher for single-parent, as opposed to two-parent, families; and so on.

About the only exception to the rule was the aged, whose numbers among the poor declined throughout this period. Senior citizens' exit from poverty, at least to a degree, was due to a number of related causes, especially the expansion and increased effectiveness of income transfer programs, particularly Old-Age Insurance, for which older Americans deserve much of the credit. By the 1960s, the aged were not only greater in number but also increasingly well organized, and, as we have seen, the "gray lobby" helped first to secure large increases in O.A.I. benefits (in 1972 and 1974) and then the automatic tying of those benefits, and S.S.I. payments as well, to increases in the cost of living. (The same was not true, it should be remembered, of benefits received by A.F.D.C. clients and others on welfare.) Thus, the aged were not as vulnerable to poverty as they had been previously or as were others less powerful and considered less worthy.

Meanwhile, memories of Watergate and his pardon of Nixon, lingering suspicions of those in power, and his inability to solve the nation's economic problems contributed to Ford's loss to Jimmy Carter, "the outsider," in the 1976 presidential contest. Carter, a little-known former governor of Georgia, exploited the public's continued discontent with professional politicians and bureaucrats and their same old programs. Insisting that the American people were searching for "new voices, new ideas, [and] new leaders" and promising that he would control inflation, redress the unemployment situation, and thereby lower the "misery rate"—the sum of the inflation and unemployment rates—to eight, Carter won the presidency and carried into office with him a huge Democratic majority in Congress. Once in the White House, however, he would have to surmount persistent doubts about his ability to govern effectively and to solve the nation's pressing social and economic (as well as diplomatic) problems.

In some ways, Carter was an old-fashioned populist who felt for the common folk; he also possessed a human rights dominated ideology. Yet he was aware of the conservative popular mood and he shared one of the major themes of public discourse during the 1976 bicentennial celebration—the idea that the nation had to accept a sense of limits to its power, its resources, and its potential for economic growth. This was particularly evident when Middle Eastern nations stopped shipment of oil to the United States in reprisal for American assistance to Israel and gasoline prices went from 37 cents a gallon earlier in the decade to $1.60 a gallon in 1977, helping to bring on double-digit inflation—and to point out to the American people, in no uncertain terms, that their destiny was not entirely in their own hands. Carter proceeded, therefore, with fiscal restraint, prompting one writer to call him "the most conservative Democrat since Grover Cleveland." And in the spring of 1977, Senator George McGovern, the previous Democratic presidential candidate, accused Carter of being addicted to "republican economics" and stated that it was difficult to remember which party had won the election.

Certainly, there was an element of truth to those allegations. Thus Carter cut the budgets of many social programs in an effort to fight inflation and to provide resources for increased military spending. Further, when Senator Hubert Humphrey and Representative Augustus Hawkins introduced a bill to create federal public service jobs when the national unemployment rate exceeded 3 percent, a measure that Gerald Ford had vetoed earlier, Carter did not vigorously support it; eventually, the Full Employment and Balanced Growth Act was passed, a diluted and relatively meaningless version of the original measure. Carter also failed to support a variety of other social measures introduced in Congress, including bills to provide comprehensive services to families headed by teenagers, to provide federal funding for child care, to provide federal subsidies to local community centers, to provide assistance to battered women, and so on.

Yet, it was both inaccurate and unfair to label Carter a "warmed-over Gerald Ford," for among other things he signed into law a strip mining control bill that Ford had vetoed, he waged many battles on behalf of the environment, he persuaded Congress to create a cabinet-level Department of Energy and then one of education (turning H.E.W. into the Department of Health and Human Services), and he appointed an unprecedented number of women and members of minority groups to judgeships and other government positions. In addition, he fostered a national youth employment bill, secured passage of a measure designed to rescue children from longtime stays in

foster homes, expanded Medicaid, enhanced the rights of the disabled, asked Congress to enact a costly measure to make mental
health facilities and treatment available to many more people, elaborated a national urban policy designed mainly to aid inner cities with
problems of chronic high unemployment, and pushed for a whole
series of other important measures, including major welfare reform.
Thus, on January 26, 1977, only six days after his inauguration, the
President appointed a study group to conduct a detailed analysis of
the nation's welfare policies and come forward with proposals for
reform of what he referred to as the "complicated and often
inequitable system."

Several months later, the President told the American people that
the nation's welfare program was even worse than he thought and that
it "should be scrapped and a totally new system implemented." And
he promised to reveal, within three months, plans for such a new system, one that would cost no more than the present scheme.

True to his promise, Carter publicly unveiled his welfare reform
proposal at a news conference in his home town of Plains, Georgia, on
August 6, 1977. The plan, introduced in Congress several weeks later,
was known as the "Better Jobs and Income Program" (B.J.I.P.). To
become effective in October 1980, if enacted into law, the sweeping
program would abolish the existing welfare system with its patchwork
of benefits, including A.F.D.C., S.S.I., and food stamps, and replace it
with a new two-tier system—a job program for those who could
work, and an income maintenance program for those who could not.

In brief, the proposal called for the creation of 1.4 million full- and
part-time jobs and job-training slots designed to allow every able-bodied head of a household on relief who could not find a job in the private sector to work at one that would pay the minimum wage or higher. The benefits received by those working full time, whether in the
private or in the public sector—two-parent families, single adults,
childless couples, and single parents with no children under age fourteen—depended on the size of their families and the amount of their
earnings. Thus, while a single individual who earned up to $3800 a
year would receive $1100, a family of four earning that amount
would get an additional $2300 from the federal government, bringing
its total annual income up to $6100. For each additional dollar
earned (beyond $3800) up to $8400, the benefits would be reduced

by only fifty cents. In addition, the earned-income tax-credit program, which increased the take home pay of low-wage workers, would be expanded to provide further benefits in the form of tax relief for the working poor in private or nonsubsidized public employment.

Those unable or unexpected to work full time, or at all, because of age, blindness, or disability, or because they were single parents with children under fourteen years of age, would receive a monthly cash benefit that, in most instances, was more generous than what they were already receiving. Hence a family of four in which no adult could work would receive a basic benefit of $4200 a year (in 1978 dollars), an elderly couple $3750, and a single person $2500. Here, too, when possible, there were incentives to supplement this guaranteed annual income. Those who secured part-time employment, including mothers with children between the ages of seven and fourteen who were expected to work while their youngsters were in school, would have their benefits reduced by only fifty cents for each additional dollar of outside income, up to $8400, when the payments would cease. And the expanded earned-income tax credit would provide added tax relief to these people as well.

The program, which would affect some thirty-two million Americans, would cost the federal government approximately $30.7 billion a year, or $2.8 billion more than the existing system. However, it would bring some $2 billion in financial relief to state and local governments during the first year and substantially more thereafter.

Carter's proposal, then, in some ways was similar to Nixon's proposed F.A.P.: Both provided a federal guarantee of minimum income, both used a negative income tax mechanism, and both had monetary work incentives. On the other hand, there were very important differences between the two: The Carter plan provided universal coverage while Nixon's proposal had concerned only families with children, the benefits were considerably higher in the Carter proposals, as were the exemptions from work for women with young children, and, perhaps most important, Carter's proposal, unlike Nixon's, included the provision of jobs. By so doing, the Carter plan, in contrast to the F.A.P.— or the E.O.A., for that matter—would have shifted the onus of poverty from the unemployed to the malfunctioning of the labor market.

On the whole, initial reaction to Carter's proposal was quite favorable, but Congress adjourned without taking action on the measure and, not surprisingly, a year later it was pronounced dead by congressional leaders. Conservatives opposed the plan's cost and the creation of public service jobs, which they feared would compete with private industry, while liberals complained that the payments (both the guaranteed annual income and the proposed wages) were too low and that the plan smacked of "workfare." Perhaps the real reason for the proposal's expiration was its comprehensive nature; incremental reform seems more suited to the American political process, especially in this very touchy area.

Meanwhile, in May 1977, Carter had proposed publicly the use of substantial amounts of general tax revenues and greater employer contributions to shore up the financially troubled Social Security System. Unfortunately, that proposal, too, was rejected; instead, Congress passed, and the President approved, large increases in the payroll tax for employees and employers alike, a costly band-aid solution, at best, that failed to get at the causes of the problem—rampant inflation, growing unemployment, and the aging of the population.

Carter also was "committed to the phasing in of a workable health insurance system" and in July 1978 he unveiled the broad outlines of such a plan, one that placed as much emphasis on curbing rising medical costs as on assuring health care for all citizens. Because the plan—to be called Health Care—was to be phased in slowly and piecemeal and because it had many budgetary (and hence service) restraints, supporters of a more immediate and a more comprehensive scheme opposed it, including Senator Edward Kennedy, A.F.L.-C.I.O. President George Meany, and other longtime supporters of compulsory health insurance. To no one's surprise, this measure, too died shortly.

So, while proposing many significant reforms, Carter was unable to get most of them through Congress, a Congress controlled by his own party. Rather than the "strong, independent, and aggressive President" he had promised to be, he appeared to be weak, indecisive, and ineffectual. In fact, his failure to exert effective presidential leadership led the *New York Times* to refer to Carter as "President Wobble."

Carter's failure to inspire confidence was highlighted by the Iranian hostage crisis—the languishing of fifty-two American citizens in the American embassy in Teheran, where they were held captive for well over a year while Carter and the nation were unable to secure their release. Then came the Soviet Union's invasion of Afghanistan, which also left many Americans feeling angry, frustrated, impotent, and disillusioned with the government's ability to resolve important problems—and with Carter's leadership, or lack of it.

Even more costly to Carter's political future and reputation, however, was his handling of the economy. In 1980, the nation witnessed the second consecutive year of double-digit inflation, the first such instance since World War I. When, with Carter's approval, the Federal Reserve Board drove up interest rates in an attempt to curb inflation, a severe recession ensued, with rising unemployment and continuing high prices. The "misery rate" stood not at eight, as Carter had promised four years earlier, but at 18.7 (7.8 percent unemployment and 10.9 percent inflation). As a result, in the summer of 1980 Carter received the lowest approval rating ever recorded for an American president, 21 percent. Not surprisingly, that fall he was swept out of office in an electoral landslide that returned the Republicans to power behind Ronald Reagan, the former movie actor who had served two terms as governor of California—a state where in June of 1978, with his support, the voters had approved Proposition 13, an amendment to the state constitution that slashed property taxes and dramatically symbolized a growing nationwide tax revolt against all sorts of government expenditures, especially costly welfare measures.

Clearly, times had changed. The certainty and optimism of the 1960s had given way to the doubts and pessimism of the 1970s—and the "mean season" was at hand; not only were liberals and "big spenders" with lots of new social programs under attack, but a war on the welfare state itself was about to commence.

Bibliography

ANDERSON, MARTIN. *Welfare*. Stanford, Calif.: Hoover Institution, 1978.

ATHERTON, CHARLES A. "The Social Assignment of Social Work," *Social Service Review* 43 (December 1969): 421–29.

AUSTIN, DAVID M. "Historical Perspectives on Contemporary Social Work," *The Urban and Social Change Review* 18 (Summer 1985): 16–18.

BURKE, VINCENT AND VEE. *Nixon's Good Deed: Welfare Reform*. New York: Columbia University Press, 1974.

CLOWARD, RICHARD A., AND FRANCES F. PIVEN. "The Weight of the Poor: A Strategy to End Poverty," *The Nation* 202 (May 2, 1966): 510–17.

CONLAN, TIMOTHY. "The Politics of Federal Block Grants: From Nixon to Reagan," *Political Science Quarterly* 99 (Summer 1984): 247–70.

DANZIGER, SHELDON, AND ROBERT PLOTNICK. "Can Welfare Reform Eliminate Poverty?" *Social Service Review* 53 (June 1979): 244–60.

DERTHICK, MARTHA. *Policymaking for Social Security*. Washington, D.C.: Brooking Institute, 1979.

DUNCAN, GREG J. *Years of Poverty, Years of Plenty*. Ann Arbor: Institute for Social Research, 1984.

FEAGIN, JOE R. *Subordinating the Poor: Welfare and American Beliefs*. Englewood Cliffs, N.J.: Prentice-Hall, 1975.

FRANKLIN, GRACE A., AND RANDALL B. RIPLEY. *CETA: Politics and Policy, 1973–1982*. Knoxville: University of Tennessee Press, 1983.

FRIEDMAN, MILTON. *Capitalism and Freedom*. Chicago: University of Chicago Press, 1962.

GERBER, LARRY. *The Limits of Liberalism*. New York: New York University Press, 1983.

GOLDBERG, GERTRUDE S. "New Directions for the Community Service Society of New York: A Study of Organizational Change," *Social Service Review* 54 (June 1980): 184–219.

GOODWIN, LEONARD. *Do the Poor Want to Work?* Washington, D.C.: Brookings Institute, 1972.

GRØNBJERG, KIRSTEN. *Mass Society and the Extension of Welfare, 1960–1970*. Chicago: University of Chicago Press, 1977.

HOFFMAN, WAYNE, AND TED MARMOR. "The Politics of Public Assistance Reform: An Essay Review," *Social Service Review* 50 (March 1976): 11–22.

KATZ, MICHAEL. *The Undeserving Poor: From the War on Poverty to the War on Welfare*. New York: Pantheon Books, 1989.

LEVIN, HERMAN. "Conservatism of Social Work," *Social Service Review* 56 (December 1982): 605–15.

LYNN, LAWRENCE E., AND DAVID DEF. WHITMAN. *The President as Policymaker: Jimmy Carter and Welfare Reform*. Philadelphia: Temple University Press, 1981.

MACDONALD, MAURICE. *Food Stamps and Income Maintenance*. New York: Academic Press, 1977.

MOYNIHAN, DANIEL P. *The Politics of a Guaranteed Income: The Nixon Administration and the Family Assistance Plan*. New York: Vintage Books, 1973.

MURRAY, CHARLES. "The War on Poverty, 1965–1980," *The Wilson Quarterly* 8 (Autumn 1984): 94–139.

OWEN, HENRY, AND CHARLES L. SCHULTZE, eds. *Setting National Priorities: The Next Ten Years.* Washington, D.C.: Brookings Institute, 1976.

OZAWA, MARTHA. "S.S.I.: Progress or Retreat?" *Public Welfare* 32 (Spring 1974): 33–40.

PAULL, JOSEPH E. "Recipients Aroused: The New Welfare Rights Movement," *Social Work* 12 (April 1967): 101–6.

PLOTNICK, ROBERT, AND FELICITY SKIDMORE. *Progress Against Poverty: A Review of the 1964–1974 Decade.* New York: Academic Press, 1975.

President's Commission on Income Maintenance Programs. *Poverty amid Plenty: The American Paradox.* Washington, D.C.: Government Printing Office, 1969.

QUADAGNO, JILL. "Race, Class, and Gender in the U.S. Welfare State: Nixon's Failed F.A.P.," *American Sociological Review* 55 (February 1990): 11–28.

RANGEL, CHARLES B. "Making the Political Process Respond to Human Needs," in *The Social Welfare Forum.* New York: Columbia University Press, 1971.

REESER, LINDA C., AND IRWIN EPSTEIN. "Social Workers' Attitudes Toward Poverty and Social Action, 1968–1984," *Social Service Review* 61 (December 1987): 610–22.

ROCHEFORT, DAVID A. *American Social Welfare Policy.* Boulder: Westview Press, 1986.

SELIGMAN, BEN B. *Permanent Poverty.* Chicago: Quadrangle Books, 1968.

SHEEHAN, SUSAN. *A Welfare Mother.* Houghton Mifflin, 1976.

C H A P T E R   16

War on the Welfare State

■ Relying on folksy and nostalgic rhetoric and his training as an actor, Ronald Reagan, the darling of the nation's conservatives, managed to capture the confidence that Carter had been unable to inspire. Promising an "era of national renewal" through a restoration of the nation's older values and institutions, its military might, and its role in world affairs, Reagan won an overwhelming victory. Not only did he capture the White House but his party also gained control of the Senate for the first time in more than a quarter of a century and added thirty-five seats in the House, with almost all of the changes involving the dislodging of liberals by conservatives. While, in fact, the outcome of the election represented less a right-wing realignment than a dissatisfaction with Carter's leadership and a concern about the nation's economic woes, especially growing unemployment and skyrocketing inflation, Reagan interpreted the vote as a mandate to move the nation in a new direction, including the dismantling of the welfare state, or at least as much of it as was possible.[1] He thus chose a cabinet dominated by conservative businessmen who shared his philosophy and immediately turned to what he called "the worst economic mess since the Great Depression."[2]

---

[1] It is true, of course, that disenchantment with the poverty problem and with welfare recipients had been growing since the latter 1960s, and that even Jimmy Carter had advocated tax cuts, reduced federal spending, and increased defense appropriations relative to social welfare, but a commitment to the welfare state had remained clear throughout the Nixon, Ford, and Carter administrations.

[2] Throughout the presidential campaign, Reagan had likened himself to Franklin D. Roosevelt, implying that when in office he, too, would be forced to take bold economic action. Reagan's legislative proposals and executive decisions, however, unlike

Reagan's positions on public issues, which he had been espousing for some time, were very clear. He detested big government, regarded free enterprise and a healthy business climate as the source of prosperity for all Americans, took a hard line on military preparedness and strength, and disliked welfare recipients, whom he believed to be "cheats" and "free loaders" who should be forced back into the labor market.

These positions, of course, and their proposed solutions—supply-side economics, or Reaganomics, as they were called, a combination of reduced government spending on social programs, a heavy dose of military expenditures, the termination of government regulations, tax cuts (especially for the well-to-do), and a balanced budget—were not new. In fact, they differed little from Herbert Hoover's ideas—and those of many of his nineteenth-century predecessors. And Reagan's director of the Office of Management and Budget, David Stockman, created a sensation, within and without the administration, when he confided to a journalist that the administration's policies were a Trojan horse full of benefits for the rich and that supply-side economics was nothing but trickle-down economic theory in disguise.

In the area of social welfare, Reagan's thinking was especially "Hooverian" or, rather, classic nineteenth century. One of the President's chief advisers on these matters, Martin Anderson, was a senior fellow at Stanford University's Hoover Institution. In his 1978 book, *Welfare: The Political Economy of Welfare Reform in the United States*, Anderson had argued that "the 'war on poverty' that began in 1964 has been won," and that a significant retrenchment in social programs therefore was in order. And another of Reagan's "mentors" was George Gilder, the conservative commentator-writer who believed that "in order to succeed, the poor need[ed] most of all the spur of poverty" (while the rich, of course, as Arthur Schlesinger, Jr., the historian, cynically observed, presumably need the spur of wealth). Gilder's 1981 study *Wealth and Poverty* held that the world was unfathomably complex and that any intervention based on "social engineering" not only was doomed to failure but was likely to do

---

Roosevelt's, curtailed the functions and responsibilities of the federal government. In fact, many of the New Deal programs were among the first to go, along with those of the New Frontier, the Great Society, and even the Nixon administration.

harm. Adam Smith's "invisible hand"—the forces of the free marketplace or, in essence, "survival of the fittest"—would ensure the general
welfare.

For Reagan, then, the nineteenth century was the golden era of
American history—a time when individualism, localism, free enterprise, and the laissez-faire philosophy prevailed. This nostalgic view of
the past and obsession with self-sufficiency precluded the President
from understanding not only the problems faced by the victims of systematic oppression—members of various racial and ethnic minority
groups confined to ghettos and women—many of whom were jobless
through no fault of their own, but the plight of millions of others as
well, including white men and women who were working but who
could not support themselves and their families on their meager earnings. These ideas also led Reagan to believe that it was essential to
reverse the historical trend that had gotten Washington heavily
involved in the area of welfare—that the key, in other words, to solving the welfare problem was not only cutting back on assistance but
also removing responsibility for the needy from the vast federal
bureaucracy, where, in his opinion, waste and inefficiency abounded,
and returning it to the states and localities. The victims of those
changes, he argued, would and should be provided for by private
foundations, churches, fraternal groups, businesses, and charitable
organizations—an assumption or hope that rested on questionable
economic and historical premises. Aside from the inability of the private sector to provide the necessary financial resources—as the Hoover
years and the Great Depression seemingly had proved—federal welfare had grown for compelling reasons: Washington had taken on
responsibilities in this area when, and only when, it was clear that
problems that were national in scope had arisen and that existing
institutional arrangements could not or would not cope with the situation. Moreover, while waste and inefficiency (and even corruption)
exist in the federal bureaucracy, they are present at lower governmental levels and in private agencies as well. In addition, one might argue,
and in fact studies and recent public disclosures (including those in
the United Way) have demonstrated, that there is more fraud and
abuse in the nation's tax system or in its defense industry or in the
health care professions or in private charities than in the public wel-

fare system—fraud and abuse that are far more costly to the nation's taxpayers.[3]

The Reagan administration provided few surprises, with perhaps the exception of the speed, tenacity, and skill with which it pursued its goals. Demonstrating remarkable political adroitness, Reagan quickly managed to increase greatly the defense budget, significantly reduce taxes (for three years, in a way that clearly favored the upper classes), terminate some social programs entirely (such as public service programs for the unemployed, including CETA), and slash government spending, by billions, on many others designed to help the poor and the ill, young and old alike—A.F.D.C., child care, school lunch and other nutrition programs, food stamps, subsidized housing, energy assistance, family planning, public and mental health services, alcohol and drug abuse counseling, legal aid, the Jobs Corps, and the like. At the same time, the President announced that additional reductions in social programs (of $95 billion and $30 billion, respectively) would be proposed in 1983 and 1984 in order to help defray the cost of the tax cuts and increased military expenditures and achieve a balanced budget.

Then, to implement his desire to transfer government functions from Washington to the state capitals, Reagan (in his 1982 State of the Union Message) called for a "New Federalism," a "great leap backwards," as one critic put it, involving forty-six programs, most notably, however, the three that had the greatest effect on the lives of the poor and dependent—A.F.D.C., food stamps, and Medicaid.[4]

---

[3]In 1980–81, there were approximately eleven million recipients of welfare in America, seven million of whom were children. Of the four million adults who received assistance, most were mothers of those children, many of whom were under six years of age; others were working (usually for inadequate wages) or had been working and were unemployed but looking for other jobs. Furthermore, studies of these people showed that the overwhelming majority of them remained on welfare for short periods of time, usually to cope with temporary unemployment, illness, or some other crisis, and that they preferred work to public assistance. So, contrary to the administration's assumption—and the prevailing belief—the number of welfare "cheats" or "malingerers" was very small. Furthermore, annual federal expenditures for A.F.D.C. in the early 1980s amounted to less than 1 percent of the federal budget, while "defense" consumed well over 25 percent of the federal budget.

[4]The remaining forty-three programs, which cost about $30 billion to maintain, would have gone to the states and would have virtually taken the federal government out of the fields of special education, youth employment, job training, and mass transportation.

Under the plan, which would have begun in 1984 and been phased in over the following three years, the states would have assumed all the costs of the first two programs, while the federal government would have completely financed the latter. State and local governments would have had the option to abandon, or reduce the scope of, the programs if they so desired, as would the federal government, and given their economic plight and the prevailing ideological climate, that was a very real possibility, something the Reagan administration no doubt had in mind.[5]

Again, however, as critics indicated, the so-called New Federalism really was not very new at all. Nixon had proposed a similar approach and had used that very term in initiating his revenue sharing scheme. In some ways, however, as Henry Steele Commager, the well-known American historian, pointed out, it really was "a throwback to the Confederacy (1781–89) when the thirteen states . . . [claimed] to be sovereign and the national government was all but impotent." Some even went further back in history, labeling it the "New Feudalism." The plan, however, won little support, among Republicans as well as Democrats, and it died stillborn.

While Reagan clearly focused his budget cuts on means tested rather than on entitlement programs, he did propose reductions in S.S.I. and in Social Security, especially in disability benefits and in O.A.I., respectively, something he had pledged not to do during his campaign for office. These proposals, however, particularly the latter, precipitated a political storm. Many prominent citizens, both members of Congress and others, condemned the President, and a new organization, Save Our Security (SOS), a coalition of various old-age groups and other liberal and labor organizations that claimed to represent thirty-five to forty million Americans, vigorously fought the proposed cuts—and the administration backed down.[6]

---

[5]For an excellent contemporary discussion of the administration's intentions and the likely effects of the "New Federalism" had it been enacted, see Frances F. Piven and Richard A. Cloward, *The New Class War* (New York: Pantheon Books, 1982), pp. 125–34.

[6]Although Reagan did not manage to cut S.S.I.—in fact, Congress increased such benefits over the President's objections—his administration succeeded in removing some 500,000 people from the program, including many with such mental disabilities as schizophrenia, by ruling that they were able to work for a living. However, when a substantial number of these people

As it turned out, however, by raising the issue and the anxiety of many Americans, the administration did the nation a service, at least in the long run, for even Social Security's most loyal advocates conceded that changes in the system were essential in order to maintain its solvency and preserve the funds of more than thirty-five million beneficiaries.

The system had been strained for some time. An increase in the number of people living to old age and their growing political clout meant a rapidly increasing amount of retirement benefits and medical costs, especially due to huge benefit increases, double-digit inflation, and the indexing of payments, which, because they were tied to the Consumer Price Index, exceeded the rate of inflation for most recipients.[7] The cash flow crisis was exacerbated by a number of other related matters, including a rapid upsurge in disability claims, a failing economy, rising unemployment, and a declining birthrate, all of which not only put a severe burden on the disability and unemployment insurance reserves but also meant that there were (and would continue to be) fewer workers contributing funds to assist the larger and larger non-working segment of the population;[8] bankruptcy or ever-increasing taxes for the working class faced the administration, neither of which was very appealing.

Seeking a solution, Reagan created a bipartisan commission and charged it with making recommendations to prevent the system's defaulting. Despite a great deal of public skepticism, the fifteen-member National Commission on Social Security Reform, under the leadership of economist Alan Greenspan, a member of Reagan's Economic Policy Advisory Board and a former chair of the President's Council of Economic Advisers, eventually came up with a compromise plan that

---

appealed those decisions, with the help of lawsuits, a great many of them had their disability benefits restored. Users of Part A of the Medicare program (hospitalization), however, suffered as the Reagan administration, troubled by rising hospital charges, established national levels of payments (DRG's) for hundreds of treatments, which did hold back increasing costs but often led to improper treatment, early dismissals, and other problems for the elderly sick.

[7] Since the C.P.I. contained numerous costly and rapidly increasing items, such as housing and gasoline, which did not affect many of the elderly, their annual benefit increases tended to be considerably greater than the annual increases in their cost of living.

[8] Also, because wage increases, in general, lagged behind COLAs, the system was "paying out" more money than it was "taking in" for that reason as well.

received widespread support not only in Congress but also throughout the nation.[9]

Briefly, the "rescue plan," which was projected to save $168 billion over the next seven years and thereby guarantee the system's solvency over the ensuing seventy-five years, consisted of the following: a delay, for six months, of an impending 5 percent cost-of-living increase in benefits; the taxing of half the benefits, starting in 1984, of higher-income retirees (single people with adjusted gross incomes, exclusive of Social Security, of more than $25,000 and couples with incomes in excess of $32,000); the bringing of new federal employees and workers in nonprofit organizations into the system; the acceleration of scheduled future payroll tax increases; and the gradual raising of the retirement age from sixty-five to sixty-seven (between the years 2000 and 2027). Thomas "Tip" O'Neill, the Democratic Speaker of the House of Representatives and one of the moving forces behind the changes, referred to them as "landmark measures," while President Reagan, when signing them into law on April 20, 1983 (before 800 people, friend and foe alike, invited to the White House for the occasion), declared, "None of us here today would pretend that this bill is perfect . . . but the essence of bi-partisanship is to give up a little to get a lot. My fellow Americans, I think we got a great deal. Older Americans," he added, "no longer need worry that their check will be stopped. These amendments reaffirm our government's commitment to Social Security."

Meanwhile, Reaganomics did not appear to be working; if anything, the President's economic program seemed to have worsened the situation. The gross national product continued to decline, interest rates remained high, and the nation was mired in the worst recession since the Great Depression. Unemployment was approaching, and soon would exceed, 10 percent of the work force. Many major industries—steel, automobiles, and others—were faced with virtual collapse. Entire regions of the nation, especially the industrial Midwest, had descended into depressionlike conditions. Business failures were

---

[9]Representative Barber Conable (R.-N.Y.), who served on the commission, perhaps best summed up the popular reaction to the proposed changes when he said of the plan: "It may not be a work of art, but it is artful work. . . . It will do what it was supposed to do: . . . save the nation's basic insurance system from imminent disaster."

occurring in unprecedented numbers and thousands of people across the nation were being thrown onto the streets, where soup kitchens and temporary shelters could not keep up with their needs. While the President contended that his domestic budget cuts had left intact a basic "safety net" for the "truly needy," the facts spoke otherwise. Not only did many needy citizens continue to suffer, in many cases more than before, but millions of others fell below the poverty line for the first time in their lives: Between 1980 and 1983, the percentage of poverty-stricken Americans went from 11.7 to 15.3, the highest rate, and the greatest number (some 35.3 million), since the mid-1960s. Furthermore, the administration, which had pledged a balanced budget, ran the highest deficits in American history—with no end in sight. Only a lower inflation rate brightened the otherwise dark economic picture.

Much of the President's initial popularity had vanished. Wall Street financiers, once his biggest supporters, called upon Reagan to reverse his course, as did many of his own advisors, who urged him to reduce military spending, delay additional scheduled tax cuts, and show more compassion for the poor by restoring some of the funds slashed from numerous welfare programs. Reagan, however, remained firm. In fact, he not only insisted on going ahead as planned but even demanded additional monies for defense and proposed further reductions in social spending, prompting a group of religious leaders representing all faiths and denominations to state that the President's budget revealed a "nation intent on a selfish and dangerous course of social stinginess and military overkill," a "real moral failure," according to the President of the United Church of Christ.[10]

As 1983 began, Reagan appeared somewhat sobered by the deep recession, by the 12 million unemployed wage earners, by the record-breaking federal deficits (which threatened to impede economic recovery and growth), by the appearance in America's cities of vast sections populated by a so-called underclass of racial minorities—school dropouts, teen-age mothers, dope addicts, hustlers, criminals, and the

---

[10]Reagan's fiscal 1983 budget, which included another tax cut that favored the well-to-do and projected a $99 billion deficit, called for a $34 billion increase in defense outlays (over 1982 levels) and, at the same time, a $27 billion reduction in spending on social programs. No wonder he was accused of callousness toward society's less fortunate members.

like—who existed at the margins of society and frequently preyed on others, and perhaps by his rapidly tarnishing image as well. In his State of the Union Message he expressed a willingness to consider cuts in defense spending—or at least a slight reduction in the proposed increases, to be balanced by additional cutbacks in welfare spending, including a temporary freeze on the indexing of Social Security and S.S.I. payments. He also indicated a readiness to support federal aid to the states for an extension of unemployment compensation to those who had exhausted their benefits. And in what clearly elicited the warmest response from his audience, the President declared, "We who are in government must take the lead in restoring the [nation's] economy"—a statement that stood in sharp contrast to one made when he had assumed the presidency two years earlier, namely that "government is not the solution to the problem; government is the problem."

True to his word, Reagan quickly signed into law a measure that Congress had long debated, one that earlier he had threatened to veto—a $9.6 billion relief package, with $4.6 billion earmarked for the creation of 300,000–600,000 public service jobs and $5 billion designated to go to twenty-seven financially distressed states to subsidize the extension of their unemployment compensation programs.

Meanwhile, there were growing signs that economic recovery was on the way. Inflation continued to drop, interest rates began to fall, the G.N.P. was growing, and the Index of Leading Economic Indicators, the administration's main economic forecasting gauge, increased for a number of successive months. Unfortunately, however, the unemployment rate dropped only slightly and millions of Americans—several million more than when Reagan took office—continued to be mired in poverty, especially women, as the "feminization of poverty" continued.[11] Thanks to the rising divorce rate, job and pay discrimination, a massive rise in the number of babies born to teen-age mothers, and the cutbacks in various social programs, especially in food stamps and A.F.D.C. (whose payments continued to vary from state to state and remain unindexed for inflation), more than two out of every three adults with incomes below the poverty

---

[11]Actually, in 1984 there were some 400,000 *more* Americans below the poverty line than in 1983, but because of the increase in population, the poverty rate had fallen from 15.3 percent to 14.4 percent.

line were women—and female-headed families were five times more likely to be poverty-stricken than two-parent families.

Still, conditions continued to improve for others, or so it appeared, and in July 1983, for the first time in fifteen months, public opinion polls indicated that more Americans approved of Reagan's handling of the economy than disapproved of it. The President's political popularity returned as well—and a little more than a year later he won a smashing victory in his bid for re-election. Reagan's attractive personality, his "tough" foreign policy, his refusal to raise taxes, his glowing optimism, and, perhaps above all, his continued celebration of time-honored American values, especially the work ethic, rugged individualism, and hostility to public "handouts," continued to strike responsive chords with the American people.[12] To Reagan and to those who supported him, poverty was un-American; the poor therefore were responsible for their condition, and welfare was wasteful and counterproductive.

These beliefs received backing from a number of articulate and aggressive neo-conservatives, especially the sociologist Charles Murray, whose controversial book *Losing Ground* (1984), more than any other work, promoted the view that welfare programs were harmful to the poor and exacerbated the poverty problem. In terms remarkably similar to J. V. N. Yates, the British Poor Law Commissioners, and other nineteenth-century commentators as well as more recent "culture of poverty" proponents, Murray argued that relief policies—especially A.F.D.C., food stamps, and even federal job training programs—tended to undermine individual responsibility, to create a state of dependency, and thus to prevent the poor from achieving self-sufficiency. By making unemployment "affordable," welfare spending created an environment, or culture, that encouraged dropping out of school at

---

[12]Reagan defeated Walter Mondale, Jimmy Carter's Vice President who was associated with liberalism and who appeared to be beholden to numerous special-interest groups, especially organized labor. When Mondale tried to make Reagan's mounting budget deficits a campaign issue, few people seemed concerned. They were greatly concerned, however, with Mondale's call for increased taxes. The election results were rather interesting—and revealed, among other things, an electorate deeply divided along class lines. According to an American Broadcasting Corporation News exit poll, Americans earning more than $30,000 a year favored President Reagan over Walter Mondale by more than two to one, but those earning less than $10,000 a year favored Mondale by landslide proportions.

an early age, abandoning low-wage jobs, and having illegitimate children, and thus perpetuated, and even worsened, the poverty problem:
"We tried to do more for the poor and produced more poor instead,"
wrote Murray.[13] The solution to the problem, he insisted, was to dis-
mantle all benefit programs for working-age people, except perhaps
for unemployment insurance.

Not all Americans, of course, shared Murray's, and the President's,
outlook. The notion that poverty was the unintended result of well-
meaning but misguided social programs, or "that the government
fought a war on poverty and poverty won," is "ideological slander, not
history," wrote Michael Katz. He and others argued that structural
changes in the economy and the *erosion* in anti-poverty programs were
the causes of the problem, and that a strengthening, not a dismantling, of the welfare state was essential in order to solve it. Such was
the theme of Michael Harrington's *The New American Poverty* (1984),
a depressing sequel to his earlier bestseller, *The Other America*, which
began with the grim pronouncement, "The poor are still there." They
are poor, however, said Harrington, not because of any personal shortcomings or decisions on their part, but because of changes in the
international economy, especially the "de-industrialization" of
America, and the way in which they have been treated, or mistreated,
here at home. They are the uprooted and the homeless, products of
de-institutionalization, cuts in welfare programs, shortages in low-rent
housing, and other social and economic forces over which they have
no control; undocumented aliens who have become the new sweat-
shop laborers; unemployed blue-collar workers victimized by the dis-
appearance of steady and relatively well-paying manufacturing jobs in
the "smokestack industries" as a result of technological advances and
global competition (including the movement of capital by American

---

[13]What Murray ignored was the fact that, between 1960 and 1972, precisely the years when
welfare programs really proliferated, poverty in America was cut in half—and the greatest
growth in poverty came during the early 1980s, when the Reagan administration curtailed and
eliminated such programs. For a view diametrically opposed to Murray's, see Robert
Haveman, *Starting Even: An Equal Opportunity Program to Combat the Nation's New Poverty*
(New York: Simon and Schuster, 1988). Also see Nicholas Lemann, *The Promised Land* (New
York: Knopf, 1991), which argues that, to the extent that the Great Society's welfare programs
were failures, it was not because they were too liberal or beneficent, but rather because they did
not go far enough in their quest to eradicate poverty.

businessmen to third world countries where labor costs were cheaper); white-collar workers who lost their jobs due to reorganization schemes in the name of efficiency, plant closings, or moves to new locations in the so-called Sunbelt; hopeless, uneducated, and untrained young blacks unable to get jobs due to racism; families headed by poor, unmarried women who could not work because they had no place to leave their young children; uprooted farmers and farm laborers hurt by the elimination of the subsistance farm and the agricultural depression; and millions of others in unskilled, unsteady (and often part-time), low-wage, dead-end, "benefit-less" jobs in the service sector of the economy—cooks in fast food restaurants, dishwashers and chambermaids in hotels and motels, janitors and cleaning women in schools, hospitals, nursing homes, and the like.[14] Harrington, Katz, and others, including Robert Greenstein, director of the Center on Budget and Policy Priorities, demanded that the government spend billions of dollars on social programs to meet the needs of these "rejects" of society.

The administration, however, continued to ignore, or discount, such demands and, despite evidence to the contrary, to argue that poverty was diminishing, and would continue to diminish, through normal market forces.[15] Thus, during his second term in office, Reagan continued to neglect the well-being of the nation's needy citizens and to concentrate, even more, on foreign policy matters, including the development of a Strategic Defense Initiative—S.D.I., or Star Wars, as it was dubbed—a space-based laser-guided anti-missile system that eventually would cost trillions of dollars and that, according to many scientists who refused to work on the project, may not even

---

[14]In December, 1988, the federal government's Bureau of Labor Statistics reported that ten million Americans lost their jobs, both blue and white collar, because of plant closings or lay-offs between 1983 and 1988, a period considered the longest peacetime economic expansion in the nation's history—and an equal number lost their jobs for the same reasons between 1973 and 1983.

[15]Interestingly, in March, 1985, just when Reagan entered office for the second time, Jay Angoff, a Congress Watch lawyer, indicated that "corporate welfare," including the investment tax credit, which cost the U.S. Treasury more than $38 billion and required taxpayers to pay 10 percent of the cost of new equipment that businesses bought, was costing the American public more than $100 billion a year—more than the cost of A.F.D.C., food stamps, and many other welfare programs combined.

be workable.[16] At times, Congress balked at the President's continued cuts in domestic spending and, on occasion, even took some modest steps to help the needy, at least the working needy: thus it increased the amount of money that working parents could claim under the Earned Income Tax Credit and it instituted two new tax credits that allowed the working poor to recoup some of their expenses for day care and health insurance. The two major pieces of legislation to emerge from Congress, however, were the Balanced Budget and Emergency Deficit Control (or Gramm-Rudman-Hollings) Act and a tax "reform" measure. The former required across-the-board cuts in domestic and defense programs if the budget did not meet specified spending reductions in the coming years, and the latter simplified federal taxes by decreasing the number of tax brackets and loopholes, increased corporate taxes, and removed approximately six million low-wage earners from the income tax rolls. At the same time, however, it gave the largest tax cuts to the well-to-do and was designed not to generate any more revenue than the old measure; thus, it would have no impact on the federal deficit—or on the government's ability to generate additional funds for badly needed social programs.

Meanwhile, conditions were going from bad to worse at the state level, where, despite evidence from previous programs (including W.I.N. I and W.I.N. II) that workfare neither provided meaningful employment opportunities for many single women nor removed large numbers of them from the welfare rolls, it was evolving from a cranky conservative notion to one with increasingly broad support.[17] In fact, by the mid-1980s workfare was an idea whose time seemed to have

---

[16]In addition, Reagan's 1987 budget included $400 million to conduct research on a supersonic "Orient Express" passenger plane which would be able to speed passengers from Washington, D.C., to Tokyo in two hours.

[17]In some ways, the impetus for these programs came from Congress which, in 1981, shortly after Reagan took office, passed legislation granting the states more flexibility in administering their W.I.N. programs. Critics of workfare argued that it merely punished people for being poor; that the vast majority of those affected by it were unwed mothers with young children who had no marketable skills and who, after attending short-term training programs, would be forced into menial, low-paying, sex-stereotyped work; that in any event there were not enough such jobs to go around, and thus for each person who might enter the workforce as a result of the program someone else would be displaced, and that the costs of the program were greater than their projected savings.

come, or more accurately, come back, in large part because of a need on the part of economically strapped states to find ways to keep budgets (and taxes) down. What could be more inviting targets for spending cuts than programs for the poor? Thus, in statehouses all across America, Democrats and Republicans joined forces to vote in favor of such programs that combined the promise of jobs traditionally favored by liberals with efforts to pare the welfare rolls advocated by conservatives. In fact, so broad was the consensus in favor of workfare—not only by lawmakers but by an increasingly hostile general public—that by 1987 as many as forty states had developed and operated such programs of one kind or another, with less than satisfactory results, at best. Thus a study of sixty-one workfare programs throughout the United States conducted by the General Accounting Office (GAO) concluded that, on the whole, they had very little effect on moving their participants off welfare.

Indeed, despite the proliferation of such programs, the plight of the nation's destitute, hungry, and homeless citizens worsened. In November, 1984, in a pastoral letter on "Catholic Social Thinking and the U.S. Economy"—a prelude to their plea for *Economic Justice for All* (1986)—American Roman Catholic bishops had called poverty in America a "social and moral scandal that must not be ignored," and stated that "works of charity cannot and should not have to substitute for humane public policy. Society's responsibility to alleviate poverty must . . . be carried out through the government acting as the agent of the common good." A little more than a year later, the Physicians Task Force on Hunger in America reported on a two-year nationwide study it had conducted and concluded that, despite fifty-eight continuous months of economic expansion, hunger was more widespread and serious than at any time in the previous fifteen years (affecting some twenty million Americans), largely, in its words, because of "governmental failure": "Supply side economics has failed as a remedy for hunger," declared Larry Brown, a professor at the Harvard School of Public Health and chair of the task force. And in November, 1986, Robert M. Hayes, a former Wall Street lawyer who at the time headed the National Coalition for the Homeless, reported that a new wave of destitute citizens could be found in the nation's streets—some 60,000 in New York City alone—a great many of whom were children and infants. The problem, in fact, which continued to grow, became so

pervasive that in early September, 1988, *Time Magazine* ran a special
cover story on "Begging in America." Something had to be done!

Something, in fact, was being done. For months, Congress had
been working on a welfare reform bill that was hailed—by the
President, by the Congress, and by the press—as a "revolutionary"
measure, one that would bring about a "sweeping overhaul" of the
nation's welfare system, making it a "job employment system not a
payment system," and thus one that would "bring a generation of
young American women back into the mainstream of American life."
Largely the work of Senator Daniel "Pat" Moynihan (D.-N.Y.), the
author, twenty years earlier, of Richard Nixon's ill-fated Family
Assistance Plan, the Family Support Act, as it was entitled, was signed
into law by Reagan in October 1988, a month before the upcoming
presidential election. The major provision of the $6.8 billion federal
statute—which was to start in October 1990 and then become fully
effective in stages over the following six years—was the Job
Opportunities and Basic Skills (or JOBS) program, one that required
single parents on welfare, chiefly women, whose children were older
than three years (unless states lowered the age to one, which they had
the authority to do) to work in order to receive assistance. If they
could not get jobs (in the public or in the private sector), they had to
enroll in education or job training courses, to be paid for by the states
and the federal government. The states were required to meet enrollment quotas and to reduce the grants of those who refused to "join"
the program.

In addition, the measure included stiff new procedures for collect-
ing child support payments from absent parents (including the gar-
nishment of wages); the guarantee of money, for one year, for child
care, transportation, and other expenses necessary to enable recipients
to work or to take part in education and/or job training programs; the
continuation of Medicaid coverage, again for one year, for those who
became self-supporting; and the requirement that all states provide
welfare benefits to families in which both parents were unemployed—
something that had been optional under A.F.D.C.-UP, but in which
only twenty-eight states had chosen to participate—with the provision
that at least one parent in such families then had to participate in the
JOBS program.

Without disparaging the new and constructive features of the measure, and there certainly were some—especially the provision of funds for child care and transportation expenses, the continuation of Medicaid coverage for those who managed to get off welfare, and the requirement that all states participate in the A.F.D.C.-UP program—the idea of forcing welfare recipients, largely women with young children, to enter the workforce in order to receive assistance was of course hardly novel, nor had it been very successful in the past; indeed, as we have just seen, the states had been trying to do that for some time, largely in vain. Furthermore, the statute, like so many previous welfare "reform" measures, was based on a number of dubious assumptions—assumptions, in fact, proved incorrect by a variety of scholarly studies: that most recipients have been on welfare for long periods of time (even generations), by choice; that they are able to get, and to hold, jobs, or would be able to do so after receiving some basic education or job training; that paid employment was the ticket out of poverty for women on welfare; and that they will enter the labor force only when required by law or threatened with starvation. Thus the statute did not mandate a federal minimum A.F.D.C. benefit or provide any incentives to the states to increase their existing ones—and hence did nothing to reverse the 40 percent decline in welfare recipients' "real" dollar purchasing power since the early 1970s.

To no one's surprise, then, despite the hoopla accorded the measure at the outset, there were some skeptics on both sides of the ideological aisle. Some conservatives denounced the measure as too costly and, thanks to its child care and extended Medicaid benefits, likely to encourage low-income working women to leave their jobs and go on welfare. Liberals meanwhile minimized the importance of the measure, claiming that it would have little effect one way or another. Time, of course, would tell. In the meantime, perhaps they could take some consolation in the fact that the poor and the dependent at least had received some attention from Washington—that it finally had been recognized in the nation's capital that the plight of the destitute needed improving, and that that would not occur simply through normal market forces.

In the meantime, the Reagan administration had become crippled by its own hostage crisis (in Lebanon, where a number of kidnapped Americans had been held captive for years), by the Iran-Contra scandal—a secret and illegal attempt by members of the administration to sell arms to Iran in return for the release of the hostages and then to funnel some of the money to the so-called Contras in Nicaragua, who were trying to overthrow their leftist government—and by its lame-duck status. Liberals, close to despair, hoped for a change with the coming presidential election.

As it turned out, the 1988 presidential election proved to be a disappointment, not only to liberals but to most Americans, record numbers of whom stayed away from the polls.[18] After a wide-open race for the nominations, including a number of hotly contested primaries, Vice President George Bush and Governor Michael Dukakis of Massachusetts emerged as the presidential candidates. Dukakis, a socially conscious but financially conservative "technocrat," had a rather impressive record of accomplishments as governor of the Bay State, especially on welfare matters, where he reduced the rolls significantly and managed to get a large number of recipients into good, decent paying jobs; in fact, his was one of the few successful state workfare programs (known as Employment and Training Choices) and served as something of a model for the new federal statute. Furthermore, during the campaign he came forward with a number of important new proposals, including an innovative college tuition loan program, a war on drugs, an energy policy, a national literacy program, and a universal health insurance scheme.

The more conservative Bush, on the other hand, campaigned on the Reagan administration's record and said very little else, other than that he favored school prayers, the death penalty, a lower capital gains tax, and a strong national defense—and he opposed abortion and a tax increase. For the most part, he simply told the American people why they should not elect his opponent, not always in an honest and fair way. In fact, while he called for a "kinder, gentler nation," he waged what most people agreed was a tough, slashing campaign against Dukakis. He used such matters as the Governor's veto of a bill requiring teachers to lead students in the Pledge of Allegiance, the state's ill-fated prison furlough program (in which he pandered to

---

[18]Throughout the race, a large number of voters expressed unhappiness with both candidates, with the negative tone of their campaigns, and with their failure to discuss significant issues. It was not surprising, therefore, when only about 50 percent of the eligible voters cast ballots, a sixty-four-year low.

racist fears by continually using in his television commercials a mug shot of Willie Horton, a black convicted murderer who had committed another murder while "on leave" from a Massachusetts prison), and the fact that the Governor was a "card carrying" member of the American Civil Liberties Union to portray Dukakis as a big-spending liberal who was out of the political mainstream—tactics that worked. Bush won the presidency by a wide margin (although the Democrats strengthened their hold on Congress), capturing almost 54 percent of the popular vote, forty states, and 426 of the 538 electoral votes.

In the end, however, the consensus was that Dukakis lost the election for a number of reasons—because he failed to respond early to Bush's negative attacks on him, because he was viewed as passionless and was unable to communicate a coherent vision of who he was and where he wanted to lead the nation, and above all, because Bush's "experience" and use of the "peace and prosperity" issue were difficult to counter. Whatever, immediately after the election, Bush claimed a mandate to continue President Reagan's policies of holding the line on domestic spending, avoiding a tax increase, and maintaining a strong national defense.

True to his word, President Bush showed little inclination to deal with the nation's domestic problems. Indeed, as the authors of *American History*, a widely used college textbook, phrased it, the "first eighteen months of the Bush presidency were notable above all for the absence of important [domestic policy] initiatives or compelling new ideas. . . ." Instead, he focused most of his attention on foreign policy, a field in which he was more experienced and felt most comfortable—and one in which his actions would win him widespread acclaim and popularity, at least for a while.

To be fair, however, Bush was hampered by a number of things for which he was not entirely responsible, including a staggering $2.6 trillion debt he inherited from the Reagan administration, huge budget deficits, a crisis in the scandal-ridden savings and loan industry that would cost the taxpayers more than $500 billion to "clean up," and an economy with various structural weaknesses that, by 1990, would lapse into an increasingly serious recession. Of course, his campaign promise of "no new taxes" did not help matters, nor did his lack of interest in domestic policy.

So it was that early in his administration the number of poverty-

stricken Americans began to climb once again, going from 12.8 percent of the population, or about 31.8 million Americans, in 1989, to
13.5 percent of the population, or nearly 33.6 million, in 1990, then
to 14.2 percent of the population, or approximately 35.7 million,
twelve months later—the most in any given year since 1964. As a
result, all across America welfare applications soared.

Battered by swelling caseloads, revenue cuts due to the recession, and
thus increasing budget deficits, many states, in efforts to save money,
again looked to their welfare programs and either froze or reduced their
A.F.D.C. benefits. Along with county governments, they cut even more
sharply (and in some cases even terminated) general assistance grants for
the needy who did not qualify for federally supported welfare programs,
throwing hundreds of thousands of former recipients and other needy
citizens onto the streets and precipitating a host of new measures that
came to be known as the "new paternalism."[19]

One of the most notable of these new initiatives—which like most
of the others needed, and received, federal approval, or "waivers"—
occurred in Wisconsin. There, the conservative Republican Governor
Tommy Thompson pushed through the legislature (or more accurately, implemented through the use of his line-item budget veto power)
"Learnfare," a program that provided for a 15 percent cut in A.F.D.C.
benefits for welfare families whose teenage children missed a prescribed number of school days. The program was a success,
Thompson later claimed, despite findings to the contrary by a state-
commissioned study prepared by the Employment and Training
Institute of the University of Wisconsin-Milwaukee, which concluded
not only that the measure had not improved overall school attendance
among high school students from welfare families, but had in fact led
to lower attendance.[20]

---

[19]In the spring of 1992, during the height of the recession, A.F.D.C. benefits throughout the
nation averaged about $390 per month for a family of three, while the official poverty level for
such a family was $905 per month.

[20]Interestingly, according to Thompson the program was successful not because it increased
school attendance but because the families of 6,600 teenagers had their benefits cut the first
year, "saving" the state some $3.3 million. Even in those terms, however, critics quickly point-
ed out that the Governor failed to factor in the cost of administering the program, which may
have been greater than the alleged savings. Undeterred, Thompson called for extending the
program to elementary school children.

Meanwhile, in New Jersey, the liberal Democratic Governor Jim Florio took credit for a new law that denied increased benefits to unmarried mothers who gave birth to additional children while on A.F.D.C. That idea spread to California, where a moderate Republican governor, Pete Wilson, pushed for passage of Proposition 165, a public referendum on the same matter, which also would have cut the state's A.F.D.C. grants by 25 percent and would have required teenage mothers to live with a parent or a guardian in order to receive those benefits. And although the measure went down to a narrow defeat, the state trimmed A.F.D.C. grants by more than 10 percent during the 1991–92 and 1992–93 fiscal years and adopted a policy (which since has been invalidated by the courts) that denied newcomers higher benefits than they had received at their prior places of residence. And so it went, in Maryland, Oklahoma, Illinois, Wyoming, Michigan, Connecticut, Rhode Island, and elsewhere.

The states' financial woes also affected their ability, or willingness, to carry out the provisions of the 1988 Family Support Act. Thus many failed to start or to expand existing job training and placement programs or to provide ample funds for child care and other supportive services required by the law and considered critical in facilitating participation in JOBS by A.F.D.C. recipients. At least those were the findings of Jan Hagen and Irene Lurie, authors of *Implementing JOBS: Initial Choices* (1992), a "summary report" of the first major study of the act since it became law. In fact, they concluded, "In none of the [ten] study states did JOBS spur state leaders to alter their public stance toward welfare ot to make a strong personal commitment to reform their welfare programs in light of the new law." Thus the likelihood that it will take large numbers of A.F.D.C. recipients off the welfare rolls and place them on the tax rolls appears to be slim, at best, as critics of the much-celebrated measure predicted. Still, Senator Daniel Moynihan, the statute's chief architect and booster, remained "very encouraged" by its prospects "Give it more time," he urged.

Meanwhile, all sorts of related social problems continued to worsen, including homelessness—which reached an all-time high since the Great Depression—unemployment, child abuse, crime, racial tensions, and the like. Proposals to deal with these and other problems, especially the needs of drug addicts, alcoholics, and AIDS victims, went nowhere or were rebuffed by the President. Thus, for example, he vetoed a civil rights bill that would have bolstered protections for minorities and women against job discrimination (on the ground that it would lead to quotas) and did the same to a measure that would have provided up to six months of unpaid leave for workers with newly born or adopted children or with family emergencies (on the ground that it was too costly and would hurt small businesses, although it applied only to establishments with fifty or more employees). Other major challenges, such as rapidly increasing medical costs and the lack of health insurance for millions of Americans, simply were ignored.

This, of course, is not to say that nothing was done. In 1990 Congress passed, and President Bush signed into law, the Americans with Disabilities Act (ADA), a measure that aroused very little controversy since it cost the federal government almost nothing and promised to get into the labor market lots of people who otherwise were unable to enter the workforce, or who for other reasons (such as discrimination) were kept out of it. Bush also eventually approved an increase in the minimum wage from $3.35 to $4.25 per hour (after earlier vetoing a similar measure with a slightly higher figure). The first change since 1981, it still left a full-time worker with a family of four $1,400 below the poverty level.

Throughout, however, the President remained exceedingly popular, thanks largey to his public image as a subdued, "good-natured" person and even more to the success of several overseas ventures, to which he committed most of his time, energy, and resources. To begin with, late in 1989 he successfully dispatched American troops to Panama to overthrow the unpopular military dictator Manuel Noriega, who was captured, brought to the United States to stand trial for drug trafficking, found guilty, and imprisoned. Then came the dissipation of the Soviet Empire and the collapse of communism in the Soviet Union and throughout Europe, ending the Cold War and making the United States the world's only "superpower," for which Bush (and former President Reagan) claimed much of the credit.

Finally, there was the highly popular Persian Gulf War—the launching of military action (in conjunction with numerous allies and under the jurisdiction of the United Nations) against Iraq, which had invaded and quickly subdued its small, defenseless, oil-rich neighbor,

Kuwait—a war that ended successfully (in February 1991) in a matter of weeks. The quick and relatively painless victory over Iraq and its hated leader, Saddam Hussein, resulted in record high popularity ratings for the President.[21]

Immediately after the war, however, the nation's attention returned to domestic issues, especially the ever deepening recession, and when it became evident that Bush had few plans to deal with it—and, in fact, for months even refused to admit its existence—his popularity declined with startling speed.[22] When finally forced to acknowledge the existence of the recession, and some of the pressing social problems resulting from it, he reminded the American people: "We have a deficit to bring down. We have more will than wallet, but will is what we need." While some questioned his will, he obviously continued to look to voluntary associations and private individuals, the "thousand points of light" he frequently spoke of during his campaign for the presidency, to meet the needs of the destitute and dependent.

The President's plea for the private sector to help the nation's needy was dealt a severe blow when, in the spring of 1992, the United Way, the nation's largest and most prestigious private charitable organization, was racked with scandal. Journalists discovered, and revealed, that William Aramony, head of the organization, not only was being paid the astounding salary, including benefits, of $463,000 a year, but that he frequently used chauffeur-driven limousines, flew first-class on airlines (and sometimes even traveled on the very expensive supersonic jet, the Concorde), had numerous hideaway apartments, appointed various members of his family to high-paying jobs

---

[21]According to public opinion polls conducted at the time, 90 percent of the American people approved of the way Bush was handling the presidency. Another result of the war and its hasty success was a new splurge of arms spending on a variety of exceedingly expensive "high-tech" weapons—Tomahawk, Maverick, Hellfire, and Patriot missiles, Multiple Launch Rocket Systems (MLRS), Apache helicopters, etc.—which, thanks in part to widespread television coverage of the conflict and good military public relations, caught the public's imagination. This, of course, meant huge profits for defense contractors while many poor women and children continued to suffer.

[22]He also was hurt by his decision in 1990 to accept a "tax revenue increase" proposed by Congress to deal with the huge budget deficit (and thereby break his promise to shun all tax increases) and, ironically, by the tardiness of his response to the chaos in the former Soviet Union that resulted from the collapse of communism there.

within the organization, and engaged in a number of other question-able (if not unethical) financial practices. At the same time, he and the President (who had just spent billions on various military ventures) were asking hard-pressed Americans for contributions for food pantries, abused children, homeless citizens, and others desperately in need. The public, of course, was outraged. As many as one hundred of the organization's 1,100 affiliates immediately stopped paying dues to the national body, and several eventually left the organization alto-gether despite Aramony's resignation.

Only weeks later, South Central Los Angeles erupted in violence, a scene that was all too reminiscent of the urban riots of the mid-1960s. While members of the Bush administration maintained that the Los Angeles riot was a product of the failed Great Society pro-grams, other less politically motivated and more accurate analysts, such as the writer Mike Davis, insisted (in a *Nation* magazine article) that it "must . . . be understood as an insurrection against an intoler-able political-economic order." The three-day incident, which involved many Hispanics and Asians as well as African-Americans and left fifty-three dead and more than $1 billion in damages, erupt-ed after a Simi Valley jury that contained no African-Americans delivered a verdict of not guilty on virtually all of the assault charges brought by the state against four white Los Angeles police officers who were accused of brutally beating Rodney King, a black citizen who they had stopped for a traffic violation. To many Americans, who had seen on television a widely replayed "home" videotape of the clubbing King had received, the acquittal of the police officers seemed to be a miscarriage of justice—and a vivid example of the racism that continued to permeate American society.[23] Indeed, a report funded by the Milton Eisenhower Foundation would con-clude (in March 1993) that the Kerner Commission's vision of two unequal Americas, "one black, one white—separate and unequal," is "more relevant today than in 1968."

---

[23]A year later, federal civil rights charges were filed against the four officers. On April 17, 1993, after a lengthy trial, a racially diverse Los Angeles jury found two of the policemen guilty and two of them innocent of the charges; the convicted officers faced up to ten years in prison and $250,000 in fines. On August 4, 1993, however, they were sentenced to two and a half years in prison and no fines. While many people felt the sentence was too lenient, to everyone's relief, calm prevailed.

While these and other events illuminated the need for a new domestic order in the minds of some Americans, as the 1992 presidential campaign approached few citizens or politicians appeared willing to come to the defense of the poor—or to reverse the punitive measures that had been directed against them during the previous twelve years.

Bibliography

ANDERSON, MARTIN. *Welfare: The Political Economy of Welfare Reform in the United States.* Stanford: Hoover Institution, 1978.

AULETTA, KEN. *The Underclass.* New York: Random House, 1982.

BARLETT, DONALD, AND JAMES STEELE. *America: What Went Wrong?* Kansas City, Mo.: Andrews and McMeel, 1992.

BLOCK, FRED, WITH RICHARD CLOWARD, BARBARA EHRENREICH, AND FRANCES FOX PIVEN. *The Mean Season: The Attack on the Welfare State.* New York: Pantheon Books, 1987.

BLUESTONE, BARRY, AND BENNETT HARRISON. *The Deindustrialization of America.* New York: Basic Books, 1982.

BROWNING, ROBERT X. *Politics and Social Welfare Policy in the United States.* Knoxville: University of Tennessee Press, 1986.

DEVINE, JOEL, AND JAMES WRIGHT. *The Greatest of Evils: Urban Poverty and the American Underclass.* Hawthorne, N.Y.: Aldine, 1993.

GILDER, GEORGE. *Wealth and Poverty.* New York: Basic Books, 1981.

HACKER, ANDREW. *Two Nations: Black and White, Separate, Hostile, Unequal.* New York: Scribner's, 1992.

HAGEN, JAN L., AND IRENE LURIE. *Implementing JOBS: Initial State Choices.* Albany: The Nelson A. Rockefeller Institute of Government at the State University of New York, 1992.

HAMILTON, CHARLES V. "Social Policy and the Welfare of Black Americans: From Rights to Resources," *Political Science Quarterly* 100 (Summer 1986): 239–55.

HANRATTY, MARIA, AND REBECCA BLANK. "Down and Out in North America: Recent Trends in Poverty Rates in the United States and Canada," *Quarterly Journal of Economics* 107 (February 1992): 233–54.

HARRINGTON, MICHAEL. *The New American Poverty.* New York: Penguin, 1988.

HAVEMAN, ROBERT. *Starting Even: An Equal Opportunity Program to Combat the Nation's New Poverty.* New York: Simon and Schuster, 1988.

JOST, KENNETH. "Welfare Reform," *CQ Researcher* 2 (April 10, 1992): 315–35.

KASARDA, JOHN D. "Urban Change and Minority Opportunities," in Paul E. Peterson, ed., *The New Urban Reality*. Washington, D.C.: Brookings Institute, 1985.

KATZ, MICHAEL, ed. *The 'Underclass' Debate: Views from History*. Princeton, N.J.: Princeton University Press, 1993.

KAUS, MICKEY. *The End of Equality*. New York: Basic Books, 1992.

KEIGHER, SHARON M. "Reagan's 'New' Federalism and the 1971 California Medi-Cal Reforms," *Urban and Social Change Review* 16 (Summer 1983): 3–8.

LEMANN, NICHOLAS. *The Promised Land*. New York: Knopf, 1991.

LEVITAN, SAR, AND CLIFFORD JOHNSON. *Beyond the Safety Net*. Cambridge, Mass.: Ballinger, 1984.

MARMOR, THEODORE; JERRY MASHAW; AND PHILIP HARVEY. *America's Misunderstood Welfare State*. New York: Basic Books, 1990.

MEAD, LAWRENCE. *Beyond Entitlement: The Social Obligations of Citizenship*. New York: Free Press, 1985.

———. *New Politics of Poverty*. New York: Basic Books, 1992.

MURRAY, CHARLES. *Losing Ground: American Social Policy, 1950–1980*. New York: Basic Books, 1984.

National Conference of Catholic Bishops. *Economic Justice for All: Pastoral Letter on Catholic Social Thinking*. Washington, D.C.: United States Catholic Conference, 1986.

PHILLIPS, KEVIN. *The Politics of Rich and Poor*. New York: Random House, 1990.

PIFER, ALAN. "Philanthropy, Voluntarism, and Changing Times," *Daedalus* 116 (Winter 1987): 119–31.

PIVEN, FRANCES F., AND RICHARD A. CLOWARD. *The New Class War: Reagan's Attack on the Welfare State and Its Consequences*. New York: Pantheon Books, 1982.

SIDEL, RUTH. *Women and Children Last: The Plight of Poor Women in Affluent America*. New York: Penguin, 1987.

STERN, MARK J. "The Emergence of the Homeless as a Public Problem," *Social Service Review* 58 (June 1984): 291–301.

WILSON, WILLIAM J. "Cycles of Deprivation and the Underclass Debate," *Social Service Review* 59 (December 1985): 541–57.

———. *The Truly Disadvantaged*. Chicago: University of Chicago Press, 1987.

CHAPTER 17

■ Toward a New Domestic Order? ■

■ Despite a stronger than expected challenge from the conservative columnist Patrick Buchanan, George Bush easily won the 1992 Republican presidential nomination. His Democratic opponent, on the other hand, Bill Clinton, the young, little-known six-term governor of Arkansas, emerged as the candidate after withstanding many personal attacks and a bruising battle with several tough contenders and a hostile press. A former Rhodes Scholar with a computer-like mind and a joyous addiction to pressing the flesh, Clinton, dubbed the "Comeback Kid," proved to be a brilliant campaigner as well as remarkably resilient. A "centrist" who combined such conservative values as responsibility and self-help with liberal ones like tolerance and generosity, he quickly took a commanding lead in the public opinion polls.

The President was deeply puzzled. He thought he had done everything right. He had staged a showy raid in Panama and deposed its hated military dictator. He had won the Cold War, expelled Saddam Hussein from Kuwait, and brought the troops home to participate in frenzied victory parades. Yet the American people seemed dissatisfied with his performance. He didn't get it. When he finally realized that the electorate cared more about the problems at home than abroad, especially increasing business failures, growing unemployment, and pinched pocketbooks, he belatedly offered it the promise of an economic recovery package. For the most part, however, that package consisted of more of the same—capital gains tax cuts, lower interest rates, and a heavier dosage of supply-side economics, which, after more than a decade, had brought mainly a declining economy, a decay in public services, a rise in social disorder, and, above all, a growing disparity in the distribution of income and wealth between the rich and the poor.[1]

When that did not work, Bush resorted to what had served him so well four years earlier: Attack politics. He attacked all sorts of "evil" forces that allegedly were conspiring against him—the "cultural elite," the "make-work" lawyers in their "tassled loafers," the "lazy poor" who rioted in Los Angeles, the "nuclear freeze crowd," "tree-hugging" environmentalists, homosexuals, and the godless, who, Bush never tired telling the American people, "forgot to put the three letters G-O-D in their party platform." He also talked about "family values," (a euphemism for his anti-abortion and anti-gay rights positions) and savagely attacked his opponent, "Slick Willy," as a "waffler," a draft-dodger, an overseas war protestor, and even as "Bozo the Clown," who knew less about foreign policy than Bush's dog Millie. Most of all, however, Bush and his supporters went after "liberals," especially those who pretended to be something other than traditional "tax and spenders."

Clinton meanwhile remained unruffled and continued to run a positive campaign, even after Ross Perot, the billionaire businessman, entered the race as an independent and spent some $60 million of his own money on his candidacy. Clinton understood the racial and class divisions in America and realized that liberalism had lost much of its political appeal when it came to be perceived as something that taxed the majority to serve the interests of African-Americans and other minorities. He sought to advance programs that would unite all Americans in a common purpose: "This is America. There is no 'them.' There is only us," Clinton reminded listeners on numerous occasions. Promising that, if elected, he would have an action-filled post-inauguration "one hundred days" reminiscent of Franklin Roosevelt's, above all Clinton emphasized broad economic issues, including the need to revitalize the economy, stimulate job growth (in part through rebuilding the nation's faltering infrastructure), and reduce taxes on the middle class. He also called for health care reform,

---

[1]For an analysis of the concentration of wealth in the hands of the rich and its effects on the middle and lower classes, and the nation, in the 1980s and 1990s, see the books by Kevin Phillips and by Donald Barlett and James Steele cited in the bibliography at the end of Chapter 16.

including universal health insurance, a family leave policy (which, you recall, Bush had vetoed earlier), campaign finance reform, a reversal on the ban on gays in the military and of the so-called gag rule on abortion, increased college loans, the creation of a National Service Trust Fund, and the need for welfare reform.

Unlike four years earlier, welfare reform actually proved to be one of the more important issues in the campaign, in some ways the "Willie Horton issue of 1992," as some saw it: "We must work to reform our dismal welfare system," Bush had declared in February 1992, as he officially announced his bid for reelection, decrying what he (and his running mate, Vice President Dan Quayle) called "the liberal version of a happy, productive, and content welfare state," a theme he repeated throughout the campaign. As it turned out, however, his only concrete "reform" was to promise to speed up federal approval of waiver requests from states wanting to change—i.e., make more restrictive—A.F.D.C. rules.

Clinton, who touted his record as Governor of Arkansas, claiming credit for implementing a successful welfare-to-work program, also made welfare reform a major theme of his campaign. Attempting to walk a tightrope on the issue—that is, to please both conservatives and liberals—he chiefly proposed setting a two-year limit on welfare benefits for the able-bodied. "I want to erase the stigma of welfare for good by restoring a simple, dignified principle: No one who can work can stay on welfare forever," Clinton repeatedly exclaimed. But when asked about New Jersey's decision to eliminate additional benefits to single women who had more children while on welfare, he denounced it and called for more spending on health and child care, on education, and, if necessary, on public service employment.[2]

So whereas the debate over welfare reform during the campaign reflected agreement on some things, most notably that the existing system was not working and needed to be changed, and that the new system needed to do better at getting recipients off welfare and into the

---

[2]Public service employment, of course, was not a new idea. It was an integral part of Franklin Roosevelt's New Deal, had been incorporated in Jimmy Carter's ill-fated "Better Jobs and Income Program," and more recently had been the focus of a plan announced earlier that spring by a group of Democratic Senators. With a few exceptions, however, including the time of the deep recession during Reagan's first term in office, it had been shunned by most lawmakers, not just by conservatives, as a threat to the marketplace.

workforce, there were significant differences between the candidates on how to achieve those goals and on the degree to which public officials should use welfare to control the personal lives of its recipients.

What effect, if any, the welfare issue had on the election results is unclear. However, when the votes were counted, Bill Clinton, the "baby boomer" from Hot Springs, Arkansas, became the nation's forty-second President-elect by securing 43 percent of the popular vote (to 38 percent for Bush and 19 percent for Perot) and, more importantly, 370 electoral votes, 202 more than his Republican rival. Although the consensus was that Bush lost the election more than Clinton won it, thanks largely to a battered economy, a deeply splintered Republican Party, and an ineffectual campaign, the results indicated something more; clearly, the American people wanted a President who was *for* something rather than someone who merely spawned numerous demons. As the *Milwaukee Journal* put it immediately following the election, Clinton's victory represented "the triumph of vision over drift, of inclusiveness over meanness, of optimism over fear." Or, as the President-elect stated on the night of his success, "It was a victory for all the people who work hard and play by the rules, a victory for the people who feel left out and left behind but who want to do better." The American people "want their future back," he added, and "I intend to help give it to them."[3]

Whether or not he would give the American people "their future back" remained to be seen. Certainly his victory seemed to pave the way for real change. He (and his influential wife, Hillary Rodham Clinton, a highly respected lawyer) had been very active in matters of social welfare, especially in promoting education and children's rights. In addition, the new President had a Congress controlled by his own party, one that had not only more new faces than at any time since 1969, but more African-Americans, Hispanics, and women than ever before in American history. Thus, even before he took office, there

---

[3]Certainly, Clinton owed his election to some luck as well. Among other things, the economy remained "flat" until right around election day, when it began to show signs of a slight recovery; Bush mistakenly allowed right-wing extremists to dominate the Republican Party convention, upsetting many women and other moderate members of the party, and just prior to the election a memo emerged and was made public which seemed to indicate that, contrary to what he had long claimed, Bush (then Vice President) was "in the loop" when crucial decisions were made in the arms-for-hostages deal with Iran during the Reagan administration.

was great optimism that Clinton would make good on his promises to change the way things worked in Washington and to be President to all of the American people.

He got off to a bad start, however, when it was discovered that his Attorney General designate, Zoë Baird, had hired illegal aliens as domestic servants and had failed to pay their Social Security taxes, as required by law; then a second nominee, Kimba Wood, admitted to having done the same; as a result, the Justice Department remained leaderless for some time as the search for a third candidate went on. That was followed by another sticky quagmire when Clinton ran into stiff opposition from the military brass and powerful legislators after announcing his intention to lift the ban on gays in the armed forces, as he had promised to do during the campaign. He also hinted that he probably would not be able to follow through on his campaign pledge to cut taxes on the middle class. Later many citizens would be furious with the new President when they learned that he had his hair trimmed aboard the presidential airplane by a Beverly Hills hairdresser (for $200 while air traffic at the Los Angeles airport came to a standstill); a scandal occurred in the White House travel office; the President withdrew his nomination of longtime friend Lani Guinier to head the Justice Department's Civil Rights Division due to conservative opposition; and he hired David Gergen, a veteran of the Nixon and Reagan White Houses, to help refurbish his sagging public image.

In addition, Clinton delayed unveiling his plans for revamping the nation's health and welfare systems, postponed his promise to push for an increase in the minimum wage, hinted that he would be willing to compromise on the issue of gays in the military, and then did so (proposing a plan dubbed "don't ask, don't tell, and don't pursue," a policy that, in effect, would make gay conduct rather than homosexual status incompatible with military service). No wonder that faith in his judgment, in his competency, and even in his trust, was shaken, not only among liberals. Indeed, in June 1993 public opinion polls indicated that only 36 percent of the American people approved of Clinton's handling of the presidency.

In the meantime, however, Clinton—a smart, energetic, and resilient person who had bounced back from political setbacks on numerous occasions in the past—scored some important political victories and began to regain some of his declining credibility and goodwill. Among other things, he got Congress to pass a Family Leave Act (similar to the one Bush had vetoed except that it provided for up to three months of unpaid leave rather than six), which he quickly signed into law. He also lifted the ban prohibiting federally subsidized family planning clinics from discussing abortion with pregnant clients, attacked the nation's pharmaceutical industry for its "shockingly high prices," launched a campaign to "guarantee [the free] immunization of every American child," and persuaded Congress to extend unemployment compensation for those suffering the most from the prolonged recession. Perhaps most important, he appointed a Task Force on Health Care Reform, headed by his wife, to draft a proposal to completely revamp the nation's health care system, one that would include measures to contain the spiraling costs of medical care and to provide affordable health insurance to all Americans. He also renewed his campaign pledge to "end welfare as we know it."

Clinton's plans to overhaul the nation's health and welfare systems—as well as to cut the deficit and revitalize the economy—depended, of course, on getting his economic package through Congress. That proved to be far more difficult than he had anticipated. To begin with, his $16 billion economic stimulus program was filibustered to death by Senate Republicans, who claimed that it was too costly and unnecessary. Then his deficit reduction (or budget) bill—which included tax *increases* for the middle as well as the upper classes—barely went through the House and then passed the Senate by only one vote (51–50, when Vice President Al Gore cast the deciding tally) after a broad-based energy tax was replaced by an increase in the gasoline tax and substantial cuts in Medicare, with Clinton's approval.

Still, buoyed by the passage of his budget bill, however slim the margin, Clinton turned next to his long-promised and much anticipated proposal for health care reform, the nation's "most urgent priority," in his words. He laid out the broad outline of his plan for a sweeping revision of the nation's health care system in an impassioned call for action before a joint session of Congress and a large national television audience on October 22, 1993: "This health care system of ours is broken," he declared, "and it is time to fix it."

In brief, the President's proposal called for a system that would guarantee quality medical treatment for all Americans from birth to death, including the 37 million citizens who were without any insurance and the 20 million others whose coverage was meager. Under the plan, every legal resident of the United States would receive a health security card that would entitle its holder to a comprehensive package of benefits that never could be taken away under any circumstance, including the loss of a job. It also would cover the costs of treating pre-existing illnesses, something that was not included in most existing plans.

On the whole, the plan would be financed by employers, who, for the most part, would be required to pay 80 percent of the premiums, with employees paying the remainder. The federal government, however, would provide subsidies to help the poor, the jobless, and small businesses pay their share of the costs—and it would finance prescription drugs and long-term care for the elderly, which were not "covered" under Medicare.

The plan would operate under a system of "managed competition," that is, through Regional Health Alliances created in each state to serve as huge purchasing pools designed to help consumers save money on their insurance premiums by giving them "buying power" or economic clout. A National Health Board would oversee quality and impose certain caps (or price controls) on physicians and hospitals, thereby keeping the costs of treatment, and thus insurance premiums, in line. Clinton hoped Congress would act on the measure by the end of 1994, which would enable the plan to become operative in some states by 1995—and cover everyone by January 1, 1998.

While many of the plan's important details were left unanswered, including what new taxes would be needed to cover the federal government's expenses, precisely how much individuals and families would be charged, and the degree to which all citizens would be free to choose their own physicians, most Americans reacted favorably to the plan and looked forward to the upcoming debate over its specifics.[4] Further, there seemed to be bi-partisan support, in and out of Congress, for the notion that the time had come for some sort of universal national health insurance scheme. The precise nature of that scheme, however, and how long it would take lawmakers to act on it, of course remained to be seen.

---

[4] A *Time*/CNN poll taken a few days after the speech was delivered indicated that 57 percent of the American people favored Clinton's health care proposal. It also indicated that, for the first time in four months, 50 percent of the American people "approved" of the way he was handling the presidency.

In the meantime, however, where does this leave the nation's destitute and dependent citizens, those not protected by Social Security, Supplental Security Income, Unemployment Insurance, and the other entitlement programs which, for the most part, withstood the assault on the welfare state during the last twelve years or so? What will happen to those needy people who have been, and others who no doubt later will be, the "rejects" of society—those who, for one reason or another, are unable to participate in educational or work training programs, or those who participate in such programs but still cannot find decent jobs at decent wages, or any jobs at all?

Certainly, the nation's economic situation is crucial for the well-being of these, as well as all other, Americans. Yet by now it should be obvious to all that even under the best of economic circumstances, America will not achieve full employment or provide living wages to all those who are employed; there always will be some, perhaps many, who will be unable to participate in the economic fruits of society, at least directly, especially in our downwardly mobile postindustrial, "high-tech" society. Again, what will happen to these people?

Clearly, the nation will not return in the near future, if ever, to the policy assumptions that fueled the New Frontier and the Great Society (and most of American history, for that matter)—the notions that Americans controlled their own destiny and that therefore nothing was impossible, including the elimination of poverty, if Americans but wished to achieve it, or that, thanks to the nation's boundless resources, poverty and dependency simply will "wither away."

That loss of confidence, or dose of reality, need not imprison us, however. In fact, it could be liberating, or even a blessing in disguise for the nation's destitute and dependent citizens, for in the absence of such beliefs perhaps Americans again will acknowledge, or be forced to acknowledge, what their colonial forebears (and on occasion others) simply took for granted, namely that the poor will be with them, always, through no fault of their own, and that therefore they too have a right to a healthy, happy, and secure life. That, of course, in turn, will depend on how central the principle of social justice is, or again becomes, to this generation of Americans.

Here, too, there are reasons for optimism, or at least wishful thinking. Times change; periods of conservatism are followed by periods of liberalism, and despite the President's "middle-of-the-road" approach and shaky, error-filled start, the ground may be fertile for such a mood swing. Unlike his immediate predecessors, who either did not recognize the nation's social problems or refused to face up to them, and who regularly engaged in government-bashing, President Clinton certainly admits that the nation has many such problems, realizes that it cannot afford to ignore them, and believes that the public sector can and should help to resolve them. Just as our colonial ancestors viewed their villages and towns as communities, he cries out for the nation to become once again a true commonwealth, for the government again to become an instrument for the improvement of its citizens' lives, especially by providing at least a minimal level of social welfare for all of its inhabitants. And while in a day of multiculturalism, rapid demographic change, and economic hardship, the challenge of rebuilding an American community is great, Clinton remains committed to that ideal. If he can sustain the momentum he managed to attain by October, 1993, and turn more of his campaign rhetoric into reality, he may not only secure his political and historical fortune but help build the foundation for a new domestic order, one that contains a universal health insurance scheme that will enable all citizens to secure sound comprehensive medical treatment and a welfare system that recognizes both the inevitability of unemployment and the utility of good, parental child care. Such a system would provide decent jobs for all who can and should work and an adequate universal income floor below which those who cannot or should not work will not be allowed to fall. Only time will tell.

Index